# SUBJECTS OR CITIZENS?

# RELIGIONS AND BELIEFS SERIES

The series includes books bearing on the religions of the Americas, the Bible in its relationship to cultures, and on ethics in relation to religion. The series welcomes manuscripts written in either English or French.

> Editorial Committee: *Robert Choquette, Director*
> *Margaret Dufour-McDonald*
> *David Jeffrey*
> *Pierre Savard*

**In the same series**

Pauline Côté, *Les Transactions politiques des croyants,* 1993

RELIGIONS AND BELIEFS SERIES, NO. 2

# SUBJECTS OR CITIZENS?

The Mennonite Experience in Canada,
1870–1925

**Adolf Ens**

**1994**

**University of Ottawa Press**

This book has been published with the help of a grant from the Canadian Federation for the Humanities, using funds provided by the Social Sciences and Humanities Research Council of Canada.

---

CANADIAN CATALOGUING IN PUBLICATION DATA

Ens, Adolf, 1933–
    Subjects or Citizens?: The Mennonite Experience in Canada, 1870–1925
(Religions and Beliefs; no. 2)

Includes bibliographical references and index.
ISBN 0-7766-0390-6

    1. Mennonites — Canada — History. 2. Church and state — Canada — History. 3. Mennonites — Government policy — Canada — History. I. Title. II. Series: Collection Religions et croyances; no. 2.

FC106.M45E68 1994             322'. 1'088287             C94-900829-X
F1035.M45E68 1994

---

Cover: Danielle Péret
Typesetting: Infographie G.L.

"All rights reserved. No part of this publication may be reproduced or transmitted in any form or any means, electronic or mechanical, including photocopy, recording, or any information storage and retrieval system, without permission in writing from the publisher."

© University of Ottawa Press, 1994
ISBN 0-7766-0390-6
Printed in Canada

## CONTENTS

| | |
|---|---|
| List of Maps | viii |
| List of Tables | ix |
| Acknowledgments | xi |
| Introduction | 1 |
|    The Mennonites: A Brief Historical Sketch | 1 |
|    Anabaptist-Mennonite Concept of the State | 3 |
|    Mennonite Church Relations with the State in Prussia and Russia | 4 |
|    The Canadian Experience to 1925: An Overview | 7 |
| Chapter I: Settlement in Canada | 11 |
|    Negotiating a *Privilegium* | 12 |
|    Group Migration | 21 |
|       The Reserves | 22 |
|       The Mennonite Loan | 24 |
|       Non-Mennonite Intruders | 27 |
|       Homestead Rights | 31 |
|       Hamlet Privilege | 35 |
|       Naturalization and Land Patents | 38 |
|       Termination of the Reserve | 41 |
|    Mennonites and the "High" Government: A Summary | 44 |
| Chapter II: Adjusting to Manitoba, 1876–1890 | 61 |
|    Public Schools: External Resources | 62 |
|    Municipal Government: External Authority | 66 |
|    Mennonite Solidarity Broken: Unequally Yoked | 75 |
| Chapter III: Westward Expansion, 1890–1910 | 85 |
|    The Reserves | 86 |
|    Government Loan | 91 |
|    Non-Mennonite Intruders | 92 |
|    Homestead Rights | 93 |
|    Hamlet Privilege | 94 |
|    Naturalization and Land Patents | 96 |

Termination of the Reserves ............................... 96
Immigration from Russia and the U.S.A. .................... 97

Chapter IV: The Rift Widens: The Education Issue in Manitoba
and Saskatchewan, 1890–1920 ............................... 105
  Manitoba Education Legislation to 1916 .................. 105
  Higher Education: Alliance of Church and State .......... 108
  School Developments, 1890–1916 .......................... 110
  The "National Schools," 1916 ............................ 116
  The *Zwangsschulen*, 1918 ............................... 123
  Compulsory Attendance: Boycott and Court Enforcement .... 138
  The Petitions: Articulating the Issues .................. 153

Chapter V: The War Issues ................................. 171
  Military Exemption Provisions ........................... 172
  The Early Years of the War .............................. 173
  The National Service Registration, 1917 ................. 173
  Implementing Mennonite Exemption:
    Military Service Act, 1917 ............................ 175
  U.S. Mennonite Immigrants and the Military Service Act .. 180
  The 1918 National Registration .......................... 181
  Financial Involvement: Red Cross and Victory Loans ...... 183
  Press Censorship ........................................ 185

Chapter VI: Emigration and Accommodation .................. 199
  The Postwar Situation ................................... 200
  The Emigration Option ................................... 201
    Reinländer ............................................ 203
    Bergthal Groups ....................................... 209
  The Accommodation Option ................................ 216

Conclusion ................................................ 231

Appendixes
  1. Order-in-Council of April 26, 1872 ................... 237
  2. Order-in-Council of September 25, 1872 ............... 239
  3. Capital Brought into Canada by Russian
     Mennonite Immigrants, 1874–1880 ...................... 241
  4. Sample Homestead Entry Receipt ....................... 242
  5. National Service Registration Card, 1917 (Front) ..... 243
     National Service Registration Card, 1917 (Back) ...... 244
  6. Mennonite Identification Certificate, World War I .... 245
  7. Canada Registration Board Cards, 1918
     (Card for Females) ................................... 246

|     | Canada Registration Board Cards, 1918 (Card for Males)............................. | 247 |
|-----|---|---|
| 8.  | Excerpts of the Paraguayan Mennonite Privilegium ....... | 248 |
| 9.  | Sommerfelder Mexican Privilegium .................. | 250 |

Bibliography ........................................... 253
   Books ............................................. 253
   Periodical Articles ................................... 258
   Theses and Dissertations.............................. 259

Index ................................................. 261

# MAPS

1. Province of Manitoba, 1875, Showing Rivers, Trails and Reserves.................................. 15
2. Mennonite West Reserve Showing the "Meno-Canuck Boundary"........................................ 29
3. Mennonite East Reserve with Hanover and Hespeler Municipalities...................................... 69
4. Municipal Boundary Changes in the Mennonite West Reserve, 1880–1916........................... 72
5. Saskatchewan Mennonite Reserves ..................... 88
6. Hague Reserve and Additions ......................... 90
7. Public School Districts in the East Reserve ............... 128
8. West Reserve Reinländer Public School Districts .......... 132
9. Hague Reserve Showing Reinländer School Districts ....... 136
10. Swift Current Reserve Showing Reinländer School Districts............................................ 137

# TABLES

1. Mennonite Immigrant Arrivals at Quebec, 1874–1880 ...... 22
2. Mennonite Immigrant Groups, Manitoba, 1874–1880 ...... 45
3. Number of Mennonite Public School Districts, 1891–1902 .. 111
4. Manitoba Mennonite District Schools Kept in Operation by Order-in-Council, 1918 ............................ 125
5. Discontinued Manitoba Mennonite District Schools Reopened by Order-in-Council, 1918–1920 .............. 126
6. Public School Districts Created in Hanover Municipality, April 8, 1919, with Greenway as Official Trustee .......... 129
7. Loans Made on Behalf of Manitoba Mennonite Districts by Official Trustee Greenway ........................ 130
8. Public Schools Created in Rhineland and Stanley Municipalities with Greenway as Official Trustee, February 21, 1920. ................................... 131
9. Saskatchewan Mennonite School Districts Created by the Department of Education, 1918–1919 ............... 135
10. School Attendance Prosecutions in Mennonite Districts, Saskatchewan, 1920 and 1921 ........................ 148
11. School Attendance Prosecutions in Five Mennonite Districts, Swift Current Area, Saskatchewan, 1922 and 1923 ......... 150
12. Mennonite School Attendance Cases Sent to Provincial Police, Hague Area, Saskatchewan, October 1921 and 1922 . 151
13. School Attendance Prosecutions in Six Mennonite Districts, Hague Area, 1923–1925. .............................. 151
14. Summary of School Attendance Prosecutions of Saskatchewan Mennonites, 1918–1925. ................ 152
15. Mennonite Groups in Manitoba and Saskatchewan, 1917 .... 154
16. Mennonite School Petitions to the Governments of Manitoba and Saskatchewan, 1916–1922 .............. 155
17. Reinländer Land-Seeking Delegations, 1919–1921 ......... 203
18. Sommerfelder–Chortitzer–Bergthaler Land-Seeking Delegations. ........................................ 210

19. Manitoba and Saskatchewan Mennonite Emigrants to
    Latin America, 1922–1930......................... 214
20. Return to Local Control of Manitoba Mennonite District
    Schools......................................... 218
21. Manitoba Mennonite Schools Under Official Trustee
    Administration as of May 6, 1930 ..................... 220

# ACKNOWLEDGMENTS

It is a privilege to thank publicly at least some of the people who contributed significantly to the realization of this book. Professor Robert Choquette served as my supervisor when I worked on it as a Ph.D. dissertation in religious studies at the University of Ottawa. My colleagues at Canadian Mennonite Bible College gave helpful general advice and generous encouragement. The more specific and pointed comments of manuscript readers were very helpful in identifying areas that needed further attention. So also were the questions and comments of lay historians who heard or read parts of its contents in earlier form. The co-operative and uncomplaining staff at the National Archives, Ottawa, the provincial archives in Winnipeg, Regina, and Saskatoon, the land titles office and several municipal offices in Manitoba, and the Mennonite Heritage Centre in Winnipeg, contributed much to make the research work more efficient and enjoyable. The steady encouragement of Suzanne Bossé of the University of Ottawa Press and the discerning work of copy editor Veronica Schami are gratefully acknowledged. The assistance and support of my wife, Anna, in the various stages of this project are deeply appreciated. To all of them my heartfelt thanks. The errors and gaps that remain are, of course, my responsibility.

Adolf Ens<br>
Winnipeg<br>
Thanksgiving, 1994

# INTRODUCTION

## The Mennonites: A Brief Historical Sketch

Mennonites constitute one of the groups that claim historical descent from the sixteenth-century Anabaptists, or from that stream of the Reformation characterized by Williams as "radical," by Bainton and Fast as the "left wing," and by Klaassen as "neither Catholic nor Protestant."[1]

One Anabaptist group emerged in Zurich around 1523 out of Huldrich Zwingli's circle of reformers. The rebaptism of several of the leaders of this group in January 1525 followed an earlier decision not to baptize infants. Since both acts were done in defiance of state law and against the wishes of Zwingli's Reformed Church, they marked the beginning of a "free church" as a body of Christians distinct from either the Catholic or Reformed state churches.[2]

Within a few years of the appearance of this circle of Anabaptists in Switzerland, similar movements surfaced in Moravia to the east and in the Low Countries to the northwest. The group in Moravia came under the strong communitarian impulse of Jakob Huter from 1533 to 1535 and has retained both the name (Hutterite) and the communal way of life to the present time. The movement in the Low Countries struggled to establish a clear identity. A revolutionary wing established the short-lived violent kingdom of Münster under the leadership of Jan Matthijs in 1534. The peaceful wing was initially led by Obbe Philips and his brother Dirk, but they were soon overshadowed by Menno Simons, a former priest, who was ordained as an Anabaptist leader in 1537 and who grew in stature and influence until his death twenty-four years later.[3] Like Huter in Moravia, Menno gave both organizational principle and his name to the movement.[4] Descendants of all three of these groups of Anabaptists have found their way to Canada.

The intense persecution to which Anabaptists in Switzerland were subjected from the outset forced them to seek refuge elsewhere. Many went eastward to Moravia. Others went north into Alsace, where the city of Strassburg provided a haven of toleration for a while. After the Thirty Years War many settled in the Palatinate. Near the end of the seventeenth century the first of the descendants of the Swiss Brethren crossed the Atlantic to settle in William Penn's colony in America. At intervals throughout the eighteenth and nineteenth centuries this migration to America continued, some of it directly from Switzerland, some of it from the Palatinate, Alsace, Bavaria, and Hesse. After the American Revolution, a movement north from Pennsylvania into Upper Canada began in 1786. A century later, westward migration from Ontario led to the formation of a number of communities of Swiss Mennonites in the Northwest Territories, beginning at High River (Alberta) in 1891.[5]

A measure of toleration for Mennonites in the Netherlands came in 1581, much earlier than it did for the Swiss. But prior to that time many had settled in the Vistula delta area of Poland, Prussia, and the Free City of Danzig. During two and a half centuries of life there, many patterns of congregational and community organization developed that were later transplanted, with some adaptations, to Canada.[6] In 1788 the first group of descendants of these Dutch Mennonites became part of a large eastward migration of Germanic people and settled near the Dnieper River in New Russia. After another century of adaptation in surroundings quite different from their earlier Polish-Prussian ones, a group of almost seven thousand of them immigrated into the new Dominion of Canada and settled in the still newer province of Manitoba during the years 1874 to 1880. Westward expansion into the Northwest Territories began a decade later.

The Hutterites, under the pressure of repeated persecution and suppression, moved eastward from Moravia to Hungary and Transylvania during the Thirty Years War, and then still further to southern Russia via Wallachia around 1770. A century later they joined the Mennonites in a mass migration to North America, settling in Dakota in 1874. During the Spanish-American War a group of them moved for a few years (1898–1905) to southern Manitoba, but returned again to the U.S.A. Near the end of World War I a large number of the Hutterites once more immigrated to Canada, eventually settling in the three prairie provinces.[7]

The present study focusses on the descendants of the Dutch-Prussian-Russian Mennonites who immigrated to Canada in the 1870s.

However, since descendants of the Hutterites and the Swiss Brethren also found their way to western Canada during the period under consideration, reference to their experience is included.

## Anabaptist-Mennonite Concept of the State

Among the points that separated the proto-Anabaptists from Zwingli at the second Zurich disputation in October 1523 was a difference in their understanding of the limits of the authority of civic government. When the magisterial reformers held that the city council should decide on how to proceed with the needed reform of the Mass, the radicals under the leadership of Conrad Grebel began to part company with Zwingli. They argued that the church, interpreting Scripture under the leading of the Holy Spirit, should decide such matters, not the state. A little more than a year later, this position had ripened to the point where a number of Zwingli's former disciples were willing to risk their lives by being rebaptized in direct contravention of the law.

It is clear from the outset of the movement, however, that these Swiss Brethren (Anabaptists) were not anarchists or revolutionaries. Their oldest extant confession of faith, the Schleitheim Confession of 1527, includes an article dealing with the relationship of believers (or of a believers' church) to the state. It begins with the significant affirmation that the office of government is ordained by God.[8] Based strongly on Romans 13 in the Bible, the article holds that the state was instituted by God in response to human sin in order to punish the evil and protect the good.[9] Christians therefore owed obedience to the secular authority as long as its claims did not violate the prior obedience owed to God (Acts 4:19).[10] In no case was rebellion acceptable.[11]

The necessity of government was primarily to maintain order among the ungodly. The Swiss Brethren held, in contrast to the Reformers, the office of magistrate could be satisfactorily filled by a non-Christian civil ruler. But since the "sword" (meaning the "judicial and police powers of the state")[12] was an ordering of God "outside the perfection of Christ," the Schleitheim articles held that a true Christian should not serve as magistrate. It was not appropriate for a follower of Christ to "pass sentence in disputes and strife about worldly matters" (Matthew 20:25–27).[13] Nor was it proper that the Christian "should use the sword against the wicked for the protection and defense of the good, or for the sake of love."[14]

Like Luther, the Swiss Brethren saw a radical distinction between the church of Christ and the world. Unlike Luther, they held that those in the kingdom of Christ had no responsibility for maintaining law and order in the "world" (1 Corinthians 5:12).[15] Conversely, they were convinced that the state had no rights or responsibilities in the affairs of the church. They were therefore opposed in principle to a state church and advocated a concept of religious liberty that would allow even Turks and Jews to be left alone to live according to their faith in the Christian nations of Europe.[16]

The Dutch and Polish-Prussian Anabaptists held similar views of the state, although they developed an openness to participating in governmental office earlier than the Swiss. Their confessions of faith and catechisms instruct submission to government, since it is ordained of God, and obedience to it in all matters not in conflict with the Word of God.[17]

The refusal of Anabaptists to swear the civil oath (Matthew 5:33–37), participate in warfare, or initiate litigation brought them into conflict with state authorities at various times in their history.[18] In time these characteristics came to be identified as Mennonite distinctives and were a point of special consideration in looking for new countries in which to settle.

## Mennonite Church Relations with the State in Prussia and Russia

Dutch Anabaptist-Mennonite refugees fleeing Spanish Catholic persecution during the middle half of the sixteenth century settled in the region of the Vistula delta and along the Baltic coast to the east. Here they found varying degrees of tolerance and freedom under four different political jurisdictions: the Catholic king of Poland, the Lutheran duke of the Königsberg-Tilsit area (later the king of Prussia), and the free cities of Danzig and Elbing. Since the rulers in most cases were absolutist, and no constitutional guarantees of religious liberty existed, Mennonites received numerous charters of privileges during the two centuries preceding the union of the entire area under the king of Prussia. These charters modified or counteracted discriminatory laws or government orders. Among the Mennonites they established a pattern of seeking their guarantee of religious toleration not in an impersonal constitution but rather in a special *Privilegium* from the reigning monarch.[19]

During the reign of Frederick the Great (1740–1786) the entire region was unified under Prussian rule. Frederick was willing to extend complete religious toleration but growing European militarism made him reluctant to allow it to include exemption from military service. The special charter of 1780 compromised by allowing Mennonites such exemption in return for an annual sum of money in support of a military academy. This uneasy settlement, weakened by a series of economic restrictions in succeeding years, made the invitation from Czarina Catherine II to settle in southern

Russia very attractive to many Mennonites. During the next fifty years, about half of the Mennonite population of the delta area migrated to the steppes of New Russia.[20]

Catherine's invitation to Germans and other Western Europeans to come to settle in the newly acquired Russian territory north of the Black Sea was first published in two manifestos in December 1762 and July 1763. In 1786 a special representative visited the Prussian Mennonite communities and sparked their interest in seeking a more favourable place to live. The two delegates who went to investigate settlement possibilities that same year not only explored the land but also negotiated a charter of privileges with the Russian government. A twenty-point *Privilegium*, worked out by Catherine's representative and the Mennonite delegates, was delivered by the Russian chargé d'affaires in Danzig on March 3, 1788.[21] The first point granted complete freedom of religious practice according to Mennonite church order and usage. The seventh accepted simple affirmation in place of an oath of allegiance and the eighth guaranteed exemption from all military service for all time for the Mennonite immigrants and their descendants. When Catherine was succeeded on the throne by Czar Paul I in 1796, *Ältester* (bishop or elder) David Epp and Minister Gerhard Willms spent two years in St. Petersburg to negotiate a renewal of the Mennonite charter.[22]

Like other foreign colonists in Russia, the Mennonites were to enjoy forever complete autonomy in the administration of their internal affairs according to the July Manifesto of 1763.[23] During their two centuries of residence in the Polish, Danzig, and Prussian territories they had never achieved full citizenship status. Now they were suddenly required to administer their own affairs at both the village and the district levels with very uneven guidance from the Curator and Director of Foreign Colonists to whom they were directly answerable.[24] This Director was appointed by the central agency of the Russian government, which was in charge of the administration of the foreign colonies. Under Catherine II this Office of Guardianship of Foreigners was modified several times without great success. Under her successors it evolved by 1818 into the Guardianship Committee of the Foreign Colonists in Southern Russia, known among the Mennonites by its German title of *Fürsorge Komitee* and located since 1828 in Odessa. Until its dissolution in 1871, just a few years prior to the first emigration to North America, this committee remained the channel for the self-governing colonies to relate to the Russian government.

The system of local administration, as spelled out in the Instruction of May 1801, made each village a separate unit of government. A community assembly, composed of one representative from each homestead, elected a *Schulze* (mayor) and two *Beisitzer* (assistants) who together formed an executive committee to administer the village. In addition to electing village and district officials, the community assembly had wide-ranging powers that included levying taxes, hiring teachers and fire-overseers, selecting preachers and herdsmen, assigning individual farmers their strips of land, and determining the crop rotation. Its decisions on purely local issues were final.

The executive committee, and especially the *Schulze*, had an even broader range of local power. Not only were they responsible for maintaining peace and order, collecting taxes, and maintaining roads and bridges, but they also had far-reaching authority over agriculture, commerce and industry, justice, fire safety, and the morals and church attendance of villagers. No decision of the committee or of the *Schulze* was binding, however, without ratification of the community assembly.

A number of village communities together formed a *volost* (district). A district assembly, composed of one or more representatives from each village, had powers comparable to a village assembly and could make decisions binding upon all of the member villages. The village *Schulze* or one of the *Beisitzer* was always one of the village representatives. A chairman of the district assembly, or *Oberschulze* (reeve), and several assistants, were elected by the voters of the villages. Together they formed the *Gebietsamt* (district government) and with the help of hired clerical staff administered the affairs of the whole district or colony. The *Oberschulze* represented the colony before the governmental agencies, particularly the *Fürsorge Komitee*. He was also responsible for maintaining peace and order in the colony and administering justice. In imposing sentences (fines, incarceration, public labour, corporal punishment) on offenders, however, it was necessary to obtain consent of the *Schulze* of the village to which the guilty person belonged.[25]

This was the system of government that the Mennonites in Russia used until the emigration of the 1870s. In economic, educational, and welfare areas it was supplemented by institutions modelled after institutions they had known in West Prussia and Danzig.[26] It was transplanted to North America by the Mennonite groups settling in Manitoba in the 1870s and continued there until it was replaced by Canadian institutions created by the federal or provincial governments.

The Anabaptist concern for a clear separation of church and state thus underwent considerable modification in its application by the Mennonites in Russia. While a clear demarcation remained between the spheres of the Mennonite community and the national government, local government was now completely in Mennonite hands so that church and mini-state were coterminous. All offices in this local government were held by members of the Mennonite church, although in some villages a national was hired to serve as constable.[27] This led to some acrimonious struggles between church leadership and civic officials in the early decades.[28]

Migration from Prussia to Russia continued from 1788 until the 1860s. The first group of some 228 families settled in 1789 at Chortitza, near the Dnieper River in the province of Ekaterinoslav. A second colony was begun in 1803 at the Molochnaia River in Taurida province, some 145 kilometres from Chortitza. Two more colonies were established farther east by direct migration from Prussia.

As the first two colonies grew to fill all locally available lands, internal migration within Russia began. The first of the so-called daughter colonies was Bergthal, founded by settlers from Chortitza in 1836. Its community and congregation had gained independence from the mother colony and congregation at Chortitza prior to the emigration to Canada. The communities at other daughter colonies (Fürstenland, begun in 1864; Borosenko, 1865; Nepluievka, 1869; Baratov, 1871) were still part of the Chortitza congregation when the emigration took place. These colonies provided most of the settlers who came to Canada during the 1870s.

## The Canadian Experience to 1925: An Overview

Between 1874 and 1880 almost 7,000 Mennonite immigrants from Russia settled in Manitoba as part of the Canadian government's effort to fill the "new Canada" recently acquired from the Hudson's Bay Company. Less than a century earlier their forebears had helped to fill "New Russia" in a similar way. As their original settlements in Manitoba filled up, expansion to the Northwest began in the 1890s, even before the provinces of Saskatchewan and Alberta had been created. This second round of pioneering allowed them to continue their pattern of block settlement and village community.

In Russia they had enjoyed a preferred foreign colonist status with virtually full local autonomy. In Canada they would need to make the transition to a system of municipal administration much more directly linked to the provincial government. In Russia they had developed their own education system, internally funded and fully controlled by the church. Here they would have to come to terms with public schools, including government funds, government inspection and teacher standards, government curriculum, and the national flag.

A good number of the immigrants left Russia because they felt that accommodation to its society had already eroded some cherished traditions. They stressed separation and reform, involving in some aspects a return to a lost tradition. Others, including many of the landless, looked for new economic opportunity and were quite prepared to participate in their new host society, accommodating themselves to it as far as their basic religious convictions permitted. As a result, two simultaneous trends may be observed: reform-separation-tradition and accommodation-participation-modernization. In obvious tension with each other, each modified the other and produced for the most part stable communities and amiable social relations.

The outbreak of the war in Europe and Canada's participation in it intensified the assimilationist pressure on all "alien" immigrants. In the context of wartime and postwar heightened patriotic nationalism, a group that lived in separate communities, spoke German, and taught pacifism faced enormous pressures. For many in the "accommodating" group the process of accommodation was accelerated; for many in the "resisting" group a new exodus seemed the only solution.

# Notes

1. George Hunston Williams, *The Radical Reformation* (Philadelphia: Westminster, 1962) is the most comprehensive account in English of the Anabaptist movement in the sixteenth century, and Cornelius J. Dyck, *An Introduction to Mennonite History*, 3rd ed. (Scottdale: Herald Press, 1993) the best concise survey of Mennonite developments to the present. Roland H. Bainton, "The Left Wing of the Reformation," *Journal of Religion* 21 (April 1941): 124–134. Heinold Fast, *Der linke Flügel der Reformation. Glaubenszeugnisse der Täufer, Spiritualisten, Schwärmer, und Antitrinitarier* (Bremen: Scheunemann, 1962). Walter Klaassen, *Anabaptism: Neither Catholic nor Protestant* (Waterloo: Conrad Press, 1973).

2. Fritz Blanke, *Brothers in Christ. The History of the Oldest Anabaptist Congregation in Zollikon, near Zurich, Switzerland*, trans. Joseph Nordenhaug (Scottdale: Herald Press, 1961), p. 15.

3. His collected writings have gone through numerous editions in Dutch, German, and English and continue to enjoy a wide circulation. The best English edition is *The Complete Writings of Menno Simons, c. 1496–1561*, ed. John Christian Wenger, trans. Leonard Verduin (Scottdale: Herald Press, 1956).

4. In the Netherlands, descendants of the sixteenth-century Anabaptists have continued to use the name *Doopsgezinde* for their church. Elsewhere, they, as well as the descendants of the Swiss Brethren, have almost universally accepted the name Mennonite.

5. Frank H. Epp, *Mennonites in Canada, 1786–1920. The History of a Separate People* (Toronto: Macmillan, 1974), especially chaps. 2 and 13, gives an account of their coming to Upper Canada and the beginnings of western settlement.

6. E. K. Francis, "Mennonite Institutions in Early Manitoba: A Study of Their Origins," *Agricultural History* 22 (July 1948): 144–155.

7. John A. Hostetler, *Hutterite Society* (Baltimore: Johns Hopkins, 1974), and Victor Peters, *All Things Common. The Hutterian Way of Life* (Minneapolis: University of Minnesota Press, 1965), both begin with a concise historical survey of the movement. The latter then focusses on Hutterites in Canada.

8. Article 6 of the "Schleitheim Brotherly Union," 1527. The complete text with an introduction and extensive notes is found in John H. Yoder, ed. and trans., *The Legacy of Michael Sattler*, Classics of the Radical Reformation, 1 (Scottdale: Herald Press, 1973), pp. 27–54.

9. Hans Hillerbrand, "The Anabaptist View of the State," *Mennonite Quarterly Review* (hereafter *MQR*) 32 (April 1958): 84–85.

10. Robert Kreider, "The Anabaptists and the State," in Guy F. Hershberger, ed., *The Recovery of the Anabaptist Vision* (Scottdale: Herald Press, 1957), p. 189. Hillerbrand, pp. 92–93, summarizes in five points the basis for Anabaptist willingness to obey governmental authority.

11. Kreider, pp. 86-87. Conrad Grebel et al., "Letters to Thomas Müntzer by Conrad Grebel and Friends," in George Hunston Williams and Angel M. Mergal, eds., *Spiritual and Anabaptist Writers. Documents Illustrative of the Radical Reformation*, Library of Christian Classics, vol. 25 (Philadelphia: Westminster, 1957), pp. 83–84, had already in 1524 warned Müntzer against attacking the princes. Menno Simons, *Complete Writings*, 671, preached against the abominations of the Münster revolt from the outset of his Anabaptist career.

12. Yoder, p. 52, n. 74.

13. Ibid., p. 40; Hillerbrand, pp. 94–96.

14. Yoder, p. 39.

15. The most extensive development of the doctrine of two worlds in the implicit theology of Anabaptism is that of Robert Friedmann, *The Theology of Anabaptism*, (Scottdale: Herald Press, 1973), and "The Doctrine of Two Worlds," in Hershberger, pp. 105–118. Balthasar Hubmaier, an early associate of Grebel, argued for a much more "responsible" role for the Anabaptist community in Moravia at the Nicolsburg disputation in 1527. However, his congregation did not survive his martyr death in 1528. Williams, *The Radical Reformation*, pp. 224–229.

16. Kreider, p. 191; Hillerbrand, pp. 89–91.

17. *Confession, oder kurzes und einfältiges Glaubensbekenntniß derer so man nennt die vereinigte Flämische, Friesische und Hochdeutsche Taufgesinnte Mennonitengemeinde* (1660; Odessa: die Gemeinde zu Rudnerweide, 1853), pp. 25–27. *Katechismus, oder: kurze und einfältige Unterweisung aus der heiligen Schrift, in Frage und Antwort*. Achte Auflage. (Elbing: die christliche taufgesinnte Gemeine in Preußen, 1837), p. 36. The version of the *Glaubensbekenntniß der Mennoniten in Preußen* included in this edition of the catechism concludes the article on the state with the remark: "We consider ourselves obligated to accept public office only in such cases where it does not conflict with our obligations to God and our *Gemeinde* [church]; we gladly leave such tasks to those who have the freedom of conscience to accept them" (pp. 30–31). Mennonites in Russia used the *Confession* above, which did not include this provision.

18. Kreider, pp. 192–193; Hillerbrand, pp. 103–107; Harold S. Bender, "Church and State in Mennonite History," *MQR* 13 (April 1939): 88.

19. Harold S. Bender and C. Henry Smith, eds., *The Mennonite Encyclopedia. A Comprehensive Reference Work on the Anabaptist-Mennonite Movement*, 4 vols. (Scottdale: Mennonite Publishing House, 1955–1959), s.v. "Privileges (*Privilegium*)," by Ernst Crous; Cornelius J. Dyck and Dennis D. Martin, eds., *The Mennonite Encyclopedia*, vol. 5 (1990), s.v. "Privileges (Privilegia)," by Adolf Ens.

20. For a brief summary of this era of Mennonite history, see John Horsch, *Mennonites in Europe*, 2nd rev. ed. (Scottdale: Mennonite Publishing House, 1950), chap. 27; C. Henry Smith, *Smith's Story of the Mennonites*, 5th ed., rev. and enl. by Cornelius Krahn

(Newton, Kans.: Faith and Life Press, 1981), chap. 5; William I. Schreiber, *The Fate of the Prussian Mennonites* (Göttingen Research Committee, 1955).

21. The entire text is reproduced by D. H. Epp, *Die Chortitzer Mennoniten. Versuch einer Darstellung des Entwickelungsganges derselben* (Odessa: A. Schultz, 1889), pp. 24–32. An English summary is found in David G. Rempel, "The Mennonite Commonwealth in Russia. A Sketch of Its Founding and Endurance, 1789–1919," *MQR* 47 (October 1973): 283–286. According to J. J. Hildebrand, *Hildebrand's Zeittafel. Chronologische Zeittafel 1500 Daten historischer Ereignisse und Geschehnisse aus der Zeit der Geschichte der Mennoniten Westeuropas, Russlands und Amerikas* (Winnipeg: By the author, 1945), p. 147, the original document in Russian was dated 22 April 1787.

22. D. H. Epp, pp. 97–101. This September 1800 charter reaffirms all relevant items of the original *Privilegium* and expands the clause on military exemption.

23. David G. Rempel, "The Mennonite Colonies in New Russia. A Study of Their Settlement and Economic Development from 1789 to 1914" (Ph.D. dissertation, Stanford University, 1933), pp. 42–43.

24. Rempel, "The Mennonite Commonwealth," *MQR* 47 (October 1973): 296, 300; 48 (January 1974): 11.

25. Rempel, 48 (January 1974): 10–15, gives a concise summary of the system of local government. A more extensive treatment is found in his "Mennonite Colonies in New Russia," pp. 113–122.

26. Francis, "Mennonite Institutions in Early Manitoba," pp. 149–151.

27. Bender's contention, "Church and State in Mennonite History," p. 98, that "actually the government approached a form of theocracy," is not accurate. The church had no power in civil affairs and no direct influence. Officials of the two organizations did not overlap. And church control of the school system implies theocracy only if it is assumed that education is clearly the responsibility of the state. On this point see also Henry J. Gerbrandt, *Adventure in Faith. The Background in Europe and the Development in Canada of the Bergthaler Mennonite Church of Manitoba* (Altona, Man.: D. W. Friesen, 1970), p. 28, and C. A. Dawson, *Group Settlement. Ethnic Communities in Western Canada*, vol. 7, Canadian Frontiers of Settlement, W. A. Mackintosh and W. L. G. Jörg, eds. (Toronto: Macmillan, 1936), pp. 95, 99.

28. See John Friesen, ed., *Mennonites in Russia, 1788–1988. Essays in Honour of Gerhard Lohrenz* (Winnipeg: CMBC Publications, 1989), pp. 56–60, 64–68; James Urry, *None But Saints. The Transformation of Mennonite Life in Russia, 1789–1889* (Winnipeg: Hyperion Press, 1989), pp. 125–137.

CHAPTER I

# SETTLEMENT IN CANADA

In 1870 Czar Alexander II inaugurated a program to assimilate German and other foreign subjects more thoroughly into the Russian nation. Special exemptions granted to these colonists a century earlier by Catherine II, including the "eternal" Mennonite *Privilegium* of 1800, came to an end. Military exemption was replaced by conscription and universal military training. The Russian language was to replace German as the official language of instruction in the schools. The *Fürsorge Komitee* in Odessa was abolished, placing Mennonites and other foreign colonists under the direct administration of municipal and provincial authorities. Realizing that such far-reaching changes might be unacceptable to some of the "foreigners" in Russia, Alexander allowed a ten-year transition period during which emigration would be permitted.

This abrupt change in government policy came as a shock to the Mennonites. Delegations were sent to St. Petersburg, at first to gain assurance that the *Privilegium* of Catherine and Paul would be honoured. When that proved impossible, a compromise was sought on the issue of military service. The promise of non-combatant alternative service persuaded about two-thirds of the fifty thousand Mennonites to remain in Russia. Over seventeen thousand, however, emigrated to North America during the decade of transition.[1]

In 1870 Canada acquired title to the huge northwest territory of North America, which had until then been under the jurisdiction of the Hudson's Bay Company. That was but one of a series of steps undertaken by the John A. Macdonald government of the young Dominion of Canada to ensure that its dream of a continent-wide national state would be realized. The U.S. purchase of Alaska from Russia in 1867, coupled with a resolution in Congress expressing concern about the new British Dominion and openly expressed annexationist sentiments in several states, understandably caused Macdonald some anxiety. Paper jurisdiction over the huge prairie region with its 1,500–kilometre undefended border meant little without a settled population occupying the land. How could more settlers best be attracted?

Under considerable pressure from its small settled population, Ottawa gave provincial status to Manitoba in 1870. However, the federal government retained control over crown lands in order to use them to lure settlers and compensate railway construction companies. A year later the first of a series of treaties was signed with the Cree and Ojibway nations, ceding aboriginal title to the land. The Dominion Lands Act of 1872 provided for homestead grants as a further inducement to settlers. The creation of the Royal Northwest Mounted Police in 1873 was to ensure law and order in the West. Good transportation was promised in the form of a transcontinental railway agreed to in the negotiations to bring British Columbia into Confederation.

Hundreds of English Canadians from Ontario and some Americans responded by relocating to Manitoba. But these came as individuals. Groups settlement schemes, initially devised to make relocation more attractive to French Canadians, became a prominent feature of prairie settlement and a significant attraction to various European groups, including the Mennonites from Russia.

## Negotiating a *Privilegium*

Early in 1872 the Canadian government was informed that some Mennonites wished to emigrate from Russia. Cornelius Jansen, Prussian consul in the Black Sea port of Berdiansk and a Mennonite, had been interested in settlement in America for some time. The British consul in Berdiansk, James Zohrab, was aware of Canada's interest in agricultural immigrants. Through this connection two Mennonite delegations made formal inquiry through Zohrab of settlement possibilities and conditions in Canada. *Ältester* Leonhard Sudermann, leader of a Molotschna colony congregation, addressed three issues. Would Mennonites, like the Society of Friends, be assured of "an entire exemption from all military service?" Could they hope for a grant or cheap purchase of land? Would "an advance from the Government" be possible in case of necessity?[2] The sympathetic stance of Zohrab encouraged a group of Hutterian Brethren to identify themselves with Sudermann's inquiry.[3]

The lines of communication to the Canadian government were rather cumbersome. The British consul in Berdiansk reported to the Foreign Office in London (sometimes via the embassy in St. Petersburg), which passed the information on to the Colonial Office, which in turn relayed it to the Canadian Governor General in Ottawa, who delivered it to the appropriate government ministries. In spite of this, Ottawa had its formal response ready by April 26, 1872. An order-in-council of that date responded to the three points in the Mennonite request. First, the Minister of Militia and Defence pointed out that by statute

> any person bearing a Certificate from the Society of Menonists shall be exempt from Military Service when balloted in time of peace or war, upon such conditions and under such regulations as the Governor-in-Council may, from time to time prescribe.[4]

Second, the Minister of Agriculture informed the Mennonites of the provisions of the Dominion Lands Act under which persons over the age of twenty-one could apply for a homestead grant of 160 acres. The Department of Agriculture also provided copies of several of its immigration publications. Third, the enquirers were informed that it was not the policy of the Dominion government to grant aid to any settlers in Canada.

By July 1872 the Mennonites in Russia had an opportunity to discuss immigration to Canada personally with a special agent of the Canadian government, William Hespeler.[5] A recent German immigrant living in Waterloo, Ontario, Hespeler had been given the special assignment of recruiting or assisting German-speaking immigrants from eastern Europe. He arrived at the British consulate in Berdiansk on July 25 and immediately made contact with Mennonites of the Molotschna colony through the connections established earlier by Consul Zohrab.[6] A representative from Bergthal colony, *Gebietsamtschreiber* (district government secretary) Jacob Friesen, also came to see Hespeler during his visit to the Molotschna area.[7]

One point on which the Mennonites sought additional clarification and reassurance was that of military exemption. The order-in-council of April seemed to make exemption subject to "such conditions and such regulations as the Governor-in-Council may, from time to time prescribe." Hespeler assured them that the law provided for absolute exemption from military duty in time of peace or war and that the Governor-in-Council could prescribe no conditions or regulations under which they could be compelled to serve.[8] The Canadian government, which had been informed of this concern by consuls Jansen and Zohrab in letters of June and July, provided the same assurance in a further order-in-council.[9] It gave "the German Mennonites in Russia the fullest assurances of absolute immunity from military service if they settle in Canada." The Governor General in Council, the report went on to say, "cannot prescribe any conditions or regulations under which, under any circumstances, the persons referred to ... can be compelled to render any military service."

Hespeler's energetic wooing of Mennonite immigrants had meanwhile attracted the unfavourable attention of the Russian authorities. In order to escape apprehension, he quietly slipped out of the country in early August but continued to correspond with the Mennonite leaders from Germany. In early November he arranged for a number of representatives from the Molotschna and Bergthal colonies to meet with him in Odessa. At this meeting he invited an official delegation to come to Canada at government expense in order to explore settlement possibilities. Representing Bergthal colony at this meeting were *Oberschulze* Jacob Peters and minister Heinrich Wiebe.[10]

In Canada, meanwhile, the government stepped up its efforts to ensure that it would obtain at least some of the Mennonite immigrants. Jacob Y. Shantz, a Swiss Mennonite businessman living in Kitchener, Ontario,[11] was sent to inspect Manitoba with the hope that his report would be a suitable inducement to the Mennonites in Russia. His *Narrative of a Journey to Manitoba*, based on his western trip in the fall of 1872, was translated into German and distributed widely among the Mennonites in Russia.[12] What particularly appealed to them were the large grants of land *en bloc* to which Shantz drew attention. These were essential for maintaining the communal style of life that they had developed during ninety years of living in colonies of villages in Russia.

The Canadian government followed up this general promise of free land by setting aside a specific block of seven townships to be "reserved for the exclusive use, by settlement, of Germans in Russia, Mennonites and others."[13] Except for a slight modification introduced a couple of months later this reserved block, located just east of the junction of the Red and Rat Rivers, became the Mennonite East Reserve (see map 1).[14]

This aggressive wooing of the Mennonites by the Canadian government, and especially the illegal activities of its agent William Hespeler, alarmed the British diplomatic staff in Russia. Lord Loftus, the ambassador in St. Petersburg, had already drawn the attention of the Foreign Minister to the fact "that the penalties imposed by Russian law on immigrants, and on those who further immigration, without the previous consent of the Imperial Government are very severe."[15] That warning came in April, before Hespeler had appeared on the scene. After his two visits with the Mennonites in Berdiansk and Odessa in July and November, British concern mounted. In early December the Foreign Office advised the Colonial Office:

> Lord Augustus Loftus appears to think that the Canadian government have been going rather too far in their endeavour to induce these

# Map 1
## Province of Manitoba, 1875, Showing Rivers, Trails, and Reserves

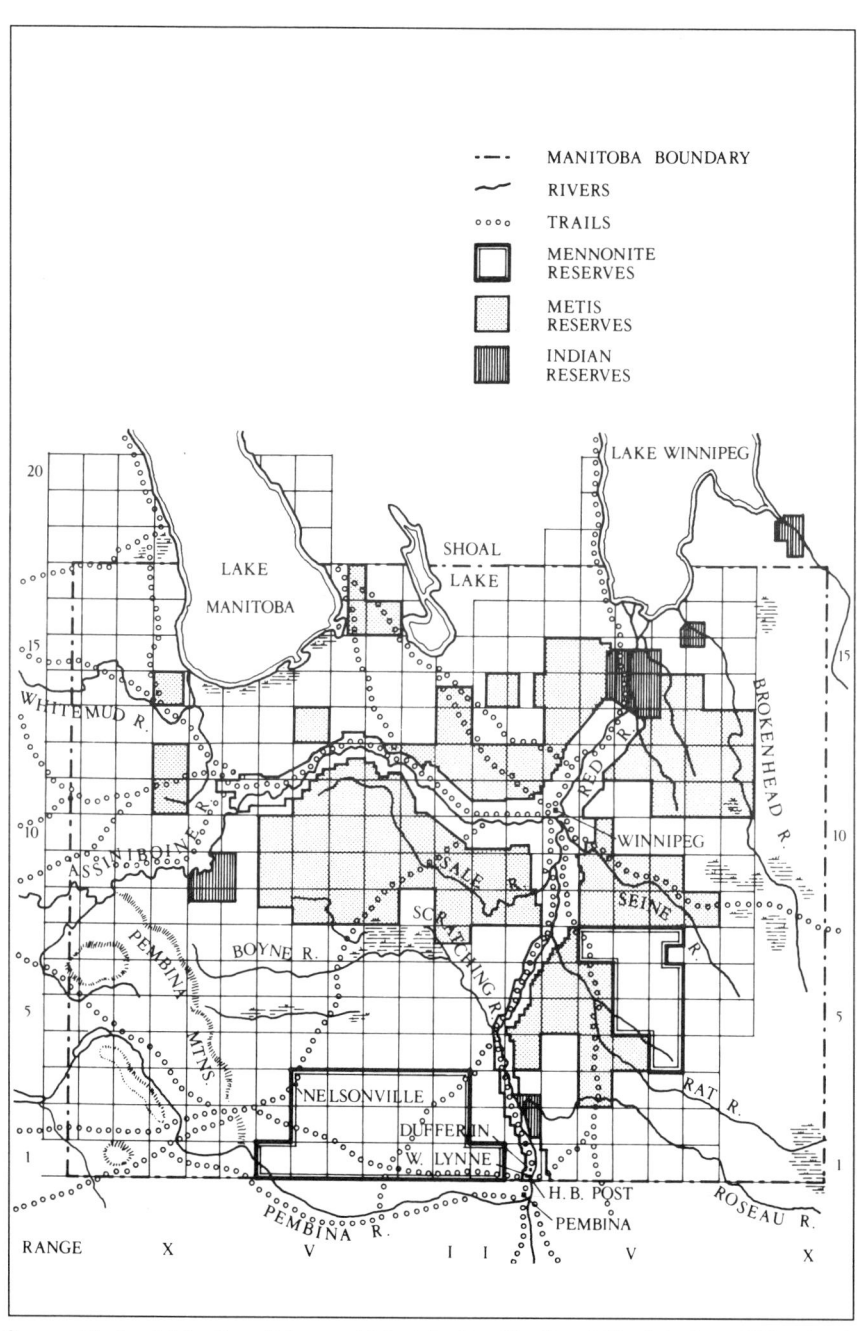

Source: Gerhard John Ens, *Volost and Municipality: The Rural Municipality of Rhineland, 1884–1984* (Altona, Man.: R. M. of Rhineland, 1984), p. 12. Used by permission.

Mennonites to immigrate to Canada if they leave Russia, and he seems to think that Mr. Hespeler (the Canadian Emigration Agent) is likely to get himself into trouble and Her Majesty's government also if he again returns to Bessarabia with the object of inducing these people to leave.[16]

The Colonial Secretary, Lord Kimberley, followed this up with a coded telegram to the Canadian government: "To avoid complications with Russia Canadian Government should take no further steps with respect to Mennonite emigration till informed that matter can be safely proceeded with."[17] From this point on all correspondence between the Canadian and British government on this subject was marked "secret."

The Canadian government acted promptly on Lord Kimberley's telegram and immediately recalled Hespeler to Canada.[18] He did return, but his work had been done. In February 1873 Consul Zohrab reported to the Foreign Office that two public meetings had been held in the neighbourhood of Berdiansk for the purpose of selecting delegates to visit the U.S.A. and Canada. Representatives of ten Mennonite colonies had attended these meetings.[19] The Bergthal colony elected its *Oberschulze* Jacob Peters and one of its ministers, Heinrich Wiebe, brother of *Ältester* Gerhard Wiebe, while the *Kleine Gemeinde* chose Cornelius Toews, a brother of *Ältester* Peter Toews, and David Klassen.[20] In all, twelve delegates were selected to visit North America representing the Mennonites and Hutterites of Russia, Volhynia in Poland, and Prussia.

The Canadian authorities attempted to provide every assistance possible to the delegates.[21] The Canadian immigration agent in Hamburg facilitated their travel through Germany and England. In Ottawa, the Minister of Agriculture was alerted of their arrival. In Kitchener-Waterloo Jacob Y. Shantz arranged for them to meet with Ontario Mennonites and then accompanied the delegates to Winnipeg. Here Hespeler arranged for them to meet the lieutenant-governor of Manitoba as well as Premier A. J. Clark and most of his cabinet.

Two land inspection tours were undertaken. The first under the leadership of J. Norquay, provincial Minister of Agriculture, and immigration agent William Hespeler, left Winnipeg on June 18, 1873, to inspect the eight townships reserved east of the Red River. Half of the delegate group saw enough mosquitoes, local population, and unimpressive terrain on that trip to give up on Manitoba. They returned to the U.S.A. The remaining six delegates, including Wiebe and Peters of Bergthal colony, as well as Klassen and Toews of the *Kleine Gemeinde*, undertook a second trip west of Winnipeg, north of the Assiniboine River on June 23. Despite their involvement in a Dominion Day brawl at White Horse Plain,[22] the delegates from Bergthal and the *Kleine Gemeinde* were sufficiently impressed with Canada not to join the other delegates in further exploring settlement possibilities in the U.S.A.

The four delegates now returned to Ottawa and on July 23 sent a letter to J. H. Pope, Minister of Agriculture, informing him of their choice of the province of Manitoba and in particular of the eight townships reserved for them. They indicated their intention to begin the migration in the spring of 1874 and expressed the hope that another location might be available to them should the soil of the present reserve prove unsuitable.[23]

John Lowe, Secretary of the Department of Agriculture, responded to their letter a few days later, outlining in fifteen points the advantages and immunities offered to the Mennonites by the Canadian government.[24] For the most part this letter was merely a summary of Canadian immigration law and Dominion Lands Act provisions. However, the first point reiterated exemption from military service for Mennonites, the second confirmed the reserve of eight townships provided for by an earlier order-in-council, and the fifth responded affirmatively to the delegates' request that Mennonites be allowed to exchange these eight townships for any other eight unoccupied townships should the original ones prove unsatisfactory. Finally, points ten and eleven affirmed full religious freedom for the Mennonites, including the privilege of educating their children and of affirming instead of taking oaths.

These points answer most of the eleven questions that the *Kleine Gemeinde* delegates were instructed to raise.[25] They follow the eight-point outline communicated three months earlier by Hespeler to J. H. Pope, the Minister of Agriculture, and are almost identical with the draft response prepared for Hespeler by the Department of Agriculture in May.[26] The four delegates to whom the letter was addressed and the church groups they represented saw this document as their new *Privilegium*.

Following legal refinements, Pope submitted the substance of Lowe's letter to the cabinet on July 28, 1873. It was approved by the Privy Council on August 13.[27] This document, rather than the earlier letter of John Lowe, was the legal statement of the Canadian government's agreement with the Mennonite immigrants, the actual *Privilegium*.

On the diplomatic front, meanwhile, the British Foreign Office continued to be concerned about Canadian activity in Russia, particularly that of its energetic special emigration agent. Lord Tenterden warned that "such a line of conduct on Mr. Hespeler's part, while permission to emigrate has not been granted to the Mennonites, is liable to create inconvenient discussions between her Majesty's Government and the Government of Russia."[28] British concern mounted in the spring of 1873 when Ambassador Loftus in St. Petersburg was requested by Prince Grachakov to warn

Consul Zohrab in Berdiansk "against being mixed up in any way in these attempts to induce the German Mennonite colonists to leave Russia."[29]

In Zohrab's response to this warning, he revealed that Hespeler had obtained possession of some of the official correspondence between Ottawa and London on this subject, and had passed some of it on to the Mennonite leaders. On discovering this the Colonial Secretary rather strongly rebuked Lord Dufferin and the Canadian government and requested a full explanation of this matter together with a list of documents given to Mr. Hespeler. Lord Kimberley drew attention to his telegram of December 7, 1872, in which he had instructed the Canadian government that it should take no further steps in the matter of the Mennonite immigration, and then added: "Your Lordship cannot fail to perceive the very serious embarrassment which may be caused by these proceedings."[30]

Ottawa's "full explanation" was prepared by Agriculture Minister Pope.[31] In his covering letter, Lord Dufferin pointed out to the Colonial Secretary that "in the present instance the communications made to Mr. Hespeler do not seem to have possessed any inconvenient significance," but that he had nevertheless warned his ministers about the impropriety of transmitting official documents to anyone without the consent of the Governor General.[32]

For the British Foreign Office the matter was taken care of with this explanation. For the Mennonites, however, the consequences of this exchange did not become apparent until almost fifty years later. Nine days after Lord Dufferin had approved their *Privilegium* in the form of Order-in-Council number 957, he sent a telegram to Pope in which he withdrew his approval of that particular Privy Council minute and asked that it "be cancelled until he can send further directions."[33] A notation reading "Suspend order accordingly and do not act on or enter it" was made on the front of the original copy of this order-in-council on August 22, and Pope's copy, the only one in circulation besides that of the Governor General, was withdrawn. Until March 1916, the official Mennonite *Privilegium* was thus not only a secret document, but also one that had been entirely removed from circulation.[34]

What was its legal status meanwhile? Since the conduct of Canada's foreign relations in 1873 was still the responsibility of the British government, the Governor General, as an imperial officer, had the power to withhold royal assent from actions of the Canadian government impinging on external affairs. Indeed, on instruction from the Colonial Secretary or the Foreign Secretary in London, it was his obligation to do so. The normal procedure for undoing the effect of an order-in-council was by passing a subsequent order-in-council revoking the former one. No such action was taken in this case. There appears to be no precedent for Lord Dufferin's withdrawing his signature from a legal document.[35] Since the significance of this action was never tested in the courts, it remains a matter of conjecture. It is clear that the Canadian government did not intend to revoke its agreement with the Mennonites. One may therefore assume that Lord Dufferin "did not seek to rescind the order-in-council but only to have it put aside until 'it could be safely proceeded with.'"[36]

Meanwhile, the two departments most directly involved with Mennonite immigration and settlement, those of Agriculture and the Interior, operated on the basis of the John Lowe letter of July 26, 1876. A Department of Agriculture memorandum in the summer of 1877 summarizes the sequence of events that led the Governor General to withdraw his name "from that order, in view of certain correspondence which had passed with the Imperial Government," and concludes: "The official letter of July 26th to the Mennonite Deputation, did, however, remain, as an act of the Government, by the Department of Agriculture."[37]

Five years later John Lowe himself explained the situation to the Secretary of the Department of the Interior. His July 26 letter "was embodied in an Order-in-Council which was passed at that time" from which Lord Dufferin afterwards withdrew his name "in consequence of some correspondence between the British Russian Ambassador and the Imperial Government." Lowe concludes: "It was, therefore, understood that the letter which was a formal act should remain as an understanding between the Canadian Govt and the Mennonites."[38]

The Mennonite delegates felt that the negotiations with the government had gone well. They were reassured on every point of concern by the letter that they had received from Lowe on July 26. As far as they were concerned, this letter was their new *Privilegium*. And in effect it was, since it remained the only record of their agreement in circulation and was the document on the basis of which the government dealt with them until the events of 1919 publicized the existence of the official order-in-council of August 13. On the basis of its assurances the delegates from Bergthal and the *Kleine Gemeinde* recommended that their people migrate to Canada, rather than to the United States.

The Bergthal delegates seem to have had their mind made up in favour of Canada even before exploring the land in Manitoba. They had travelled as far south as Texas in the U.S.A. but did not like the country. Even more important to Rev. Heinrich Wiebe was the question of exemption from military service. Hutterite delegate Paul Tschetter noted the following conversation with Wiebe in his diary entry under St. Paul, May 25:

> We talked about nonresistance and how he liked the country here. He said the country did not appeal much to him and that after all the

question of military service is the most important. He thought that it would not be possible to secure total exemption from military service in the United States, but that the English government would be more liberal and grant a charter guaranteeing exemption from military service which was better than what this country could offer.... He said that one should not only consider the land question but also not forget the matter of freedom, for that is the reason why we came to this country and are making this long journey.[39]

*Ältester* Gerhard Wiebe, in reporting the return of the delegates to his Bergthal church, mentions only that they brought with them two written guarantees of freedom from military service. Quality, quantity, and price of land were obviously of secondary importance to him also. The Bergthal community chose Canada, wrote Wiebe, "because it was under the protection of the Queen of England; and we believed that our freedom from military service would survive longer there and also that church and school would remain under our own jurisdiction."[40]

This confidence in Canada was undoubtedly based primarily on the fact that the delegates had received a written *Privilegium* from the federal government, something they had been unable to procure from Washington. But Wiebe's reference to the Queen of England also suggests that they were prepared to place more trust in a monarchical than a republican form of government.[41] In Russia, Mennonites had preferably negotiated directly with the Czar and had always tended to place their faith in the highest authority.[42] A Bergthal descendant, writing fifty years later in Canada, strongly reflects this attitude. For the beleaguered Mennonites in Russia in 1870, rescue came sooner than expected, he wrote in 1923.

A turn for the better began in 1872. Queen Victoria of England was looking for immigrants for the lands which England had freed for settlement in Canada. It was through her that the way for the Mennonites from Russia to Canada was opened, and just as Empress Catherine of Russia had once appeared as the saviour of the Mennonites, so the Queen of England now appeared in almost the same way.[43]

The emphasis that the Bergthal and *Kleine Gemeinde* delegates placed on a *Privilegium* is seen even more strongly when their choice is compared with that of the Molotschna delegates who recommended settlement in the U.S.A. When bishops Jacob Buller and Leonhard Sudermann were delegated by their congregations to make the inspection trip to North America, they received written instructions to consider the following points as absolutely essential in their negotiations with the government: legal assurance of complete religious freedom, including specifically full exemption from every kind of military service; sufficient land of good quality either free or at low prices and easy terms; and assurance of the kind of closed settlement, use of the German language, and local self-government such as they had enjoyed in Russia.[44] In spite of the fact that the two most important of these demands, the first and the third, were not met by the United States government, both Buller and Sudermann recommended Kansas as the place of settlement to their people.[45] They did so, knowing that the Canadian government was prepared to meet these demands if they would settle in Canada. Juhnke suggests that the persuasive salesmanship of American railroad representatives made the difference.[46] Toews and Klassen of the *Kleine Gemeinde* chose Canada, in spite of a footnote in their delegate mandate which asked "that during the selection of a place of refuge they are first of all to keep the United States in mind."[47]

## Group Migration

On their arrival back in Russia the delegates of the Bergthal colony and of the *Kleine Gemeinde* in Borosenko recommended Canada to their people as the place to settle. Both congregations endorsed the recommendation and prepared to emigrate as entire communities. The first immigrants from both groups arrived in Quebec in July 1874. By then John A. Macdonald's Conservative government had resigned in disgrace over the "Pacific scandal" and been replaced by the Liberals under Alexander Mackenzie. The next year, the peak of the immigration, they were joined by large numbers from the Fürstenland, Chortitza and a few smaller colonies. Although the latter settlements had not sent any delegates to North America, and did not emigrate as entire colonies, many of their members accepted the report of the Bergthal delegates as their basis for emigrating.[48] The congregation in Fürstenland was led by *Ältester* Johann Wiebe, a relative of the Bergthal bishop Gerhard Wiebe.

Almost seven thousand Mennonites from these four groups in Russia arrived at Quebec during the years 1874 to 1880 and went on to settle in Manitoba. The "postage stamp" province had a population of under 12,000 in 1871, largely Métis and English half-breeds. Indians (558) and whites (1,565) were a distinct minority. Catholics slightly outnumbered Protestants. In 1875 and 1876 Mennonites constituted well over a quarter of all immigrants coming to the province, but by the end of the decade they were an insignificant drop in the bucket. (See table 1 for annual totals.) Nevertheless, Mennonites constituted over ten percent of the province's 1881 total population of 65,954.[49]

The Canadian government provided passenger warrants from Hamburg to Fort Garry in the amount of thirty dollars per person over the age of eight and fifteen dollars for children. Jacob Klotz was appointed special immigration agent in Hamburg and directed "to bestow particular attention to the embarkation of the Mennonites who may sail from Hamburg for

Table 1
**Mennonite Immigrant Arrivals at Quebec, 1874–1880**

| | Year | | | | | | | Total Arrivals |
|---|---|---|---|---|---|---|---|---|
| | 1874 | 1875 | 1876 | 1877 | 1878 | 1879 | 1880 | |
| Mennonite Arrivals | 1,543 | 3,261 | 1,352 | 184 | 323 | 208 | 69 | 6,940 |
| Total Immigrant Arrivals | | 11,970 | 34,000 | | | 11,500 | 18,000 | |

Source: Adolf Ens and Rita Penner, "Quebec Passenger Lists of the Russian Mennonite Immigration, 1874–1880," *MQR* 48 (October 1974): 530; Delbert Plett, *Profile of the Mennonite Kleine Gemeinde 1874* (Steinbach: DFP Publications, 1987), p. 66, identifies an additional ship with ten Mennonite passengers in 1874. Totals have been adjusted accordingly. W. L. Morton, *Manitoba: A History*, 2nd ed. (Toronto: University of Toronto Press, 1967), pp. 176–177.

Canada."[50] Along with him, immigration agents all along the line reported regularly on the flow of Mennonites, from the Agent General in London, England, to the agents in Quebec and Montreal, the travelling agent between Quebec and Toronto, the agents at Toronto and Winnipeg, and the special agent at West Lynne on the Manitoba–U.S.A. border.[51] In addition to these, Jacob Y. Shantz, working for both the Canadian government and the Russian Mennonite Aid Committee, organized by him among Ontario Swiss Mennonites, was a tremendous help in keeping the flow of immigrants moving smoothly and in helping the new arrivals through the first few weeks on location in Manitoba.

## The Reserves

When the province of Manitoba was founded in 1870, its crown lands remained under the jurisdiction of the federal Department of Agriculture, which handled immigration matters, and the Department of the Interior, which was in charge of crown lands. The latter department was therefore responsible for administering clauses four and five of the *Privilegium*, which promised that additional or alternative townships would be reserved for Mennonite settlement should the original eight prove insufficient or unsuitable.

The approximately thirteen hundred Mennonites who arrived in Manitoba in 1874 took up 386 homesteads in the eight townships reserved east of the Red River and founded two villages on the Scratching River west of the Red.[52] In reporting this to the Surveyor General, Winnipeg immigration agent William Hespeler expressed the hope that an additional reserve would soon be granted, for he considered that only about two-thirds of the eight townships were fit for settlement. The investigation subsequently ordered by the Minister of the Interior showed Hespeler's estimate to be generous. Three of the eight townships were described as "principally marsh lands," and three others as "bad," "very inferior," and "totally unfit for farming purposes." The Surveyor General estimated that not more than fifty additional families could obtain reasonably good homesteads on the reserve.[53]

The Chortitza and Fürstenland settlers who arrived the following year expressed a preference for the "treeless plain between the River and Pembina Mountain." The Dominion Lands agent in Winnipeg therefore recommended creating a second reserve, consisting of the first three townships immediately north of the U.S. border stretching from range one east to range five west of the principal meridian. He assured Ottawa that "no objection will be raised by Canadian settlers as tracts unfit [for] settlement by them being destitute of timber."[54]

Following some bargaining between the Mennonites and officials of the Department of the Interior, the government agreed to a second reserve of seventeen townships whose boundaries were officially ratified in the spring of 1876.[55] Although some of these townships were still in the process of being surveyed, eighteen villages were laid out in the summer of 1875 by the incoming settlers.[56] Two major settlements, in addition to the smaller one at Scratching River, were now established (see map 1).

To the extent that geography and pioneer conditions permitted, these settlements reproduced as nearly as possible the communal conditions that Mennonites had learned to appreciate in Russia.[57] The two reserves on either side of the Red River formed natural communities. As soon as a village had been laid out, its family heads proceeded to elect a *Dorfschulze* (village mayor), *Brandschulze* (to enforce fire safety regulations and act as appraiser for the mutual fire insurance), and *Hirtenschulze* (to regulate matters relating to the common pasture of the village). The *Dorfschulzen* of the various villages together formed the *Gebietsamt*, a council for the whole reserve, and elected an *Oberschulze* (reeve) for the whole community.[58] In the East Reserve Jacob Peters, delegate in 1873 and *Oberschulze* of the Bergthal colony since 1850, occupied this position after his arrival in 1877. In the West Reserve Isaak Mueller was elected to the office on his arrival at the West Lynne immigrant sheds in 1875.

The church continued with the leadership already elected in Russia. *Ältester* (bishop) Gerhard Wiebe initially continued his leadership over the entire Bergthal congregation even though the geographical separation of the two reserves made that impractical. For *Ältester* Peter Toews the shorter distance from the East Reserve to the Scratching River villages of the *Kleine Gemeinde* was more manageable. *Ältester* Johann Wiebe's continuing leadership of the Fürstenland congregation was natural. Since the congregation had been an affiliate of the Chortitza church in Russia until the time of the emigration, it was a relatively easy matter for immigrants from that congregation to join the Fürstenland group. This enlarged congregation was known as the Reinländer church in Manitoba. All three congregations had a number of additional ministers and deacons, who constituted the *Lehrdienst* under the leadership of their bishop. The village schools and the *Waisenamt* (orphan's office), which administered inheritances and the care of widows and orphans, functioned under the direction of the *Lehrdienst*.

Thus all of the basic needs of the community were taken care of from the outset by an organization brought along from Russia. Roads, bridges, and dams were constructed as needed. Taxes and statute labour were assessed in order to accomplish these public works. Schools were opened in the first year of settlement. Basic welfare was provided for the victims of accident by fire or death.

## The Mennonite Loan

Most of the Mennonites who immigrated to Canada during the 1870s were relatively poor. The six villages of the Fürstenland colony were located on rented land. The Bergthal colony's acreage had been purchased in 1836, but by 1874 the number of landless families in the colony comprised two-thirds of the total.[59] The landless situation in the two mother colonies, Chortitza and Molotschna, was severe enough that, in spite of extensive emigration to North America, four daughter colonies involving twenty-two villages were founded in Russia during this decade.[60] Many of the emigrating families were already so poor in Russia that they required financial assistance for their passage to Canada.[61] The limited amount of capital that they brought with them to Canada, estimated at an average of $125 per person,[62] was insufficient in many cases to provide basic food and shelter for the first winter and to obtain the necessary implements and seed for spring farm work.

Aware of this poverty, the delegates from Bergthal met with representatives of the Swiss Mennonites in Ontario a second time on their way home in 1873 to approach them about a loan for the new settlers.[63] The Russian Mennonite Aid Committee, which Jacob Y. Shantz served as secretary-treasurer, became the channel for Ontario Mennonite aid to the immigrants. Money loaned to the Manitoba Mennonite settlers through this Committee came to about $50,000.[64]

During the winter of 1874 it became obvious both to the Ontario Mennonites and to the leaders of the immigration that the direct resources of the Ontario Mennonites would be insufficient to meet the need. Accordingly, a deputation of leading Mennonites from Ontario went to Ottawa in 1875 to request from the government an advance of one hundred thousand dollars to assist the immigration. This loan was to be repaid in ten annual instalments, with the deputation becoming personally responsible for the repayment. The Liberal government of Alexander Mackenzie introduced a bill for this purpose to the House of Commons, which was approved on April 7, 1875, after considerable debate.[65] Funds from the loan were made available as needed and were handled by Shantz, representing the Mennonite Aid Committee of Ontario.[66] Some of the money was used for the purchase of farm equipment, but much of it was required to save the new settlers from starvation during the early years when grasshoppers and drought destroyed the harvest.[67]

Between March 25, 1875, and November 7, 1877, a total of $96,400 was loaned.[68] During the first four years simple interest was to be charged at six percent per annum, and during the remaining six years compound interest at the same rate. The new settlers were unable to meet that payment schedule. In fact, by the middle of 1883 only three payments had been made amounting to $20,653.30 of the $76,844.34 due by then. Since Ontario Mennonites had posted bonds against this loan, the Treasury Board decided briefly during June 1883 to have the Justice Department collect the monies due from the bondsmen. The Minister of Agriculture interceded and obtained an agreement from cabinet not to press for immediate payment.[69]

By February 29, 1888, the Mennonites had repaid a total of $115,805.38 but by this time the interest had mounted so that the balance owing was still $51,480.76.[70] Later that year the Mennonite Aid Committee reported that they had "entirely exhausted the collections which it is possible for them to make from the settlers in Manitoba from the absolute inability of the remaining debtors to make any more payments." The Committee therefore requested from the government "a commutation of the rate of interest of six percent compounded, to four percent simple interest on the amount of capital advanced." That would leave a balance of $12,950.22 which the committee proposed to pay in final liquidation of the debt. The government adopted that course of action.[71]

The matter was not quite taken care of yet. Since the original terms of the loan had been set by an Act of Parliament, the Justice Department pointed out that it would require an action of Parliament to change those terms now.[72] Assent was duly given to the required Act on May 2, 1889,[73] clearing the way for cabinet to authorize returning the bonds to the Mennonite Aid Committee of Ontario.[74]

Because the government was experiencing difficulties in collecting any monies at all on similar loans made to other groups of immigrants,[75] the Minister of the Interior was rather effusive in reporting the successful termination of the Mennonite loan in 1892.

> The history of any country does not afford, I undertake to say, a case in which an obligation to the government on the part of any society, company or individual has been fulfilled with greater faithfulness than this....[76]

The inaccuracy in the Minister's further remark may be due to the fact that immigration matters were transferred from the Department of Agriculture to the Department of the Interior that year, so that both he and his staff were unfamiliar with the history of the Mennonite loan. His report continued:

> It is pleasant to be able to add that, as far as I know, neither from the persons to whom the advance was made nor from the Waterloo Society, who became accountable for its repayment, has there ever been any suggestion, far less any formal demand (as has been too frequently the case in regard to other loans made by the government), for a relaxation of the terms of refund, either as regards principal or interest, nor has there been any attempt either on the part of the settlers themselves or of their bondsmen to escape liability in even one individual case.

Largely as a result of this statement, "a veritable legend grew around the event and the faithful mode of repayment by its beneficiaries."[77] But the Mennonite settlers of Manitoba were not aware of this legend nor did they feel that they were doing anything heroic. Gerhard Wiebe, bishop of the Bergthal congregation, treated the entire loan as payable to the Ontario Mennonites, and was very aware of and thankful for substantial reductions made by them.[78] His counterpart on the West Reserve, *Ältester* Johann Wiebe, urged his congregation to greater diligence in repaying their debt.

> To strive with all one's will power to repay natural debts is an essential aspect of the Christian and God-pleasing way. Even more so with respect to our government debt, because she has taken us Mennonites into her land and given us protection and freedom of religion.[79]

He too was humbled and deeply grateful for the assistance given by the Ontario Mennonites.[80]

From the side of the Manitoba Mennonites, relations with both the government and Shantz's committee in Ontario had been so satisfactory in this matter that they were willing to try it again. When the first group migration to the Northwest Territories began in 1895 it was once more

Jacob Shantz who was requested to ask the Canadian government for a loan to assist the resettlement. But by 1895 government policy on such loans had changed and the request was politely refused.[81]

## Non-Mennonite Intruders

The possibility of forming closed communities by means of reserves created for them by the government was a very important factor in attracting Mennonites to settle in Canada rather than in the U.S.A. They discovered very quickly, however, that an order-in-council in the cabinet secretary's files did not protect them from receiving uninvited neighbours.

On the East Reserve this did not become a problem. The Anglo-Saxon Clear Springs settlement, founded four years before the Mennonite immigration, had inadvertently been included in the reserve. Its nine square miles in township 7, range 6 east were officially removed from it before the Mennonites arrived in Canada.[82] The few French-speaking Métis who briefly asserted a prior claim to lands in the East Reserve did not take up residence on them and did not mention their claim until years later.[83] The poor quality of the land and the rapidity with which available homesteads were taken deterred non-Mennonites from attempting to move in once the migration had started. In fact, from 1878 to 1881 well over half of the Bergthal families, dissatisfied with their land on the East Reserve, had moved to the western one or were planning to do so.[84] The non-Mennonites who entered the East Reserve later (1889–1896) either worked for Mennonite farmers or businessmen, or purchased land from them.[85]

This was not the case on the West Reserve. The open prairie stretching from the Red River to the Pembina escarpment, which Canadian settlers had regarded as "unfit for settlement" until recently, suddenly became "one of the most valuable tracts of land in possession of the Dominion."[86] Matters were complicated by the fact that many Mennonite settlers had located there before the boundaries of the reserve were officially established.

Several Canadian families from Ontario, located in the wooded area in the northwest corner of the reserve, quickly petitioned Ottawa to remove townships 2 and 3 in range 5 west from the Mennonite Reserve. They had come there with a view to settling the entire area "of the said townships with British subjects from Canada." The creation of the Mennonite Reserve, they argued, now deprived them of "the possibility of a Canadian neighbourhood."[87] Other immigrants from Ontario, who had squatted in the same area, complained directly to the Prime Minister.[88]

The complaint of the Canadian settlers was that they were too few in number to start their own schools and churches and now had no hope of others of their compatriots joining them, and that their holdings had depreciated in value since being placed in the reserve. The Mennonites, on the other hand, complained that the squatters and legal non-Mennonite settlers in the western portion of the reserve illegally restrained them from cutting timber in those townships. They also claimed that the English-speaking settlers were threatening to tear down any village that the Mennonites might attempt to found in that area. The Dominion Lands Surveyor, reporting these complaints in November 1877, recommended ejecting the squatters and offering compensation to legitimate non-Mennonite settlers to induce them to move.[89]

An official investigation ordered by the Minister of the Interior revealed that the central concern of the Mennonites was that they continue to have access to the woodlands of the western townships for timber and fuel.[90] Since the Mennonites felt very strongly about this, the government was anxious to effect a speedy solution to the problem lest the continuing immigration from Russia suffer a serious setback. Following discussions with the Minister of the Interior and John Lowe of the Department of Agriculture the Surveyor General recommended that squatters be ejected from the reserve and that a team of government representatives negotiate with the Mennonites to surrender their claim to townships 2 and 3 in range 5 west, or at least to those parts occupied by legitimate English settlers, in return for one or two townships adjoining the Mennonite Reserve in range seven and eight west. William Pearce, Dominion Lands Surveyor, and Donald Codd, Dominion Lands Agent, representing the Department of the Interior, and William Hespeler, representing the Immigration Department, all located in Winnipeg, were appointed to this commission.[91]

The commission met most of the English-speaking settlers involved in the dispute and then had a meeting with "all the reeves of the various villages" in the Mennonite Reserve. Its report in early 1878 resulted in instructions to the Dominion Land Agent at Emerson, George F. Newcombe, to implement its recommendations.[92] This involved ejecting squatters and cancelling a number of legitimate claims for failing to meet the requirements of the Homestead Act.[93] It also involved redrawing the western boundary of the reserve in townships two and three of range five west in such a way as to exclude the remaining legitimate non-Mennonite settlers from the reserve. The new boundary, which Newcombe called the "Meno-Canuck boundary," is indicated on map 2.[94] In return for the portions of townships two and three in range five west that the Mennonites had surrendered, amounting to just over one township, they accepted the first township in ranges seven and eight west.[95]

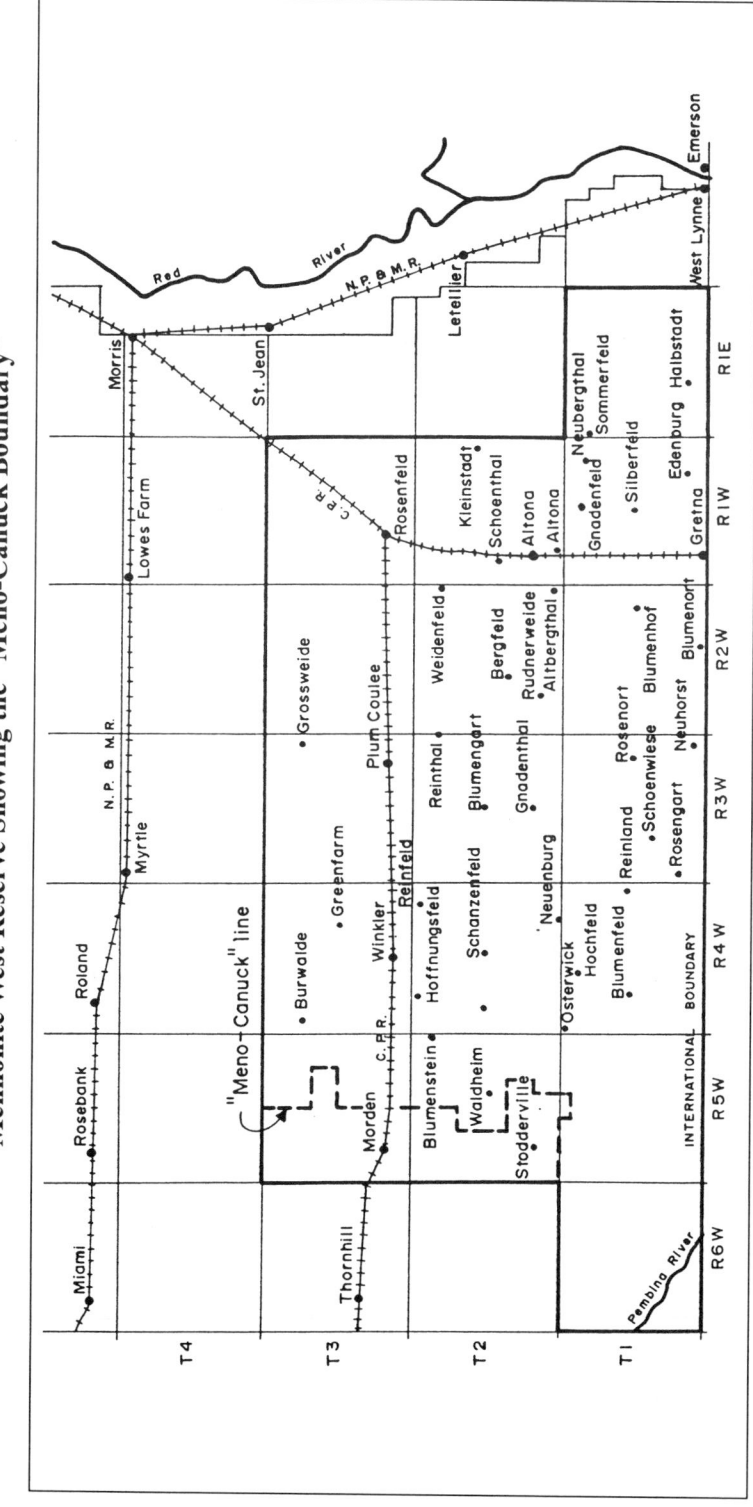

Map 2
Mennonite West Reserve Showing the "Meno-Canuck Boundary"

Source: Based on Report of George F. Newcomb to Donald Codd, April 30, 1878, NA, RG 15, vol. 232, no. 3129.

Unfortunately, the problem was not solved by this redrawing of boundaries. Non-Mennonite squatters continued to come into the western end of the reserve every year until the problem was further compounded by rumours that Ottawa was going to throw open the Mennonite reserves to general settlement.[96] Finally, in 1880, the Mennonite leaders protested formally to the Prime Minister that the Nelsonville Land Office was not enforcing the "Meno-Canuck" line, which they had always respected. Some of their young men were again before the magistrate, they complained, for cutting a load or two of dead firewood on their own timber lands.[97] It is difficult to determine whether the Dominion Lands Agent was unwilling or unable to enforce the provisions of the reserve. In any case, when William Hespeler reported an open clash between Mennonites and squatters in June 1881 and urged the Surveyor General to settle the Mennonite Reserve question, another special investigation was ordered.[98] The lengthy report filed by R. Rauscher in October of that year included a two-page list of non-Mennonite squatters on lands for which Mennonites held homestead entries, and another two-page list of non-Mennonite settlers who had not obtained entries to the lands they occupied. These squatters, Rauscher wrote, "form an unbroken Phalanx of Guardians against their Menonite [sic] neighbours, who they violently drive back when coming to fetch fuel or building timber, near the territory of which they (the Squatters) took forcible possession."[99] He recommended that the wooded portions of these townships be set aside as "Wood and Timber lots" under government inspection.

Nothing seems to have come of that suggestion, but Rauscher's lists drew attention to the magnitude of the squatter problem and to the loose administration of the Dominion Lands Office at Nelson. By the following summer the Commissioner of Dominion Lands in Winnipeg was pressing for further thorough investigation and calling the attention of the Minister of the Interior to "the growing confusion in the Reserve."[100] Much of that confusion, as it turned out, was in the Department's own administration. The books of the Winnipeg office were found to have over 450 homestead and pre-emption entries more than those in Ottawa.[101] Discrepancies were also found to exist between the departmental records in Ottawa and the entries in the books of the Nelson office.[102] The latter were found to be particularly unreliable.[103]

In view of that kind of inept administration by the Dominion Lands Office in Nelson, and the "misunderstanding and blundering of local officials," which Hespeler and Pearce had noted in their report of 1878, it is not surprising that the problem of non-Mennonite intruders was not solved by decisive government action. Rather, it disappeared as arable lands were taken up by settlers and woodlots cleared of their useful timbers.

## Homestead Rights

The Mennonite *Privilegium* outlined the provisions of the Dominion Lands Act by which settlers could obtain their homesteads. The second clause provided that "any person who is the head of a family or has attained the age of twenty-one years, shall be entitled to be entered for one quarter section or less quantity of unappropriated Dominion lands, for the purpose of securing a homestead right in respect thereof." The seventh provided that "the Mennonite settler, will receive a patent for a free grant after three years residence, in accordance with the terms of the Dominion Lands Act." And the ninth indicated "that from the moment of occupation the settlers acquire a homestead right in the land."[104]

The East Reserve, which had been created before any Mennonites came to Manitoba, was surveyed and ready for occupancy when the first settlers arrived. Already in 1874, the first year of the immigration, 386 made entries and exercised their "homestead right."[105] A sample receipt for the ten-dollar application fee for a homestead right is found in appendix 4.[106]

Matters were less organized for the settlers who took up land west of the Red River in 1875 and later. The boundaries of the reserve there were not set until the spring of 1876. What was more serious was the fact that the survey plans of those townships along the U.S. boundary were not completed until the spring of 1877.[107] In the meantime, the arriving Mennonite settlers had laid out entire villages, erected houses and other buildings, and had begun to break the land, all the while having the status of mere squatters. Many of them had spent their entire capital resources in making these improvements and did not have the ten dollars cash to pay the homestead entry fee. In this difficulty William Hespeler, now an immigration agent in Winnipeg, appealed to the Department of the Interior to allow the over 450 settlers waiting to make their homestead entries to do so without the immediate payment of the application fee.[108] The Department agreed to honour this request, partly to help "a most industrious and valuable class of settlers," partly to avoid the serious inconvenience that was sure to arise if the settlers remained as squatters much longer, and because the situation was in fact caused by the delay in the survey.[109] The Surveyor General even added that "there will be no necessity for the steps suggested of securing the fees by mortgage as the undersigned has no doubt that they will adhere to the agreement to pay the same in two annual instalments." In any case, the Department was protected since the issue of the patent could be delayed until the debt had been paid.[110]

A second example of government accommodation to Mennonite wishes occurred a few years later. *Obervorsteher* Isaak Mueller in the summer of 1880 requested permission from the Minister of the Interior for West Reserve Mennonites to affirm land applications before the local Justice of the Peace, rather than having to go eighty miles to Winnipeg to do so.[111] The Department responded by transferring the West Reserve land business to the office at Nelsonville, a town just outside the northwest corner of the reserve. The inefficient and somewhat ineffective service given by this office has been noted earlier. Mueller, who showed himself to be a very capable administrator in his own right, already observed this after a few months. He therefore took it upon himself to advise the Minister of the Interior, none other than Prime Minister John A. Macdonald himself, how this office should be run. He had obviously learned fairly quickly that by signing a letter "your obedient servant," one could get away with quite a bit.[112]

A third problem encountered by the West Reserve Mennonites in seeking to exercise their homestead rights proved more difficult to solve. In the 1878 federal election Canadians, tired of almost five years of Liberal "slow-down," returned the Conservatives and Macdonald to power. Their "National Policy" included building the transcontinental railway and a new drive for immigrants. To achieve the former a syndicate of Canadian and British capitalists organized the Canadian Pacific Railway Company and negotiated a contract with the government to complete the rail line to the Pacific. Part of the government's contribution consisted of twenty-five million acres of western land.

On July 9, 1879, the Department of the Interior identified the first instalment of railway lands: all odd-numbered sections of land lying within 110 miles on either side of the proposed rail line west of the Red River. The notice also published the conditions and terms under which these lands could be purchased effective August 1.[113] Two weeks later the Dominion Land Agent in Winnipeg, Donald Codd, was authorized to begin selling these lands. Assuming that this included previously reserved lands, Codd authorized the agent in Emerson to sell odd-numbered sections in the West Reserve to bona fide Mennonites.[114] When this was discovered in Ottawa six months later, the Minister ordered an immediate halt of such sales.[115] In the interval, however, over eight thousand acres had been sold, which sales Codd now proceeded to cancel.[116] At this Hespeler complained to the Surveyor General that lands that had been purchased by Mennonites through him, "their agent," were being cancelled by Codd.[117] Isaak Mueller, administrator of the West Reserve, wanted to know why Mennonites were now "forbidden to either purchase or homestead odd-numbered sections."[118]

The village settlement pattern, which the Mennonites were instituting in the Russian model on both reserves, required a block of contiguous land. Access to odd-numbered sections was therefore essential. Both Codd and Hespeler pointed this out to the Surveyor General and argued that withholding the odd-numbered sections was unjust to the Mennonites.[119] Russell considered their plea "groundless" since any qualifying Mennonite was free to homestead on either even or odd sections "by order LR," and informed the Winnipeg office accordingly.[120]

This ruling by the Department solved the problem for most of the individuals affected. In the Nelsonville office, however, confusion over whether Mennonites could get homestead entries in the reserve on both odd- and even-numbered sections, or on even only, continued for another two and a half years.[121]

This first phase of the railway lands problem was compounded by a change in the Homestead Act in 1879 that limited the size of a homestead to eighty acres instead of the earlier one hundred and sixty. The original figure was soon restored, but in the meantime it affected a considerable number of Mennonite homesteaders. These were now permitted to apply for an additional eighty acres for which they would qualify after having met residence requirements for three years on the original homestead.[122] By February 1881 fifty-four West Reserve Mennonites had filed such application.[123] Dominion Lands Inspector William Pearce reported in September 1882 that the problems related to the eighty-acre homesteads were not yet all solved. By that time a new round of administrative difficulties with the railway lands had begun.[124]

Sometime during 1882 all of the odd-numbered sections south of the Canadian Pacific Railway line were withdrawn from sale.[125] Later that year and early in 1883, two orders-in-council were passed describing the lands granted to the Canadian Pacific Railway Company in Manitoba.[126] The second of these granted to the Company all of the odd-numbered sections south of the main line of the CPR from the Red River to the original western boundary of the province.[127] The CPR immediately advertised these lands for sale. When the Deputy Minister of the Interior noticed that Mennonite West Reserve lands were included in this advertisement, he objected. Since the Mennonite Reserve had been created before "any right of the Company had accrued," the CPR could not sell reserve lands without an enabling order-in-council.[128]

A year later the new Deputy Minister, A. M. Burgess, gave the CPR clearance to sell odd-numbered sections in the Mennonite Reserve, but noted that an order-in-council would be required to do so.[129] The Railway Secretary responded that in his reading of the January 1883 order-in-council the grant "was clearly understood to cover the Mennonite lands except insofar as individual claims existed against particular sections."[130] The Minister of the Interior, however, "did not admit the right of the Company to any of the lands in the said Reserve."[131] The CPR was not satisfied with the ministerial word and wanted to be informed "on what ground or principle" the odd-numbered lots in the Mennonite Reserve were excluded from the CPR grant.[132]

Meanwhile, some lands had in fact been sold under the tentative permission granted in late 1883. The Department now agreed to the issuing of patents for the lands thus sold, without, however, yielding its stance on the question of the proprietorship of the odd sections.[133]

A further complication was introduced in the spring of 1885 by an order-in-council according to which the exclusive privilege to Mennonites in both reserves was to cease on October 1.[134] The question whether the odd-numbered sections would now revert to the CPR, since they were no longer reserved, was referred to the Justice Department for an opinion.[135] Its Deputy Minister ruled early in 1886 in favour of the CPR.[136] The Interior Department asked him to reconsider his opinion, contending that the orders-in-council of 1882 and 1883 only gave the CPR those odd-numbered sections vested in the Crown at that time.[137] The matter was then juggled back and forth between the two departments without a clear decision until the Minister of the Interior on December 9, 1889, submitted the entire problem once more to the Privy Council. But the Cabinet apparently was also not inclined to make a decision on the matter, for on May 9, 1890, the clerk of the Privy Council noted that the matter was referred once more to the Minister of Justice. Finally, in midsummer of 1893, four deputy ministers of justice later, the definitive ruling was handed down: Only those lands at the disposal of the government at the time of the grant were in fact granted to the CPR by the 1883 order-in-council.[138]

The Interior Department had obviously been anticipating this decision for some time, since already in 1888 earlier sales of odd-numbered sections in the Mennonite Reserve were being cancelled,[139] and by the spring of 1889 all Mennonite sales had been cancelled except three that were still under negotiation.[140]

For the Mennonites the problem was that without access to the odd-numbered sections no new villages could be founded. During the period of indecision from 1883 to 1888 these lands were at times completely out of circulation and at other times sold by both the government and the CPR, resulting in double entries and cancelled sales.[141] This uncertainty, and the delay in obtaining refunds for cancelled sales,[142] led some of the younger landless generation to explore settlement possibilities in Oregon.[143] For the Deputy Minister the choice in that situation was clear: "If it be a question between giving the land to the Canadian Pacific Railway Company as a part of their land grant, and allowing the Mennonites to go out of the country, I don't think we should hesitate as to the course to pursue."[144] The government's solution to this CPR land problem apparently was successful, for only a few families actually migrated to Oregon.[145]

These problems hardly affected the Mennonites in the East Reserve. Their problems stemmed rather from abundant rainfall and poor drainage. Beginning in 1878 many there found that they could no longer farm their original homesteads and decided to join the Fürstenland and Chortitza Mennonites on the West Reserve. But taking up a second homestead was not legal under the Dominion Lands Act until a revision in 1883.[146] Nevertheless, the Department of the Interior permitted some of them officially to abandon their original homestead (see appendix 4) and thereby become eligible to homestead once more on the West Reserve.

## Hamlet Privilege

When the first 228 families from Prussia founded a Mennonite settlement in Russia in 1789, they did so "in accordance with the land law of March 1764, which provided that the allotments be assigned in one contiguous plot, with the recipient to live on his separate 'farm.'"[147] This practice was soon abandoned, however, and the old *Holländerdorf* (village) was adapted to the Russian steppes. During the century of Mennonite experience in Russia, this semi-communal village system of land holding became thoroughly established.

Under this system, each farmstead in the village consisted of 175 acres of land, but not in one contiguous block. Instead, each family cultivated a strip of land in the village proper, on which its dwelling and other buildings were erected. All had a share in the community pasture, which was usually situated at one end of the village. The rest of the land was divided into strips, so that all shared more or less equally in the good land and the poorer parcels, in land close to the village and that farther away.

The Mennonite immigrants of the 1870s, therefore, like the Métis and their French Canadian river lot system, did not fit into the newly adopted Canadian landholding system with its sectional survey and individual homesteads. While their 1873 *Privilegium* from the Canadian government did not speak directly to this question, they assumed that the setting aside of reserves for them implied the right to regulate landholding patterns internally. On both Manitoba reserves, therefore, settlement from the outset took place in villages. The Dominion Lands Act, however, required settlers to reside on their homesteads for three years before being eligible to obtain a patent to their quarter section.

An amendment to the Act in 1876 granted Mennonites (along with Icelanders settling west of Lake Winnipeg) the privilege of fulfilling homestead residence requirements while living in villages.[148] The amended version provided

> that, in the case of settlements being formed of immigrants in communities, (such for instance as those of Mennonites or Icelanders,) the Minister of the Interior may vary or waive, in his discretion, the foregoing requirements as to residence and cultivation on each separate quarter-section entered as a homestead.[149]

A further amendment in 1883 gave a rationale for the waiver, specified a minimum community size, and limited the area of the Minister's discretion.

> In case of a number of homestead settlers, embracing not less than twenty families, with a view to greater convenience in the establishment of schools and churches, and to the attainment of social advantages of like character, ask to be allowed to settle together in a hamlet or village, the Minister of the Interior may, in his discretion, vary or dispense with the foregoing requirements as to residence, but not as to the cultivation of each separate quarter-section entered as a homestead.[150]

Since this provision of the Act did not apply to all settlers automatically but only at the Minister's discretion, it came to be known as the "Hamlet Privilege," somewhat distinct from the Homestead Right, which every incoming settler obtained.

In spite of these amendments the Department continued to use the regular "Application for Homestead Patent" forms on the Mennonite reserves. The second affirmation on this application read:

> I obtained entry in Dominion Lands Office at .... on the .... day of .... 187.. , and have been actually residing on my homestead and cultivating the same continuously since the .... day of .... 187.. , and I am still residing upon and cultivating the said lands.[151]

In November 1882 the West Reserve *Obervorsteher* asked the Department to prepare forms "that will meet the case of my people who are settled in villages."[152] A revised "Application for Homestead Patent" was accordingly issued by the Department. The new form, No. 11, prepared in accordance with the 1883 Dominion Lands Act, replaced the old residence clause with the following:

> That I made my Homestead Entry in the Dominion Lands Office at .... and perfected the same by commencing to actually reside in the village of .... to which said Homestead is appurtenant and cultivate my portion of the land belonging to the said village on the .... day of .... 188..... .

The Dominion Lands Office in Winnipeg only began using these forms in early 1885.[153] But the privilege itself was enjoyed by the Mennonites from the outset of their settlement and no difficulties with the government were ever encountered on this point. In fact, it is quite likely that in a number of villages at least one or two settlers received patent to their quarter section of land without meeting the cultivation requirement of the 1883 Act, since each village had a large community pasture that was left as virgin prairie.

While hamlet privilege made settling in villages much easier and enabled the implementation of this semi-communal landholding system, Canadian land laws did not protect the village against one of its members withdrawing his land from the community. In Russia the situation was different. There the land belonged to the community and state law prevented farmsteads from being subdivided or alienated from the colony. Because hamlet privilege in Canada did not provide similar protection, voluntary agreements were drawn up in a number of villages binding settlers not to sell their holding without the consent of two-thirds of all the farmstead owners.[154] Some of these agreements were not legally exact (e.g., Neuenburg, June 26, 1882, did not specify the precise lands involved),[155] some were not registered with the Land Title Office, where any sale would have to be processed,[156] and some may not even have been in writing.[157] Since holding each other to the agreement was an internal church matter rather than an external legal one these technicalities were not important.

Between 1885 and 1889 hamlet privilege was officially terminated, in piecemeal fashion, through a series of somewhat confusing orders-in-council.[158] In preparing to draft the order to end hamlet privilege entirely, the Department ordered a search of the files to discover when the Minister had exercised his discretion to implement it. An unidentified departmental aide reported: "I can find nothing in the early files where the Minister of the Interior distinctly states that Mennonites might settle in Hamlets, though the permission is implied all through."[159] In his opinion the permission to settle in hamlets was part of the agreement with the Mennonite delegates made in 1873, and the 1876 amendment of the Dominion Lands Act was made in accordance with that agreement. An unsuccessful attempt was made to have the Department of Agriculture, which negotiated the 1873 agreement, clarify this point.[160] In spite of the absence of "any record of the Minister having exercised the discretion vested in him by sub-clause 11 of clause 34 of the Dominion Lands Act, 1879," the Deputy Minister did not have any doubt "that it was intended to have been exercised, and the indications are that it was exercised, patents having always been issued to Mennonite homesteaders without regard to the condition of residence on the land."[161] Having established that the hamlet privilege existed in fact, if not on paper, the Minister of the Interior was now free to ask cabinet to abolish it.[162]

Some communities apparently thought that hamlet privilege had afforded them protection against the disintegration of their village. For them the ending of this privilege caused concern and led in some cases to formal agreements such as those signed by other villages in the 1870s.[163] Even after the privilege had been officially withdrawn, it did not cease in practice. In both reserves until 1894 Mennonites were apparently permitted to fulfil the residence requirement of the Homestead Act without living on their actual homestead under what was now referred to as the "Two Mile Radius Conditions."[164]

## Naturalization and Land Patents

The final goal of exercising homestead rights was, of course, the acquisition of title to the land. The preceding two sections documented the extensive interaction between the Mennonites and the government in Ottawa in connection with making homestead entries and fulfilling the residence requirements. A third requirement for obtaining title to the land was that the claimant must be a subject of Her Majesty by birth or naturalization.[165] An immigrant wishing to become naturalized was required to take the oath of allegiance.[166] For the Mennonites this presented a twofold difficulty. First, they had religious scruples about swearing an oath. Second, they were concerned that should they become naturalized citizens they would be called upon to take up arms. Some leaders considered this a very serious matter. Reverend David Stoesz, a senior minister in the Bergthal congregation, apparently relinquished his homestead claim in May 1877, rather than risk the loss of military exemption.[167]

This matter was reported to the Surveyor General, who checked it with the Deputy Minister of Justice and received the opinion that Mennonites could take the oath of allegiance and become naturalized citizens without becoming subject to military service according to the 1868 Militia Law.[168] In August Governor General Lord Dufferin visited the East Reserve. In a rousing speech he exhorted the Mennonites to become full citizens, "to share with us on equal terms our constitutional liberties, our municipal privileges, and ... to assist us in choosing the members of our Parliament." He assured them that even as citizens they would not have to serve in any army.[169] An order-in-council was then passed later that month confirming that for Mennonites to take the oath of allegiance would "not be construed as interfering with the immunity from military service secured to them" by the order-in-council of September 25, 1872.[170]

In spite of this official reassurance, not all Mennonites were convinced. Some saw implications in the taking out of citizenship far beyond the mere fulfilling of homestead requirements. It would indicate their desire to become part of the people of the province instead of remaining a separate *Gemeinschaft*. By becoming citizens they would become subject to jury duty, to the provincial school law, and to taxation by a municipal government without regard to Mennonite village organization.[171] These warnings were not taken very seriously, however, and by 1880 many of the Bergthal people were becoming naturalized and applying for their homestead patents.[172] In the *Kleine Gemeinde*, however, concern persisted because the certificate of naturalization that each applicant had to sign included the promise to defend His Majesty the King "to the utmost of my might." A brotherhood meeting on January 26, 1880, agreed to seek to have the wording changed.[173]

Among the Chortitza and Fürstenland settlers the majority began to seek naturalization only in late 1882.[174] Some members of this group were reluctant to make the affirmation required for obtaining a certificate of naturalization, "considering same to be against their religious belief," and attempted to purchase their homestead land instead.[175] Others risked remaining on their homestead without obtaining title to it. At least one applicant amended the certificate of naturalization by promising to defend the British monarch only "in so far as it does not go against Christ's teaching."[176] Although the number of Mennonites choosing these options was quite small, apprehension about the oath of citizenship persisted well into the twentieth century.[177] Perhaps it was this persistence that caused officials in Ottawa to assume in later years that "Mennonites do not as a rule take steps to become naturalized, such action being contrary to one of the tenets of their faith."[178]

With the procedures for naturalization cleared, many Mennonites became in quick order citizens of Canada and owners of their land. In the summer of 1881 a new obstacle arose that delayed the granting of homestead patents for quite a number of them, particularly on the West Reserve. Payments on the 1875 government loan, secured by the Mennonite Aid Committee of Ontario, were running far behind schedule. In June 1881 the Treasury Board suggested therefore that no homestead patents be issued to Manitoba Mennonites for the time being.[179] William Hespeler protested this suggestion, arguing that the loan was guaranteed by the Ontario Mennonites and not by mortgages against Manitoba Mennonite lands.[180] John Lowe supported Hespeler's understanding of this point and claimed that "the Mennonite loan has no relation to anything of this kind."[181]

Legally this interpretation was quite correct and on the basis of it most East Reserve Mennonites and many Bergthal settlers on the West Reserve obtained their patents irrespective of any indebtedness to the government. The Chortitza–Fürstenland leaders, however, in their desire to make sure that their people would repay the loan, tried to make repayment a condition for obtaining homestead patent. Since *Obervorsteher* Isaak Mueller loosely represented the entire West Reserve, these efforts also affected the Bergthal people settled on the eastern part of the reserve. They now made representation to the Minister of the Interior complaining that Mueller was holding up their patents.[182]

The problem, as Mueller saw it, was that once Mennonites had patents for their homesteads, it would be a simple matter for them to make loans against their land and that this possibility would be exploited by undesirable outside elements. In Nelsonville there existed "a ring of sharpers" just waiting to set upon his people. To prevent that from happening, Mueller requested that the former Emerson land agent, George Newcomb, remain in Ottawa during the winter and that all patent applications be sent directly to the Ottawa Office. This request, he said, was supported by "nearly the entire number of my people and all of those that wish to pay their just debts to the government."[183]

In late 1882 the Ontario Mennonite Aid Committee requested the Department of the Interior to withhold the granting of homestead patents to Mennonites in Hamilton and Manchester Counties in Manitoba. The Committee wanted the debt of the Manitoba Mennonites to be a first charge on their lands.[184] In Manitoba, meanwhile, Mueller prepared a list of the 190 persons who had not yet repaid their share of the loan in full and gave the location of the homestead of each of them. A statement accompanying this list indicated that it was agreed that the Mennonite loan "should be a first lien or charge upon the respective homesteads and preemptions" of the debtors.[185] Jacob Shantz forwarded the list and the agreement to the Department of the Interior.[186] At the urging of several persons, including the president of a Toronto loan company, the government passed an order-in-council to hold up patents on the 190 applications on the list until proof of repayment in full of their loan was furnished.[187] The way was thus cleared for patents to be issued to all the other applicants from the Chortitza–Fürstenland portion of the West Reserve. This stimulated those still indebted to repay their loan quickly and the Department of the Interior arranged with Shantz that a receipt given by Mueller in Manitoba would clear the way for the issuing of a homestead patent.[188] The Ontario Committee then negotiated a similar agreement with the Bergthal settlers on the eastern portion of the West Reserve and on the East Reserve. A second list of 146 debtors was submitted to the Department in May 1883.[189] Because of some irregularities in the list, however, an order-in-council dealing with these was not passed until the end of the year.[190]

Once it became known that the Mennonites could readily obtain title to their homestead as soon as their debt to the Ontario Mennonite Aid Committee was paid, some loan companies paid these debts in order to be able to make individual loans to the Manitoba Mennonites against their land title.[191] By 1892 the final payment of the Mennonite loan was made and thereby the last obstacle to Manitoba Mennonites receiving their patents removed.[192]

## Termination of the Reserve

Unlike the Indian Reserves, which the federal government was creating in the Northwest at the time of the Mennonite immigration, the reserves set aside for particular immigrant groups were not intended to be permanent ones. Rather, they were to serve as an inducement to would-be immigrants by enabling groups or colonies to settle as homogeneous communities on the open prairies. They did this by restricting the acquisition of land (by homesteading or purchase) in the designated reserves to specific groups for a limited period of time.

In the case of the Mennonite reserves, neither of the two orders-in-council creating them specified a time limit. As a result the government was forced to try to determine after the fact what had been intended when the reserves were created. According to John Lowe, at whose initiative the East Reserve was set aside in 1873, the implied termination date was 1882, the year mentioned in clause 14 of the *Privilegium*.[193] The Mennonites in Manitoba, like most of Ottawa's officialdom, had not caught the implication.

Actually, the first suggestion that the reserves be terminated came much earlier than 1882. Already in 1879 the Dominion Lands Agent in Winnipeg recommended this to the Surveyor General.[194] By then the Mennonite immigration had dropped off sharply and the West Reserve was still far from full. According to the Agent's understanding, completely settling the area was a condition for holding it as a reserve. In passing this suggestion on to the Deputy Minister, the Surveyor General added his opinion that "it would be a great injustice to go on retaining for the children of these foreigners land that we refuse our own people to enter and cultivate at once; and that is precisely what continuing the reservation means."[195]

At this point the Minister of Agriculture requested William Hespeler "to ascertain from the leaders of the Mennonites if they have any reasons to assign against throwing open the reservation ... for general settlement."[196] The Department of the Interior, meanwhile, continued to receive petitions from persons and groups as diverse as the provincial treasurer of Manitoba, the Municipality of Dufferin South, and a group of Ontario settlers, to open all or part of the West Reserve.[197] An enterprising member of Parliament from Ontario, Hugo Kranz, asked for the whole remaining unoccupied lands in the West Reserve to "be set aside for settlement by myself." He planned to bring in German, Swedish, Norwegian, or Scotch settlers and fill all the lands in three years.[198] By 1881 the Minister yielded to the "great pressure ... brought to bear upon him by persons desirous of securing the unoccupied portion of those lands," and obtained approval from the cabinet to have unoccupied West Reserve lands sold at a Winnipeg public auction in June.[199]

This action by the government produced different reactions among the various interested parties. "A rush of squatters comprising all classes including many persons from across borders" took up lands on the reserve, reported the Land Agent at Emerson, "with the view of having prior claim if said Reserve be thrown open as rumoured."[200] Hugo Kranz now offered to buy all the available lands for his planned German settlement.[201] A great number of prospective settlers and land speculators wrote to the departments of the Interior and Agriculture asking for advance concessions, sales, and other favours.[202]

Two of the persons more directly involved in carrying out the order-in-council raised tough administrative questions. Isaak Mueller, administrator of the West Reserve Mennonite community, wanted to know how the proposed sale would affect the many claims in process of those who had received eighty-acre homesteads or those who had made entry for homestead or pre-emption on lands formerly identified as railway lands.[203] Donald Codd of the Winnipeg Land Office was aware of this problem and pointed out to the Surveyor General that the lands had to be thoroughly checked before being offered for sale.[204] Faced with these practical reminders, the Department found it "impossible to have the necessary arrangements made for selling those lands" in June, and asked cabinet to postpone the date of the sale to September, at the same time raising the upset price from two to three dollars per acre.[205]

The Deputy Minister now published a three-page list of lands in the Mennonite Reserve to be sold by public auction.[206] That list was quickly discovered to be "not reliable at all, for it comprises as vacant the very sites of large villages."[207] A few days later four members of Parliament, including those representing the areas affected by the sale, cabled the Minister of the Interior: "utmost fear and anxiety caused by advertised sale of lands ... not to delay the sale of these lands here will have the most disastrous effect."[208] But the government decision-making apparatus was already in motion and the following day cabinet fixed September 19 as the date for the sale.[209]

The protests were not in vain however. Three days later all the lands in the Mennonite Reserve within fifteen miles of the international boundary were withdrawn from the sale.[210] That restricted the proposed sale to the largely unoccupied three-mile-wide strip along the northern edge of the reserve. The greatly reduced sale, postponed once more, finally took place on October 19, 1881.[211] In spite of administrative precautions and postponements, some occupied lands were still inadvertently sold at the auction.[212] More serious than this inconvenience for the Mennonites was the fact that for over a year before the sale and almost a year after, the reserve was plagued by an unusual number of squatters. Furthermore, Mennonite settlers were hampered by the fact that both of the Dominion Lands Offices were reluctant to make any new entries on the reserve.[213]

On the East Reserve the question of termination first came up in late 1883 when the leadership requested permission for younger members of the community to take up homesteads abandoned earlier by Bergthal immigrants transferring to the West Reserve.[214] The Secretary of the Department of the Interior saw this as an occasion for deciding the entire Mennonite Reserves question and initiated discussions on this matter with the Department of Agriculture.[215] This led to a cabinet decision opening even-numbered sections for homesteading and odd ones for sale to Mennonites exclusively up to July 1, 1885. After that date odd-numbered sections would be opened for sale to the public.[216] A Mennonite delegation to the Commissioner of Dominion Lands in Winnipeg, claiming the right to make homestead entries on odd-numbered as well as even-numbered sections, and William Hespeler's complaint about the "blind injustice" of the Department, succeeded only in postponing the date for opening the reserve from July 1 to October 1.[217]

The order-in-council making this change of date went a step further than the previous one had. After October 1 even-numbered sections on the East Reserve were to be opened to the public for homesteading and odd-numbered sections for sale, and both even- and odd-numbered sections on the West Reserve were to be offered for public sale after that date.[218] In the summer of 1886 the Commissioner of Dominion Lands in Winnipeg recommended that the odd-numbered sections in both Mennonite reserves be opened for homestead entry instead of for sale.[219] The Minister ignored the advice and recommended instead that on termination of the reserve, now set for January 1, 1887, even-numbered sections on the West Reserve should be opened to the public for homesteading. He then rescinded the previous order-in-council of May 6, 1885, without making alternative provisions for the East Reserve.[220]

In early 1887 the East Reserve leadership, unaware that the 1885 order-in-council throwing open their reserve had been rescinded, petitioned the Minister of the Interior to retain their reserve and if possible to open also the odd sections for settlement.[221] The Minister, apparently equally unaware of the consequences of the 1886 order-in-council, replied that he had considered the petition but would adhere to the decision already made.[222]

When the Department discovered in 1888 that for a year and a half it had had no guidelines for dealing with lands in the East Reserve and with odd-numbered sections in the West Reserve, it submitted a new proposal to the Privy Council. Both reserves were now to be treated in the same way, with even-numbered sections open for homesteading and odd-numbered sections for sale to Mennonites only up to June 1, 1889.[223] With no reasons being given, this deadline was twice extended by one year in annual orders-in-council.[224] By 1891 nearly all the available land in the reserves had been taken up and the Minister recommended that "in the public interest" they be continued indefinitely.[225] Apparently this was done at the insistence of the Department of Agriculture, which considered that "good faith to the Mennonites requires that we shall continue these reservations indefinitely until the lands have all been taken up by Mennonites."[226] But each time the opening up of the reserve was postponed, there was disappointment among the many outsiders who had hoped to obtain lands on them.[227]

This concept, that "the Department is bound to keep such reservation intact unless by consent of the Mennonites themselves," became the standard response during the next number of years to all who urged opening up the reserves.[228] By 1895, however, reports were reaching Ottawa that Mennonites themselves were selling land on the reserve to outsiders, and even William Hespeler began to suggest that the time had come to throw open the reserves.[229] As reports of such sales increased during 1896, more and more officials of the Department began to share Hespeler's view, and the decision was reached to throw open the reserves after six months. This decision was promptly protested by the Reeve and Treasurer of Hanover Municipality.[230] The Mennonite bishops, who had been consulted on this question in October 1896, also expressed the hope that the reserves might continue unchanged.[231] For one final time the government agreed to postpone the date.[232]

But the reserves had really outlived their usefulness. A map of vacant lands in May 1898 showed only a few openings on the western fringe of the West Reserve and a larger number of sections in the swampiest two townships of the East Reserve. The West Reserve was finally terminated on August 1, 1898, and the East Reserve on November 30 of the same year.[233] By that time the Manitoba Mennonites had already obtained a new reserve between the forks of the Saskatchewan River in the Northwest Territories.

## Mennonites and the "High" Government: A Summary

Three fairly distinct Mennonite groups arrived in Canada during the 1870s. A summary of their approximate numbers, location, and leadership is given in table 2. Most of the *Kleine Gemeinde*, numbering fewer than seven hundred immigrants, settled in half a dozen villages on the East Reserve and two villages at Scratching River. This group had separated from the main congregation in Russia in 1812, in part because the leadership of the large church did not distance itself clearly enough from the civic administration. In 1873 it had instructed its delegates to North America to ascertain:

> May we be exempted from all state service and offices of authority as well as from any dealings in which the commandment of God "to love your neighbour as yourself" would be infringed? And would we be freed from participating in elections for any offices beyond what was allowed by our conscience?[234]

In keeping with this stance and as a minority on the East Reserve, the *Kleine Gemeinde* villages restricted themselves to administering their own local village affairs and left the more numerous Bergthal people to handle most of the administration of the reserve, including relations with the government in Ottawa. The minority position of the *Kleine Gemeinde* was further weakened during the winter of 1881–1882 when about half of the congregation, including *Ältester* Peter Toews, joined the U.S.-based Church of God in Christ, Mennonite, led by John Holdemann.[235]

Table 2
**Mennonite Immigrant Groups, Manitoba, 1874–1880**

| Group | Vorsteher | Ältester | Location | Number |
|---|---|---|---|---|
| *Kleine Gemeinde* | | Peter Toews[a] | East Reserve | 696 |
| | | Jacob Kroeker[b] | Scratching River | |
| Bergthal | Jacob Peters | Gerhard Wiebe | East Reserve | 2,833 |
| – Chortitzer | | David Stoesz | East Reserve | |
| – Bergthaler | | Johann Funk | West Reserve | |
| Chortitza–Fürstenland (Reinländer) | Isaak Mueller | Johann Wiebe | West Reserve | 3,411 |

a. Toews joined the Holdemann group 1881.
b. Kroeker was elected 1883 to succeed Toews who had joined the Holdemann group. P. J. B. Reimer, ed., *The Sesquicentennial Jubilee. Evangelical Mennonite Conference, 1812–1962* (Steinbach, Man.: Evangelical Mennonite Conference, 1962), p. 24.
Source: Totals given by Adolf Ens and Rita Penner, "Quebec Passenger Lists of the Russian Mennonite Immigration, 1874–1880," *MQR* 48 (October 1974): 531, have been revised on the basis of data given in Delbert Plett, *Profile of the Mennonite Kleine Gemeinde 1874* (Steinbach: DFP Publications, 1987), pp. 61–71, and Cathy Friesen Barkman, "Quebec Passenger Lists with Names Compared to the Hamburg Passenger Lists and Families Cross-Referenced to Church Registers," in John Dyck, ed., *Bergthal Gemeinde Buch* (Steinbach: Hanover Steinbach Historical Society, 1993), pp. 257–333.

Virtually the entire Bergthal colony and congregation came to Canada as an organized community of over 2,800 people, bringing with them civil leadership in *Vorsteher* Jacob Peters and a church leader in *Ältester* Gerhard Wiebe. This group initially settled on the East Reserve but after 1876 also settled on the eastern part of the West Reserve. To serve this scattered church adequately, David Stoesz was elected as assistant bishop in 1879.[236] By the early 1880s the two sections of this congregation were developing into fairly distinct groups, leading to the ordination in 1882 of Johann Funk by Stoesz as *Ältester* for the West Reserve Bergthal people.[237] The West Reserve portion retained the name Bergthaler, while the East Reserve church under Stoesz came to be known as the Chortitzer, after the village of *Ältester* Wiebe.

On the western portion of the West Reserve, the immigrants from the Chortitza and its newer daughter colonies (Fürstenland, Borosenko, Nepluievka, Baratov), numbering about 3,400, became one ecclesiastical and civil community. The largest group, it was also for a while the strongest and the most influential under the capable leadership of *Obervorsteher* Isaak Mueller and *Ältester* Johann Wiebe. In Canada the combined group took the name Reinländer congregation.

During the immigrant generation very little difference can be discerned among these three groups in their attitude toward the government of Canada. First, it was for them "*die hohe Regierung*" (the high government) in Ottawa. They preferred to deal with the Prime Minister rather than the Minister of Agriculture or the Interior; with the Minister of the Interior rather than his Deputy; with the Department in Ottawa rather than the Commissioner's Office in Winnipeg. That tendency was stronger in the Reinländer leadership than in that of the Chortitzer, Bergthaler, or *Kleine Gemeinde*. Second, their relationship to the government in Ottawa focussed on their agreement, the *Privilegium*. They expected the government to honour it and were prepared themselves to be bound by it. It defined their relationship to the state. They were quite prepared to be subjects of the realm, but reluctant to accept the privileges and obligations of full citizenship in the nation. In internal matters within the reserves they assumed a free hand. Third, the Mennonite administration from both reserves preferred to deal with the government through intermediaries. William Hespeler and J. Y. Shantz were much more than translators for immigrants who had not yet mastered the English language. They were quasi-governmental figures who helped to form a buffer between church and state. Later on W. P. Leslie, a justice of the peace, J. B. McLaren, an attorney, and Enoch Winkler, a lumber merchant, moved into this role. Fourth, the Mennonites tended to assume governmental benevolence, whether it be in extending a loan, providing protection against squatters, or granting hamlet privilege.

The Government of Canada, for its part, showed itself genuinely accommodating during this period. It was repeatedly willing to go far beyond the letter of the agreement. The solicitousness with which the delegates and the immigrants were treated on arrival was also experienced by the settlers during the first two decades. The Mennonites, in turn, retained their basic respect for the government in spite of numerous administrative difficulties, and lack of efficient service or co-operation from local officials.

## Notes

1. For a general treatment of the migration and the negotiations involved, see Epp, *Mennonites in Canada*, chaps. 8 and 9; Gerbrandt, chaps. 4 and 6; and E. K. Francis, *In Search of Utopia. The Mennonites in Manitoba* (Altona: D. W. Friesen, 1955), chaps. 2 and 3.

2. L. Sudermann to J. Zohrab, 3 January 1872, in Ernst Correll, "Mennonite Immigration into Manitoba: Sources and Documents, 1872, 1873," *MQR* 11 (July 1937): 210–211.

3. P. Lohrenz to J. Zohrab, 13 January 1872, ibid., p. 211.

4. P.C. no. 827B, 26 April 1872. National Archives of Canada (hereafter NA), RG 2, 1, vol. 108. The entire order-in-council is reproduced in appendix 1. Mennonite exemption from military service was already on the Canadian statute books as a result of the efforts of Quakers and Swiss Mennonites during the colonial era. William Janzen, *Limits on Liberty: The Experience of Mennonite, Hutterite, and Doukhobor Communities in Canada* (Toronto: University of Toronto Press, 1990), p. 12. It was incorporated into the Militia Act passed by the first assembly of Upper Canada in 1793, retained in the amended militia law of the united Canadas in 1841, and again in the Militia and Defence Act of the new Dominion of Canada in 1868. The latter is referred to in the order-in-council mentioned above. For a more detailed account of this background, see J. A. Toews, *Alternative Service in Canada during World War II* (Winnipeg: Publishing Committee of the Canadian Conference of the M.B. Church, 1959), pp. 14–16; and Epp, *Mennonites in Canada*, chap. 4.

5. For a brief biography see Werner Entz, "William Hespeler, Manitoba's First German Consul," *German-Canadian Yearbook*, 1973, pp. 149–152.

6. William Hespeler, Strassburg, to J. H. Pope, Minister of Agriculture, 28 August 1872, NA, RG 17; reproduced in Correll, "Sources and Documents, 1872, 1873," pp. 226–227.

7. Klaas Peters, *The Bergthaler Mennonites*, trans. Margaret Loewen Reimer (Winnipeg: CMBC Publications, 1988), p. 12. Originally serialized in *Die Mennonitische Rundschau*, January–April 1890, Peters' *Die Bergthaler Mennoniten und deren Auswanderung aus Russland und Einwanderung in Manitoba* was published in book form by the Mennonite Brethren Publishing House, Hillsboro, Kansas, in the early 1920s.

8. Epp, *Mennonites in Canada*, p. 187, based on Hespeler's 28 August 1872 report to the Department of Agriculture.

9. P.C. no. 1043D, 25 September 1872, NA, RG 2, 1. Its text is reproduced in appendix 2.

10. Klaas Peters, p. 12.

11. For a comprehensive biography of Shantz see Samuel J. Steiner, *Vicarious Pioneer. The Life of Jacob Y. Shantz* (Winnipeg: Hyperion Press, 1988).

12. J. Y. Shantz, *Narrative of a Journey to Manitoba, Together with an Abstract of the Dominion Lands Act, and an Extract from the Government Pamphlet on Manitoba* (Ottawa: Department of Agriculture, 1873). Steiner, pp. 163–181, reprints the text of Shantz's report as sent to the Minister of Agriculture on 28 February 1873. Excerpts of the *Narrative* are found in Ernst Correll, "Mennonite Immigration into Manitoba: Documents and Sources, 1873–1874," *MQR* 24 (October 1950): 44–47; and Lawrence Klippenstein and Julius B. Toews, eds., *Mennonite Memories* (Winnipeg: Centennial Publications, 1977), pp. 41–44.

13. P.C. no. 226, 3 March 1873, NA, RG 2, 1. This was done at the request of John Lowe, Secretary, Department of Agriculture, to J. C. Aikens, Secretary of State, 19 February 1873, RG 15, vol. 246, no. 27630.

14. An order-in-council of 23 May 1873, NA, RG 2, 1, withdrew a small portion of one township from the reserve because eleven Canadian families had already settled there.

15. Dispatch no. 60, Lord Loftus to Earl Granville, 3 April 1872, NA, RG 2, 5, vol. 14, no. 883B.

16. Foreign Office to Colonial Office, 2 December 1872, NA, CO 42, vol. 712, Canada no. 12062, microfilm B-523.

17. Telegram, Lord Kimberley to Lord Dufferin, 7 December 1872, ibid. The received cable in cipher form is in RG 7, G 13, vol. 5.

18. J. H. Pope, report to the Privy Council, 9 July 1873, NA, CO 42, vol. 718, pp. 351–362, microfilm B-527. The letter recalling Hespeler was dated 10 December 1872.

19. Consular dispatch no. 13, J. Zohrab to Earl Granville, 10 February 1873, NA, RG 2, vol. 19, no. 174-C.

20. The official commission for Peters and Wiebe, dated 20 February 1873, is reproduced in John Dyck, *Oberschulze Jakob Peters 1813–1884. Manitoba Pioneer Leader* (Steinbach, Man.: Hanover Steinbach Historical Society, 1990), pp. 49–51; that for Toews and Klassen, dated 10 February 1873, appears in Delbert Plett, *Storm and Triumph. The Kleine Gemeinde (1850–1875)* (Steinbach: DFP Publications, 1986), p. 280.

21. Correll, "Documents and Sources, 1873–1874," pp. 47–48, reproduces half a dozen telegrams and several letters sent by John Lowe to Hespeler, Shantz, and various other immigration officials in connection with the arrival of the delegates.

22. Told in dramatic fashion by Peters, pp.14–16, and soberly analysed by Gerbrandt, pp. 54–56.

23. Gerbrandt, chap. 5, describes the entire delegate trip in considerable detail and reproduces the 23 July 1873 letter in its English translation. William Schroeder, *The Bergthal Colony*, rev. ed. (Winnipeg: CMBC Publications, 1986), pp. 64–70, maps the two Manitoba trips of the delegates and provides an outline of their itinerary.

24. John Lowe to David Klassen et al., 26 July 1873, NA, RG 15, vol. 1507, pp. 167–169. Gerbrandt, pp. 57–59; Francis, *In Search of Utopia*, pp. 44–45; and Schroeder, pp. 125–126, reproduce this letter in full. The German translation is found in *Gedenkfeier der Mennonitischen Einwanderung in Manitoba, Canada* (Steinbach, Man.: Festkomitee der Mennonitischen Ostreserve, 1949), pp. 123–124. The date of this letter is given variously as 23, 25, or 26 July.

25. Plett, p. 280.

26. Hespeler to Pope, 26 April 1872; Department of Agriculture to Hespeler, 3 May 1873; reproduced in Ernst Correll, "Mennonite Immigration into Manitoba," *MQR* 11 (October 1937): 280–281; 22 (January 1948): 48–94.

27. P.C. no. 957, 13 August 1873, NA, RG 2, 1, vol. 83. For a discussion of the most significant change and its effects on the Mennonites, see chap. 4, under "Compulsory Attendance: Boycott and Court Enforcement."

28. Lord Tenterden, Foreign Office, to Under Secretary, Colonial Office, 13 December 1872, NA, RG 2, 5, vol. 17, no. 13-C.

29. Consular dispatch no. 15, A. Loftus to Earl of Granville, 16 April 1873; included in secret dispatch, Lord Kimberley to Lord Dufferin, 1 May 1873, NA, RG 2, 5, vol. 20, no. 256-C.

30. Secret dispatch, Lord Kimberley to Lord Dufferin, 11 June 1873, NA, RG 2, 5, vol.20, no. 313-C.

31. J. H. Pope, report to the Privy Council, 9 July 1873, NA, CO 42, vol. 718, pp. 351–362, microfilm B-527.

32. Secret dispatch, Lord Dufferin, Charlottetown, to Earl of Kimberley, 21 July 1873, NA, CO 42, vol. 718, pp. 349–351.

33. Lord Dufferin's later explanation of this action to Sir John A. Macdonald does not sound as if cancellation of the action was his intent. From the Citadel, Quebec, 1 October 1873, he wrote: "Some time ago a Minute of Council came for my signature authorizing an agreement between the Dominion and the Mennonites, but on referring to a Despatch from Lord Kimberley I found I was instructed not to sanction further proceedings in respect of these persons until instructed from home that I might do so. I therefore wrote to Mr. Pope to beg him to hold his hand." NA, MG 26 A, vol. 79, pp. 30931–32.

34. This information is written on the top and left hand margins of the original copy of P.C. no. 957, 13 August 1873. On 3 March 1916 the Deputy Minister of Agriculture received a copy.

35. Norman B. Williams, Project Officer, Research Branch of the Library of Parliament, to Senator Eugene A. Forsey, 19 July 1977, p. 2. Copy in possession of the author, courtesy of the late Senator Forsey.

36. Ibid., p. 4.

37. Memorandum, Department of Agriculture, 3 August 1877, NA, John Lowe Papers, MG 29 B13, vol. 9.

38. John Lowe to A. M. Burgess, Secretary, Department of the Interior, 28 September 1882, NA, RG 15, vol. 232, no. 3219(2A).

39. Hofer, p. 199.

40. Gerhard Wiebe, *Causes and History of the Emigration of the Mennonites from Russia to America*, trans. Helen Janzen (Winnipeg: Manitoba Mennonite Historical Society, 1981), p. 34. Wiebe's *Ursachen und Geschichte der Auswanderung der Mennoniten aus Russland nach Amerika* was first published by the Nordwesten at Winnipeg in 1900.

41. C. Henry Smith, *The Coming of the Russian Mennonites. An Episode in the Settling of the Last Frontier, 1874–1884* (Berne, Ind.: Mennonite Book Concern, 1927), p. 104.

42. Gerbrandt, p. 44.

43. J. H. Doerksen, *Geschichte und Wichtige Dokumente der Mennoniten von Russland, Canada, Paraguay und Mexico* (n.p., 1923), p. 40.

44. Leonhard Sudermann, *Eine Deputationsreise von Russland nach Amerika vor vierundzwanzig Jahren* (Elkhart, Ind.: Mennonitische Verlagshandlung, 1897), pp. 9–10; idem, *From Russia to America. In Search of Freedom*, trans. Elmer F. Suderman (Steinbach, Man.: Derksen Printers, 1974), p. 3. George Leibbrandt, "The Emigration of the German

Mennonites from Russia to the United States and Canada, 1873–1880," *MQR* 7 (January 1933): 6, and James C. Juhnke, *A People of Two Kingdoms. The Political Acculturation of the Kansas Mennonites* (Newton, Kans.: Faith and Life Press, 1975), p. 15, translate the expression "*abgeschlossene Gemeindeverfassung*" in the third request as "closed settlements"; it could be understood in the more restricted sense of "separate community constitution" as Suderman translates it.

45. Leibbrandt, pp. 9–10. See also the 5 September 1873 response of Hamilton Fish (for President Grant) to the petition of the Hutterite delegates, in Hofer, p. 217.

46. Juhnke, pp. 15–16.

47. Plett, p. 280.

48. Johann Wiebe, *Die Auswanderung von Russland nach Kanada, 1875* (Cuauhtemoc, Mexico: Campo 6.5 Press, 1972), p. 27, reports that about 150 families from Fürstenland were planning to emigrate. Peter Friesen, "Eine Begebenheit aus Russland und Kanada Manitoba," ibid., pp. 65–66, indicates the dependence of the Fürstenland people on the Bergthal delegates. See also Dyck, *Oberschulze Jakob Peters*, p. 60. *Mennonite Encyclopedia*, s.v. "Manitoba," by Cornelius Krahn, reports Wiebe as stating that 1,009 persons were ready to leave Fürstenland for Canada.

49. W. L. Morton, *Manitoba: A History*, 2nd ed. (Toronto: University of Toronto Press, 1967), pp. 145, 176–177.

50. John Lowe, Secretary, Department of Agriculture, to Jacob E. Klotz, Preston, Ontario, 11 February 1874, NA, RG 17, vol. 1509, p. 56.

51. Canada, Parliament, *Sessional Papers*, vol. 8, 1875, no. 40, "Report of the Minister of Agriculture," app. 2, Quebec Agent, p. 16; app. 4, Toronto Agent, p. 25; app. 5, Montreal Agent, p. 31; app. 12, Winnipeg Agent, p. 53; app. 13, West Lynne Agent, p. 55; app. 18, Agent General, London, p. 78; app. 41, Dominion Travelling Agent, p. 153. Similar reports are found in subsequent annual reports of the Minister of Agriculture.

52. William Hespeler, Winnipeg, to J. S. Dennis, Surveyor General, 4 March 1875, NA, RG 15, vol. 230, no. 1047. Thirty families of the *Kleine Gemeinde* arrivals in Manitoba in 1874 chose to homestead on the Scratching (now Morris) River instead of on the reserve. Jacob Y. Shantz, "Menonites [sic] to Manitoba. This Book Contains the Names and Number of Families and Souls that Moved to Manitoba," handwritten ledger compiled 1874 to 1880, copy in Mennonite Heritage Centre Archives (hereafter MHCA), Winnipeg, vol. 989, p. 8. Shantz's note, p. 33, that some of the 1874 immigrants remained with Ontario Mennonites for the winter, accounts for the difference between the 1,533 arrivals at Quebec and the 1,300 settling in Manitoba.

53. D. Laird, Minister of the Interior, to L. Letellier, Minister of Agriculture, 3 April 1875, NA, RG 15, vol. 232, no. 3129. The Department was aware at the time when the eight townships were selected to form the reserve that some drainage would be required. William Hespeler to Donald Codd, Dominion Lands Agent, Winnipeg, 20 September 1879, ibid. Fifteen years after its creation, slightly over thirty-one sections of it were turned over to the Province of Manitoba under the Swamp Lands Act by Order-in-Council P.C. no. 1272, 7 June 1888, RG 2, 1, vol. 394.

54. Telegram, Donald Codd to J. S. Dennis, Surveyor General, 23 July 1875, NA, RG 15, vol. 232, no. 3129.

55. Dennis cabled ministerial approval of the final boundaries (townships 1-1E, 1 to 3 in ranges 1 to 5W, and 1-6W) to Codd on 30 July 1875. Ibid. Formal reservation by order-in-council did not occur until almost a year later. P.C. no. 397, 25 April 1876, NA, RG 2, 1, vol. 142.

56. John H. Warkentin, "The Mennonite Settlements of Southern Manitoba" (Ph.D. dissertation, University of Toronto, 1962), p. 64.

57. Francis, "Mennonite Institutions in Early Manitoba," pp.145–148.

58. J. B. McLaren, "The North-west: The Mennonites," in George Monro Grant, ed., *Picturesque Canada: The Country as It Was and Is*, 2 vols. (Toronto: Belden Bros., 1882), vol. 1, p. 324; Abe Warkentin, *Reflections on Our Heritage. A History of Steinbach and the Rural Municipality of Hanover from 1874* (Steinbach: Derksen Printers, 1971), p. 57. Peter Elias, unpublished Memoirs [1913], p. 11, MHCA, vol. 1078, suggests that the two *Beisitzer*, traditionally elected to assist the *Schulze* in Russia, functioned in Manitoba as *Brandschulze* and *Hirtenaufseher*. Peter D. Zacharias, *Reinland: An Experience in Community* (Reinland, Man.: Reinland Centennial Committee, 1976), p. 58, draws attention to the fact that the term *Obervorsteher* was preferred to *Oberschulze* by some of the Manitoba groups because it was less suggestive of worldly authority.

59. Gerhard Wiebe, p. 41. Schroeder, p. 34, indicates the steady growth of Bergthal's landless problem.

60. *Mennonite Encyclopedia*, s.v. "Russia," by Cornelius Krahn.

61. J. E. Klotz, Canadian immigration agent in Hamburg, reported 145 Mennonite indigent families in 1875 and 71 in 1876. Some were supported by their wealthier brethren; most were extended assistance for their ocean passage on instructions from Shantz. Klotz paid $15,256 for this purpose in 1875 and $4,451.49 in 1876. Canada, Parliament, *Sessional Papers*, 1876, IX.8, app. 21, p. 86; ibid., 1877, X.8, app. 28, p. 89.

62. *Gedenkfeier*, p. 150, and Epp, *Mennonites in Canada*, p. 201, give a fairly detailed breakdown of the amounts of capital brought in as recorded by the Russian Mennonite Aid Committee of Ontario. The table in appendix 3 shows a somewhat higher total on the basis of annual amounts reported by government immigration sources. The $125 per capita figure is based on this higher total.

63. Klaas Peters, p. 15.

64. Francis, *In Search of Utopia*, p. 58. For a discussion of the Bergthal portion of this loan see Dennis E. Stoesz, "A History of the Chortitzer Mennonite Church of Manitoba 1874–1914" (M.A. thesis, University of Manitoba, 1987), pp. 115–123. For a more detailed discussion of the Mennonite loan and an Ontario Mennonite perspective, see Steiner, chap. 7.

65. Ernst Correll, "The Mennonite Loan in the Canadian Parliament," *MQR* 20 (October 1946): 257–272, has reproduced the entire Commons debates (15, 19, and 26 February) regarding the Mennonite loan. The statute, 38 Vic. chap. 3 (1875) was given royal assent on 8 April. Ibid., pp. 272–273. The new Icelandic community at Gimli received a loan of $80,000 in 1876. Peter B. Waite, *Canada 1874–1896. Arduous Destiny* (Toronto: McClelland and Stewart, 1971), p. 62.

66. The first instalment of $50,000 was "placed at the credit of" Shantz by P.C. no. 445, 5 May 1875, NA, RG 2, 1, vol. 123.

67. Francis, *In Search of Utopia*, p. 58. Zacharias, p. 67, gives a sample of how one village community spent its portion of the loan. See also Peter Wiens, secretary of the Reinland Mennonite Colony, to J. Y. Shantz, 4 February 1877, in Ernst Correll, "Sources on the Mennonite Immigration from Russia in the 1870's," *MQR* 24 (October 1950): 349–350.

68. P.C. no. 2317, 15 November 1883, NA, RG 2, 1, vol. 267. Stoesz, p. 115, reports that approximately $35,000 of this amount went to the East Reserve Mennonites.

69. Ibid.

70. "Mennonite Loan," NA, MG 29, B-13, vol. 9.

71. P.C. no. 1147, 4 June 1888, NA, RG 2, 1, vol. 394.
72. P.C. no. 572, 18 March 1889, NA, RG 2, 1, vol. 415.
73. The text is reproduced in Correll, "The Mennonite Loan," pp. 274–275.
74. P.C. no. 1149, 22 May 1889, NA, RG 2, 1, vol. 420.
75. Francis, *In Search of Utopia*, p. 57.
76. Canada, Parliament, *Sessional Papers*, 1893, no. 13, "Annual Report of the Department of the Interior for the Year 1892," p. xxxii.
77. Correll, "The Mennonite Loan," p. 255. *Mennonitische Blätter*, published in Danzig and widely read by Mennonites in Russia, reported the story on 16 May 1893, p. 74, *"Die Kanadische Regierung und die Mennonitische Anleihe."* Klaas Peters, pp. 39–40, popularized the Minister's remarks in his booklet prepared on the occasion of the fiftieth anniversary of the immigration. Others have picked it up from him. See, for example, Gerhard Lohrenz, *"Die Mennoniten kommen nach Manitoba,"* *Der Bote*, 16 July 1974, p. 2; I. I. Friesen, "The Mennonites of Western Canada with Special Reference to Education," (M.Ed. thesis, University of Saskatchewan, 1934), pp. 55–56; Smith, *The Coming of the Russian Mennonites*, pp. 189–190. Even Leibbrandt, *MQR* 7 (January 1933): 35–36, who had access to the sources, falls victim to this "legend."
78. Gerhard Wiebe, p. 56. See also the open letter of thanks by his brother Heinrich to the Ontario Mennonites, 5 March 1894, *Herold der Wahrheit*, 1 April 1894, reproduced by Correll, "Sources on the Mennonite Immigration," pp. 350–352.
79. Johann Wiebe to *Reinländer Gemeinde*, 1881, MHCA, vol. 1099, no. 28. Wiebe repeats his admonition in January 1882, ibid., no. 29. An excerpt of his letter of thanks to the Ontario Mennonites is reproduced by Epp, *Mennonites in Canada*, p. 226.
80. For further detail on the role of Ontario Mennonites in these loans, see Steiner, pp. 143–147.
81. J. Y. Shantz, Berlin, Ontario, to Department of the Interior, 9 April 1895; J. R. Hall, Secretary, Department of the Interior, to Shantz, 22 April 1895; NA, RG 15, vol. 233, no. 3129(4).
82. By order-in-council of 23 May 1873, NA, RG, 2, 1.
83. Warkentin, "The Mennonite Settlements," p. 50, indicates that no Métis had settled within the borders of the reserve. Charles Sauvé, St. Vital, to Prime Minister Wilfrid Laurier, 16 January 1896, NA, MG 26 G, vol. 35, pp. 11441–46, microfilm C-746, claims that around 1872 some thirteen persons had "taken possession" of certain lots in townships 6 and 7 of range 5E of the reserve.
84. Stoesz, pp. 36–37.
85. Ibid., pp. 171–172; Lydia Penner, *Hanover: One Hundred Years* (Steinbach: Derksen Printers, 1982), p. 41; Abe Warkentin, pp. 320–323.
86. Lindsay Russell, Surveyor General, to J. S. Dennis, Deputy Minister, Department of the Interior, 11 February 1881, NA, RG 15, vol. 232, no. 3129.
87. Petition to the Department of the Interior, 17 August 1876, NA, RG 15, vol. 235, no. 6411.
88. Abilard Parker to Sir John A. Macdonald, and John Johnston to Macdonald, both 26 December 1877, NA, MG 26 A, vol. 347, pp. 159626–27, microfilm C-1712.
89. William Pearce to Donald Codd, Dominion Lands Agent, Winnipeg, 14 November 1877, NA, RG 15, vol. 232, no. 3129.
90. Pearce to Codd, 22 November 1877; Codd to J. S. Dennis, Surveyor General, Ottawa, 29 November 1877; NA, RG 15, vol. 232, no. 3129.

91. J. S. Dennis to the Minister of the Interior, 14 December 1877, NA, RG 15, vol. 232, no. 3129.

92. William Hespeler and William Pearce to the Minister of Agriculture and the Minister of the Interior, 15 January 1878, NA, RG 15, vol. 232, no. 3129.

93. Codd to Surveyor General, 1 March 1878, NA, RG 15, vol. 232, no. 3129.

94. George F. Newcomb to Codd, 30 April 1878, NA, RG 15, vol. 232, no. 3129.

95. Codd to Surveyor General, 1 May 1878, NA, RG 15, vol. 232, no. 3129. The change was effected by Departmental order rather than by order-in-council. On 31 May 1880 Lindsay Russell, Surveyor General, recommended to J. S. Dennis, Deputy Minister of the Interior, to withdraw them officially. This recommendation was approved by the Minister, J. A. Macdonald. Since Mennonites entered township 1-6W only in a marginal way, the two new ones, 1-7W and 1-8W, never really "belonged" to the reserve. See Baldwin Berg, comp., *Our 1-6 Heritage. A History of the School Districts of Deer Creek—Lindal—Elk Creek—Diamond* (Morden, Man.: One-Six History Book Committee, 1976) for the limited Mennonite involvement in this area.

96. Codd to Surveyor General, telegrams, 10 June 1878 and 25 June 1879; letter, 19 May 1880; NA, RG 15, vol. 232, no. 3129.

97. Isaak Mueller, General Manager, Reinland Mennonite Association, and Johann Wiebe, Bishop, Neuhorst, to Head of Government, 21 July 1880, NA, RG 15, vol. 232, no. 3129. The letter was written by W. P. Leslie, Justice of the Peace, H. M. Customs, Spencerfeldt, who on several occasions assisted the West Reserve leadership in this way.

98. William Hespeler, Winnipeg, to Lindsay Russell, Surveyor General, 16 June 1881, NA, RG 15, vol. 232, no. 3129(2A).

99. R. Rauscher, Dominion Lands Surveyor, to L. Russell, Surveyor General, 22 October 1881, NA, RG 15, vol. 232, no. 3129(2A).

100. A. Walsh to Surveyor General, 29 July 1882; Walsh to Deputy Minister of the Interior, 17 August 1882; NA, RG 15, vol. 232, no. 3129(2).

101. G. W. Newcomb, Winnipeg, to Deputy Minister of the Interior, 3 November 1882, NA, RG 15, vol. 232, no. 3129(1-2 & 2a).

102. J. R. Hall, Secretary, Department of the Interior, to A. Walsh, Commissioner of Dominion Lands, Winnipeg, 16 May 1884, NA, RG 15, vol. 232, no. 3129(1-2 & 2a).

103. Agent of Dominion Lands to Secretary, Department of the Interior, 11 February 1893, NA, RG 15, vol. 232, no. 3129(1-2 & 2a).

104. P.C. no. 957, 13 August 1873.

105. William Hespeler, Winnipeg, to J. S. Dennis, Surveyor General, 4 March 1875, NA, RG 15, vol. 230, no. 1047.

106. Homestead Entry Receipt made out to Johann Dueck, 11 October 1875, NA, RG 15, vol. 233, no. 3129(3).

107. Donald Codd, Dominion Lands Agent, Winnipeg, to J. S. Dennis, Surveyor General, letter, 8 March 1877, and telegram, 14 March 1877, NA, RG 15, vol. 236, no. 7665.

108. William Hespeler to Codd, 25 April 1877, NA, RG 15, vol. 236, no. 7665. Zacharias, p. 152, shows that in Reinland, a village founded in 1875 in township 1-4W, the earliest homestead entries were made on 30 May 1877.

109. Codd to Dennis, 14 May 1877, NA, RG 15, vol. 236, no. 7665.

110. Dennis to the Minister of the Interior, 28 May 1877, NA, RG 15, vol. 236, no. 7665.

111. Mueller to Minister of the Interior, telegram, 30 August 1880, NA, RG 15, vol. 232, no. 3129.

112. Mueller to Minister of the Interior, 8 October 1880, NA, RG 15, vol. 232, no. 3129.

113. J. S. Dennis, Deputy Minister of the Interior, and Lindsay Russell, Surveyor General, "*Verordnung betreffend der Dominion Länder für den Zweck der Canadian Pacific Eisenbahn*," NA, RG 15, vol. 233, no. 3129(3). The text in English is reprinted in John Rempel and William Harms, *Atlas of Original Mennonite Villages, Homesteaders and Some Burial Plots of the Mennonite West Reserve, Manitoba* (Altona: by the authors, 1990), pp. 134–135.

114. Codd, Winnipeg, to Russell, Ottawa, telegram, 25 February 1880, NA, RG 15, vol. 233, no. 3129(3).

115. Russell to Codd, telegram, 18 February 1880, NA, RG 15, vol. 233, no. 3129(3).

116. Codd to Russell, telegrams, 28 February and 8 March 1880, NA, RG 15, vol. 233, no. 3129(3). R. Rauscher's report of 22 October 1881 to Russell listed fifty-four Mennonites who had obtained entries on railway lands and from whom second payment was now being refused. NA, RG 15, vol. 232, no. 3129(2A). Assuming each entry to be for a quarter section, this amounts to 8,640 acres.

117. William Hespeler to Russell, telegrams, 20 and 21 February 1880, NA, RG 15, vol. 233, no. 3129(3).

118. Codd to Russell, telegram, 15 February 1880, NA, RG 15, vol. 233, no. 3129(3).

119. Codd to Russell, 14 March 1880; Hespeler to Russell, 11 March 1880; NA, RG 15, vol. 233, no. 3129(3).

120. Pencilled note, 23 March, on Codd's 14 March 1880 letter. This was communicated to Codd in a letter from Russell, 27 March 1880, NA, RG 15, vol. 233, no. 3129(3).

121. J. B. McLaren, Solicitor for the Mennonites, Nelsonville, to Surveyor General, 12 July 1882, NA, RG 15, vol. 232, no. 3129(2A).

122. Lindsay Russell to W. P. Leslie, who had inquired for Isaak Mueller, 8 January 1881, NA, RG 15, vol. 232, no. 3129(2A).

123. Rauscher report to Russell, 22 October 1881, NA, RG 15, vol. 232, no. 3129(2A). J. B. McLaren, Nelson, to Surveyor General, 28 August 1882, NA, RG 15, vol. 232, no. 3129(1-2 & 2A).

124. William Pearce, Winnipeg, to Lindsay Russell, Deputy Minister of the Interior, 1 September 1882, NA, RG 15, vol. 232, no. 3129(1-2 & 2A).

125. A. Russell, for Surveyor General, to A. G. Mason, Stodderville, 18 July 1882, NA, RG 15, vol. 232, no. 3129(1-2 & 2A).

126. 3 November 1882 and 25 January 1883.

127. P.C. no. 110, 25 January 1883, NA, RG 2, 1, vol. 245.

128. Lindsay Russell, Deputy Minister of the Interior, to C. Drinkwater, Secretary, CPR, Montreal, 8 November 1882, NA, RG 15, vol. 303, no. 67992.

129. Burgess to Drinkwater, 5 December 1883, NA, RG 15, vol. 303, no. 67992.

130. Drinkwater to Burgess, 29 February 1884, NA, RG 15, vol. 303, no. 67992.

131. Burgess to Drinkwater, 2 June 1884, NA, RG 15, vol. 303, no. 67992.

132. Drinkwater to Burgess, 27 August 1884, NA, RG 15, vol. 303, no. 67992.

133. J. R. Hall, Secretary, Department of the Interior, to Drinkwater, 16 September 1885, NA, RG 15, vol. 303, no. 67992.

134. P.C. no. 937, 6 May 1885, NA, RG 2, 1.

135. J. R. Hall, Acting Deputy Minister of the Interior, to G. W. Burbidge, Deputy Minister of Justice, 24 September 1885, NA, RG 15, vol. 303, no. 67992.

136. Burbidge to Hall, 28 January 1886, NA, RG 15, vol. 303, no. 67992.

137. A. M. Burgess, Deputy Minister of the Interior, to Burbidge, 31 August 1887, NA, RG 15, vol. 303, no. 67992.

138. E. L. Newcombe, Deputy Minister of Justice, to Burgess, 18 July 1893, NA, RG 15, vol. 303, no. 67992. A copy of this ruling was sent to CPR Secretary Drinkwater on 19 February 1897! The Deputy Ministers of Justice involved were Burbidge, A. Power, Robert Sedgewick, and Newcombe.

139. William Rempel, Clerk, Municipality of Rhineland, to Thomas Greenway, Premier of Manitoba, 26 November 1888, Public Archives of Manitoba (hereafter PAM), MG 13, E 1, p. 1276.

140. Secretary, Department of the Interior, to C. Drinkwater, Secretary, CPR, April 1889, NA, RG 15, vol. 303, no. 67992.

141. W. D. Scott to Thomas Greenway, 10 December 1888, PAM, MG 13, E 1, p. 1558. J. R. Hall, Assistant Secretary of the Interior, to Drinkwater, 24 September 1888, NA, RG 15, vol. 303, no. 67992.

142. Corbet Locke to H. H. Smith, Commissioner of Dominion Lands, Winnipeg, 22 January 1889, NA, RG 15, vol. 571, no. 179925(2). Locke, acting as attorney for the Mennonites, argued in a 13 May 1889 letter to Smith that "a great wrong" was being done to those Mennonites who had purchased CPR lands with borrowed money and were now without land but paying interest because of the delay of refunds.

143. H. H. Smith to A. M. Burgess, Deputy Minister of the Interior, 19 June 1888, passing on information he had received from Premier Greenway, NA, RG 15, vol. 570, no. 179925(1). George Young, Dominion Lands Agent, Manitou, reported on 21 June 1888 to H. H. Smith that "a deputation has been sent from the neighbourhood of Gretna, to Oregon, Washington Territory and British Columbia to select a suitable location for 500 Mennonites," giving as a reason the numerous applications for odd-numbered sections that were being refused. NA, RG 15, vol. 570, no. 179925(1). Klaas Peters, leader of this deputation, reported extensively on the exploratory trip in *Mennonitische Rundschau*, 17, 24, 31 July, and 7 August 1889. Henry C. Jacobsen, Dominion Government Intelligence Officer, Winnipeg, reported 7 September 1889 to Smith on his assignment to see the twelve to fourteen West Reserve families reportedly wanting to leave for California. NA, RG 15, vol. 571, no. 179925(2).

144. Burgess to Smith, 25 June 1888, NA, RG 15, vol. 570, no. 179925(1).

145. News items in *Die Mennonitische Rundschau*, 6 February and 12 March 1890, indicate a group of ex-Manitoba Mennonites in Oregon large enough to have their own school with twenty-one pupils enrolled. For a brief account of this settlement venture, see Leonard Doell, "Klaas Peters (1855–1932): A Biography," in Klaas Peters, *The Bergthaler Mennonites*, pp. 48–49; John Dyck, "The Oregon Trail of Manitoba Mennonites," *Mennonite Historian*, September 1988, pp. 1–2; December 1988, pp. 4, 8.

146. Francis, *In Search of Utopia*, p. 70.

147. D. G. Rempel, "The Mennonite Commonwealth in Russia," p. 297.

148. John Warkentin, "Manitoba Settlement Patterns," *Papers of the Historical and Scientific Society of Manitoba*, series 3, no. 16, 1961, p. 73.

149. Canada, *Statutes*, 1876, p. 75, 39 Vic., ch. 19, sec. 9, amending sub-sec. 11 of sec. 33 of the 1874 Act.

150. Ibid., 1883, pp. 288–289, 46 Vic., ch. 17, sec. 32.

151. NA, RG 15, vol. 246, no. 27630(1).

152. Isaak Mueller, Spencerfeld, to Lindsay Russell, Deputy Minister of the Interior, 28 November 1882, NA, RG 15, vol. 232, no. 3129(1-2 & 2a).

153. P. B. Douglas, Assistant Secretary, Department of the Interior, to A. H. Whitcher, Dominion Lands Agent, Winnipeg, 2 April 1885, NA, RG 15, vol. 232, no. 3129(1-2 & 2a).

154. See Royden Loewen, *Blumenort. A Mennonite Community in Transition, 1874–1982* (Steinbach: Blumenort Mennonite Historical Society, 1983), pp. 81–82, for the nine-point "Verbindungsschrift der Dorfsgemeinde Blumenort: 1878," and John Dyck, ed., *Working Papers of the East Reserve Village Histories, 1874–1910* (Steinbach: Hanover Steinbach Historical Society, 1990), p. 45, for the contract of the village of Chortitz, 15 October 1877.

155. Gerhard John Ens, *Volost and Municipality. The Rural Municipality of Rhineland, 1884–1984* (Altona, Man.: Rural Municipality of Rhineland, 1984), pp. 253–254.

156. A. Walsh, Commissioner of Dominion Lands, to L. Russell, Deputy Minister of the Interior, 2 March 1882, NA, RG 15, vol. 232, no. 3129(1-2 & 2a).

157. The fifth WHEREAS of the Blumenort (West Reserve) "Cancellation of Village Agreement," 1 December 1923, reads: "it is not known if said Agreement was reduced to writing or not." Land Titles Office, Morden, Manitoba, copy in MHCA.

158. P.C. no. 937, 6 May 1885, ended it for the West Reserve; orders-in-council of 26 and 28 October 1886 confused the issue; P.C. no. 1938, 14 August 1889, terminated it entirely. NA, RG 2, 1. H. H. Smith, Commissioner of Dominion Lands, reflects this confusion in a letter to A. M. Burgess, Deputy Minister of the Interior, 13 August 1889. RG 15, vol. 571, no. 179925(2).

159. Unsigned memo, Department of the Interior, 23 March 1889, NA, RG 15, vol. 246, no. 27630(2).

160. A. M. Burgess, Deputy Minister of the Interior, to John Lowe, Deputy Minister of Agriculture, 1 April 1889, NA, RG 15, vol. 246, no. 27630(2).

161. Burgess to H. H. Smith, Commissioner of Dominion Lands, Winnipeg, 3 August 1889, NA, RG 15, vol. 246, no. 27630(2). The wording of the relevant clause of the 1879 Act is still identical with that of the 1876 amendment.

162. P.C. no. 1938, 14 August 1889, NA, RG 2, 1.

163. Jacob Derksen, "Bergthal," in Dyck, *Working Papers*, p. 24. See contracts for Bergthal, 4 March 1891, and Osterwick, 1 February 1894, from the East Reserve, ibid., pp. 27–31, 75–77; Sommerfeld, 11 March 1892, in Ens, *Volost*, pp. 255–262, and Alt Bergthal, 10 March 1891, in MHCA, vol. 3720, no. 3.

164. R. A. Ruttan, Agent of Dominion Lands, Edmonton, to T. R. Burpé, Secretary to the Commissioner of Dominion Lands, Winnipeg, 11 June 1896. NA, RG 15, vol. 571, no. 179925(2).

165. Dominion Lands Act, sec. 33, quoted in P.C. no. 786/1877, NA, RG 2, 1.

166. Alien Law, 31 Vic., ch. 66, quoted in P.C. no. 786/1877, NA, RG 2, 1.

167. Jacob Derksen, "Bergthal," in Dyck, *Working Papers*, p. 18.

168. A. Belch, Dominion Lands Agent, Winnipeg, to J. S. Dennis, Surveyor General, Ottawa, 14 July 1877; Dennis to the Minister of the Interior, 26 July 1877; NA, RG 15, vol. 237, no. 8974.

169. The full text of Lord Dufferin's address is given in Schroeder, p. 105.

170. P.C. no. 786, 27 August 1877, NA, RG 2, 1.

171. Anonymous contributor, Winnipeg, 29 November 1877, *Herold der Wahrheit*, January 1878, p. 9. The American editor suggested that the Mennonites take their time to find out the duties and obligations of British subjects; if the advantages were significant and if the Mennonite non-resistant status was not jeopardized, then they could take out citizenship.

172. William Hespeler, Winnipeg, to A. N. Whitcher, Dominion Lands Agent, Winnipeg, 14 October 1880, NA, RG 15, vol. 246, no. 27630(1).

173. *Ältester* Peter Toews, "Diary," in Delbert Plett, ed., *Profile of the Mennonite Kleine Gemeinde 1874* (Steinbach: DFP Publications, 1987), p. 170.

174. James R. Bonny, Justice of the Peace, Nelson, to the Minister of the Interior, 24 November 1882, NA, RG 15, vol. 232, no. 3129(1-2 & 2a); Isaak Mueller to Lindsay Russell, Deputy Minister of the Interior, telegram, 12 January 1883, NA, RG 15, vol. 246, no. 27630(1). The village of Reinland, usually a bellwether for the Fürstenland-Chortitza group, submitted applications for homestead patents from eleven of its residents on 22 March 1883, and certificates of naturalization on 20 April 1883. NA, RG 15, vol. 275, no. 50322.

175. Bonny to the Minister of the Interior, 13 June 1883, writing on behalf of Gerhard and Henry Elias, NA, RG 15, vol. 232, no. 3129(1-2 & 2a).

176. H. H. Ewert, Übersetzung des Bürgereides," *Der Mitarbeiter* 2 (March 1908): 47.

177. Peter A. Elias, ibid., p. 46, and editorial response, p. 47.

178. Lord Byng, Governor General, to Winston Churchill, Secretary of State for Colonies, London, 22 February 1922; O. D. Skelton, for the Secretary of State for External Affairs, to Secretary of State for Dominion Affairs, London, 26 February 1929; NA, RG 7, G 21, no. 37523.

179. Secretary, Treasury Board, to the Minister of the Interior, 20 June 1881, NA, RG 15, vol. 246, no. 27630(1).

180. Hespeler to Lindsay Russell, Surveyor General, 22 July 1881, NA, RG 15, vol. 246, no. 27630(1).

181. John Lowe to Russell, 4 January 1882, NA, RG 15, vol. 246, no. 27630(1).

182. E. F. Burnham, Barrister, Emerson, writing on behalf of some eighty Mennonites, to the Minister of the Interior, 7 June 1882; J. B. McLaren (Solicitor of Nelson), Kingston, to Minister of the Interior, 13 November 1882; NA, RG 15, vol. 232, no. 3129(2A).

183. Isaak Mueller to the Minister of the Interior, 28 November 1882, NA, RG 15, vol. 232, no. 3129(1-2 & 2a).

184. H. W. C. Meyer, Wingham, Ontario, to Lindsay Russell, Deputy Minister of the Interior, 5 December 1882, NA, RG 15, vol. 232, no. 3129(1-2 & 2a). The West Reserve was included in these two counties, but not the East one.

185. Agreement signed at Reinland by Isaak Mueller, General Manager, and Peter Wiens, Secretary and Treasurer, of the Reinland [West] Reserve, 16 December 1882, NA, RG 15, vol. 246, no. 27630.

186. George Newcomb to Lindsay Russell, 11 January 1883, NA, RG 15, vol. 246, no. 27630(1).

187. P.C. no. 251, 6 February 1883, NA, RG 2, 1.

188. Department of the Interior to J. Y. Shantz, 25 April 1883; Shantz to Minister of the Interior, 28 April 1883; NA, RG 15, vol. 246, no. 27630.

189. F. W. Meyer and Bernhard Klippenstein, 13 April 1883, received by the Department of the Interior, 21 May 1883, NA, RG 15, vol. 246, no. 27630(1).

190. P.C. no. 2426, 13 December 1883, NA, RG 2, 1.

191. J. Y. Shantz to the Minister of the Interior, 1 September 1885, NA, RG 15, vol. 281, no. 54018.

192. J. Y. Shantz, Secretary of the Waterloo Society [Ontario Aid Committee], to the Secretary, Department of the Interior, 26 April 1892, NA, RG 15, vol. 246, no. 27630(2).

193. John Lowe, Department of Agriculture, to Lindsay Russell, Deputy Minister of the Interior, 25 September 1882; Lowe to A. M. Burgess, Secretary, Department of the Interior, 28 September 1882; NA, RG 15, vol. 232, no. 3129(2A). In his 26 July 1873 letter to the Manitoba delegates from Russia, as well as in the order-in-council of 13 August 1873, clause 14 assured potential Mennonite immigrants that the price of passenger warrants from Hamburg to Fort Garry would not rise above $40 per adult up to the year 1882.

194. Donald Codd to Lindsay Russell, 26 September 1879, NA, RG 15, vol. 232, no. 3129.

195. Russell to J. S. Dennis, Deputy Minister of the Interior, 4 October 1879, NA, RG 15, vol. 232, no. 3129.

196. H. B. Small, Acting Secretary, Department of Agriculture, to Dennis, 25 November 1879, NA, RG 15, vol. 232, no. 3129.

197. J. Norquay, Provincial Treasurer's Office, Manitoba, to Dennis, 13 July 1880; Robert McKay, Warden, and six councillors, Alexandria, petition, 3 May 1880, to remove township 1 in ranges 5 and 6W; petition by nineteen Ontario settlers to Privy Council, 21 July 1880, to open township 1, range 5W; NA, RG 15, vol. 232, no. 3129.

198. Hugo Kranz, Ottawa, to Sir John A. Macdonald, Minister of the Interior, 27 January 1881, NA, RG 15, vol. 232, no. 3129.

199. P.C. no. 381, 24 March 1881, NA, RG 2, 1.

200. J. E. Tetu, Dominion Lands Agent, Emerson, to John Lowe, telegram, 16 June 1880, NA, RG 15, vol. 232, no. 3129.

201. Kranz to the Minister of the Interior, 18 March 1881, NA, RG 15, vol. 232, no. 3129. Kranz to John A. Macdonald, 30 March 1881, MG 26 A, vol. 374, pp. 174501-3; Kranz to J. S. Dennis, 14 April 1881, RG 15, vol. 232, no. 3129(2A).

202. NA, RG 15, vol. 232, no. 3129(1-2 & 2a).

203. W. P. Leslie, Spencerfeld, to Surveyor General, 21 March 1881, NA, RG 15, vol. 232, no. 3129. The problems connected with eighty-acre homesteads and the 1879 railway land sales have been discussed under "Homestead Rights."

204. Donald Codd, Acting Inspector of Dominion Lands Agencies, to Surveyor General, 30 March 1881, NA, RG 15, vol. 232, no. 3129(2A).

205. P.C. no. 1123, 29 July 1881, NA, RG 2, 1.

206. Lindsay Russell, Acting Deputy Minister of the Interior, 13 August 1881, NA, RG 15, vol. 232, no. 3129(2).

207. R. Rauscher, Dominion Lands Surveyor, to Russell, 1 September 1881, NA, RG 15, vol. 232, no. 3129(2A). Rauscher indicated that the village sites of Halbstadt, Edenburg, Neuanlage, Blumenort, Neuhorst, Schönwiese, Rosengart, and Grünfeld were

being offered for public auction! Heinrich Wiebe, Emerson, cabled Russell on 14 September 1881 to ask whether such occupied lands would be sold. NA, RG 15, vol. 232, no. 3129(1-2 & 2A).

208. J. Schultz, T. Scott, J. Ryan, and J. Royal, Winnipeg, to Hon. D. L. McPherson, telegram, 6 September 1881, NA, RG 15, vol. 232, no. 3129(2). The announced sale was to include lands in some of the Red River parishes as well as the Mennonite Reserve, and much of the "fear and anxiety" was among settlers in the former.

209. P.C. no. 1270, 7 September 1881, NA, RG 2, 1.

210. A. Campbell, Acting Minister of the Interior, to Lindsay Russell, Acting Deputy Minister, 10 September 1881, NA, RG 15, vol. 232, no. 3129(2).

211. Russell to A. H. Whitcher, Dominion Lands Agent, Winnipeg, telegram, 15 September 1881, NA, RG 15, vol. 232, no. 3129(2).

212. Whitcher to Surveyor General, 17 November 1881, NA, RG 15, vol. 232, no. 3129(2A); G. Newcomb, Nelson, to Deputy Minister of the Interior, 10 November 1881, no. 3129(1-2 & 2a).

213. Correspondence files no. 3129(2) and no. 3129(2A) indicate that undesirable after-effects of the sale continued in the Lands Office until September 1882.

214. Peter Toews, *Vorsteher*, and David Stoesz, Bishop, to Sir John A. Macdonald, December 1883, NA, RG 15, vol. 246, no. 27630.

215. J. R. Hall to G. Newcomb, 7 February 1884, NA, RG 15, vol. 246, no. 27630(1). The discussions took place in August.

216. P.C. no. 2309, 17 January 1885, NA, RG 2, 1.

217. A. Walsh to Minister of the Interior, 27 February 1885; William Hespeler to Walsh, 19 February 1885; NA, RG 15, vol. 246, no. 27630(1).

218. The change of date was made by P.C. no. 937, 6 May 1885, NA, RG 2, 1.

219. H. H. Smith to A. M. Burgess, Deputy Minister of the Interior, 23 June 1886, NA, RG 15, vol. 246, no. 27630(2).

220. P.C. no. 1848, 28 October 1886, NA, RG 2, 1.

221. Bishop David Stoesz, et al., Bergthal, to the Minister of the Interior, 12 February 1887, NA, RG 15, vol. 246, no. 27630(2).

222. P. B. Douglas, Assistant Secretary, Department of the Interior, to Stoesz, 28 March 1887, NA, RG 15, vol. 246, no. 27630(2).

223. P.C. no. 1696, 11 July 1888, NA, RG 2, 1.

224. P.C. no. 1317, 15 June 1889; and P.C. no. 1421, 11 June 1890, NA, RG 2, 1.

225. P.C. no. 1047, 18 May 1891, NA, RG 2, 1.

226. A. M. Burgess, Deputy Minister of the Interior, to H. H. Smith, Commissioner of Dominion Lands, Winnipeg, 13 May 1891, NA, RG 15, vol. 570, no. 179925(1).

227. E. F. Stephenson, Dominion Lands Agent, Winnipeg, to H. H. Smith, 28 April 1891, NA, RG 15, vol. 571, no. 179925(2); *Mennonitische Rundschau*, 2 July 1890, p. 1.

228. L. Pereira, Assistant Secretary, Department of the Interior, to J. H. Smith, Morden, 8 May 1894; A. M. Burgess, Deputy Minister, to J. R. Hall, Secretary, Department of the Interior, 28 November 1895; NA, RG 15, vol. 570, no. 179925(1).

229. T. R. Burpé, Secretary, Dominion Lands Commission, Winnipeg, to Secretary, Department of the Interior, 17 October 1895, NA, RG 15, vol. 570, no. 179925(1).

230. Burpé to Secretary, Department of the Interior, 20 January 1897, NA, RG 15, vol. 570, no. 179925(1). Hanover Municipality was coterminous with the East Reserve.

231. Johann Funk, Bishop, Altona, representing the Bergthal portion of the West Reserve, to H. H. Smith, Commissioner of Dominion Lands, 18 January 1897; Peter Toews, Reeve, and David Stoesz, Bishop, representing the East Reserve, to Smith, 18 February 1897; Johann Wiebe, Bishop, Reinland, representing the Chortitza-Fürstenland portion of the West Reserve, to the Hon. Government in Ottawa, 24 February 1897; NA, RG 15, vol. 570, no. 179925(1).

232. Clifford Sifton, Minister of the Interior, to Bishop Johann Wiebe, 5 March 1897, NA, RG 15, vol. 570, no. 179925(1).

233. P.C. no. 1266, 27 June 1898, NA, RG 2, 1.

234. Plett, *Storm and Triumph*, p. 280.

235. Clarence Hiebert, *The Holdemann People. The Church of God in Christ, Mennonite, 1859–1969* (South Pasadena: William Carey Press, 1973), pp. 133–147.

236. Ordained 4 April 1879. *Herold der Wahrheit*, 1 May 1888.

237. Stoesz, who lived in Bergthal, East Reserve, functioned as leader of the entire Bergthal church after Wiebe's "retirement" in 1882. He ordained Funk, of the village of (Alt) Bergthal, West Reserve, on 11 April 1882. David Stoesz, diary entry of 25 April 1882; copy in MHCA, vol. 1559. Gerbrandt, p. 84, and Epp, *Mennonites in Canada*, p. 294, mistakenly report that Funk was ordained by Gerhard Wiebe in 1887.

CHAPTER II

# ADJUSTING TO MANITOBA, 1876–1890

The preceding chapter focussed exclusively on relations with the government in Ottawa. All of the issues related to the agreement concluded with the federal government in 1873. The Mennonites initiated both that agreement and the subsequent negotiations. By contrast, relations with the provincial government of Manitoba, which took place during the same time period, were initiated by Winnipeg and were not explicitly connected to the *Privilegium*. It is not surprising then that they created tensions in some parts of the Mennonite community.

The province of Manitoba was still in its infancy. Its birth out of the Riel uprising had been painful. Its narrow boundaries and unequal status within the federation (other provinces controlled their own crown lands) were grounds for ongoing tension with Ottawa. Both Ontario and Quebec saw in Manitoba a potential extension of their influence. The dual nature of its population, almost equally divided along Francophone-Catholic and Anglophone-Protestant lines, lent itself to that tug-of-war. The Germanic-Anabaptist Mennonites fit into neither camp.

At the beginning the government of the new province struggled to provide basic elements of administration. It counted on a good deal of initiative on the part of local communities. Hence, legislation in the areas of education and local government was at first merely enabling. Much of the time and energy of the lieutenant-governor was devoted to preparing the way for further immigration by negotiating treaties with the Indian nations in the rest of the prairie lands. Resolving the issue of land grants to the semi-sedentary Métis and half-breeds, a large majority of the initial population of the province, presented a thorny issue. The influx of white settlers threatened the continuance of their rights and those of the Indians in the land of their birth. The Mennonites who poured into the province in 1874 represented the first large-scale invasion of these foreigners.

The communities founded on the two Mennonite reserves embodied a certain continuity with the old country. Village and colony configuration were as they had been. In some cases, neighbours again lived side by side. Village names were for the most part the familiar German ones from Russia and from Prussia before that. Ethnic cohesion, a common church membership, and familiar social institutions provided a solid basis for community order without external authority. The *Oberschulze* and his council had no legal means of enforcing their decisions in Canada as had been the case in Russia. Self-government worked because of the moral force of local democracy and church sanction. Most of the leaders favoured this kind of freedom from external authority. For the more individualistic members of the community, however, and for those who disagreed with the direction set by the leaders, external authority offered a way out from under the traditional leadership.

In Russia the members of these communities had also accepted as natural that the community itself bear not only the cost of self-government, but also of public works projects and schools. They naturally assumed that they would pay for these services in Canada as well. The hardship of pioneering conditions and the almost total poverty of many of their members caused them to realize very quickly that financial independence at this stage would come at a considerable sacrifice in the quality of services available. They gladly and gratefully accepted loan assistance from their Ontario co-religionists and from the government in order to survive the first few years and to obtain the minimum necessary to start a farm operation. Other community services were carried on as well as possible. The Mennonite communities were therefore vulnerable at the points of external authority and external resources. Under what conditions were these acceptable? When did their acceptance constitute inappropriate compromise?

## Public Schools: External Resources

Manitoba's "public" schools were at this point for the most part denominational schools. Established on local or denominational initiative and administered by local trustees, they were eligible for government support by placing themselves under the broad superintendence of either the

Protestant or the Catholic section of the Provincial Board of Education.[1] The *Kleine Gemeinde* group was the first to explore the possibility of entering such an arrangement. At a brotherhood meeting on November 19, 1875, it was agreed that the leadership of the congregation would act as school board and that "the financial support for schools arranged by Hespeler was to be accepted."[2]

The Bergthal congregation was more cautious. "We had been here only a few years," wrote *Ältester* Gerhard Wiebe, "when we were offered money for the assistance and support of our schools, which seemed very risky to us because we feared it might cause us to lose the educational independence which the government had guaranteed us."[3] Nevertheless, they asked the Superintendent of Education for Protestant Schools for information as to the steps to be taken in order to receive their share of the legislative grant. After some correspondence between the Board and the Mennonites through the mediation of William Hespeler, the Protestant section of the Board in October 1878 appointed a special committee to work toward organizing school districts on the Mennonite Reserve.[4]

The committee followed this up with a letter to the Mennonite churches reiterating the promise of financial support for their schools and spelling out the conditions. They were invited to organize their various villages into school districts according to their own discretion. They were assured of the continued use of their own teachers and of the right to teach in their own language. Their congregations were given full control over all instruction. The government support of eighty to a hundred dollars per year would not in any way affect their rights and freedoms. The Mennonites were then invited to send delegates to a meeting on November 6 in Hespeler's office.[5]

By November 18 the Superintendent had received letters from the two East Reserve Mennonite bishops (Gerhard Wiebe of the Bergthal group, whose congregation was known as Chortitzer, and Peter Toews of the *Kleine Gemeinde*) asking the Board to erect thirty-six Mennonite villages into as many school districts. The government showed "its interest in this movement by appointing Mr. Hespeler a member of the Board of Education."[6] By mid-December of 1878 the two *Kleine Gemeinde* villages in Scratching River and thirty-five East Reserve villages had participated in the annual census of school children conducted by the Protestant section of the Board, reporting a total of 750 children between the ages of six and fourteen.[7] Thirty-three of these villages, and three that had not participated in the census, were duly erected into public school districts in 1879.[8]

Financial support from the Board was not entirely without strings, however. The Superintendent of Protestant schools held an examination for Mennonite teachers in early 1879 and issued a one-year licence to thirty-one teachers.[9] The Protestant Board and the Superintendent obviously regarded this examination as a very natural, matter-of-fact occurrence. For some of the Mennonites, however, it raised new apprehensions. William Hespeler, who was on the Board of examiners for 1879, suggested that the Mennonite leaders should divide their teachers into three classes. This corresponded to the Board's current system of issuing first, second, and third class certificates. When Gerhard Wiebe asked why they should do this, Hespeler replied: "Well, you don't think that the government would pay money to those who are cowherds in summer and schoolteachers in winter, do you?"[10] Wiebe, always easily offended, was prepared to break off negotiations on the spot. Hespeler diplomatically assured the Mennonites that the Board would overlook their shortcomings until they were able to do better. A considerable number of Bergthal villages then agreed to become public school districts, but the implied threat of Hespeler's words had made the Bergthal leaders profoundly suspicious.

For the first half of 1879 thirty-five Mennonite school districts actually functioned. During the second half of the year three of these were reported closed and ten others gave no report.[11] During 1880 the number of Mennonite school districts was reduced to twenty-two with a peak enrolment of 401. The Superintendent thought this came "from various causes, the chief of which was, I believe, the breaking up of the Rat River Reserve."[12] Gerhard Wiebe saw the reason elsewhere:

> It did not take long until we realized where matters were leading and we speedily withdrew and accepted no more funds. Oh how we wished that the *Kleine Gemeinde* had acted in the same way ... but they said that as soon as they would see any danger, they would also refuse the money.[13]

The Protestant section of the Board of Education tried to be as accommodating as possible. The Examiners before whom the Mennonite teacher candidates had to appear in 1879 consisted of William Hespeler and two Mennonite laymen, Jacob Friesen and Abraham Isaak. The next year the examining committee consisted of Hespeler and the two Mennonite bishops, Peter Toews and Gerhard Wiebe.[14] Nevertheless, the number of Bergthal schools declined from twenty-nine to sixteen in that year, although all six *Kleine Gemeinde* schools remained in operation. For 1881 the Superintendent reported only six Mennonite teachers examined and licensed for one year.[15] Four of them were now district school teachers for the third consecutive year. The Superintendent's report for the year ending January 31, 1882, indicated only seven Mennonite district schools left in operation, six of them from the *Kleine Gemeinde*.[16] The Bergthal group had almost totally withdrawn.[17]

The Protestant Board also sought to accommodate the Mennonites by providing them with a German-speaking inspector, William Hespeler, who served from 1879 through 1881.[18] During the third year of his inspectorship, the actual visiting of schools was done by Jacob Friesen, who also wrote the Inspector's Report to the Superintendent and signed it for Hespeler.[19]

After the low point of seven district schools in 1881, the total increased to nine the following year under Inspector Jacob Friesen, and to thirteen in 1883.[20] For the first time a few district schools were opened on the West Reserve, including one in Reinland, the administrative centre of the Chortitza–Fürstenland group. Although this school operated against the wishes of the church leadership and in competition with the local church-operated school, it had an enrolment of twenty-three.[21] The other West Reserve districts were all in Bergthal villages. The Reinländer church was still unalterably opposed to government involvement in education and excommunicated parents who sent their children to the district school.[22]

In December 1884 the former teacher of the Reinland district school was appointed Inspector of Mennonite schools by the Protestant section of the Board.[23] Wilhelm Rempel was one of the best-educated and most capable teachers in the Mennonite community. Since January 1884 he had been serving as secretary of the newly created Municipality of Rhineland.[24] During the first year of his inspectorship the number of district schools increased to twenty-two, including ten on the West Reserve.[25] In spite of this increase, Rempel was basically pessimistic in his prognosis. Some communities he saw as "being under the impression as if the advancing of the school would lead the Mennonites into inconvenience and conscientious troubles."[26] In other communities he found indifference or "even opposition as to several of the subjects to be taught, and it seems to me as if we will have to wait for years to come till our wrongly informed people surmount that aversion prevailing amongst them regarding the better education of our rising generation."[27] It was this fear of the dangers of a broader education, rather than objection in principle to their involvement with the government in education, that kept the Bergthal communities from converting to public school districts more rapidly. Most of the *Kleine Gemeinde* villages already had district schools, while the Reinländer church still remained closed to the idea in principle.

A new factor was introduced with the conversion of both reserves to municipal government in January 1884. According to the 1881 Public Schools Act of Manitoba, it was "the duty of the council of municipalities to establish and alter when necessary the school districts within their bounds."[28] Instructions on how to proceed in forming school districts were received by the Rhineland Municipality from the Superintendent of Education in Winnipeg in December 1884.[29] The council acted promptly on these instructions and early in 1885 introduced a by-law effecting a division of the municipality into twenty-two school districts "provided however that the formation of the same be petitioned for by the ratepayers."[30]

While this action greatly simplified the process of converting church-operated schools to district schools, the response from the community was a mixed one. For example, the village of Schanzenfeld petitioned the municipal council, which then duly passed a by-law in the spring of 1885 creating a district school.[31] When only four ratepayers appeared at the first meeting and one of the three elected trustees refused to function, the council sought the advice of the Winnipeg education office on the matter.[32] In contrast to the four ratepayers supporting the district school, thirteen others signed a petition to the reeve of the municipality absolutely rejecting the district school.[33] In view of that kind of community opposition, Superintendent J. B. Sommerset stated that it was "not his desire at all to force school districts upon the people" and advised leaving Schanzenfeld alone. The municipal council accepted his advice.[34] Schanzenfeld, like Reinland, was a community of the Chortitza–Fürstenland group. Several other villages of this community attempted to form district schools in the next several years.[35]

Rempel's inspectorship came to an end in January 1888 when the Superintendent initiated a new system by which all inspectors were to hold full-time year-round appointments.[36] His replacement, W. Thiem-White, while trained at Normal School and knowledgeable in the German language, met with even more resistance than Rempel had found. A special committee appointed by the Board of Education found conditions in the Mennonite district schools so inadequate that it wondered whether the annual legislative grants of $150 should continue to be paid to such schools.[37] The Board therefore resolved to apply the conditions for receiving grants more rigorously. At the same time it also terminated the services of Thiem-White in June 1889. A successor was not appointed until after the new Manitoba School Act 1890 had been passed. The passage of this legislation began a new era in education in the province.

## Municipal Government: External Authority

Group migration, block settlement, and the expectation of a basic continuity of community structures greatly facilitated the transition from Russia to Manitoba. In the Bergthal colony, which emigrated virtually as an entire group, the transition was effected almost without a break. Having lived together somewhat isolated from the rest of the Mennonite settlements in Russia since 1836, they wanted to continue in Canada the way of life that the new order in Russia had threatened. Jacob Peters, who had served them as *Oberschulze* since 1850 and as *Beisitzer* before that, resumed a leading role upon his arrival in the East Reserve in 1877.[38] The *Kleine Gemeinde*, which occupied a small minority of the villages in the East Reserve, passively accepted the administrative leadership of the much larger Bergthal group.[39]

The people settling on the West Reserve were a less cohesive body. The largest group came from Chortitza, the oldest colony in Russia. However, since the large Chortitza congregation had overwhelmingly voted in favour of remaining in Russia, most of its leadership had not joined the emigrants.[40] Over one thousand came from Fürstenland, a daughter colony of Chortitza founded in 1864. Smaller numbers originated in other Chortitza daughter colonies, including Borosenko (1865), Iasykovo (1869), Nepluievka (1870), and Baratov (1871).[41]

The one natural leader among all of these immigrants was *Ältester* Johann Wiebe of Fürstenland. Since his congregation was an affiliate of the parent church in Chortitza, of which he was an assistant bishop, it was natural for immigrants from other Chortitza satellite communities to consider themselves part of the same congregation. But it could not be assumed that they would automatically accept Wiebe as their *Ältester*. Accordingly, he called a brotherhood meeting at the immigrant sheds at West Lynne shortly after his arrival in July 1875. After he was confirmed as bishop of the whole group, Wiebe proceeded immediately with the election of a *Vorsteher* (a term he preferred to *Oberschulze*) for the new settlement they were about to found.[42] The choice was Isaak Mueller (1824–1912), a fifty-year-old farmer and miller from the Chortitza village of Neuhorst.[43] Together with the precise and orderly fifty-five-year-old Peter Wiens from the Chortitza village of Kronsthal as secretary, and the still youthful thirty-year-old Franz Froese from Fürstenland as treasurer, Mueller gave leadership to the community during its formative first twelve years.[44] The jurisdiction of this *Gebietsamt* over the Bergthal villages founded in the eastern portion of the West Reserve was not as clearly established.[45] However, as of yet no clear evidence of a second *Gebietsamt* on the West Reserve has come to light, and the *Oberschulze* of the East Reserve did not attempt to exercise any jurisdiction over the West Reserve Bergthal communities.[46]

This system of local administration, completely independent of the provincial government, continued until 1880 in both reserves. The Municipal Act of 1873 was essentially enabling legislation. For a community to establish itself as a municipality required a "petition of at least two-thirds of the male free holders or householders, being respectively of the full age of twenty-one years, and resident in any township or parish in which locality there shall be not less than thirty male residents as aforesaid."[47] In

1880, however, the provincial government took the initiative of drawing boundaries for suggested municipalities. Under this legislation, Hespeler Municipality was established with boundaries coterminous with the East Reserve.[48] A year later the reserve was divided into two municipalities, as shown on map 3, Hespeler comprising the more densely settled grassland area in the north (township 7, ranges 4 to 6), and Hanover the remaining five townships of less densely populated woodland area.[49] In 1890, the two portions were again reunited under the name Hanover.[50] The arbitrary division that existed during this decade was ignored by the East Reserve population, which functioned with one council for the whole area.[51]

In spite of this explicit legislation, it is difficult to determine precisely when the transition from *Gebietsamt* to municipality occurred. Practical changes in administration took place so gradually that the villages hardly noticed them. Minutes continued to be taken in German. Representatives of the *Waisenamt*, which, among other things, handled the loan from the Canadian government, and the fire insurance organization continued to participate in the municipal council from time to time as they had in the earlier *Gebietsamt*.[52] All village *Schulzen* were invited to at least one council meeting per year until the villages began to disintegrate. The designation "reeve" was not used in council minutes until December 1889.[53] Council passed no by-law until 1895 "because they wanted to avoid the Canadian legal system."[54] There appears to have been no opposition in principle to the introduction of municipal government. Indeed, some of the leaders seem to have viewed its coming positively as an aid in the task of local self-government, particularly that of tax collecting.[55] It is not clear when elections were first held according to the stipulations of the Municipal Act.[56] As late as 1891 the municipal council called together the village *Schulzen* to a "meeting to elect new council members for 1892."[57] That is, reeve and councillors were not elected by the voters as a whole, but by their village representatives. As in the earlier *Gebietsamt*, *Kleine Gemeinde* members abstained from voting and running for office, so that the new administration was made up of Bergthal people.[58]

In contrast to this smooth transition in the East Reserve, the coming of municipal government became an explosive issue on the West Reserve. The Reinländer church, the official name of the combined Chortitza–Fürstenland congregation led by Johann Wiebe, opposed its introduction in principle. On the other hand, the increasing number of Bergthal people in the eastern portion of the West Reserve, as well as Reinländer dissidents, welcomed it as a way of countering the power of the *Gebietsamt* and its *Obervorsteher*, *Kaiser* Isaak Mueller.[59]

As on the East Reserve, the municipality first appeared via the provincial legislation, which determined the municipal boundaries of 1880.

# Map 3
## Mennonite East Reserve with Hanover and Hespeler Municipalities

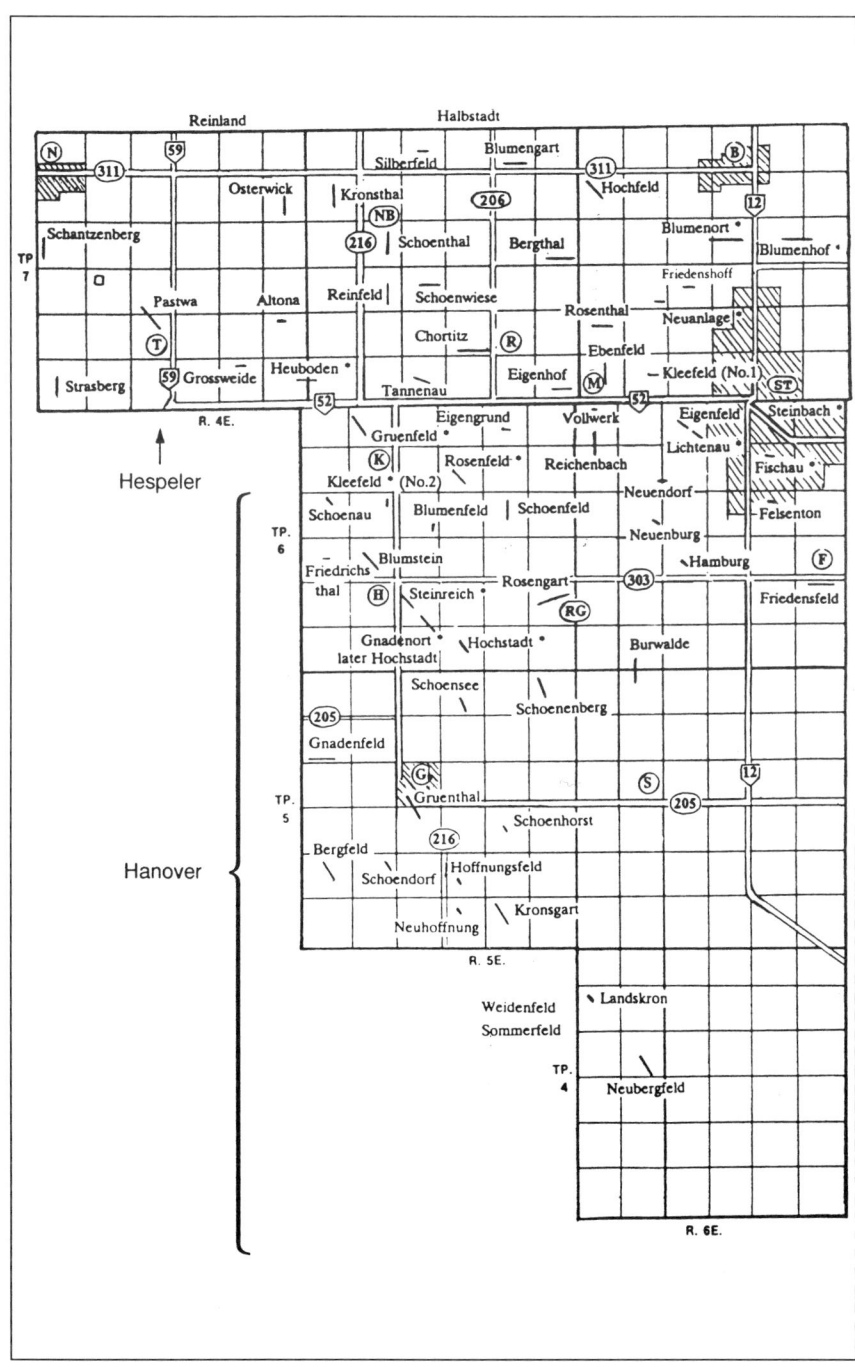

Source: John Dyck, ed., *Working Papers of the East Reserve Village Histories, 1874–1910* (Steinbach: Hanover Steinbach Historical Society, 1990), p. 11. Used by permission.

Under this Act, the municipality of Rhineland consisted of the entire Mennonite portion of the West Reserve, with the western boundary running approximately along the "Meno-Canuck" line.[60] The press reported strong Mennonite opposition to this imposition of external authority, with some threatening to emigrate if municipal government was actually forced on them.[61] It was quickly discovered, however, that this opposition existed only on the West Reserve; East Reserve Mennonites were ready to accept the change.[62] The *Manitoba Free Press* even claimed that the people in the West Reserve, too, were willing to accept municipal government, but that *Kaiser* Isaak Mueller was resisting it. To persuade Mueller and his people to accept it, Premier Norquay, assisted by William Hespeler, visited the reserve and suggested that the Mennonites appoint candidates for the various positions on the municipal council, which the government would then confirm. This solution was apparently accepted.[63] Accordingly, the government acted in May 1880 to appoint Mueller as Warden of the Municipality of Rhineland and six others as councillors.[64] These were duly affirmed into office by the government representative, Mr. Lester.[65]

Mueller now proceeded to collect vital statistics (births, deaths, and marriages) in accordance with the form prescribed by the government, and announced the deadline by which he needed to report these to Winnipeg. Similarly, at the request of the government, he instructed each village to prepare a map indicating all the lands belonging to it.[66] In 1883 the *Gebietsamt*-municipality gave a summary report to the Deputy Minister of Agriculture in Winnipeg indicating the state of the colony lands, population, livestock, and fixed and movable property.[67] From 1880 to 1883 Mueller thus seems to have functioned in the dual capacity of *Obervorsteher* of the Reinländer *Gebietsamt* and Warden of the Municipality of Rhineland.[68]

But his authority did not go unchallenged. In 1882, the twenty-five Bergthal villages on the eastern portion of the West Reserve elected their own *Obervorstand*.[69] In the western half of the reserve meanwhile, an excommunicated Reinländer, Jacob Giesbrecht, opposed Mueller for the position of reeve and attempted to use the courts to confirm himself in that position.[70] Mueller's authority was thus threatened in both portions of the reserve. Nevertheless, in the elections in late 1882 to choose an *Obervorsteher* for 1883 and 1884, Mueller easily defeated Giesbrecht, his closest rival, by a vote of 268 to 70.[71]

In 1883, the provincial government once more altered municipal boundaries, apparently at the suggestion of William Hespeler, dividing the West Reserve into two main portions (see map 4). The western (Reinländer) part retained the name Rhineland, while the eastern (Bergthaler) portion was created into the new municipality of Douglas. The eastern extremity of the Reserve remained in Montcalm and the western one in

South Dufferin.[72] Under this legislation the government appointed electoral officers to hold elections in both municipalities. In Douglas no opposition was encountered. Otto Schulz was elected reeve and his Mennonite council moved at its second meeting to petition the legislature for permission to conduct its meetings in German. The same meeting also instructed municipal clerk Franz Kliewer to assure the constituency that taxes would not rise sharply as a result of salaries for municipal officials.[73] Finally, the meeting appointed a committee to negotiate with Montcalm Municipality to move township 1-1E, which was part of the Mennonite Reserve, into Douglas. The introduction of municipal government thus raised only practical concerns for the Bergthal people of the West Reserve: language of operation, costs, and boundaries. Reservations about co-operation with the provincial government were not raised. In fact, Kliewer indicated that they, as well as the government, had come to realize that the methods used in Russia were no longer appropriate.[74]

In Rhineland, C. F. Collins, County Court Clerk of Nelson, served as returning officer for the elections in December 1883. Reeve Jarvis Mott, a Baptist from Ontario and one of the few Anglo-Saxons in the municipality, and all six Mennonite councillors were elected by acclamation. At the first meeting of Council, Collins administered the oath of office to Mott and the "declaration of office" to the five Mennonite councillors present.[75] The Reinländer dissidents and their Bergthal allies had succeeded in their struggle against Mueller's Reinländer regime during the two years prior to the election. Thanks to the authority of the provincial government their council was now the official local government. The Reinländer congregation, whose *Gebietsamt* still functioned, countered by forbidding its members to do any business with the municipality.[76] Councillor Johann Dueck of Osterwick, a Reinländer church member, was thus prevented from taking his seat on the municipal council. The Municipal Act of 1883 provided that "any mayor, reeve or councillor refusing to act, after having been duly elected, shall thereby incur a penalty of forty dollars ... and any mayor, reeve or councillor wilfully neglecting to attend and subscribe to the oath of office as prescribed in this Act shall be evidence of his refusal to act."[77] In April the municipal council of Rhineland invoked this clause against Dueck and instructed its solicitor, J. B. McLaren, to proceed to collect the penalty.[78] It also declared Dueck's seat vacant and passed a by-law for the election of his replacement.[79] Whether the municipality succeeded in collecting the forty-dollar fine from Dueck or the Reinländer church remains unclear.[80] He could hardly be said to have been "duly elected" in view of the procedures used in December 1883.

A communication received in January 1884 from the deputy of the Provincial Secretary assured the newly elected municipal council of official government recognition, adding that Mr. Mueller had no power to

## Map 4
**Municipal Boundary Changes in the Mennonite West Reserve, 1880–1916**

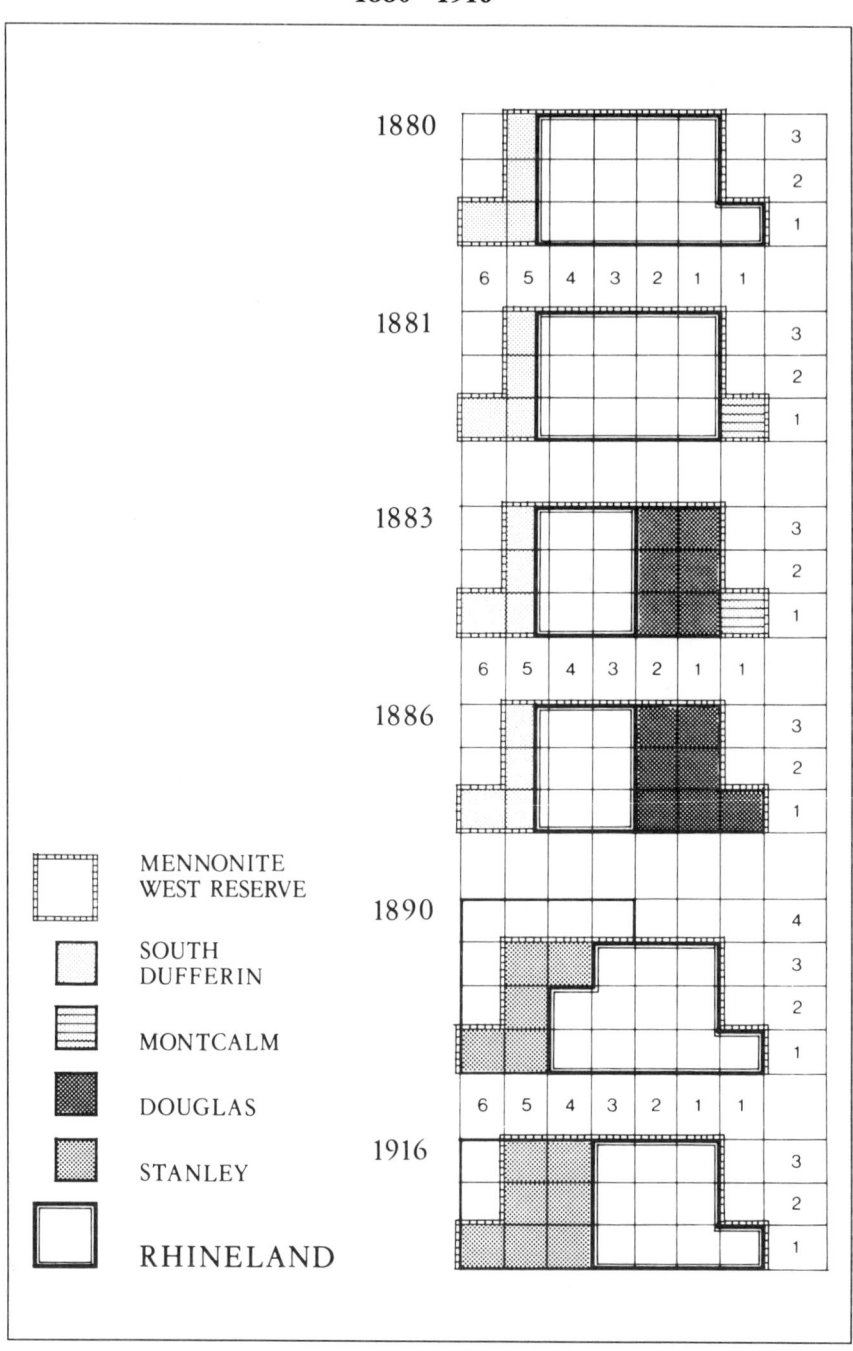

Source: Gerhard John Ens, *Volost and Municipality: The Rural Municipality of Rhineland, 1884–1984* (Altona, Man.: R. M. of Rhineland, 1984), p. xi. Used by permission.

form a council for 1884.⁸¹ Having achieved formal power, the council now proceeded to transfer actual power to itself from the Reinländer *Gebietsamt*. It requested the Provincial Secretary to write to Mueller informing him that his council was no longer recognized and requesting him to furnish to the proper department a statement of taxes levied and monies paid out during the past four years. It then proceeded to set up a joint committee with the new Municipality of Douglas to apportion the assets and liabilities of the "former Municipality of Rhineland between this Municipality and the Municipality of Douglas."⁸²

Meanwhile, Mueller had gone to Winnipeg in February to determine what the rights of his *Gebietsamt* were and had discovered that he was "justified in retaining in possession any assets or books whatever" until a proper apportionment and distribution had been made under the provisions of the Municipal Act.⁸³ He therefore chose not to give any account to the new councils, although he met with Bergthaler representative Bernhard Klippenstein regarding the dividing up of some road equipment.⁸⁴

The new municipal councils found it difficult to begin their work without access to the assessment records of previous years, and filed a complaint with the Provincial Secretary.⁸⁵ Representatives from Winnipeg then came down to the Douglas municipal office in Neuanlage and summoned a meeting with officials of the Reinländer *Gebietsamt*. Inspection of the records showed that its books were definitely not legal municipal property, so Mueller was allowed to retain possession of them.⁸⁶ With that kind of resistance from Mueller, the new Rhineland Municipality did not find out until November what its financial situation was.⁸⁷

During the first year the Rhineland municipal council met in the home of councillor David Reddekopp in Schanzenfeld. In 1885 Jacob Giesbrecht of Reinland served as reeve, and since the appointed secretary-treasurer, Wilhelm Rempel, also lived in Reinland, the municipal office was transferred to their village, which also served as headquarters of the Reinländer *Gebietsamt*.⁸⁸

The council now conducted a series of farmers' meetings to determine which body should have possession of the administrative office building in Reinland. By a majority of 162 to 69 these farmers voted to allow the municipality possession of the building. Isaak Mueller learned of the decision through an intermediary.⁸⁹ He promptly informed all of the *Dorfschulzen* of this development, pointing out that the vote of Reinländer church members, a large majority of the ratepayers in the municipality, opposed this move. Since the building was being used as a district school, Mueller proposed that it be sold by public auction in order to avoid further strife.⁹⁰ Finding its intentions blocked in this way, the council presented the matter to the Provincial Secretary, D. H. Wilson, for his opinion and advice.⁹¹ Wilson's response is no longer available, but it apparently supported the verdict of the farmers' meetings. In any case, the municipal council took matters into its own hands, removed all of the *Gebietsamt* materials from the building, and occupied it. In that manner another stage in the transition from *Gebietsamt* to municipality was effected.⁹²

The *Gebietsamt* lost its office building, but not its office. Two weeks after the municipal council held its first meeting in 1884, Isaak Mueller sent all the village *Schulzen* the proposed new regulations governing statutory labour, and exemptions for *Dorfsvorsteher, Brandältester*, etc. The instruction was signed by Mueller as *Bezirksvorsteher*.⁹³ Having the consent of the community, he could successfully request statutory labour from his constituency. The municipal council, on the other hand, derived its authority from the provincial government and functioned in Rhineland without the consent of the majority of its ratepayers. It accordingly petitioned the Legislative Assembly to amend the 1884 Municipal Act "so as to give the Municipal Councils the right to impose statute labour according to local want."⁹⁴

The municipal council realized that its effectiveness in providing local administration would be limited as long as the majority of the constituency failed to participate in municipal elections. It thus tried very hard to encourage Reinländer church members to participate in these elections. The church leaders opposed this and were fairly successful in keeping solidarity among their members on this point.⁹⁵ In the 1885 elections, for example, it is estimated that barely a tenth of the eligible voters in Rhineland Municipality cast their ballots.⁹⁶ Therefore, candidates for office could be selected from less than one-tenth of the eligible men, since the Reinländer church permitted neither voting nor holding of office in the municipality. However, almost every year a member of the Reinländer church was in fact elected to council and then either had to resign from that office or be excommunicated from his church.⁹⁷ The church was not left in peace on this point until Bishop Johann Wiebe appeared before the court in Morden and apparently convinced the judge on Biblical grounds that his church could not be forced to participate in elections.⁹⁸

A pattern of peaceful co-existence between *Gebietsamt* and municipality gradually developed and with it an acceptable *modus vivendi*.⁹⁹ Exactly when this was achieved is difficult to pinpoint but by the end of 1887, Franz Froese, who succeeded Isaak Mueller as *Obervorsteher* of the *Gebietsamt* that year, required of his tenant prompt fulfilment of municipal tax and road requirements.¹⁰⁰ That the municipal council was not anti-clerical is indicated by an 1885 by-law exempting Mennonite clergymen in the municipality from statute labour and land taxes "because they get no pay for their clerical and frequently troublesome services."¹⁰¹

## Mennonite Solidarity Broken: Unequally Yoked

The most serious consequence of accepting the external resources available through public schools and the external authority available through municipal government was that the original solidarity of the Mennonite immigrants was broken. Just as Bergthal *Ältester* Gerhard Wiebe lamented the fact that the *Kleine Gemeinde* did not stand with his congregation in opposing district schools, so Reinländer *Ältester* Johann Wiebe regretted the absence of Bergthal support in opposing municipal government. While Gerhard Wiebe was almost as strongly opposed to the latter development as Johann was, his resignation in the spring of 1882, because of what he apparently considered to be a serious moral lapse on his part, rendered him ineffectual.[102] The other Bergthal bishops, David Stoesz and Johann Funk, were not seen as opponents of municipal government by the Reinländer bishop.[103]

The basic reason for opposition to municipal government and district schools was that to accept them was seen as a violation of their understanding of the roles of church and state and their emphasis on not being "unequally yoked together with unbelievers."[104] This had been a major reason that Bishop Johann Wiebe and his Fürstenland congregation had left Russia. The church there no longer practised discipline according to Matthew 18, but dealt with nearly all cases according to secular law and with secular authority. Adulterers were still disciplined according to God's word, but many other offences were dealt with according to state law, which included corporal punishment. This law was administered by a member of the congregation, elected by voters who were all members of the same congregation, but affirmed in office by the Russian government.[105] The two Wiebe bishops had decided to abandon this whole system in Canada by reintroducing a clearer distinction between the spheres of authority of church and state. According to the Municipal Act, however, the reeve of a municipality functioned ex officio as Justice of the Peace.[106] For the church to co-operate with the municipality under those terms meant a return to the Russian system, which they had rejected in principle.

Experience showed that these concerns were not unjustified. Several disputes or conflicts were brought before the municipal council of Rhineland as early as 1885, and in at least one case the parties involved were simply given a deadline to settle their dispute or else it would be taken to the municipal solicitor in Nelson.[107] To the church leadership it did not seem right that disputes between members of their church should be settled by outside authorities. Even more serious was the way in which the council dealt with those who were in arrears in their financial obligations. Already in its second year of operation the council of Rhineland Municipality decided to turn over to the Secretary of the Eastern Judicial District the accounts of all those who had not paid their municipal taxes for 1884 in order that the Court "collect the taxes by selling the lands...."[108] Such a thing would not happen if the office were handled in accordance with apostolic teaching, wrote one observer. Instead, a careful investigation would reveal whether or not the person was capable of paying these back taxes. If he were found incapable, then voluntary contributions would be gathered in the church to pay for the delinquent's debts.[109] Others felt that to participate in elections or in government service would present a danger that "on the day of war they would rue." Accepting government positions and restructuring their internal administration according to the laws of the land would so blur the distinction between them and other nations that the government would no longer be able to recognize that they were Mennonites.[110] Furthermore, the introduction of municipal government, insofar as it replaced the *Gebietsamt*, indirectly threatened the continued existence of the village landholding system and much of the communal social organization that went with it.[111] Fear of the unforeseen consequences of "the infiltration of practices and directives coming from a government beyond the jurisdiction of the elders and the discipline of the congregation" also undoubtedly provided part of the motivation for opposing the municipality.[112]

The differences between the Reinländer congregation and those who participated in municipal government and the public schools were thus a matter of principle. Since the latter were accepted into the Bergthaler church, Reinländer members were for several years forbidden to have any contact with Bergthal people.[113] By 1888, hopes for a reconciliation seemed very slim.[114] By 1890, the large Bergthal group was itself disintegrating under the pressure of these outside influences. The portion on the East Reserve developed its own identity as the Chortitzer church. On the West Reserve a larger portion of Bergthal people became dissatisfied with the leadership of Bishop Johann Funk and gradually developed a separate identity, which came to be known as the Sommerfelder church.

In spite of their resistance to district schools and municipal administration, Mennonite church leaders continued to maintain complete confidence in the "high government." They blamed unfaithful elements within the Mennonite constituency itself for erosion of their freedom. Gerhard Wiebe wrote: "As far as the government is concerned we still have our full liberty, for it remains faithful to the agreement with our deputies, but we ourselves are trampling this freedom with our feet."[115] Johann Wiebe's assessment of the federal government was even more positive: "And if the high government had not been so gracious to us, they [our opponents in the Mennonite Reserve] would have already forced us to join with them in taking on secular power. But thanks to God and to the government we are still able to live out our faith according to God's word in our schools and churches."[116] For these two the ideal was still clearly to remain subjects of the "high government" but to refrain from the degree of involvement that full citizenship would entail.

## Notes

1. Morton, pp. 185–187.

2. Peter A. Toews, "Diary," in Delbert Plett, *Profile 1874*, p. 167.

3. Gerhard Wiebe, p. 54. John J. Bergen, "The Manitoba Mennonites and Their Schools from 1873 to 1924" (M.Ed. term paper, University of Manitoba, 1950), pp. 44–54, gives a good summary of this period of Mennonite education in Manitoba.

4. Manitoba, Legislative Assembly, *English School Reports, 1872–1883*, "Report of the Superintendent of Protestant Schools in the Province of Manitoba, 1877," p. 6; *Journals*, 1879, "Report of the Superintendent of Education for Protestant Schools for the year 1878," appendix, p. 18. Gerhard Wiebe, p. 54, and Johann C. Reimer, "*Unsere Schulen*," in *Gedenkfeier der Mennonitischen Einwanderung*, p. 79, indicate the mediating role of Hespeler. The latter, quoting from the notebook of pioneer Steinbach teacher G. G. Kornelsen, gives the date as 1879.

5. W. Cyprian Pinkham, Superintendent, James Robertson, and Stuart Mulvey, Winnipeg, to the Mennonite churches, 17 October 1878. The German version of the letter is reproduced as received in *Gedenkfeier*, pp. 78–79; an English translation in P. J. B. Reimer, ed., *The Sesquicentennial Jubilee: Evangelical Mennonite Conference, 1812–1962* (Steinbach, Man.: Evangelical Mennonite Conference, 1962), pp. 160–161.

6. "Report of the Superintendent ... 1878," pp. 18–19. A compilation by Debra Fast of the Mennonite portions of these annual reports for the years 1877–1926 is located in MHCA, "vertical file."

7. "Report ... 1878," p. 50. Dyck, *Working Papers*, appendix 6, pp. 183–184, lists the thirty-three East Reserve villages and gives their location; cf. map, p. 11.

8. Ibid., pp. 63–64. Kornelsen's list in *Gedenkfeier*, p. 79, and Reimer, p. 161, is incomplete. The suggestion of John Jacob Bergen, "A Historical Study of Education in the Municipality of Rhineland" (M.Ed. thesis, University of Manitoba, 1959), pp. 43–44, that six of these could be West Reserve villages is quite improbable since the Board was negotiating only with the East Reserve bishops.

9. "Report ... 1878," pp. 20–21, lists the thirty-one teachers examined and the entire Board of Examiners for 1879. Kornelsen's notes indicate that the examination was held at Chortitz on 10 March 1879 with Hespeler, now German consul in Winnipeg, and teachers Abraham Isaak, Schoenau, and Jacob Friesen, Tannenau, as examiners. *Gedenkfeier*, p. 83; Reimer, p. 163; Paul J. Schaefer, *Woher? Wohin? Mennoniten!*, vol. 3, *Die Mennoniten in Canada* (Altona, Man.: Mennonite Agricultural Advisory Committee, 1946), p. 68.

10. Gerhard Wiebe, p. 54.

11. Manitoba, Legislative Assembly, *Journals*, 1880, "Condensed Report of the Superintendent of Education for Protestant Schools for the Year Ending January 31st, 1880," appendix, pp. 76–77, 79. During 1879 the thirty-five Mennonite schools constituted over one-third of the ninety-nine schools operating in Manitoba under the Protestant section of the Board, although their enrolment of 632 made up only 17.5 percent of the 3,614 total. Appendix, p. 70.

12. Ibid., 1881, "Tenth Annual Report of the Superintendent of Education for Protestant Schools for the Year Ending 1880," appendix, p. 148.

13. Gerhard Wiebe, p. 55; translation by the author because the English translation has omitted a line in this passage. Later on, p. 64, Wiebe writes: "If only the Kleine Gemeinde would work together with our *Älteste*, but no [while] ... they give the appearance of still holding back, ... they lead the way, that is, with their schools."

14. "Condensed Report ... 1880," p. 72. Twenty-two Mennonite teachers were given one-year certificates.

15. "Tenth Annual Report," p. 150.

16. "Report of the Superintendent of Education for Protestant Schools for the Yending E1st January 1882," pp. 23–24. Subsequent reports will be cited in short form only. Until 1888 the school reporting year ended January 31.

17. Stoesz, "History of the Chortitzer Mennonite Church," pp. 139–140, gives 15 March 1881 as the probable official date of the withdrawal of the Bergthal villages from the public school system.

18. "Condensed Report ... 1880," p. 74.

19. "Report ... 1882," pp. 23–24.

20. "Report ... 1883," p. 68; "Report ... 1884," p. 41.

21. Elias, 2:12; Zacharias, p. 248; Peter Friesen in Johann Wiebe, pp. 70–71.

22. Elias, 2:12–13.

23. *Mennonitische Rundschau*, 11 April 1888, p. 1.

24. Rhineland Municipality (old), *Minutes*, 1884–1891, 8 January 1884, p. 1.

25. "Report ... 1886," pp. 85–86. For a brief biographical sketch of Rempel, see Zacharias, pp. 248–252.

26. "Report ... 1886," p. 86.

27. "Report ... 1887," pp. 53–54.

28. Manitoba, Legislative Assembly, *Statutes*, 1880, p. 54, sec. 12 of 44 Vic., ch. 4, "An Act to Establish a System of Public Schools in the Province of Manitoba."

29. Rhineland Municipality (old), *Minutes*, 9 December 1884, p. 39.

30. Rhineland Municipality (old), *By-laws*, 1884–1890, no. 20, 30 January 1885, pp. 58–62.

31. Rhineland Municipality (old), *Minutes*, 3 March 1885, pp. 60, 74; *By-laws*, p. 72.

32. Rhineland Municipality (old), *Minutes*, 19 November 1885, p. 86.

33. David Peters, et al., "*Schanzenfelder Gemeinde Spruch*," n.d., in *Gemeinde Buch der Kolonie Reinland*, no. 11, p. 264, PAM, MG 8, A 18-7, microfilm M-216, Mennonite Settlement Registers; copy in MHCA, microfilm no. 44.

34. Rhineland Municipality (old), *Minutes*, 1 December 1885, p. 92.

35. Ibid., 3 March 1885 (Kleefeld and Kronsgart), p. 60; 10 November 1886 (Schönfeld), p. 146; 1 April 1887 (Blumstein), p. 172. Douglas Municipality, *Minutes*, 1884–1888, 6 May 1884 (Blumenort and Kronstal), p. 47.

36. *Mennonitische Rundschau*, 11 April 1888, p. 1.

37. Manitoba, Legislative Assembly, *Sessional Papers*, 1889, no. 18, "Report of the Superintendent for Protestant Schools for the Period of 11 Months from February 1 to December 31, 1888," pp. 32–33.

38. Dyck's *Oberschulze Jakob Peters* is the most comprehensive biography of this pioneer leader. P. Braun, "*Kolonie-Verwaltung*," in *Gedenkfeier*, p. 121, and Francis, *In Search of Utopia*, p. 84, assume unbroken continuity in Peters' leadership. But it is clear that during the very important first few years in Canada someone else held this crucial role. Francis erroneously identifies the *Oberschulze* as Franz Peters.

39. Francis, *In Search of Utopia*, p. 87.

40. Jacob Epp, diary, vol. 5, 1871–1880, 24 April 1874; MHCA, vol. 1017.

41. Peter Wiens, "Anschreibe Buch der Auswanderer welche nach Amerika ziehen wollen," book no. 44, Mexico collection, MHCA, microfilm no. 655.

42. Johann Wiebe, pp. 34–35.

43. Zacharias, p. 58. Directives from Mueller to village *Schulzen* beginning 1876 are found in the Reinland village papers, MHCA, vol. 1091; Rosenort village papers, vol. 1099; and Gnadenthal village papers, vol. 2198. Francis, *In Search of Utopia*, p. 84, erroneously assumes that Mueller had been *Oberschulze* in Fürstenland until his emigration and continued in that office without election in 1875.

44. John Dyck, "Biography of Isaac Mueller," unpublished manuscript in possession of the author. Mueller was re-elected in December 1878, following a three-year term in office as was the practice in Russia. MHCA, vol. 1099, #27, 2 December 1878. He was then re-elected to two-year terms in 1880, 1882, and 1884. *Reinland Gemeinde Buch*, no. 8, pp. 4–5, MHCA, Mexico collection.

45. The Reinländer Church records, PAM, MG 8, A 18-7 (MHCA, microfilm no. 44), contain assessment data for West Reserve Bergthal villages, but the Mueller directives, MHCA, vol. 1091 and 1099, seem to have gone mostly to Chortitza–Fürstenland villages. The detailed instructions Mueller gave regarding construction of the Post Road from Emerson to Mountain City, for example, were not directed to any village east of Blumenort, the boundary of Bergthal territory. Vol. 1099, no. 27, 17 March 1878.

46. But Gerbrandt's statement, p. 71, that "those moving from the East Reserve were considered severed from the Chortitzer Church after 1878," is too strong, since there is ample evidence of Bishop Stoesz's ministry on the West Reserve well into the 1880s.

47. Manitoba, Legislative Assembly, *Statutes*, 1873, sec. 2 of 36 Vic., chap. 24, "An Act Respecting Municipalities," assented to 8 March 1873.

48. John H. Warkentin, "The Mennonite Settlements," p. 81.

49. Ibid., p. 82; Manitoba, Legislative Assembly, *Statutes*, 1880, secs. 176 and 177 of 44 Vic., chap. 3, "An Act Respecting Municipalities," assented to 4 March 1881.

50. John H. Warkentin, "The Mennonite Settlements," p. 84.

51. Ibid., p. 82. Warkentin mentions that "for statistical purposes the boundaries were always respected." Francis, *In Search of Utopia*, p. 92.

52. Stoesz, "History of the Chortitzer Mennonite Church," p. 156.

53. Penner, pp. 157, 163.

54. Stoesz, p. 158.

55. Abe Warkentin, p. 58: "The change-over to municipal government went smoothly and little actually changed except that the *Oberschulze* now had real authority and did not have to depend on the assistance of the church." John H. Warkentin, "The Mennonite Settlements," p. 81: "The change in administration was made without difficulty in the East Reserve. It is impossible to say whether this is because the situation of the Reserve in the forgotten corner of Manitoba made it appear to be safe from outside influence, or because the leaders thought that municipal government would in any case make no infringements on

the Mennonite way of life." P. Braun in *Gedenkfeier*, pp. 121–122, suggests that difficulties encountered by the villages in raising local school taxes led to a search for methods of local government more suited to the Canadian situation. Thus arose the new municipality. Francis, *In Search of Utopia*, pp. 91–92: "It seems that the step was well prepared by Hespeler who was able to point out that compliance with the wishes of Legislature and Government would make the Mennonites eligible for Provincial subsidies and public works. The Mennonites themselves recognized that the functioning of self-government in the colony, particularly tax collection, would be facilitated if their own officers enjoyed official status instead of having to rely exclusively on their personal authority and that of the church." Calvin Wall Redekop, *The Old Colony Mennonites. Dilemmas of Ethnic Minority Life* (Baltimore: Johns Hopkins Press, 1969), p. 9: "In the East Reserve, the Bergthaler soon adopted the reeve system for two reasons: (1) they were not very concerned about keeping their own organization alive; and (2) they were not able to maintain control because many farmers lived on farms outside the villages."

56. A. Warkentin, p. 58, and Francis, *In Search of Utopia*, pp. 91–92, date them on 27 December 1882, although Reeve Gerhard Kliewer and his council were apparently not confirmed in office until January 1884. Loewen, p. 90, dates the organizational meeting of the municipality 1 January 1883. Penner, pp. 7–9, 163, indicates Kliewer in office as reeve since 1880 and succeeded by Peter Toews in 1883.

57. Loewen, p. 91, quoting from "Gebietsamts Briefen" found in the *Blumenort Village Papers*. Braun, *Gedenkfeier*, p. 121, confirms that for many years the reeve was elected by "the old method of electing *Schulz, Brandältester*, etc."

58. Francis, p. 92; Loewen, p. 90. Reimer, p. 26, reports the official position of the *Kleine Gemeinde* in 1899 as follows: "No member can accept any government position or take any part in a government election. That had been its basic position already before coming to Canada." Epp, *Mennonites in Canada*, p. 292.

59. McLaren in Grant, vol. 1, p. 324, seems to think that "*Kaiser*" was the title of the office of *Obervorsteher*. Zacharias, p. 62, correctly points out that it was Mueller's nickname, resulting from his somewhat imperious manner in giving directives and from his wide-ranging powers.

60. See map 2. Township 1-6W and the western four miles of townships 1 to 3 in range 5W, part of the original Mennonite Reserve, were now part of the new non-Mennonite Municipality of South Dufferin. This prompted the Council of the latter to inquire of Ottawa whether it had the authority to tax the Mennonite lands. Robert McKay, Warden, Municipality of South Dufferin, to the Minister of the Interior, 25 July 1880, NA, RG 15, vol. 232, no. 3129.

61. *Manitoba Free Press* (hereafter *MFP*), 16 April 1880, p. 1.

62. *MFP*, 17 April 1880, p. 1.

63. *MFP*, 29 April 1880, p. 2; 1 May 1880, p. 4; *Mennonitische Rundschau*, 22 February 1888, p. 1; Elias, 2:11.

64. *Manitoba Gazette*, vol. 9, no. 7, 8 May 1880, p. 65. Appointed as councillors were two Bergthal members, Peter Friesen and Bernhard Rempel, Halbstadt; and four from the Reinländer group: David Giesbrecht, Neuhorst; Johannn Loewen, Rosengart; Gerhard Neufeld, Hochfeld; and Bernhard Hildebrand, Rosenthal. The name of the municipality in the *Gazette* is given as "Rineland," a misspelling of either "Reinland" (the village which served as the seat of the *Gebietsamt*), or of the region in Germany known as "Rhineland."

65. Elias, 2:11, thinking that they took the *oath* of office, explodes that this was "*plat gegen die evangelische Lehr*" [totally against evangelical teaching]!

66. Directives of 11 December and 16 August 1882, MHCA, vol. 1099, no. 29.

67. *Reinland Gemeinde Buch*, no. 12, p. 109, PAM, MG 8, A 18-7 (MHCA, microfilm no. 44). The following year the reporting of vital statistics was done by the municipality, not the *Gebietsamt*. See communication from Acton Burrows, Deputy Minister of Agriculture, Winnipeg, in Rhineland Municipality (old), *Minutes*, 6 November 1884, p. 33. John H. Warkentin's claim, "The Mennonite Settlements," p. 83, that no municipal organization was forthcoming from the West Reserve Mennonites in 1881 and 1882, does not seem justified in the light of this activity by Mueller's council.

68. Both the boundaries (see map 4) of the municipality and the spelling of its name were changed by the legislation of 1881, which gave both Rhineland and Montcalm jurisdiction over townships 1 to 3 in ranges 1 and 2W. Manitoba, Legislative Assembly, *Statutes*, 1880, secs. 162 and 181 of 44 Vic., chap. 3; assented to 4 March 1881.

69. H. Hiebert, Gnadenfeld (West Lynne), *Mennonitische Rundschau*, 15 August 1882, p. 1. Hiebert mentions that they had also newly elected Johann Funk as *Ältester* of their congregation.

70. Elias, 1:11–12, 2:11–14, is confusing in the actual dates cited. But the sequence of municipal administrations he describes has Mueller serve two years, then Giesbrecht two, Mott one, and then Giesbrecht again. Since Mott served as reeve in 1884, Giesbrecht's first challenge of Mueller's authority is dated 1882. Elias claims that Giesbrecht and his supporters were successful in forming the municipal council during 1882–1883, although he admits that Giesbrecht lost his suit against the Reinländer bishop Johann Wiebe in Morden. In any case, Mueller was clearly in charge of affairs during those years. The Rhineland Municipality (old), *Minutes*, p. 13, 15 March 1884, identify him as "warden of this Municipality for several years past."

71. *Reinland Gemeinde Buch*, Mexico Collection, no. 8, pp. 4–5. MHCA microfilm.

72. Manitoba, Legislative Assembly, *Statutes*, 1883, secs. 21 and 30 of Part 1, 46 and 47 Vic., chap. 1; assented to 7 July 1883. F. G. Enns, *Gretna: Window on the Northwest* (Gretna, Man.: Village of Gretna History Committee, 1987), p. 46. See Ens, *Volost*, appendix 1, p. 253, for a summary of legislation regarding boundary changes from 1880 to 1916. J. F. Galbraith, *The Mennonites in Manitoba, 1875–1900. A Review of Their Coming, Their Progress, and Their Present Prosperity* (Morden, Man.: Chronicle Press, 1900), pp. 14–15, suggests that the government effected this division in such a way as deliberately to include some English-speaking people "accustomed to municipal institutions" in each of the two new municipalities. Warkentin, "The Mennonite Settlements," p. 85, saw that as a means to hasten Mennonite assimilation. If that was indeed the government's intention, it would have been much more effective to move the western boundary so as to include all of range 5 in Rhineland. More acceptable is the suggestion in *Mennonitische Rundschau*, 22 February 1888, p. 1, that the area of the old Reinland Municipality was too extensive for one municipal council. According to C. Ewart, "The Municipal History of Manitoba," *University of Toronto Studies: History and Economics* 2 (April 1904): 136, the legislators of the 1883 Act were preoccupied with "following very closely the Act then in force in Ontario." They likely gave scant attention to details of internal Mennonite politics. If these were considered, then the division of the reserve into two municipal jurisdictions probably reflects recognition by Winnipeg of the new Bergthaler *Obervorstand* in the eastern portion.

73. Douglas Municipality, *Minutes*, 2 February 1884, p. 17. Annual salaries of Reinländer *Gebietsamt* officials were from $120 to $300 each for secretary and *Obervorsteher* between 1875 and 1883. MHCA, Gnadenthal papers, vol. 2198, no. 1. That Kliewer could communicate this via the *Mennonitische Rundschau*, 27 February 1884, p. 1, shows how widely this Elkhart, Indiana paper was read in Manitoba.

74. Douglas Municipality, *Minutes*, 2 February 1884, p. 17.

75. Rhineland Municipality (old), *Minutes*, 8 and 26 January and 1 November 1884, pp. 1, 3, 39. Mott lived on the only half section (W1/2 of 23-3-5W) of land in the municipality that was not part of the reserve. He was among those non-Mennonite settlers who had procured their land within the original boundaries of the reserve in a legitimate manner and hence was on good terms with the Mennonites. William Pearce, Dominion Land Surveyor, Winnipeg, to Donald Codd, NA, RG 15, vol. 232, no. 3129. The five councillors present were: Jacob Giesbrecht, Reinland; David Reddekopp, Schanzenfeld; Heinrich Reimer, Schöndorf; Jacob Nickel, Burwalde; and Bernard Hilbrandt. The sixth, Johann Dueck, Osterwick, had not appeared. The list given by Galbraith, p. 17, is not complete nor entirely accurate.

76. Francis, *In Search of Utopia*, p. 94; Gerbrandt, pp. 74–75.

77. Manitoba, Legislative Assembly, *Statutes*, 1883, sec. 156 of part 1, 46 and 47 Vic., chap. 1; assented to 7 July 1883.

78. Rhineland Municipality (old), *Minutes*, 15 and 29 April 1884, pp. 15–17.

79. Rhineland Municipality (old), *By-Laws*, no. 6, 15 April 1884. Peter Zacharias was elected "by nomination" to fill the vacant seat on April 26. *Minutes*, 29 April 1884, p. 17.

80. Galbraith, p. 17.

81. Rhineland Municipality (old), *Minutes*, 26 January 1884, p. 3.

82. Ibid., 1 March 1884, p. 9. The corresponding action of Douglas Municipality created "a committee to ask from the old struckout municipality of Rhineland a reckoning up of accounts so that this part of the former municipality of Rhineland may get its share from the funds now in the hands of that municipality." Douglas Municipality, *Minutes*, 8 January 1884, pp. 5–7.

83. Rhineland Municipality (old), *Minutes*, 15 and 29 April 1884, pp. 13, 17.

84. Ibid., 7 June 1884, p. 25. Klippenstein was not a member of the Douglas Municipal Council. He may have been *Vorsteher* of the West Reserve Bergthaler *Gebietsamt* referred to above, since he was Mueller's counterpart in the 1883 negotiations with Ottawa regarding the Mennonite loan. See chap. 1, under "Group Migration: Naturalization and Land Patents."

85. Rhineland Municipality (old), *Minutes*, 5 July 1884, pp. 28–29.

86. Friesen in Johann Wiebe, pp. 72–73.

87. Rhineland Municipality (old), *Minutes*, 1 November 1884, p. 35. McEwan, Dunsford and Co., Nelson, informed them that their municipality was debt-free and had a cash balance of $20.

88. Ibid., 13 January 1885, p. 48. Subsequent meetings of council were held in Reinland.

89. Ibid., 3 March 1885, pp. 63–65.

90. Directive of 7 March 1885, MHCA, vol. 1099, no. 30.

91. Rhineland Municipality (old), *Minutes*, 2 June 1885, pp. 80–82.

92. Friesen, in Johann Wiebe, p. 72, reports that the council threatened to shoot anyone who would dare to buy the building at the auction proposed by Mueller.

93. Directive of 22 January 1884, MHCA, vol. 1099, no. 30. Mueller and his successors continued to function as head of the Reinländer *Gebietsamt* until the church emigrated to Mexico in the 1920s.

94. Rhineland Municipality (old), *Minutes*, 3 March 1885, p. 60.

95. Andrew Willows, "A History of Mennonites, Particularly in Manitoba," (M.A. thesis, University of Manitoba, 1924), p. 87; Dawson, p. 148.

96. Johann Froese, *Mennonitische Rundschau*, 3 February 1886, p. 1.

97. The case of Johann Dueck in 1884 has been discussed above. The *Dorfsgemeinde* of the village of Blumengart protected itself against this eventuality in 1885 by sending a petition to the municipal office indicating that its members would not participate in the elections nor accept any office. Rhineland Municipality (old), *Minutes*, 1 December 1885, pp. 91–92. In 1886, again only five councillors took office at the January meeting of the Rhineland Council. The sixth elected member, Abram Neufeld, on April 6 announced to council before the meeting began that he would be unable to take office because of physical weakness ("*Körperschwäche*"). Idem, 6 April 1886, p. 105. In his case a letter of resignation was requested by council before it passed a by-law to declare the seat vacant and to hold a new election. Idem, 6 and 24 April 1886, pp. 106, 116; *By-Laws*, no. 32, 24 April 1886, p. 96. In 1887, elected councillor Wilhelm Reddekopp "pretends to be unable to serve" and was similarly asked for a "legal resignation" if he wanted to be released from the position. *Minutes*, 1 February 1887, p. 164. Reddekopp then got Dr. Fraser to certify that he was unable to serve "for reasons of health." Idem, 1 March 1887, p. 187. In 1888, the sixth councillor, Peter Peters, was appointed under sec. 206 of the Municipal Act 1886. Idem, 17 January 1888, p. 200. Friesen, in Johann Wiebe, pp. 73–74, indicates that some Reinländer church members who were thus elected to municipal council chose to serve their term of office and thereby "*von der Gemeinde sind losgekommen*" (were severed from their church connection).

98. Friesen, in Johann Wiebe, p. 74; Elias, 1:12. The Reinländer Church maintained this position until its emigration to Mexico in the 1920s. Bishop Johann Friesen, in a letter of 4 January 1917 to Prime Minister Borden, wrote: "We are not allowed to elect governmental offices or to serve in them according to Jesus' own words Mark 10:42f." NA, MG 26 H, 1(c), vol. 214, p. 121078.

99. Francis, *In Search of Utopia*, p. 95.

100. "*Gemeindespruch*," between Franz Froese, Reinland, owner, and Johann Penner, Chortitz, renter, 17 December 1887, in *Reinland Gemeinde Buch*, no. 11, after p. 264, PAM, MG 8, A 18-7 (MHCA, microfilm no. 44). Mueller's popularity is reflected in the fact that when he announced his retirement at the end of 1886 after twelve years as *Obervorsteher*, he still received only nine fewer votes than Froese in the election even though he was not officially on the ballot. *Reinland Gemeinde Buch*, Mexico Collection, no. 8, p. 35.

101. Rhineland Municipality (old), *By-Laws*, no. 19, 30 January 1885, p. 56. Douglas Municipality had already taken similar action the year before. *By-Laws*, 1:11, no. 8, 6 May 1884.

102. Gerhard Wiebe, p. 64, indicates his strong opposition to worldly office and recourse to the ballot box, but admits that he has no power to stop this trend in his church. The precise nature of his moral lapse is nowhere mentioned explicitly, but he discusses its consequences at some length on pp. 57–58, 73. Johann Wiebe, pp. 75–78, wrote him a pointed letter about this sin and advised him concretely how to be restored to his former effective leadership. His resignation is noted in the official church register, *Kirchenbuch der Gemeine zu Chortitz* (1887), Litter A, no. 1. MHCA, microfilm no. 184. His co-bishop, David Stoesz, noted in his *diary*, MHCA, vol. 1559, that Wiebe returned from duties in the West Reserve on 15 or 16 March 1882 and did not serve in the congregation after that time.

103. Elias, 1:9–10, 33–34, indicates that problems between the two groups became serious about 1880 because the Bergthaler accepted into membership excommunicated Reinländer. Stoesz and Johann Wiebe were unable to resolve their differences on this point. Funk's Bergthaler church, at least in later years, was opposed to having its members serve

as justice of the peace, which was one of the official functions of a municipal reeve. Bergthaler Church, Ministerial, *Minutes*, 11 March 1895, MHCA, vol. 716.

104. Elias, 1:11, quotes this passage from 2 Cor. 6:14, as well as Eph. 5:11. Francis, *In Search of Utopia*, p. 75, calls it an "ever-recurring theme." See, for example, Gerhard Wiebe, pp. 61, 65, 68; Johann Wiebe, pp. 40–41.

105. Johann Wiebe, pp. 31–34.

106. Manitoba, Legislative Assembly, *Statutes*, 1883, sec. 210 of part 1, 46 and 47 Vic., chap. 1; assented to 7 July 1883.

107. Rhineland Municipality (old), *Minutes*, 2 April and 19 November 1885, pp. 69, 88–90.

108. Ibid., 3 March 1885, pp. 62–64.

109. Jacob Kroeker, Reinland, *Mennonitische Rundschau*, 22 February 1888, pp. 1–2.

110. Johann Froese, *Mennonitische Rundschau*, 3 February 1886, p. 1. An anonymous response to this argument urged Mennonites to participate in municipal elections, maintaining that a God-fearing municipal officer could do much good if blessed by God. Idem, 24 February 1886.

111. Redekop, p. 9.

112. *Mennonite Encyclopedia*, s.v. "Manitoba," by Cornelius Krahn.

113. Elias, 2:14, 1:11; Gerbrandt, p. 74.

114. *Mennonitische Rundschau*, 22 February 1888, p. 1.

115. Gerhard Wiebe, p. 76.

116. Johann Wiebe, p. 41. Johann Friesen, who succeeded Wiebe's son as bishop of the Reinländer church in 1913, wrote in much the same vein years later in Mexico: *"Ist die Obrigkeit in Kanada Schuld daran gewesen, dass wir unter dem weltlichen Gesetz, unter den Schulzwang kommen mussten oder sind wir selbst Schuld daran ... ?"* (Was it the fault of the Canadian government that we were subjected to the forced schools, or was it our own fault?) Idem, p. 53.

CHAPTER III

# WESTWARD EXPANSION, 1890–1910

By the time the two Manitoba reserves were opened to general settlement, most of the good homestead land had been taken up. Except for the swampy southern part of the East Reserve and the hilly western townships of the West Reserve, no empty blocks of land large enough to establish a new village were left. The withdrawal of ministerial permission to fulfil homestead requirements under the "Hamlet Privilege" clause in 1889 presented a further obstacle to the founding of new villages. For the Reinländer church, which insisted on the semi-communal village life, this meant that its new families had no place to go once the existing villages were filled. The more individualistic Mennonites who wanted to escape the strictures of village life, and those who wished to expand their landholdings beyond what was possible on the Manitoba reserves, were ready to go farther afield to achieve their goals.

There was some migration to the United States in the early years of the settlement. One group of about twenty-eight Bergthal families relocated to the Mountain Lake, Minnesota area in the 1870s while a few others settled in Oregon in the late 1880s.[1] A few families settled in North Dakota, but a Reinländer delegation found that reserving land, settling in villages, and operating their own schools would not be possible there. Hence, in spite of being very pleased with the land, the Reinländer congregation decided against emigration.[2]

The completion of the transcontinental railway in 1885 and the subsequent construction of spur lines running north and south of it greatly improved settlement possibilities in the Northwest Territories of Canada. At the same time the second Riel uprising at Batoche finally convinced Ottawa to give more serious attention to the West if settlement of that region was to progress. This resulted in the creation of a representative legislative assembly in 1888. Individual Mennonite families and small groups began to homestead between the north and south branches of the Saskatchewan River in 1891 and in the Bow River Valley east of Calgary a year later.[3]

A small group of Reinländer Mennonites led by Reverend Gerhard Petkau settled at Gleichen (Alberta) around 1890. They had apparently agreed before leaving Manitoba to join another group settling at Rosthern (Saskatchewan) or else have the latter group join them at Gleichen. When the Gleichen settlers were not convinced that this area was suitable for large-scale Mennonite settlement, part of Petkau's group returned to Manitoba with him, while five families relocated to Rosthern.[4] Swiss Mennonites from Ontario founded communities at Didsbury and High River during the 1890s but further migration from Manitoba to this area did not resume until 1901 when a group of Bergthal people settled at Didsbury.[5]

The area south of Duck Lake, however, quickly caught on among Manitoba Mennonites as a suitable area for relocation. Both Reinländer and Bergthal Mennonites were involved in the movement, the latter sending an exploratory delegation to the area in 1891.[6] Beginning in 1891 Mennonite immigrants arriving directly from Russia or Prussia began to give Saskatchewan as their destination.[7] The Reinländer group that had moved west with Reverend Petkau and settled at Rosthern in 1892 joined the congregation of new immigrants founded under the leadership of Bishop Peter Regier of the Rosenort congregation of Prussia.[8] A Bergthal congregation was begun in the Rosthern area around 1893.[9] Interest in this area was also reported among Russian Mennonites living in Nebraska and Kansas.[10] From these various sources the Rosthern area had achieved a Mennonite population of about four hundred by 1894.[11]

Up to this point the Mennonite migration was basically a movement of individual families or small, informal groups. They took up homesteads in the normal Canadian pattern, although the presence of church leaders helped the process of community formation. In 1895, however, an organized group movement began, following very much the pattern established twenty years earlier in the Manitoba settlements. In order to highlight this similarity, the following summary will follow the outline used in chapter 1.

## The Reserves

The original Mennonite colonies in Russia had begun a pattern of taking care of their surplus population through the periodic establishment of daughter colonies. The Reinländer Mennonite Church of Manitoba now applied this principle to the Canadian setting by turning to the government in Ottawa for a tract of land large enough to establish a series of new villages. Since the provinces of Alberta and Saskatchewan were not established until 1905, all of the crown lands in the Northwest Territories were still under the jurisdiction of the Department of the Interior in Ottawa. Whereas the leadership in locating suitable land and negotiating with the government had been taken by the *Kleine Gemeinde* and Bergthal delegates in the 1870s, it was the Reinländer church that now took the initiative. Two reserves were eventually set aside for the Mennonites by order-in-council: the Hague Reserve, near Rosthern, in 1895, and the Swift Current Reserve, southeast of Swift Current, in 1904.

Early in 1894, J. B. McLaren, a solicitor from Morden who had served the Mennonites on frequent occasions, indicated to the Department of the Interior that the West Reserve Mennonites were interested in securing another reserve further west.[12] The two widely separated townships about which he inquired were not yet surveyed and would not likely receive railway service for a considerable time to come.[13] Since the Mennonites had no special preference for these townships their attention now shifted to the Prince Albert area.[14]

During the fall of 1894 two separate requests for a reserve in the Rosthern area were made by Mennonite representatives. One came from scattered Bergthal settlers already living in the area, for whom Klaas Peters of Gretna, Manitoba, was to act as agent.[15] There is no indication that Peters followed up this inquiry. The second request came in a meeting of *Ältester* Johann Wiebe and *Obervorsteher* Franz Froese of the Reinländer Mennonites with the Minister of the Interior in Winnipeg.[16] By now they knew exactly what they wanted, and McLaren, who was also present at the meeting, handled the necessary negotiations until a reserve of four townships, shown on map 5, was created by order-in-council early in 1895. The government order recognized "that the principle of establishing reservations of land for settlement by Mennonites" had been in effect since 1873, and that the new reserve was required to accommodate both the natural increase, which had taken place in the Manitoba settlements, and the influx of new immigrants from the United States and Europe.[17]

Because orders-in-council now had to be gazetted four times before they went into force, news of the Hague Reserve did not reach the Manitoba Mennonites until late February. Some of the families who were ready to move had meanwhile begun to agitate for a settlement in North Dakota because of this delay.[18] As soon as official word of the reserve was received, plans for a spring migration were made. A special Canadian Pacific Railway train of eighteen cars carrying thirteen families of settlers

# Map 5
## Saskatchewan Mennonite Reserves

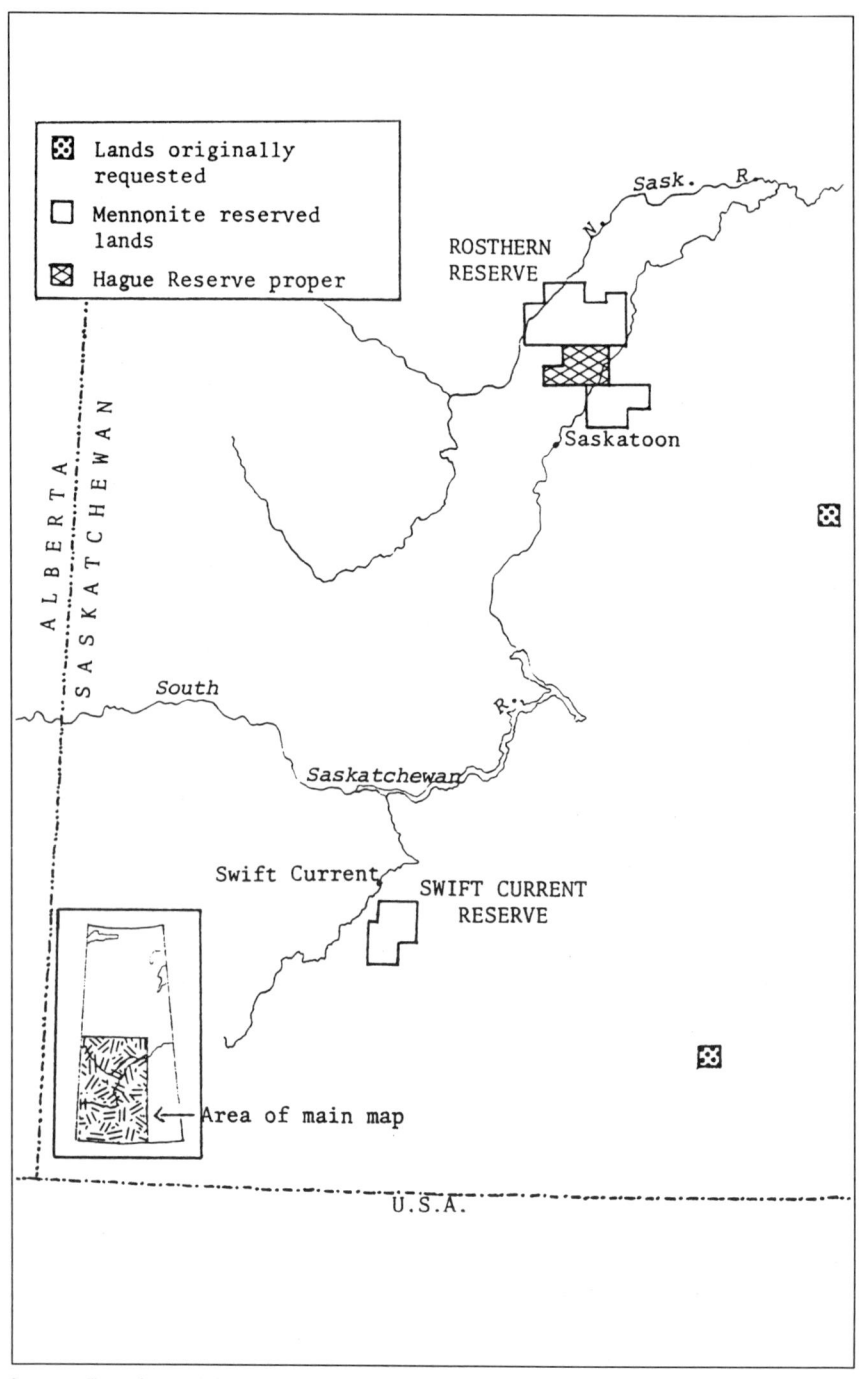

Source: Based on Richard J. Friesen, "Old Colony Settlements in Saskatchewan," M.A. thesis, University of Alberta, 1975, p. 69.

and their effects was scheduled to leave the Manitoba settlement in early May for Hague, Saskatchewan.[19] The first village established in the new colony was appropriately named Neuanlage (new settlement).[20]

Early in 1898 the Mennonites began negotiations to exchange township 40, range 5 for township 41, range 3 in order to make the reserve more compact and because the new township had better water.[21] The Deputy Minister checked out local feelings about this proposed change before responding.[22] By April it was apparent that a large contingent of Mennonite families was planning to move to the reserve from Manitoba so that *Obervorsteher* Froese now requested that township 41, range 3 simply be added to the reserve without dropping township 40, range 5.[23] This was promptly done by the Department, although the formal order-in-council was not passed until June.[24] These five townships, as shown on map 6, may be considered as the Hague Reserve proper.

An additional five townships, adjoining the southeast edge of the reserve, were set aside in August 1898 for exclusive homestead entry by Mennonites for a period of four years.[25] Later in the same year settlers in the Rosthern area made a second request for a reserve, this time in the name of Peter Abrams. This involved an area of eleven townships adjacent to the northern edge of the Hague reserve to be set aside "for a German Mennonite settlement for five years."[26] Both additions are shown on map 6.

The request was received favourably both by officials of the Department of the Interior and by the local member of Parliament, although the proposed five-year term was considered too long.[27] The reservation was accordingly effected for one year by Departmental order even though about three-fourths of the available homestead lands in it had already been taken up by Mennonites.[28] Abrams and the Mennonites were probably not aware that the Young Chippewayan Indian Reserve no. 107 had only one year before been removed from townships 43 and 44 in range 5 by government order-in-council. The band to which the reserve had been assigned under Treaty no. 6 had not taken up residence on it and may not have known that Ottawa had alienated it from band jurisdiction.[29] Serious opposition to a reserve of this size was expressed the following year by a group of German Lutheran settlers in the Rosthern area. They complained to the Minister that their settlement was too small to support church and school and that their co-religionists from Manitoba and North Dakota were now prevented from joining them.[30]

Correspondence regarding the administration of this reserved area during its one-year lifetime indicates that it was poorly conceived by those who requested the additions and haphazardly administered. As mentioned above, less than a quarter of the homestead sections were still available when the reserve was requested. Abrams subsequently admitted that one

# Map 6
## Hague Reserve and Additions

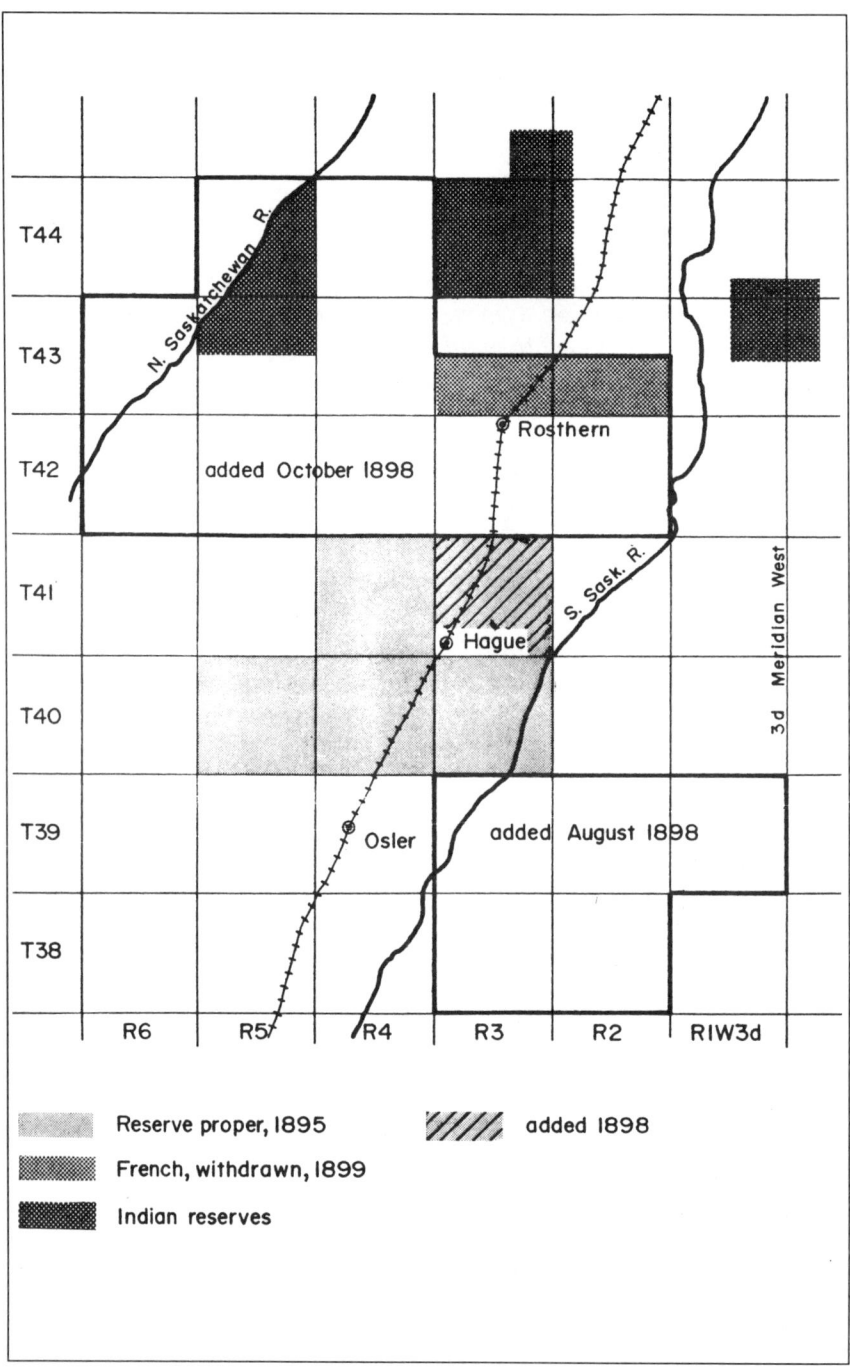

Source: Based on map attached to P.C. no. 188, January 23, 1895, NA, RG 15, vol. 652, no. 480126.

township in the Mennonite reserve was already largely occupied by French settlers and had been requested through a misunderstanding.[31] Further difficulties were encountered when Abrams authorized the Dominion Lands Agent at Prince Albert to grant homestead entries on the reserve to three Anglo-Saxons. When the agent acted on this after it had been confirmed by the Assistant Secretary of the Department, Abrams joined Bishop Regier in protesting to the Minister of the Interior about this intrusion on the reserve.[32]

A decade after Reinländer Bishop Johann Wiebe and *Obervorsteher* Franz Froese had initiated negotiations for the Hague Reserve with Minister of the Interior Daly, McLaren and Froese again met with the Minister, now the Honourable Clifford Sifton, to request another reserve, this time in the Swift Current area.[33] Annual migration to the Hague reserve had continued on a modest scale throughout the decade and available lands had virtually all been taken up.[34] Sifton's goodwill toward the Mennonites and his confidence in them are shown in the promptness with which he acted on this request and in his comment to his Deputy: "These lands are not at present suitable for farming and the Department would not encourage any settlers to locate there, but the Mennonites are quite capable of knowing whether they can succeed or not."[35] The text of the order-in-council publicly affirmed this confidence. It set aside six townships, shown on map 5, to be reserved for a period of three years for the exclusive use of the Reinland Mennonite Association of Manitoba.[36]

## Government Loan

Although the hundred thousand dollar loan advanced by the Canadian government to the immigrant settlers in Manitoba in 1875 had only recently been repaid, a new one of twenty thousand dollars was requested to assist settlers on the newly created Hague Reserve in 1895.[37] Government policy had changed meanwhile, and the request was politely turned down in view of "the present condition of revenue," although it was noted that the Minister appreciated "most highly the scrupulous good faith with which the Mennonites and their friends observed all the conditions on which the previous advance was made."[38]

Many of the migrants were poorer people, however, and needed financial assistance to relocate to Saskatchewan. The Reinländer Mennonites therefore took the advice of the Minister and advanced loans to the needy families against the security of a first mortgage on the homestead land as provided for by the Dominion Lands Act.[39] Since the church had earlier excommunicated members for signing a mortgage with a bank or land company, some of its critics now protested this reversal whereby the church itself required a mortgage from its own members as security.⁴⁰ That the protest was unsuccessful is an indication of the increasing Mennonite openness to accepting suggestions from the government. It also shows how the tendency toward greater individualism, strengthened by an instrument like the homestead system, was beginning to undermine the communal commitment of the church.

## Non-Mennonite Intruders

In 1896, the tired Conservatives, unable to find a capable replacement for John A. Macdonald after his death in 1891, lost the federal election to the Liberals under Sir Wilfrid Laurier. The vigorous immigration policy adopted by the new government under the leadership of its energetic Minister of the Interior, Clifford Sifton, and the creation of the provinces of Alberta and Saskatchewan in 1905, increased the flow of settlers to the Northwest in the years immediately after the creation of the two Mennonite reserves.

The Reinländer experience with outsiders living on the western edge of their Manitoba reserve made them additionally cautious in checking for homestead entries on lands they intended to reserve in Saskatchewan. Problems on the Hague Reserve therefore did not arise until the fall of 1898, when an energetic General Colonization Agent of the government located some Galician settlers on it.⁴¹ The fact that there were in effect two Mennonite reserves side by side was confusing to the government agents. Mennonites on the northern section, who homesteaded more or less individually, apparently consented fairly readily to outsiders taking up land in their reserved area. But for the Reinländer group who settled in villages and held their land semi-communally, any outsider seriously disrupted their settlement pattern. This group therefore protested the Galician intrusion through their solicitor, their *Obervorsteher*, and directly by petitions.⁴²

For the government it was a delicate situation. On the one hand, "there was a very great trouble experienced in retaining those Galicians in the district and any appearance of breach of faith with them might lead to undesirable results."⁴³ On the other hand, an agreement had been made with the Mennonites and "after the Department has set apart certain lands for a colony it is certainly not pleasant to be obliged to tell the people that these lands have been withdrawn."⁴⁴ Both the Deputy Minister of the Department of the Interior and the Superintendent of Immigration remained in touch with their agents, who attempted to effect a reconciliation. In at least one protracted and difficult case the Northwest Mounted Police eventually became involved.⁴⁵ The tone of official Reinländer protest indicates less confidence in the federal government's administration than was evident in the parallel situation in Manitoba two decades earlier.

These experiences on the Hague Reserve stimulated the Reinländer Mennonite leadership to take additional precautions in arranging the Swift Current Reserve. They not only made sure that the lands chosen were unoccupied and unclaimed; they "deliberately selected lands which had been in the market for nearly a generation, and [on] which ... Department did not feel warranted in encouraging new settlers to locate."[46] The terms of the reserve, as spelled out by the order-in-council, provided "that no one, unless aided by the [Reinland Mennonite] Association, or otherwise approved by the Department of the Interior, is to be allowed to make homestead entry within the tract mentioned."[47]

In spite of these precautions, eighteen homestead entries involving nine sections of reserve land were made by non-Mennonites in June and July 1904, while negotiations for the reserve were in process.[48] To ensure that this would not continue to happen, the attorney for the Mennonites instructed the Dominion Lands Agent in Regina henceforth to issue entries only to persons having a certificate from Franz Froese, *Obervorsteher* of the Reinland Mennonite Association.[49] In that way the Association in Manitoba could keep track of available lands on the reserve and make it possible for intending settlers to select their lands before leaving Manitoba. By 1906, administrative watchfulness in the Regina office had begun to slip once more and eight non-Mennonites were permitted to make entries on the reserve.[50] As a result, seven Mennonite families who had made their land selection in Manitoba and then gone west with all their effects found themselves "stranded on the prairie" because their homestead choices had been given to outsiders.[51]

A strongly worded intervention by attorney McLeod on behalf of the Mennonites in the summer of 1906 seems to have been effective. Complaining of "the most harassing treatment from the officials in the Department," he asked the Minister "to take the trouble to personally make the underlings in the Department give these people reasonable treatment in regard to the Reserve."[52] While Department officials could not find "any cause for making such a charge," the Ottawa files give no evidence of further problems.[53]

## Homestead Rights

Both of the Saskatchewan reserves were created after railway construction had penetrated the area. Varying portions of the odd-numbered sections of crown land had therefore been granted to railway companies. These could obviously not be included in any reserve now created by the government. On the Manitoba reserves, by contrast, homestead entries had been permitted on all even- and odd-numbered sections, except those assigned to the Hudson's Bay Company or set apart as school lands.

On the Hague Reserve, homesteading was possible only on even-numbered sections. The Reinländer style of village settlement required, however, that all lands of a given block belong to members of the community. The Mennonite leadership therefore asked assistance from the Minister of the Interior to arrange with the Canadian Pacific Railway "to reserve these lands for sale to the Mennonites for a term of say at least five years, at a maximum price of say $2.50 per acre."[54] The Minister pointed out that the odd-numbered sections of the reserve formed part of the Qu'Appelle, Long Lake and Saskatchewan Railroad and Steamboat Company grant, not the Canadian Pacific, and suggested that the Mennonites contact the firm of Osler, Hammond and Nanton who were agents for this company.[55] A satisfactory arrangement was then apparently made in respect to the odd-numbered sections, enabling the Mennonites to lay out some fifteen villages and a total of about thirty agglomerated settlements during the course of the next decade.[56]

The order-in-council creating the Swift Current Reserve in 1904 allowed settlers to homestead the even-numbered sections as well as those odd-numbered ones at the disposal of the government. Since the Canadian Pacific Railway grant included the odd sections of only one and a half townships of the reserve, it did not create any significant difficulty for arriving settlers.

On a different matter the government once more showed itself to be accommodating. To facilitate the migration, the Manitoba leadership requested permission to make homestead entries for Swift Current Reserve lands in the Winnipeg Land office rather than on arrival in Regina. While this request was not granted, permission was given to appoint and authorize a person in Regina to make such entries for specific homesteads, rather than require each homesteader to make entry in person.[57] This greatly facilitated the migration.

## Hamlet Privilege

Like the 1870s immigrant generation in Manitoba, the second generation of Mennonites homesteading in the Northwest Territories required ministerial permission to perform homestead duties under the "Hamlet Privilege" clause of the Dominion Lands Act in order to settle in villages. The order-in-council setting aside a reserve for the Mennonites in the Saskatchewan Valley in 1895 took this need into account and included a provision "to give the intending settlers an assurance that they will be enabled to carry out the principles of their social system, and to settle together in hamlets (for which provision is made by section 37 of the Dominion Lands Act) by obtaining entries for contiguous lands."[58]

In 1899, when the first applications for patents were being processed, they were refused "on the ground that by section 37 of the Dominion Lands Act the Minister has no power to dispense with the requirements as to cultivation of each separate homestead."[59] The Mennonite leaders appealed to the Minister, pointing out that they had been promised hamlet privileges when the settlement was begun.[60] At his recommendation cabinet then passed an order-in-council, which revived the hamlet privilege for the Hague Reserve even though it had been abolished by an order-in-council in 1889.[61] Once again Ottawa had clearly demonstrated its willingness to accommodate the Mennonites wherever possible.

The order-in-council creating the Swift Current Reserve did not mention anything about hamlet privilege for the homesteaders. The Reinländer leaders wanted to be sure that this method of settlement would again be available to their people and petitioned the Minister of the Interior accordingly. First, they argued, the very rapid development of the reserves in Manitoba and at Hague was due in large part to settlers being "permitted to perform their homestead duties under the hamlet system." Second, owing to the semi-arid nature of the district in which the new reserve was located, difficulty was anticipated in procuring a satisfactory supply of water for domestic and farm purposes. A number of settlers living close together in a hamlet could share costs and effort in facilitating a water supply for common use. Third, they pointed to the "greater convenience in the establishment of schools and churches and to the attainment of social advantages" if residence in hamlets were permitted.[62]

Ottawa was very sympathetic to the petition, but Interior Department officials pointed out that clause 37 of the Dominion Lands Act now required that an application be signed by at least twenty homestead families before a "hamlet" could be recognized as such.[63] Since this migration did not progress very quickly, none of the eight hamlets in process of formation on the reserve had the required twenty families by the end of 1906.[64] Officials of the Department had meanwhile urged that the settlers go into residence on their respective homesteads.[65] Instead of endorsing this, the Reinländer leaders appealed once more for hamlet privilege, this time to the Prime Minister himself.[66] By now almost two years had elapsed since the first homestead entries on the reserve had been made, but legal "residence" on most homesteads had not yet begun, since the Mennonites had settled in villages. In these circumstances the Minister decided to protect the settlers' homestead entries "whether they are performing their duties under the hamlet clause or not."[67]

Early in 1907 the Department abolished the "Hamlet Privilege" clause, but the Minister consented to extend it for the Swift Current Reserve since the settlement there had been begun before the change in regulations.[68] Four villages acquired the necessary twenty homesteaders during the course of 1907 and registered their status with the Department.[69] By 1909 no new villages were begun with a view to performing homestead duties under the hamlet system. However, several villages were formed, with the homesteaders purchasing adjacent forty-acre lots on which they erected their buildings and thus performed their homestead duties "by residence on farmlands owned by them in the vicinity" of their actual homestead quarter section.[70]

## Naturalization and Land Patents

Mennonite immigrants arriving directly from Europe or the United States and homesteading in the Rosthern area had to be naturalized before they could obtain title to their homestead land. No difficulties appear to have been encountered in this process.

Mennonites from Manitoba who relocated to the Northwest Territories were either Canadian-born or previously naturalized in Manitoba. Nevertheless, at one point in 1908 the Dominion Lands Agent in Swift Current required all Mennonite homesteaders to produce certificates of naturalization in order to get patents. Some of them, not having such a certificate, went "to the expense of applying to be naturalized a second time as they, quite different from the English-speaking homesteaders, rely absolutely on what the Agent of Dominion Lands or any other official of the Department tells them."[71] This incident is indicative of the readiness of even Reinländer Mennonites to co-operate with the federal government on land and reserve matters. It also suggests that the initial reluctance to become naturalized citizens had been overcome.

## Termination of the Reserves

The order-in-council that created the Hague Reserve in 1895 did not specify the length of time that the Mennonites were to have exclusive right to homestead in it. Neither did the order-in-council of June 1898, which added a fifth township to the original reserve. The five townships that were annexed to the reserve by order of the Commissioner of Dominion Lands in August 1898 were to be reserved until November 1902.[72] It may be assumed that this termination date was intended to apply to all ten townships reserved thus far. The eleven townships set aside for exclusive Mennonite entry at the request of Rosthern settlers in October 1898 were reserved for only one year. These time limits seem to have been adequate for the purpose intended by the requesting Mennonites.

The order-in-council creating the Swift Current Reserve stipulated that it should continue for a period of three years. When the termination date of August 13, 1907, arrived, however, Ottawa apparently took the initiative in instructing its Moose Jaw office not to take any action regarding the reserve until further instructed.[73] Periodic checks were made by the Department regarding the amount of available homestead land remaining in the reserve.[74] Since no formal action was taken to extend its original life, the reserve legally terminated August 13, 1907. Almost two years later the informal extension given to its life by Departmental officials was made official.[75] Actual termination of the reserve did not take place until September 1, 1909, when the Interior Department served public notice that all available lands were open to homesteading by the general public.[76]

## Immigration from Russia and the U.S.A.

While the Canadian government was pleased with the way in which Mennonite migration from the Manitoba communities was opening up settlement in Saskatchewan, the main thrust of its Immigration Department was to bring in new settlers from abroad. In this effort it was supported and encouraged by Mennonites, who were happy with their choice of Canada, and by the Canadian Pacific Railroad, which was eager to sell some of its huge grants of land.

Klaas Peters, a thirty-five-year-old farmer and teacher near Gretna, first ventured into settlement promotion with an exploratory trip to Oregon in 1888. Two years later this developed into an assignment as special agent of the CPR and his first trip to Russia to recruit immigrants among the Mennonites. In 1891 he was involved in settling the Rosthern area as agent for the law firm representing the Qu'Appelle, Long Lake and Saskatchewan Railroad and Steamboat Company. In 1893 he worked in Kansas and Nebraska as a special agent of the Canadian Department of the Interior in the interest of Mennonite immigration. That winter he returned once more to Russia for the CPR.[77]

In late 1895 Peters was approached by two of his friends to accompany them on a trip back to Russia to visit relatives. On their way they met with Department of the Interior officials in Ottawa and agreed to "promote to the best of their ability the immigration of their fellow countrymen" and to "give the greatest prominence to the absolute good faith with which they have been treated by the government of Canada."[78] Canadian immigration officials responded by assisting the travellers en route and even raised the question of appointing a government agent in Russia.[79]

A year later Gerhard Ens of Rosthern picked up this idea and indicated that he would like a position as immigration agent for bringing

Russian Mennonites to Saskatchewan.[80] Ens was himself a recent immigrant, having arrived from Russia in 1890, and was regarded as the founder of Rosthern.[81] Neither he nor Peters was actually appointed to the position, but Ens continued to stimulate and support such immigration in various ways during the next several decades. In 1902, for example, he attempted to arrange financial support among Saskatchewan Mennonites for the immigration of their needy co-religionists from the Fürstenland Colony in Russia.[82]

While Ens did not succeed in being appointed immigration agent to Russia, the Canadian government put him to work among Mennonites in the United States.[83] As a result of his work during the first four months of 1898, mostly in the Kansas area, Ens was able to report twenty-two parties of U.S. Mennonites who had taken up land in Canada bringing with them over seventy thousand dollars in capital.[84] After another four-month special assignment the following year, Ens received a permanent appointment as land guide and interpreter in the Immigration Department.[85]

Other immigration agents were subsequently appointed for special assignment among U.S. Mennonites. The result of their work was the founding of some twenty-four new communities in Alberta and Saskatchewan by immigrants from the United States between 1894 and 1914.[86] As in the case of Mennonite immigrants arriving from Russia during this time, the Americans also came in through regular immigration channels that did not involve any special negotiations with the government.

A significant difference was fairly quickly apparent between those Mennonites coming to the Northwest as individuals and homesteading as ordinary Canadians and those coming as part of a group migration and settling on reserves. The latter continued very strongly to practise their separatist ways as defined by the *Privilegium* and implemented by *Ältester* and *Obervorsteher*. The former were much more quick to adopt Canadian ways. In most respects they were prepared to accept full citizenship privileges and obligations. Thus, when Alberta and Saskatchewan became provinces in 1905, Cornelius Hiebert, a Bergthal Mennonite living in the Didsbury, Alberta area was elected to the legislature as a Conservative by the Rosebud constituency.[87] In the first general election in Saskatchewan, Gerhard Ens was elected to represent Rosthern as a Liberal.[88] Hiebert was still a Mennonite, apparently in good standing, though geographically on the fringe of the Bergthal community; Ens had already become a member of the Church of the New Jerusalem (Swedenborgian).[89]

# Notes

1. Gerhard Wiebe, p. 54; Schroeder, p. 112; chap. 1, under "Group Migration: Homestead Rights."

2. The delegation consisted of Heinrich Martens, Isaak Schmidt, and Abram Giesbrecht. *Mennonitische Rundschau*, 15 May 1895.

3. *Old and New Furrows. The Story of Rosthern* (Rosthern: Rosthern Historical Society, [1977]), p. 19. Richard John Friesen, "Old Colony Mennonite Settlements in Saskatchewan: A Study in Settlement Change" (M.A. thesis, University of Alberta, 1975), chap. 4, and Epp, *Mennonites in Canada*, chap. 13, give a summary of settlement history in Saskatchewan and Alberta.

4. Elias, Memoirs, 2:19; F. D. Guenther, *Meine innern und äusseren Erlebnisse in Mexico und Canada* (Inwood, Man.: by the author, 1957), p. 12; Klaas Peters, "Zur Geschichte der Mennonitenansiedlung bei Rosthern," *Mennonitische Rundschau*, 20 December 1893; John H. Warkentin, "The Mennonite Settlements," p. 201.

5. Epp, *Mennonites in Canada*, pp. 306–311.

6. Elected 19 May 1991 were Gerhard Klassen, "unser damaliger Gebietsvorsteher," and David Friesen of Sommerfeld. Rev. Heinrich Wiebe, one of the 1873 delegates from Russia, was added at the request of the government, and Klaas Peters as a railway land agent accompanied the group. *Mennonitische Rundschau*, 20 December 1893.

7. Canada, Parliament, *Sessional Papers*, 1892 and following, report Mennonite immigrant arrivals indicating Saskatchewan as their destination. Klaas Peters, Eduard Wiebe, *Mennonitische Rundschau*, 3 February 1892; Gerhard Wiebe, *Mennonitische Rundschau*, 10 February 1892; and Jakob Kroeker, *Mennonitische Rundschau*, 3 May 1893, report on the progress of these settlements. See also Francis, *In Search of Utopia*, pp. 146–147. Walter Klaassen, *"The Days of Our Years." A History of the Eigenheim Mennonite Church Community: 1892–1992* (Rosthern: Eigenheim Mennonite Church, 1992), chap. 2, details the arrival of one group from Russia in 1892.

8. Elias, Memoirs, 2:20.

9. Walter Quiring, *Rußlanddeutsche suchen eine Heimat. Die deutsche Einwanderung in den paraguayischen Chaco* (Karlsruhe: Heinrich Schneider, 1938), p. 28; John D. Rempel, *History of the Hague Mennonite Church, 1900–1975* (Rosthern: Valley Printers, 1975), p. 1. Leonard Doell, *The Bergthaler Mennonite Church of Saskatchewan, 1892–1925* (Winnipeg: CMBC Publications, 1987), pp. 6–11.

10. Canada, Parliament, *Sessional Papers*, 1894, no. 13, "Annual Report of the Department of the Interior for the Year 1893," appendix 1, p. 9.

11. Richard J. Friesen, p. 78.

12. J. B. McLaren to Secretary, Department of the Interior, 21 February 1894, NA, RG 15, vol. 652, no. 480126. Richard J. Friesen's account of this reserve is based largely on materials found in RG 15, no. 270476.

13. A. M. Burgess, Deputy Minister, to T. Mayne Daly, Minister of the Interior, 13 March 1894, NA, RG 15, vol. 652, no. 480126. The townships inquired about were 7-27W2d and 33-20W2d. See map 5.

14. McLaren to Secretary, Department of the Interior, 18 April 1894, NA, RG 15, vol. 652, no. 480126.

15. H. E. Ross, Prince Albert, to Secretary, Department of the Interior, 10 October 1894, NA, RG 15, vol. 652, no. 480126. On Peters' career in settlement promotion, see Leonard Doell, "Klaas Peters (1855–1932): A Biography," in Klaas Peters, *The Bergthaler Mennonites*, pp. 48–62.

16. Daly to Burgess, 3 November 1894, NA, RG 15, vol. 652, no. 480126, reports on his meeting with Wiebe, Froese, and McLaren.

17. P.C. no. 188, 23 January 1895, NA, RG 2, 1. The townships requested were 40 in ranges 3, 4, and 5, and 41 in range 4 west of the 3d meridian. Since no land had so far been taken up in any of these four townships, the Minister recommended the formal creation of the reserve to cabinet on 24 December 1894.

18. McLaren to Daly, 20 February 1895, NA, RG 15, vol. 652, no. 480126.

19. *Mennonitische Rundschau*, 1 May 1895, p. 1; 15 May 1895.

20. Leo Driedger, "A Sect in Modern Mociety. A Case Study of the Old Colony Mennonites of Saskatchewan" (M.A. thesis, University of Chicago, 1955), p. 24.

21. McLaren to the Minister of the Interior, 27 January 1898, NA, RG 15, vol. 652, no. 480126.

22. James D. Smart, Deputy Minister of the Interior, to T. O. Davis, M.P., 10 February 1898, NA, RG 15, vol. 652, no. 480126. The one negative response, from Charles Fisher, Duck Lake, to Davis, 26 February 1898, who disapproved of this kind of favouritism, was apparently ignored.

23. McLaren to Minister of the Interior, 7 April 1898, NA, RG 15, vol. 652, no. 480126.

24. The addition was effected by departmental order, Smart to Goodeve, 28 April 1898, ibid., and confirmed by P.C. no. 1627, 24 June 1898, NA, RG 2, 1.

25. Township 39 in ranges 1, 2 and 3W3d, and township 38 in ranges 2 and 3W3d. Richard J. Friesen, p. 75, based on SAB, file no. 917620. The reservation was effective until 1 November 1902 by order of the Commissioner of Dominion Lands, 19 August 1898. It is not known by whom this extension was requested.

26. Peter Abrams, Rosthern, to T. O. Davis, M.P., 13 September 1898, NA, RG 15, vol. 652, no. 480126.

27. Davis to Minister of the Interior, 19 September 1898; Smart to Goodeve, 27 September 1898, NA, RG 15, vol. 652, no. 480126.

28. Goodeve to Smart, 29 September 1898. Smart to Davis, 18 April 1899, NA, RG 15, vol. 652, no. 480126, indicates that the reservation was effective for the year ending 1 October 1899, and involved townships 42, 43A, and 43 in ranges 2-6W3d, and township 44 in ranges 4 and 5W3d. C. Sifton, Minister of the Interior, memo to cabinet, 14 February 1900, NA, RG 15, vol. 652, no. 480126, indicates that the departmental order was dated 14 October 1898.

29. Order-in-Council, 11 May 1897. Leonard Doell, Lesson 9, in "Teachable Moment" study kit, Mennonite Central Committee Canada. Klaassen, *Eigenheim*, p. 11.

30. Franz Schroeder and eleven others, Rosthern, to Minister of the Interior, 3 April 1899, NA, RG 15, vol. 652(1), no. 480126. C. W. Speers, General Colonization Agent, to Frank Pedley, Superintendent of Immigration, 11 April 1899, NA, RG 15, vol. 652(1), no. 480126, mentions another group of Germans from Nebraska who are dissatisfied with the large Mennonite reservation.

31. Peter Abrams, Rosthern, to Deputy Minister of the Interior, 19 April 1899, NA, RG 15, vol. 652(1), no. 480126. The area referred to, township 43A-3 and 43A-2W3rd, had indeed been requested by him, but not included by the Department.

32. Abrams, Rosthern, on letterhead of "Bashford & Co., Dealers in Agricultural Implements," to Agent of Dominion Lands, Prince Albert, 5 May 1899, giving permission for Messrs. Galloway, Bashford and Adamson to enter homesteads; Lyndwode Pereira, Assistant Secretary, Department of the Interior, to Agent, Prince Albert, 16 May 1899; Rev. P. Regier, Tiefengrund, and Abrams, to Minister of the Interior, 20 May 1899; NA, RG 15, vol. 652(1), no. 480126.

33. A. M. McLeod (of McLaren, McLeod, and Black), Morden, to Sifton, 6 July 1904, NA, RG 15, B-1(a), vol. 292, no. 917620(1).

34. Forty-four families arrived in 1898, 49 in 1899, 18 in 1900, 36 in 1901, 31 in 1902, 25 in 1903, and 15 in 1904. MHCA, vol. 1091, no. 13.

35. Sifton to Smart, 14 July 1904, NA, RG 15, B-1(a), vol. 292, no. 917620(1). The tract of land requested, he added, was "regarded as useless by most settlers." Sifton, 15 July 1904, actually recommended to cabinet an area larger than McLeod had requested. The request was for townships 13 and 14 in range 12W3rd, 12 and 13 in range 13W3rd, and the eastern half of 12-14W3rd; Sifton added 14-13W3d, E1/2 of 13-14W3d. See map 5.

36. P.C. no. 1605, 13 August 1904, NA, RG 2, 1.

37. J. Y. Shantz to Department of the Interior, 9 April 1895, NA, RG 15, vol. 233, no. 3129(4). Richard J. Friesen, p. 72, apparently was unaware of this request.

38. J. R. Hall, Secretary, Department of the Interior, to Shantz, 22 April 1895, NA, RG 15, vol. 233, no. 3129(4).

39. T. M. Daly, Minister, to A. M. Burgess, Deputy Minister, 3 November 1894, NA, RG 15, vol. 652, no. 480126. The firm of solicitors McLaren, McLeod and Black of Morden had special forms printed to record these mortgages.

40. Elias, 2:24–26.

41. Secretary, Department of the Interior, to Dominion Lands Agent, Prince Albert, 29 September 1898, NA, RG 15, vol. 652, no. 480126.

42. McLaren, McLeod and Black, Morden, to Secretary, Department of the Interior, 12 April and 9 May 1899; Franz Froese, Reinland, to Clifford Sifton, Minister of the Interior, 26 August 1899; petition, B. J. Friesen and twenty-eight others, Rosthern, to Department of the Interior, 14 August 1899, NA, RG 15, vol. 652, no. 480126.

43. Dominion Lands Agent, Prince Albert, to Secretary, Department of the Interior, 6 October 1898, NA, RG 15, vol. 652, no. 480126.

44. J. A. Smart, Deputy Minister of the Interior, to C. W. Speers, General Colonization Agent, 7 April 1899, NA, RG 15, vol. 652, no. 480126.

45. Abram Penner, Hague, complained 23 September 1899 to the Secretary of the Department of Agriculture that his entry to the northeast quarter of 24-41-3W3d had been cancelled in favour of a Galician. Both Penner and Sikora proved to be stubborn customers and the feud escalated to the point where the Royal Northwest Mounted Police were called in when Sikora allegedly resorted to armed defence of his farm. Speers, Regina, to Frank Pedley, Superintendent of Immigration, 25 April 1901, NA, RG 15, vol. 652, no. 480126. Penner finally abandoned his claim on 11 June 1901.

46. McLaren et al. to Frank Oliver, Minister of the Interior, 26 March 1906, NA, B-1(a), vol. 292, no. 917620.

47. P.C. no. 1605, 13 August 1904, NA, RG 2, 1.

48. P. G. Keyes, Secretary, Department of the Interior, to A. M. McLeod, Morden, 20 September 1904, NA, RG 15, B-1(a), vol. 292, no. 917620.

49. McLeod to Dominion Lands Agent, Regina, 12 September 1904, NA, RG 15, B-1(a), vol. 292, no. 917620.

50. Dominion Lands Agent, Regina, to Secretary, Department of the Interior, 27 February 1906, NA, RG 15, B-1(a), vol. 292, no. 917620.

51. McLeod to Oliver, 26 March 1906. As had been the case with the Galicians on the Hague Reserve, so here also the homestead entries of non-Mennonites that had occurred through administrative oversight were allowed to stand. W. W. Cory, Deputy

Minister of the Interior, to N. O. Côté, Chief Clerk, Land Patents Branch, 6 April 1906, NA, RG 15, B-1(a), vol. 292, no. 917620.

52. McLeod to Oliver, 4 July 1906, NA, RG 15, B-1(a), vol. 292, no. 917620.

53. N. O. Côté to J. W. Greenway, Commissioner of Dominion Lands, 30 July 1906, NA, RG 15, B-1(a), vol. 292, no. 917620.

54. J. B. McLaren to T. M. Daly, 2 April 1895, NA, RG 15, B-1(a), vol. 652, no. 480126.

55. Daly to McLaren, 2 May 1895, NA, RG 15, B-1(a), vol. 652, no. 480126.

56. Richard J. Friesen, pp. 73, 79, 81, 103–104, 145; Driedger, pp. 24–25.

57. A. M. McLeod to Clifford Sifton, Minister of the Interior, 3 January 1905; P. G. Keyes, Secretary, Department of the Interior, to McLeod, 6 April 1905, NA, RG 15, B-1(a), vol. 292, no. 917620(1).

58. P.C. no. 188, 23 January 1895, NA, RG 2, 1. This provision is repeated in P.C. no. 1627, 24 June 1898, which enlarged the original reserve.

59. J. B. McLaren, Winnipeg, to Clifford Sifton, 24 November 1899, NA, RG 15, vol. 652, no. 480126.

60. A. M. McLeod and Franz Froese to J. A. Smart, Deputy Minister of the Interior, 6 February 1900, NA, RG 15, vol. 652, no. 480126.

61. P.C. no. 441, 6 March 1900, NA, RG 2, 1. P.C. no. 1938, 14 August 1889, actually specifically abolished hamlet privilege for the Manitoba East Reserve, although the text reads: "the time has now arrived when it is desirable that this privilege should be abolished altogether."

62. Johann Wiebe, Bishop, and Franz Froese, Agent, Reinland Mennonite Association, to Minister of the Interior, 12 December 1904, NA, RG 15, B-1(a), vol. 292, no. 917620(1).

63. W. W. Cory, Deputy Minister, to Minister of the Interior, 10 April 1905; P. G. Keyes, Secretary, Department of the Interior, to J. B. McLaren, 6 April 1905, NA, RG 15, B-1(a), vol. 292, no. 917620(1).

64. McLaren to Secretary, Department of the Interior, 4 December 1906, NA, RG 15, B-1(a), vol. 292, no. 917620(1).

65. Keyes to J.W. Greenway, Commissioner of Dominion Lands, 13 September 1906; Keyes to McLaren, 20 September 1906, NA, RG 15, B-1(a), vol. 292, no. 917620(1).

66. Bishop Peter Wiebe, Reinland, to Head of the Government of Canada, 15 November 1906, NA, MG 26 G, vol. 435, p. 116199.

67. McLaren to Secretary, Department of the Interior, 4 December 1906; W. W. Cory, Deputy Minister of the Interior, to N. O. Côté, 6 December 1906, NA, RG 15, B-1(a), vol. 293, no. 917620(2).

68. A. M. McLeod to Hon. Frank Oliver, Minister of the Interior, 2 February 1907; P. G. Keyes to McLeod, 20 April 1907, NA, RG 15, B-1(a), vol. 293, no. 917620(2).

69. They were Schoenfeld (Bernhard Ens to Department of the Interior, 19 February 1907); Chortitz, Blumenhof, and Blumenort (McLeod to Keyes, 10 July 1907, NA, RG 15, B-1(a), vol. 293, no. 917620(2)). Richard J. Friesen, pp. 168–170, reproduces the Schoenfeld petitions of 19 February and 31 May 1907.

70. McLeod to Secretary, Department of the Interior, 9 June 1909, reports five such "hamlets." NA, RG 15, B-1(a), vol. 293, no. 917620(2).

71. McLaren to Secretary, Department of the Interior, 15 August 1908, NA, RG 15, B-1(a), vol. 293, no. 917620(2).

72. Richard J. Friesen, p. 75.

73. F. Dixon, Acting Commissioner of Dominion Lands, to Agent of Dominion Lands, Moose Jaw, telegram, 13 August 1907, NA, RG 15, B-1(a), vol. 292, no. 917620(1).

74. Land Patents Branch, to N. O. Côté, 27 May 1908, reported seventy-eight quarter sections remaining. P. G. Keyes, in a public notice of 31 July 1909, listed about sixty quarters. NA, RG 15, B-1(a), vol. 293, no. 917620(2).

75. P.C. no. 729, 8 April 1909, NA, RG 2, 1, vol. 1103.

76. P. G. Keyes, Secretary, Department of the Interior, public notice, 31 July 1909, NA, RG 15, B-1(a), vol. 293, no. 917620(2).

77. Doell, "Klaas Peters," pp. 49–56.

78. L. Pereira, Assistant Secretary, Department of the Interior, to T. R. Burpé, Secretary, Dominion Lands Board, Winnipeg, 16 March 1896, NA, RG 15, vol. 570, no. 179925(1).

79. J. G. Colmer, Secretary, Office of the High Commissioner, London, to A. M. Burgess, 17 April 1896, NA, RG 76, vol. 50, no. 2183-1.

80. Ens to T. O. Davis, M.P., 22 March 1897, NA, RG 76, vol. 150, no. 35848.

81. *Old and New Furrows*, pp. 19–20.

82. Ens to Obed Smith, Commissioner of Immigration, Winnipeg, 7 January 1902, NA, RG 76, vol. 50, no. 2183-1.

83. He was first appointed at the suggestion of Immigration Agent J. S. Crawford, Kansas City, and the recommendation of Davis, to Hon. Clifford Sifton, Minister of the Interior, 6 December 1897, NA, RG 76, vol. 150, no. 35848. The notice of appointment, Lyndwode Pereira, Asst. Secretary, Department of the Interior, to Ens, is dated 16 December 1897. Doell, "Klaas Peters," pp. 57–59, details the political manoeuvres that led to the choice of Ens over Peters.

84. Ens, Rosthern, to the Department of the Interior, 12 June 1898, NA, RG 76, vol. 150, no. 34848. A delegation of Hutterites from South Dakota also came at his suggestion.

85. F. Pedley, Superintendent of Immigration, to W. F. McCreary, Commissioner of Immigration, Winnipeg, telegram, 5 May 1899, NA, RG 76, vol. 150, no. 34848.

86. Epp, *Mennonites in Canada*, pp. 310, 317.

87. Lawrence Klippenstein, "Cornelius Hiebert: MLA (1905–1909)," *Mennonite Historian* 1 (September 1975): 1–2.

88. *Canadian Parliamentary Guide*, 1908, pp. 440, 445, 453.

89. Other "Mennonites" prominently involved in these early settlement efforts, who had joined the New Church, included Klaas Peters and Peter Abrams. See Adolf Ens and Leonard Doell, "Mennonite Swedenborgians," *Journal of Mennonite Studies* 10 (1992): 101–117.

CHAPTER IV

# THE RIFT WIDENS: THE EDUCATION ISSUE IN MANITOBA AND SASKATCHEWAN, 1890–1920

One of the most important provisions of the *Privilegium* assured the Mennonites their religious and educational freedom. Clause 10 of John Lowe's 1873 letter read:

> The fullest privilege of exercising their religious principles is by law afforded to the Mennonites without any kind of molestation or restriction whatever, and the same privilege extends to the education of their children in schools.[1]

Mennonites understood this not as a promise of public financial support for their schools but rather as a guarantee of the right to operate their own schools at their own expense. The educational crisis for them therefore came not in 1890, when the Manitoba Public Schools Act restricted public support to "entirely non-sectarian" public schools,[2] but rather in 1916, when compulsory attendance legislation was used to drive Mennonite private schools out of existence. Similar legislation went into effect in Saskatchewan in 1917.

## Manitoba Education Legislation to 1916

The confessional school system in existence in the Red River colony prior to its annexation by Canada was guaranteed continuing existence by the

Manitoba Act of 1870. In language that closely parallels section 93 of the BNA Act, it provides that the provincial legislature may

> exclusively make Laws in relation to Education, subject and according to the following provisions:— (1) Nothing in any such Law shall prejudicially affect any right or privilege with respect to Denominational Schools which any class of persons have by Law or practice in the Province at the Union.[3]

This proviso differs from the corresponding subsection of the BNA Act only by the addition of the words "or practice," which seems to broaden the protection offered to denominational schools. Under the Manitoba School Act of 1871, denominational schools could be established on local initiative and administered by local trustees under the superintendence of the Protestant or Catholic section of a provincial Board of Education. While independent of the provincial government, the Board received grants from it, which the two sections divided among their schools. All Manitoba schools were thus in principle confessional schools.

> Anglicans, Catholics, Mennonites, and Lutherans, all to a greater or less degree, brought to Manitoba the European union of church and school born of the fierce religious struggles of the Reformation when control of the education of the young was necessary for denominational survival.[4]

Ontario settlers, coming into the province in large numbers during the 1870s and 1880s, brought with them a quite different tradition characterized by an "atmosphere of secular and utilitarian democracy, not that of traditional religious custom."[5] Already in 1876 their influence led to an attempt to make Manitoba's elementary education more uniform and more English.[6] With the redistribution of electoral districts in 1879 and again in 1888, the basis was laid for the political domination of the English, Protestant majority in the province. The new Liberal government of Premier Thomas Greenway no longer had faith in the quality of Catholic schools, which, in the opinion of some members of cabinet, received larger grants than the Protestant ones while Catholics were paying less taxes.[7]

Accordingly, it decided in 1889 to abolish the denominational schools. The Manitoba School Act of 1890 provided for a system of nondenominational schools to be administered by local boards of trustees and a Department of Education with a Minister responsible to the legislature. It dit not even allow, as the Ontario legislation did, for "separate schools," to which Catholic ratepayers could designate their school taxes.[8]

Vigorous opposition to this new School Act by Manitoba Catholics escalated the local controversy into a national issue and eventually contributed to the defeat of the federal Conservative government in 1896. But this whole controversy involved the Mennonites only marginally. A large majority of their schools had not been receiving government support even under the old system and they were quite content to remain fully in charge of and responsible for their schools.

Among those who supported the move toward establishing public schools, an Education Society had been formed the year before to operate a teacher training institute at Gretna in the southeastern portion of the West Reserve. The resignation of its principal and only teacher, former inspector Wilhelm Rempel, forced the school to close in 1890. The new Department of Education now came to the assistance of the Society by helping it to recruit a new principal from among the Mennonites of Kansas and to support its work financially by appointing him inspector of Mennonite schools.[9] Archbishop Taché was thus justified in his complaint that while the government was dismissing all Catholic inspectors, it was creating a new inspectorship for the Mennonites.[10] Anglophone Catholics tested the constitutionality of the 1890 School Act in the courts, contending that Ottawa had guaranteed their school rights in the Manitoba Act of 1870. While this was in process, other efforts to solve the problem were undertaken. In 1893 there was some hope that the Manitoba legislature would take action "towards placing the French on a par with the Germans (Menonites) [sic] in the matter of a normal school."[11]

A second major act of the Manitoba government in 1890 was to end the status of French as an official language in the legislature and courts of the province. Until now the language of instruction in publicly supported schools had been left completely open. Although the School Act of 1890 was not specific on this point, it was widely assumed that English would be the main language of the new public schools. The Conservative government in Ottawa considered this issue in preparing remedial legislation to redress the "prejudicial effects" of the Manitoba School Act. D'Alton McCarthy, leader of the Ontario-based Protestant "Equal Rights Association," argued the case for the Manitoba government before the federal cabinet of Prime Minister Mackenzie Bowell in 1895:

> There were 15,000 Mennonites, speaking their own tongue, demanding a separate system of schools, and as far as I can see, with just as much right to have the public money appropriated to their schools as the French.... The desire of the provincial legislature was to do away with illiteracy among the people, to make the people Manitobans and Canadians, not French or Mennonites, not Poles or Polish Jews.[12]

When the courts upheld the Manitoba School Act and the federal Conservatives did not remain in power long enough to pass their remedial legislation, the Manitoba school question was eventually solved by a compromise worked out between Premier Greenway and the new Liberal government of Sir Wilfrid Laurier. The key language issue was dealt with in such a way that rural schools in which ten or more pupils spoke a language other than English were permitted to teach "in French, or such other language, and English upon the bi-lingual system."[13] According to Laurier's biographer, "the language clause was framed in general terms by the provincial authorities in order to make it apply to the German Mennonites as well as to the French Catholics."[14] This revised legislation of 1897 was acceptable to those Mennonites interested in the public school movement since it allowed them to continue using German in their schools. Those Mennonites who had in principle retained their church-operated schools were allowed to continue them unmolested.

## Higher Education: Alliance of Church and State

Wilhelm Rempel, inspector of Mennonite schools from 1884 to 1888, soon discovered that the level of teacher preparation in the Mennonite communities was far from adequate. In the fall of 1885 he met with other progressive Mennonite educators and the leadership of the West Reserve Bergthal church to discuss ways and means of improving education in general and instruction in English in particular in the Mennonite schools. No decision was reached but by the fall of 1888 an appointed committee was at work to draw up a constitution for a Mennonite teacher training school. Bishop Johann Funk of the West Reserve Bergthaler congregation supported this move but soon found that the majority of his membership did not. Nevertheless, a School Society was organized in February 1889. It proceeded to erect a three-storey school building in Gretna and to hire William Rempel as teacher to begin instruction in September.

When Rempel resigned after one year of teaching the school was forced to close. The Society then negotiated an agreement with the Manitoba government under which the next teacher of the school would also be appointed inspector of Mennonite schools for the Department of Education. This would reduce costs to the Society while avoiding outright government support for their school. Thus it was that Dr. George Bryce, a member of the Advisory Board of the Department of Education, went to Kansas in 1890 to recruit H. H. Ewert for this twofold task. Ewert's meeting with the Education Minister, Clifford Sifton, convinced him of the government's goodwill toward the Mennonites and of its broad tolerance toward the use of the German language. Thus he began his joint appointment as teacher for the Mennonite School Society and inspector for the Department of Education in September 1891. Connected with the latter appointment was the task of organizing public school districts in the Mennonite communities. For the next twelve years Ewert functioned in this dual capacity.

Ewert was born in 1855 in West Prussia, where he received his elementary and intermediate education. He was nineteen when his family moved to Kansas as part of some eleven thousand Mennonites who emigrated from Russia and Prussia to the U.S.A. in the 1870s. He studied arts, theology, and education at schools in Iowa, Missouri, and Kansas, and graduated with an M.A. degree. When Bryce recruited him in 1890, he was principal of Halstead Academy, an institution then in process of becoming a liberal arts college.

From the side of Ewert and the Society this alliance with the state apparently presented no difficulty. Their intentions and those of the government were so similar that a harmonious working relationship was anticipated. But the larger Mennonite community felt quite differently. Bishop Funk, who supported the Society, now found his leadership restricted to a very small minority of the West Reserve Bergthaler congregation. The majority, who opposed the Society and its educational goals, remained with the East Reserve bishop, David Stoesz. When it became clear by 1893 that reconciliation with Funk's group was unlikely, Stoesz supervised the election of a second West Reserve bishop, Abraham Doerksen. Since Doerksen resided in the village of Sommerfeld, this new church body came to be known as the Sommerfelder congregation.[15] The large Reinländer congregation on the West Reserve under the leadership of Bishop Johann Wiebe continued to remain aloof both from the new normal school and the public system as such. This was also the case in the East Reserve Chortitzer church under the leadership of Bishop Stoesz.[16]

Ewert remained principal of the school in Gretna until his death in 1934. During those years he made it into a major source of teachers for the many elementary schools in Mennonite districts in southern Manitoba and later on in Saskatchewan. These teachers helped many communities to make the transition from private to district school.[17]

Opposition to Ewert's work came not only from those church groups that opposed district schools in principle, but also from within the supporting constituency of the Society. Some of his opponents supported the Conservative party in the provincial election of 1903. The newly elected Roblin government promptly dismissed Ewert, "hoping to curry favour politically with the large unprogressive majority among the Mennonites" who disliked Ewert's promoting of the public schools.[18] This brought to the surface a growing division within the Society. The need for a new building in Gretna provided the opportunity for this division to take concrete forms. Between 1905 and 1908 a series of actions were taken that resulted in the Society moving its school to Altona, where it retained the name Mennonite Educational Institute. A new society continued the school in Gretna under a new name, Mennonite Collegiate Institute, with Ewert as principal.[19]

The small part of the Mennonite constituency interested in supporting higher education had already had difficulty maintaining one school in Gretna, especially since 1903, when its principal no longer received the inspector's government salary. When the Altona school opened in the fall of 1908 there were two such schools to support. In those circumstances John Hiebert, business manager of the Altona school, in November 1909 accepted a Manitoba government appointment as "organizer" of public schools among Mennonites. Since this was an official function of the Mennonite school inspector, J. M. Friesen, Hiebert's appointment was seen as a purely political one. His salary of one hundred dollars a month went entirely for the upkeep of the Altona institute.[20] The following year J. I. Baergen of Plum Coulee, a member of the Gretna association, received Hiebert's appointment and salary; this money went into the treasury of the Gretna institute. While both arrangements lasted only a year, they represented a kind of politicized government support with which no Mennonite group could be at ease.

## School Developments, 1890–1916

When Ewert took over as inspector of Mennonite schools in 1891 there were only eight district schools, including the six in *Kleine Gemeinde* villages on the East Reserve and at Scratching River.[21] During the twelve years of his inspectorate he was involved in the "extremely delicate task ... of persuading a people for the most part strongly averse from the idea of public schools to the establishment of such schools."[22] In this task there was steady progress, as indicated in table 3, which shows a total of forty-one district schools at the end of Ewert's term.[23] The fact that the Manitoba School Act permitted religious instruction for one-half hour each day was a great help. By 1902 the Bergthaler congregation that Ewert had joined, together with the Mennonite Brethren and the Sommerfelder church, had developed a curriculum for religious instruction in the public schools. The churches also appointed their own inspectors to see that this religious instruction was carried out properly.[24]

Ewert's dismissal as inspector in 1903 was a blow to the Mennonite School Society and to supporters of the public schools.[25] His immediate successors in the inspectorship, Henry Graff (1904–1905) and J. M. Friesen (1906–1909) were not nearly as successful in this cause.[26] Friesen, like Ewert, was an ordained minister in the Bergthaler congregation.[27] A particularly disturbing event during Friesen's inspectorate was the announcement made in Winnipeg in September 1906 that all Manitoba public schools were to fly the Union Jack. At a meeting of young Conservatives Premier Roblin gave a rationale for this move: "I think the man who comes from a foreign country in order to benefit his circumstances, and who objects to perpetuating the glories of our flag and declines to have his children infused with British patriotism, is a man that is undesirable."[28] In that context it is not surprising that the new law raised anxieties in the pacifist Mennonite community. The flag-flying policy was to go into effect on January 1, 1907, but this date had to be postponed to May 24, due to the difficulty of securing flagpoles for all the schools.[29]

Ewert, who in addition to being principal of the Gretna school also served as editor of a Mennonite church paper, *Der Mitarbeiter*, responded to Roblin's announcement in the November 1906 issue. He feared that the daily flying of the flag would awaken a militaristic spirit in the young people and thus create a conflict with the Mennonite confession of non-resistance. He asked other ministers and teachers to give their views regarding this issue.[30] Bishop Peter Toews of the Holdemann church shared Ewert's concern, but feared that non-compliance could be understood as a violation of the law. He therefore expressed his preference for private schools.[31]

The East Reserve *Kleine Gemeinde* church held a brotherhood meeting about this issue in December 1906. It wondered whether it was possible for a person to claim allegiance to the flag of Christ and at the same time also to the flag of this world. Would flying the national flag over the church school not represent being "unequally yoked with unbelievers" (2 Corinthians 6:15)? They feared that the flag would be only the first step in a gradual loss of non-resistance. The church therefore decided that if the government would strictly enforce the law, they would be inclined to withdraw while that way still remained open for them.[32]

Table 3
**Number of Mennonite Public School Districts, 1891–1902**

| Year | Number | Year | Number |
|------|--------|------|--------|
| 1891 | 8 | 1897 | 30 |
| 1892 | 11 | 1898 | 32 |
| 1893 | 19 | 1899 | 34 |
| 1894 | 21 | 1900 | 35[a] |
| 1895 | 24 | 1901 | 39 |
| 1896 | 27 | 1902 | 41 |

a. Two new districts were added during 1900, but one former public school reverted to private status.

Source: Compiled from H. H. Ewert's annual reports in Manitoba, Legislative Assembly, *Sessional Papers*, 1892–1903, "Report of the Department of Education."

A Saskatchewan Mennonite leader advocated a mediating position. He had seen the flag at public schools in Kansas for years and felt that it did not present a real threat to the Mennonite conscience, provided that one's inner loyalty to the flag of Christ was strong.[33] Editor Ewert, however, continued to call for a clear position. The flag for him was the proud symbol of military honour. True Christians should show their love for the fatherland by prayers and intercession for the king and all others in high positions, according to 1 Timothy 2:1–2.[34]

The Bergthaler leaders decided in a meeting in late December 1906 that they could not in good conscience obey this law. They communicated this decision to Premier Roblin, drawing attention to the *Privilegium* they had received from Ottawa in 1873, and asking to be exempted from the flag policy.[35] The government responded by assuring the Mennonites that it did not intend to force anything on them that was against their conscience and *Privilegium*.[36] That meant that they were free to relinquish the government subsidy if they chose not to fly the flag.

In late 1907 the issue was still unresolved. The Bergthaler church had decided to organize a delegation to go to Winnipeg. Bishop Toews had provided Premier Roblin with a copy of the Mennonite *Privilegium* at Roblin's request. And editor Ewert had continued his campaign with articles such as "After the flags come guns."[37] A delegation representing the Bergthaler, *Kleine Gemeinde*, and Holdemann churches had an audience with government ministers on December 30 and presented their petition.[38] The government's response came in a speech in the legislature by Education Minister Coldwell and reached the Mennonites through press reports. The flag law applied to them just as it did to any other citizens and was to be obeyed by all schools receiving government grants.[39]

Eleven district schools, including all the *Kleine Gemeinde* ones, reverted to private status over the compulsory flag-flying issue in 1907.[40] The Bergthaler found some comfort in the government's explanation that in the British tradition the flag was not primarily a military symbol. Ewert, whose attitude to the flag was shaped by his Prussian background, now modified his position.[41] But those Mennonite groups that had been slow to accept public schools thus far now became even more reluctant. According to A. A. Willows, who became Inspector a few years later, "they feared that this was just the thin end of the wedge which might ... result ultimately in the abrogation of the privilege they had received when they came to Manitoba, viz. exemption from military service."[42] The *Manitoba Free Press*, reviewing this incident a few years later, remarked that with "the substitution of a grain of wisdom for the pigheadedness, blusteringly manifested in that connection, these schools might have been saved to the national system."[43] The Liberal *Morden Chronicle* realized that Mennonite objection to the Union Jack did not mean that they would prefer any other flag. They regarded all flags as "symbols of the war-like spirit which they sought to escape when they immigrated to Canada." It recommended more teaching on "the true meaning of the British flag" instead of compulsion.[44]

When A. A. Weidenhammer took over as inspector in January 1910, the number of Mennonite district schools was thirty-seven compared to forty-one at the time of Ewert's dismissal seven years earlier. While Weidenhammer was not a Mennonite, he spoke German fluently and was at least as acceptable to the conservative Mennonite groups as Ewert had been. During the first three years of his inspectorate the number of Mennonite district schools increased from thirty-seven to sixty-three.[45] By 1915 enrolment in Manitoba's German bilingual schools totalled over 2,800. This included nearly 2,600 Mennonite children compared with just over 1,100 of them in district schools at the end of 1908. There were, however, still at least a thousand children in the Mennonite private schools who were getting little or no English teaching.[46] This included all of the Reinländer schools on the West Reserve and all or most of the Chortitzer schools on the East Reserve.

During the 1890s, when Ewert was still Inspector of Mennonite schools, he organized local teacher conferences.[47] These monthly meetings of the teachers of district schools served as opportunities for in-service training. In 1900 a larger organization, "the German-English Teachers' Association of Southern Manitoba," was founded.[48] Teachers of both district and private schools were invited to its meetings, which were usually addressed by invited representatives of the Department of Education. While this association primarily served the function of professional improvement of teachers, it included among its objectives "the discussion of the laws governing the educational affairs of the Province and to recommend desirable legislation."[49]

In 1913 the Sommerfelder congregation took the initiative in organizing a Mennonite *Schulkommission* in which the Bergthaler and Mennonite Brethren congregations of the West Reserve also participated.[50] While its main purpose was to encourage the instruction of German and religion in all Mennonite district and private schools, it was also given the special task of negotiating with the government authorities whenever Mennonite school freedom was threatened. Early in 1914 the Commission sent a delegation to Winnipeg to present a brief to Premier Roblin asking the government to recognize it as the official voice of the Mennonite communities.[51]

A school attendance act passed by the Manitoba government in early 1914 raised some concern for Ewert and the Mennonites.[52] Inspector Weidenhammer, who had by this time won the confidence of a good number of Mennonites, placed himself squarely behind any efforts the government would undertake towards compulsion.[53] By late 1915 it was becoming increasingly clear that the Manitoba government would not only enforce compulsory school attendance but would make even more drastic changes in its school legislation.

The pattern of Mennonite school development in Saskatchewan was similar to that in Manitoba, but settlements there were founded ten or fifteen years later. Mennonite immigrants coming to the Rosthern area either directly from Europe or from American Mennonite settlements during the 1890s for the most part had no reservations about accepting public schools. Bergthal Mennonites arriving from Manitoba were somewhat less ready to do so but found it difficult to organize and support private schools since they did not develop block settlements. The Reinländer community, which obtained a reserve in the Hague area in 1894, erected only private schools and did not permit its members to send their children to district schools. This was also the case on the Reinländer Reserve founded south of Swift Current in 1905.[54]

Those Mennonites who had accepted the public schools founded the German–English Academy at Rosthern in 1905 to train bilingual teachers. Graduates of this academy were also trained to teach the religious curriculum in their district schools. Between 1905 and 1917 the principal and driving force behind the academy was David Toews, a Russian Mennonite who had emigrated to Kansas in 1884 and had come north to Canada in 1893. Toews had studied under H. H. Ewert in Kansas and taught for four years in Mennonite district schools in Manitoba under Ewert's inspectorship.[55] Since 1913 he was also bishop of the Rosenort congregation, succeeding its founder, Bishop Peter Regier.

Two years after Saskatchewan received provincial status, Inspector E. B. Hutcheson reported twenty-two Mennonite public school districts organized with buildings and furnishings better than in any other districts. More teachers were still needed even though good salaries were paid.[56] At the same time tension was developing in communities where a minority had opened a district school. Reinländer church members who sent their children to these district schools were excommunicated. The accompanying shunning or avoidance had severe social and sometimes economic effects. By the summer of 1908 the Saskatchewan government had received a sufficient number of complaints about this situation to begin to look for a remedy. In August Premier Scott instructed his attorney general:

> The time has come for the government to act in the matter of the pressure placed by a certain section of the Mennonite church upon certain of their adherents whose only offence is their willingness to obey the laws of the province, particularly in relation to education. I beg that

you will look into the law on the matter as early as possible and let me know what action is possible for us to take.⁵⁷

By September, following discussions with Rosthern MLA Gerhard Ens and some excommunicated Reinländer Mennonites, the Premier was ready with two concrete suggestions:

(1) to inform the Mennonite heads that unless they leave free those of their people who wish to use the public school we will compel the formation of public school districts wherever there are enough children of school age and will force the payment of taxes; (2) to inform them also that we will deprive them of the legal right to solemnize marriages.⁵⁸

This action, it was believed, would convince the Mennonite heads to restore the rights of the church to excommunicated members.

When this threat did not produce any immediate results, the government decided to investigate the situation more thoroughly. A Commission of Inquiry headed by Frank Ford, Deputy Attorney General, and D. P. McColl, Deputy Commissioner of Education, held hearings at the school house at Warman on December 28 and 29, 1908, producing some ninety pages of evidence, much of it from excommunicated members of the Reinländer church. In early January the Commission interviewed a deputation from the congregation itself.⁵⁹

The threat posed by these new government initiatives led the Reinländer congregation to hold brotherhood meetings, both in Saskatchewan and in Manitoba, to determine its further course of action. One of the excommunicated members, hardware merchant I. P. Friesen of Rosthern, reported these church meetings to Premier Scott and Education Minister Calder. The congregation had decided to be more strict in enforcing its rules among their members, he said, adding that the economic boycott even in Rosthern was getting to be quite strong. "Unless the Government takes prompt action, there are only two ways open to me either to leave the Country or join the Church again, and keep my Children from attending decent Schools."⁶⁰

The government had concluded, however, that district schools established by force in the Reinländer districts would not achieve their purpose. The 1908 Commission report had convinced them that "even if it were possible to establish public schools among these people they would not send their children as their religious beliefs prohibit them from doing so."⁶¹ The bishops and other leaders of this group of Mennonites claimed the support of the 1873 *Privilegium* for their schools. A "strong discussion on the matter" between the Mennonite bishop of Hague and a representative from the Department of Education in 1910 resulted in some fifteen private Mennonite schools continuing to operate as before.⁶²

On the Swift Current Reserve to the south only two public school districts had been organized by 1915. In Dunelm, which included only three square miles of reserve land, the decision to organize passed by a majority of only one. The school district of Wymark, with the railway town of that name as its centre, was organized a little later. It could obtain a majority for organizing only by eliminating the southeast section on which the village of Schönfeld was located.[63]

By the fall of 1915 Mennonite parents who failed to send their children to an available public school were beginning to be fined.[64] In spite of repeated fines these parents had no intention of sending their children to public schools, claiming exemption under the 1873 *Privilegium*. Premier Scott was coming to the conclusion that in order to remedy the problem of education in the Mennonite communities there would

> have to be a revolutionary change made in the school law and a different law enacted from any up to date existing in any of the provinces of Canada. Under existing law the Mennonite private schools cannot be suppressed.... The root of this trouble lies in the Mennonite church. Jail may prove to be the only necessary remedy—not for the delinquent parents but for the heads of the church who coerce parents.[65]

In the Mennonite communities outside of the two Reserves meanwhile, both the Mennonite leaders and the government felt that they were making progress. Bishop Toews had a successful interview with Attorney General Turgeon regarding the use of German in Mennonite district schools.[66] Inspector Meyer reported substantial improvements in the Mennonite districts west and south of Rosthern and in the Waldeck, Rush Lake, and Herbert areas near Swift Current.[67]

Thus, in spite of some inevitable tensions, Mennonite relations with the two provincial governments on the matter of education were generally positive as the prolonged war in Europe began to weaken Canadian toleration for the non-British elements in its midst.

## The "National Schools," 1916

"Multiculturalism" and the "Canadian mosaic" were not part of the ideology of the Canadian West at the turn of the century. During the decade of large-scale immigration while Clifford Sifton was Minister of the Interior (1896–1905), the goal was to populate the vast prairie. This required sturdy farmers who could survive the harsh winters and difficult pioneer conditions. Most of these came not from Britain or France, the "founding nations" of Canada, but from Eastern Europe. Sifton, like many other westerners, assumed that all these newcomers "should be inculcated with

British democratic ideals and that the English language should be the language of public life and public communication."[68]

This attitude was already evident in the 1890 acts of the Manitoba government in abolishing denominational schools and official use of the French language. Sifton, a member of that government, agreed with this policy, which sought, in D'Alton McCarthy's words, "to make the people Manitobans and Canadians, not French or Mennonite, not Poles or Polish Jews."[69] Yet it was Sifton who negotiated the Laurier–Greenway compromise, which allowed bilingual public schools in Manitoba, and it was his department that continued the policy of allowing immigrant groups to settle in blocks. Both delayed assimilation but were seen as necessary expedients in achieving the urgent task of filling the West.

The nationalism of the Conservative government of Premier Rodmond Roblin was perhaps more imperialistic but not less "English" in tone. Roblin's 1906 remark that the immigrant "who objects to perpetuating the glories of our flag and declines to have his children infused with British patriotism, is a man that is undesirable," found an echo in many other voices of the time. Saskatchewan school inspector and later premier J. T. M. Anderson criticized the routine manner of granting Canadian citizenship to immigrants after three years of residence. "Surely," he wrote, "the right to become a living link in the great earth-girdling chain of the greatest Empire on earth is too lightly regarded in the apparent anxiety to 'increase production' and develop 'material resources.'"[70] A prominent leader in the Methodist Church, S. D. Chown, worried that in 1910 only a third of Saskatchewan's population was British-born:

> it means that one third of the people have the unprecedented burden thrust upon them of converting two-thirds of the population to the high ideals of Canadian citizenship ... The question of questions is which shall prevail: the ideas of southern Europe, or the noblest conceptions of Anglo-Saxondom?[71]

There were also assimilationists who saw the process as less of a one-way street. The enormously popular novelist, Presbyterian cleric Charles W. Gordon of Winnipeg (Ralph Connor), prefaced his 1909 book *The Foreigner* with this remark:

> Out of breeds diverse in traditions, in ideals, in speech, and in manner of life, Saxon and Slav, Teuton, Celt and Gaul, one people is being made. The blood strains of great races will mingle in the blood of a race greater than the greatest of them all.[72]

Harold W. Foght, a specialist in the U.S. Bureau of Education whom the Saskatchewan government employed in 1917, gave this advice:

> The one important fact to be kept in the foreground is how best to assimilate and Canadianise this heterogeneous mass of people, without

forcing the process of transition so rapidly that the best inheritance from foreign shores becomes lost. This calls for exceptional patience and firmness.[73]

But even Foght was convinced that the "one Canadian-speaking and thinking people" should be shaped primarily by "the splendid Anglo-Saxon heritage transplanted to the new soil."[74]

Most of these assimilationists agreed with Anderson that "it should never be expected that the older people will become 'true Canadians' and no attempt should be made to do what is impossible."[75] The public schools were therefore essential in winning the next generation. Denominationalism had been removed from them in Manitoba in 1890. The argument now was "that unless English was made the sole language of all schools in the West, a Canadian 'nation' could never emerge from the polyglot western population."[76] In 1914 the *Free Press*, in which Sifton held controlling interest, began a vigorous campaign to abolish bilingual instruction from Manitoba public schools.[77] The Conservative *Morden Empire* had already argued this position in 1899:

> National schools must mean, at least, schools devoted to the nation, as distinguished from other nations, or from parts or sections of the country. Then our schools to be national must be Canadian, or if you don't like that term, our schools must be British.

A German professor imported from the United States for the German normal school at Gretna, or an inspector for French schools "imported from Quebec," did not fit into that concept of national schools.[78]

When the Conservative government of Sir Rodmond Roblin was replaced by the Liberals under T. C. Norris in Manitoba in August 1915, some changes in policy were expected. In Saskatchewan the Liberals remained in power but W. M. Martin succeeded Walter Scott as premier in 1916. In spite of these changes, both of the new administrations had reason to hope that their progress in introducing district schools in Mennonite areas would continue. However, the Great War interfered with those hopes.

> This "peaceful penetration" of the sect by the "world" might have continued indefinitely had a crisis not been precipitated by Canadian educational authorities, particularly in the province of Manitoba. The Great War brought a violent reaction against all things German, and military organizations and the press brought pressure to bear on the provincial government to suppress the teaching of the German language.[79]

In Manitoba the Bergthaler and Sommerfelder leaders were prepared to deal with the new Liberal government. Aware of the campaign to have bilingual instruction abolished, they sought to exert their own influence in favour of continuing it. Valentine Winkler, whom they had helped to elect to the Manitoba legislature, was appointed Minister of Agriculture and Immigration in the new cabinet. Before the end of 1915 members of the *Schulkommission* were in conversation with him about pending changes in the Manitoba School Act.[80] The Commission's responsibilities included "to attempt to exert an influence on political parties and candidates for election, so that they would not support educational legislation unfavourable" to Mennonite schools.[81]

In keeping with this clause, members of the Commission met with Winkler at Rosenfeld on January 7, 1916 and presented him with an eleven-point petition, which read in part:

1. The majority of the Mennonites have so far put their confidence in the Liberal party and have uninterruptedly sent a Liberal representative to the legislature. They would not like to be betrayed by the Liberal party.

2. If they were betrayed, they would feel so offended that they would cease to support the Liberal government.

3. The Liberal party has no mandate from the people to abolish bilingual schools. They said in their platform only that they would see to the efficient teaching of the English language.[82]

In order to make the bilingual school law more readily enforceable, the delegation recommended that a majority of the ratepayers of a district be required to request instruction in a language other than English. This would replace the present law, under which ten non-English children in a district were sufficient grounds for demanding bilingual education. The brief ended by requesting that the School Commission be informed if and when a change in the present education law was contemplated. It would then want to send a delegation to Winnipeg to present the Mennonite concerns.

Winkler suggested that if the bilingual clause of the present school act were changed, it should require a seventy-five percent vote of the ratepayers before bilingual instruction were granted. The Commission, however, felt that in some of the railway towns it would not be able to command three-fourths of the vote and so urged that a simple majority be decisive. It also pressed for the opportunity of presenting a brief to the government "before the bill to be put before the House has received shape or form."[83]

Winkler arranged a meeting with members of the Norris government for February 15.[84] The Commission appointed as its members in the delegation H. J. Friesen and J. D. Klassen of the Sommerfelder church, B. Loewen and Benjamin Ewert of the Bergthaler church, and J. M. Elias of the Mennonite Brethren. At Winkler's request H. H. Ewert was also included. When the East Reserve Mennonites heard of these plans they sent representatives to join it in Winnipeg. The Chortitzer and the *Kleine Gemeinde* churches were represented by their bishops, Johann K. Dueck and Peter R. Dyck. The smaller Holdemann and Bruderthaler churches were represented by the ministers Jacob T. Wiebe and Peter Schmidt. The total delegation, numbering some twenty to twenty-five people, met with Premier Norris, Education Minister Thornton, Provincial Treasurer Brown, and Agriculture and Immigration Minister Winkler.[85]

Briefs on behalf of the Mennonite delegation were presented by the two Ewert brothers. H. H. Ewert began with a general defence of bilingual instruction but moved quickly to the particular concerns of the delegation. Mennonite parents felt a profound responsibility to God for the education of their children, he argued, and would never admit the right of the state to make substantial demands in this area. He then cited clause 10 of the Mennonite *Privilegium*. Although there was some question about the competence of the Dominion government to give this promise, Ewert argued that the government in Ottawa had clearly considered itself authorized to do so.

> We would not want to believe for a moment that it was trying to be deceptive. It would be a grave disappointment to the Mennonites if the provincial government would now choose to ignore this promise and consider it "a mere scrap of paper."

With respect to the German language, Ewert argued that it had become very intimately connected with religion among the Mennonites and was now considered a necessary means to maintain the faith. He ended by pleading for patience on the part of the government, pointing to the two teacher training institutes operated by the Mennonites at their own expense as a hopeful sign.[86]

Benjamin Ewert began by pointing out that the majority of schools among the Mennonite people were still private schools. The groups maintaining these felt that they could discharge their Christian obligation to their children only by maintaining complete control over education. Should they no longer be left "unmolested and unrestricted" in this, as had been promised by the Dominion government, they would emigrate. He noted that attendance at private schools was still permitted under the School Attendance Act recently passed, and expressed the hope that further changes in the Manitoba School Act would leave the private schools open.[87]

The government members assured them that their private schools would remain unmolested, but gave no assurance on the bilingual public schools.[88] There were other signs that the latter would be abolished. The *Manitoba Free Press* and other leading newspapers were campaigning for this. *Free Press* editorials in January 1916 were especially blunt in demanding abolition of the bilingual clause.

> It does not err on the side of tolerance nor on the side of persecution. It only errs on the side of impracticableness and utter absurdity.[89]
>
> There are no rights, legal, vested, or constitutional, beyond those created by the province itself by its legislation of 1897. The province gave these rights and if it sees fit, can take them away.[90]
>
> If the Roblin regime, with its fatal policy of granting concessions to racial groups in return for political support had continued for another four years, nothing could have saved Western Canada from becoming a congeries of warring races, each pursuing its own national ideal.[91]

Many organizations passed resolutions asking for abolition of the bilingual clause and sent delegations to the government. Most members of the Legislative Assembly were in favour of this move. H. H. Ewert responded with an editorial of his own, deploring this promotion of "the narrowest, most limited kind of nativism."[92] The bill to repeal the bilingual clause of 1897 (section 258) was passed on February 29, 1916, and came into force August 21.[93]

The Reinländer and Chortitzer churches had opposed district schools so steadfastly that not a single one had survived in their midst thus far.[94] These groups therefore remained initially unaffected by the legislation of 1916. Since the delegation in February had been assured that the government would leave the private schools unmolested, the other groups now made plans to change their district schools into private ones. Apparently the Minister of Agriculture and Immigration had advised this course of action.[95] A meeting of Sommerfelder and Bergthaler leaders unanimously agreed in May 1916 to recommend to their congregations that all district schools be changed to private status.[96] The reasons for this move, in addition to the elimination of German as language of instruction, were decreasing Mennonite influence in district schools, the removal of the normal school course from Gretna to Morden and then to Manitou, and the replacement of the Mennonite inspector by a non-Mennonite German-speaking one who was now to be replaced by an English one.

The Sommerfelder *Bruderschaft* (membership approx. 2,500) in late May decided almost unanimously to convert all of the district schools in their area into private ones. The Mennonite Brethren were inclined toward private schools, but first wanted to see the curriculum and make plans for financing such a venture.[97]

The five-hundred-member Bergthaler congregation at a brotherhood meeting in early June agreed to the recommendation of its leaders and voted to organize private schools where possible. To finance these schools it agreed to approach the municipal council to see whether school funds could be collected via taxation. It also agreed to use the interest on deposits in the *Waisenamt* for this purpose.[98] A second meeting of the leadership of the Bergthaler, Sommerfelder, and Mennonite Brethren congregations of the West Reserve appointed a committee to work out a curriculum for the private schools and asked Bishop Abraham Doerksen to report their move to the Manitoba government.[99]

Ewert defended this reversion to private schools in an editorial in the *Mitarbeiter*. He did not see it as a rejection of the English language, nor as an act of disloyalty. English was to be given ample consideration in these private schools and the entire program of education was to be such as to satisfy the government. According to him, this action should not be seen as a protest to embarrass the government. The churches had modestly and openly stated their case before the government, indicating that instruction in the mother tongue, or more properly "church language," was essential. When this had not succeeded, the Mennonites had not resorted to a press campaign or to political pressure but had simply proceeded to organize their own schools in such a way as they owed it to God and their conscience.[100]

The first concrete sign of trouble for the private schools in Manitoba appeared in the inspector's report for the year ending June 30, 1916. Inspector Weidenhammer, who had recently Anglicized his name to Willows, included a general survey of the Mennonite church schools in his annual report to the Department of Education. Of the Chortitzer and Reinländer schools he wrote: "Not a word of English is taught in them and very little of anything else." His evaluation of the Sommerfelder and *Kleine Gemeinde* private schools was not quite as negative, but even the best of these "were still a year or two behind the public schools."[101] But the government did not initiate any action against private schools as yet. In fact, by August ten West Reserve districts were ready, or almost so, to open the new school year as private schools.[102] And by October the new curriculum for private schools was coming off the press.[103] Those bilingual Mennonite district schools that had not reverted to private status in the fall of 1916 continued to teach German even though the teaching of a second language in elementary district schools was not permitted under the new law.[104]

In Saskatchewan, agitation for stronger government control over education was spearheaded by the Reverend Dr. Edmund H. Oliver. As principal of Presbyterian Theological College in Saskatoon and vice-president of the Saskatchewan Public Education League, he wielded considerable influence. His 1915 address on "The Country School in Non-English Speaking Communities in Saskatchewan" was printed in pamphlet form and given wide circulation. Arguing that it was the primary function of the public school to make the child into "an intelligent and patriotic citizen," and "not to make Mennonites, nor Protestants, nor Catholics, but Canadian citizens," Oliver decried the fact that many Saskatchewan children, including some eight hundred in thirty-four Mennonite private schools in the Hague and Swift Current reserves, were not receiving such education.[105]

Within the Department of Education calmer heads prevailed for the moment. Responding directly to Oliver's campaign, the Deputy Minister of Education in early 1916 urged: "Just at this time when it is easy for any agitator to rouse the prejudices and the passions of people on racial matters it behooves our better men to require from others calmness, deliberation and foresight."[106] Rather pointedly he added: "Those who shout on Saskatchewan platforms about Canadian citizenship being endangered because 800 children in Saskatchewan are being educated in Mennonite schools are hysterical fools."[107] The Minister of Education, Premier Scott, equally decisively dissociated his government from the Oliver report.[108]

While there was no strong movement among Saskatchewan Mennonites to change their district schools back to private status, at least one such attempt was made in the Hague area.[109] By late 1916 the inspector of the Swift Current area, unable to make any headway in introducing district schools on the Mennonite reserve, began to advocate "a more drastic compulsory system of education."[110]

In both provinces thus, patience was beginning to wear thin in government circles, making a more direct clash with the least co-operative Mennonite groups seemingly inevitable.

## The *Zwangsschulen*, 1918

The Manitoba school legislation of 1916 was not directed primarily against bilingual schools in Mennonite districts. For some time after its enactment, therefore, the Norris government "considered the Mennonite schools a rather minor problem."[111] This external calm brought about a certain amount of laxity within the Mennonite educational system. On the one hand, the church leadership complained that the movement toward more adequate supervision of religious instruction in the Mennonite district schools was slipping. Although the situation had changed somewhat with a number of district schools reverting to private status, a number of Mennonite communities were still served by the public school system. In some of the latter schools religious instruction had ceased, leading to what Ewert called a "Rückgang ins Heidentum" (reversion to heathendom).[112] On the other hand, the civic leaders deplored the irregular attendance of some children in district schools in the Mennonite area and petitioned the provincial government to appoint an attendance officer.[113]

The movement toward "national" schools had by no means ceased with the legislation of 1916. As the war dragged on and pressure on the government intensified to implement the full force of the legislation, anxiety in some Mennonite districts rose. A sign of renewed passive resistance to the public school system came from a couple of districts in the area south of Morden, which in the spring of 1918 failed to submit the annual census of school-aged children. The Minister of Education was thereupon authorized by order-in-council to take this census as provided in section 309 of the Public Schools Act.[114] That summer another ten school districts of the West Reserve indicated that they planned to operate as private schools in September. As can be seen from table 4, most of these districts had been erected during or prior to Ewert's inspectorate. The press interpreted this move as a power grab by the Mennonite leaders.

> It appears that the leaders of the Mennonite body seizing an opportunity favourable to the assertion and extension of their authority, started a movement ... to run their schools as private schools when the time came to reopen after the summer vacation.[115]

The government, apparently sharing that interpretation, responded with power of its own. It decided to impose public schools on non-co-operating Mennonite districts. To effect this, it appointed John F. Greenway, Assistant Deputy Minister of Education, as official trustee to continue the operation of each school as a public school.[116] Mennonites referred to these schools as *Zwangsschulen* ("forced schools"). Explaining this action a few years later, Education Minister Thornton still sounded alarmist.

> The situation became acute in 1918. Early in that year a campaign was inaugurated to destroy our public school system in the rural districts. Meetings were held, urging the ratepayers to give up the government grants and run the schools as private schools.[117]

Several of these school districts were in communities of the Bergthaler congregation. Confronted with this decisive government action, its leadership decided not to do anything further in the matter.[118] The ratepayers of Wakeham School District, however, adopted a policy of organized resistance and boycotted the public school when it was kept open in September by the Department of Education through its official trustee.[119] Charges were promptly laid under the School Attendance Act and a court session in Morden on September 27 imposed fines on eleven of the offending parents.[120] The defendants based their non-co-operation on the 1873 agreement with the federal government. Deputy Attorney General J. Allen, who conducted the case for the Department, convinced the two magistrates that no officer of the federal government could, in school matters, bind the

Table 4
## Manitoba Mennonite District Schools Kept in Operation by Order-in-Council, 1918

| District | District No. | Year Founded | Greenway Appointed Official Trustee | |
|---|---|---|---|---|
| | | | Date | Order-in-Council |
| Edenburg | 330 | 1883 | July 5 | 29748 |
| Neu Hoffnung | 1310 | 1904 | July 5 | 29749 |
| Wakeham | 773 | 1893 | July 16 | 29800 |
| Kleinstadt | 781 | 1893 | July 19 | 29825 |
| Glencross | 71 | 1878 | July 23 | 29841 |
| Steinfeld | 1128 | 1901 | July 30[a] | 29870 |
| Amsterdam | 885 | 1896 | August 6 | 29911 |
| Steinreich | 820 | 1894 | August 6 | 29912 |
| Eichenhoff | 1591 | 1911 | August 20 | 29970 |
| Edenthal | 756 | 1893 | August 23 | 29992 |

a. The motion for Steinfeld on July 30 was submitted by Acting Minister of Education J. W. Armstrong. A second minute (no. 29916), with only slightly different wording, was passed August 8, 1918.
Source: Compiled from PAM, RG 2, A 1.

province, which enjoys full control of education according to the provisions of the British North America Act.

Having successfully reversed the trend toward private schools in the Mennonite communities, the Minister of Education next took action to revive those public schools that had been managed as private schools for varying periods of time. This was accomplished in the case of nineteen districts by appointing Greenway as official trustee by separate orders-in-council during the 1918–1919 school year. Included in this action, as is indicated in table 5, were several schools that had reverted to private status in 1907 in connection with the government's flag-flying policy.

A total of twenty-nine Mennonite communities had thus been restored to the public school system and one new one (Barkfield) added to it. While that task was still in process, Dr. Thornton was already looking ahead. In his report to the Manitoba Legislature in early 1919 he said:

> There will still remain to be dealt with the areas where only private schools have so far existed and we are asking in the Public School act amendments for authority to create public school areas, so that we can proceed to put the public school within reach.[121]

## Table 5
## Discontinued Manitoba Mennonite District Schools
## Reopened by Order-in-Council, 1918–1920

| District | District No. | Year Founded | Greenway Appointed Official Trustee | |
|---|---|---|---|---|
| | | | Date | Order-in-Council |
| Grossweide | 786 | 1893 | Oct. 4, 1918 | 30174 |
| Neu Bergthal | 1594 | 1911 | Oct. 4, 1918 | 30175 |
| Alt Bergthal | 1296 | 1904 | Oct. 4, 1918 | 30176 |
| Kronsweide | 1030 | 1899 | Oct. 18, 1918 | 30225 |
| Rosefarm | 1577 | 1911 | Oct. 18, 1918 | 30726 |
| Blumenort[a] | 62 | 1878 | Jan. 17, 1919 | 30727 |
| Gruenfeld[a] | 63 | 1878 | Jan. 17, 1919 | 30728 |
| Blumenhof[a] | 64 | 1878 | Jan. 17, 1919 | 30729 |
| Neu Kronsthal[a] | 1147 | 1901 | Jan. 28, 1919 | 30776 |
| Houston[a] | 214 | 1884 | Jan. 28, 1919 | 30777 |
| Schanzenfeld | 420 | 1885 | Jan. 28, 1919 | 30778 |
| Halbstadt | 886 | 1896 | Jan. 28, 1919 | 30789 |
| Weidenfeld | 988 | 1898 | Jan. 28, 1919 | 30780 |
| Reichenbach | 1198 | 1902 | Jan. 28, 1919 | 30781 |
| Barkfield[b] | 1951 | 1919 | Mar. 5, 1919 | 31000 |
| Silberfeld | 1590 | 1911 | Mar. 25, 1919 | 31139 |
| Gruenthal | 1592 | 1911 | Mar. 25, 1919 | 31140 |
| Gandenfeld | 1593 | 1911 | Mar. 25, 1919 | 31141 |
| Rudnerweide | 1752 | 1914 | Mar. 25, 1919 | 31142 |
| Hoffnungsort[c] | 821 | 1893 | May 19, 1920 | 34000 |

a. Reverted to private status in 1907 in protest of the compulsory flag-flying policy. Houston had operated as a public school 1913–1916, reverting to private status a second time when the bilingual clause was abolished. *MFP,* July 17, 1919, p. 1.
b. Barkfield was a new district.
c. Operated as a public school to June 30, 1900.
Source: Compiled from PAM, RG 2, A 1.

Such legislation, if passed, would affect particularly the Reinländer church communities on the West Reserve and the Chortitzer communities on the East Reserve, both of which had steadfastly resisted the public school movement thus far. The former, with the assistance of the Morden law firm McLeod, Black and Company prepared a ten-page "Memorandum re Mennonite Schools" addressed "To the Honourable Members of the

Legislative Assembly of Manitoba."[122] This document was prepared for submission to the legislature when Thornton's proposed amendment to the School Act was being considered. The plan failed because the Mennonites did not receive notice when to attend.[123]

Armed with new legislation that empowered it to impose public schools on non-co-operative districts, the Department of Education proceeded to create eleven new public school districts in the Mennonite East Reserve. It did so on the grounds that "no provision has been made for the proper education of the children resident on these lands in accordance with the provisions of 'The Public School Act.'"[124] Map 7 shows that these new school districts were located mainly in those portions of Hanover Municipality occupied by the Chortitzer church people.

That the Department was not very diplomatic in its approach can be seen in the names assigned to these new school districts. As table 6 shows, existing communities were entirely overlooked and a set of unmistakably English names imposed. The community of Grunthal, for example, regarded the name of its school district, Aldershot, as "a slur on Mennonite pacifism," and never operated a school under that name.[125] Other districts also boycotted these imposed public schools. Among the teachers to experience this dilemma was James Fletcher, son of the later Deputy Minister of Education, who after his first year of Arts studies at the University of Manitoba "babysat an empty school building for six weeks" in one of these districts in 1919.[126]

In some West Reserve communities Mennonite resistance to the compulsory schools began to increase. The Reichenbach community near Rosenfeld unanimously decided in the spring of 1919 to continue its private school.[127] Since Greenway had been appointed official trustee of that district in January, he informed the ratepayers of the community that "in this case there is nothing left for me to do but ... take immediate steps to erect a new school in Reichenbach school district."[128] The private school board then appealed to their MLA, Valentine Winkler, for help.[129] As Minister of Agriculture, Winkler was naturally committed to cabinet solidarity and could not oppose Education Minister Thornton.

The Weidenfeld community also decided to continue operating its private school when Greenway was appointed official trustee. When the Department sent them three different public school teachers during the course of one month, each of whom took over their private school building for a while, they strongly protested "against this continuous and unwarranted interference" with their "rights and liberties" by the Department."[130] At the same time they also protested the prosecutions of various Mennonite parents for not sending their children to the public schools. In the newly

## Map 7
## Public School Districts in the East Reserve

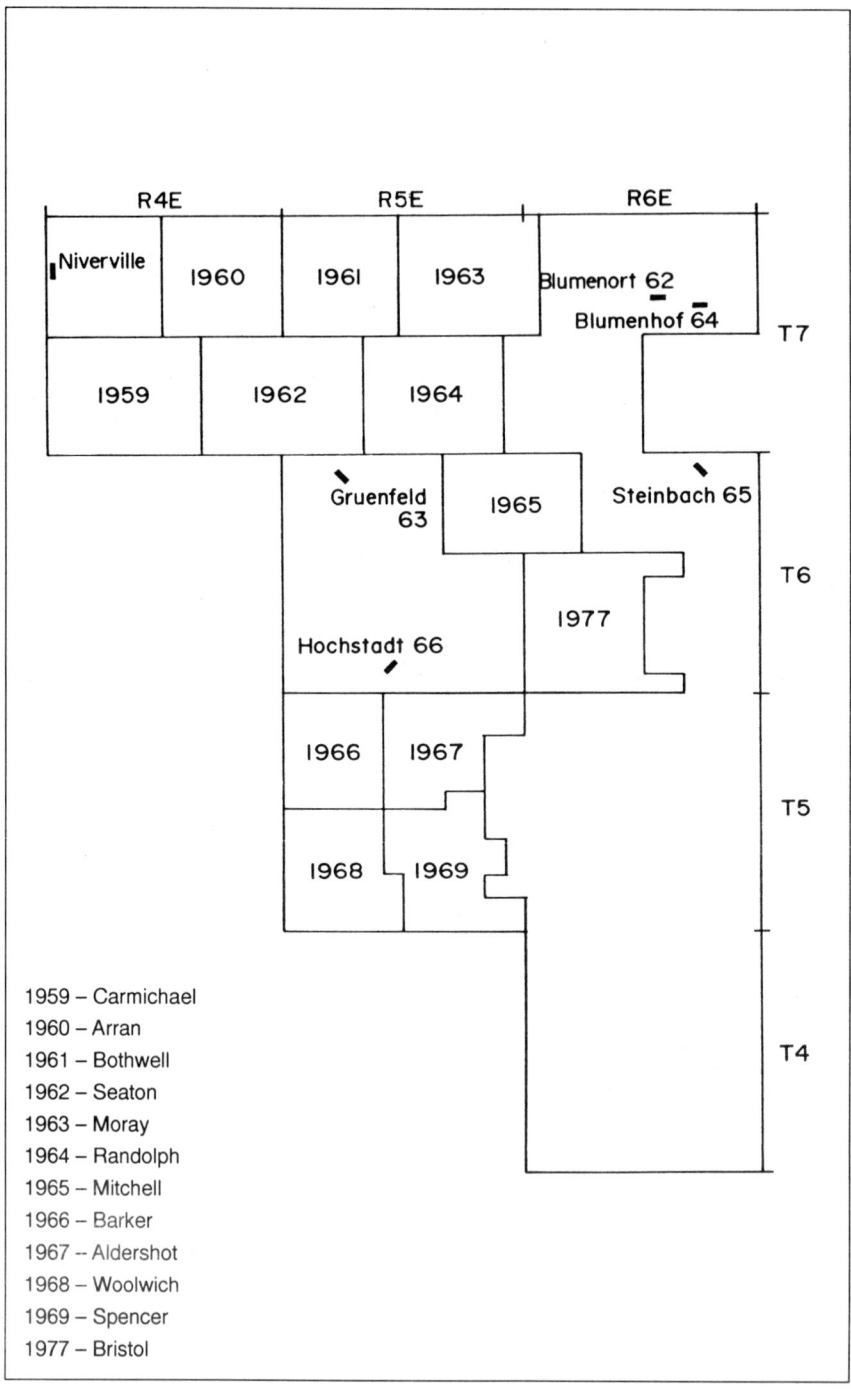

Source: Based on orders-in-council of April 8 and June 10, 1919, PAM, RG 19, B 1, box 5.

## Table 6
## Public School Districts Created in Hanover Municipality, April 8, 1919, with Greenway as Official Trustee

| District | District No. | Communities | Order-in-Council |
|---|---|---|---|
| Spencer | 1969 | Kronsgart | 31208 |
| Woolwich | 1968 | Bergfeld | 31209 |
| Aldershot | 1967 | Grunthal | 31210 |
| Barker | 1966 | Gnadenfeld | 31211 |
| Mitchell | 1965 | Reichenbach | 31212 |
| Randolph | 1964 | Chortitz | 31213 |
| Moray[a] | 1963 | Blumengart | 31214 |
| Seaton | 1962 | Altona, Heuboden | 31215 |
| Bothwell | 1961 | Kronsthal | 31216 |
| Arran | 1960 | Osterwick | 31217 |
| Carmichael | 1959 | Schanzenberg | 31218 |
| Bristol | 1977 | Neuendorf, Neuenburg | 31575[b] |

a. The April 8 order had neglected to name Greenway as the official trustee. When the omission was discovered a second order-in-council (no. 31350) was passed April 29, 1919.
b. Passed June 10, 1919.
Source: Compiled from PAM, RG 2, A 1, box 83.

reopened school districts of Neu Kronsthal and Grossweide, Mennonite parents were also withholding their children.[131] This kind of passive resistance escalated the confrontation between Mennonites and the government, provoking the latter to enforce its school law by court action.

Meanwhile, the Department of Education continued its policy of extending public school services by order-in-council. In November 1919 two of the newly created public school districts in Hanover Municipality entered into an agreement with the Department to acquire a school site, erect a school building, employ a qualified teacher "satisfactory to the inspector and the Department," and erect a teacher's residence. Or, rather, their government-appointed official trustee entered into an agreement with the government on their behalf. The irony of the situation did not escape the ratepayers even though most of them never saw the "Memorandum of Agreement" between the Minister of Education and his Assistant Deputy Minister with its interesting preamble: "WHEREAS THE DEPARTMENT is anxious to co-operate with the trustees of the said DISTRICT...."[132] As table 7 shows, Greenway entered into similar agreements on behalf of a large number of the Mennonite districts in his charge.

Table 7
**Loans Made on Behalf of Manitoba Mennonite Districts by Official Trustee Greenway[a]**

| District | District No. | Amount ($) | Date | Order-in-Council |
|---|---|---|---|---|
| Gruenfeld | 63 | 800 | Nov. 14, 1919 | 32561 |
| Randolph | 1964 | 3,000 | Nov. 14, 1919 | 32565 |
| Arran | 1960 | 3,000 | Nov. 14, 1919 | 32566 |
| Arran | | 1,000 | July 16, 1920 | 34454 |
| Barkfield | 1951 | 1,000 | Nov. 14, 1919 | 32567 |
| Moray | 1963 | 3,000 | Apr. 19, 1920 | 33768 |
| Moray | | 2,500 | Oct. 20, 1920 | 35186 |
| Carmichael | 1959 | 3,000 | Apr. 19, 1920 | 33770 |
| Carmichael | | 1,000 | Dec. 21, 1920 | 35664 |
| Spencer | 1969 | 3,000 | Apr. 19, 1920 | 33773 |
| Mitchell | 1965 | 3,000 | Apr. 19, 1920 | 33775 |
| Blumenort | 62 | 3,000 | July 2, 1920 | 34231 |
| Schanzenfeld | 420 | 2,000 | July 2, 1920 | 34232 |
| Schanzenfeld | | 1,000 | July 26, 1920 | 37121 |
| Hoffnungsort | 821 | 5,000 | Oct. 22, 1920 | 35187 |
| Exeter | 1994 | 5,000 | Apr. 30, 1921 | 36423 |
| Wells | 1998 | 5,000 | Apr. 30, 1921 | 36424 |
| Meath | 1992 | 5,000 | Apr. 30, 1921 | 36425 |
| Snowdon | 1995 | 5,000 | Apr. 30, 1921 | 36426 |
| Birkenhead | 1996 | 5,000 | July 26, 1921 | 37122 |
| Gruenthal | 1592 | 5,000 | Aug. 23, 1921 | 37340 |

a. Details of Greenway's appointment as Official Trustee of these districts are given in tables 5, 6, and 8.
Source: Compiled from PAM, RG 2, A 1.

The last area of resistance to public schools in Manitoba was dealt with in February 1920. Ten new school districts were created in the Reinländer church area in the municipalities of Rhineland and Stanley. As the names listed in table 8 indicate, the government once more ignored local feelings in imposing unmistakably English names on the new districts. Even more serious was the fact, indicated on map 8, that most of these new districts included two to four existing private schools, each serving its village community. Both of these circumstances made the public schools unacceptable to Reinländer Mennonites.

Events in Saskatchewan closely paralleled those in Manitoba. Under pressure from an intolerant public and some powerful organizations, the government enacted new school attendance legislation.[133] However, the only groups offering resistance to these new school laws were the Reinländer church communities on the two reserves. As in Manitoba, individual Mennonites from the so-called "progressive" groups were quite willing to assist the government in extending public schools into the resisting areas.[134] When Saskatchewan's new School Attendance Act went into force in May 1917, it initially affected only those Reinländer Mennonites whose villages happened to be part of existing public school districts. They promptly offered passive resistance to the annual spring census of school-aged children.[135]

Premier W. M. Martin visited the Reinländer private schools in the Hague area in the summer of 1917 in his capacity as Minister of Education, and had an extended interview with Bishop Jacob Wiens. By the spring of 1918 the Department of Education had come "to the conclusion that it was high time that some improvement should take place."[136] In order to retain their private schools, the communities would be required to employ qualified teachers recognized by the Department, use the authorized textbooks, and provide instruction in English.

Table 8
**Public Schools Created in Rhineland and Stanley Municipalities with Greenway as Official Trustee, February 21, 1920**

| District | District No. | Communities | Order-in-Council |
|---|---|---|---|
| Thames | 1991 | Bergfeld | 33336 |
| Wells | 1998 | Gnadenthal | 33337 |
| Mersey | 1997 | Chortitz, Osterwick | 33338 |
| Birkenhead | 1996 | Neuenburg, Hochfeld | 33339 |
| Snowdon | 1995 | Reinland, Rosengart, Schoenwiese | 33340 |
| Exeter | 1994 | Rosenort, Neuhorst, Kronsthal | 33341 |
| Grimsby | 1993 | Blumengart | 33342 |
| Meath[a] | 1992 | Reinfeld, Friedensruh | 33343 |
| Clyde | 1990 | Rosenfeld | 33344 |
| Barker[b] | 2058 | Sommerfeld | 36038 |

a. The northern part of Meath was separated by Order-in-Council no. 37117 on July 26, 1921, and formed into Calder School District no. 2075.
b. Barker was created February 11, 1921. Since the name had already been used for school district no. 1966 (see table 6), school district no. 2058 was eventually called Sommerfeld.
Source: Compiled from PAM, RG 2, A 1, box 84.

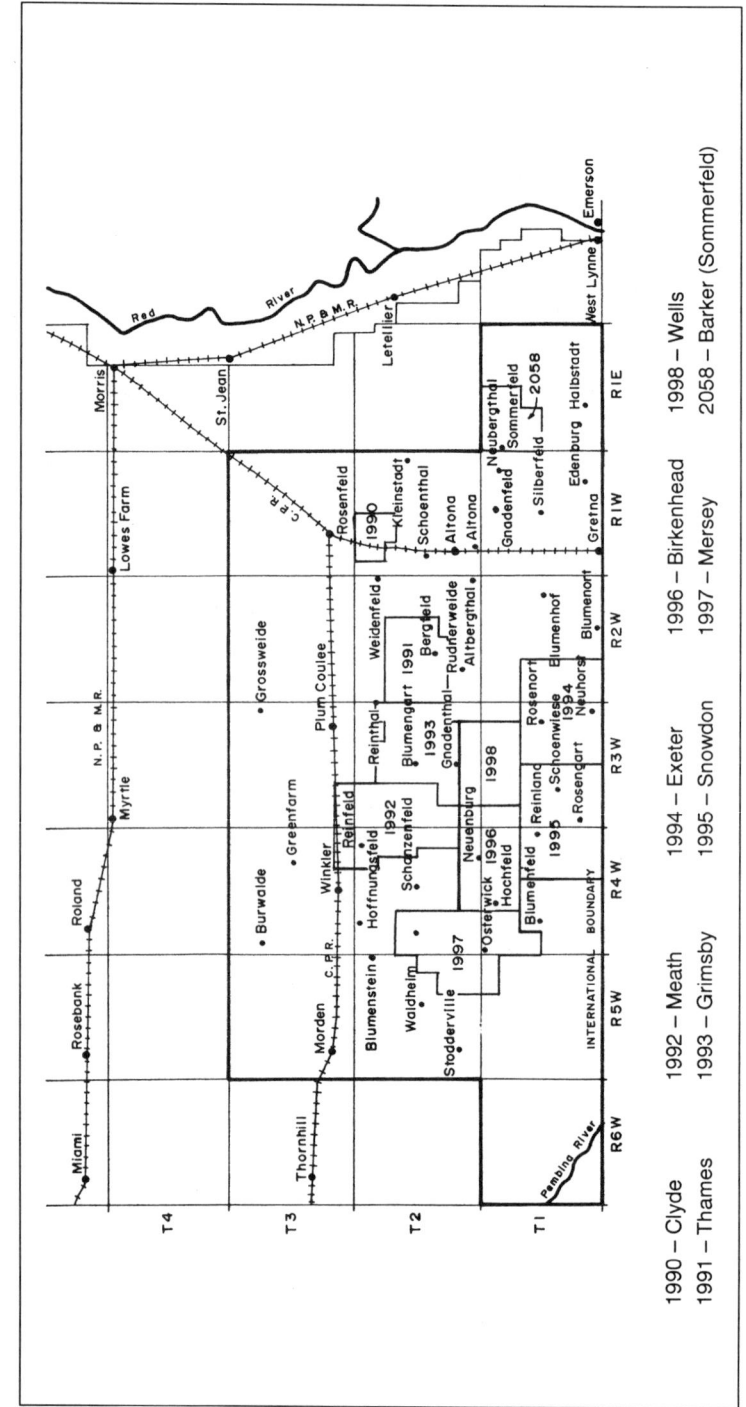

Map 8
West Reserve Reinländer Public School Districts

Source: Based on orders-in-council of February 21, 1920, and February 11, 1921, PAM, RG 2, A 1, box 84.

Instead of responding to Premier Martin that they intended "to act along these lines," as he had hoped, the Hague church sent a delegation to Ottawa to complain about the "invasion on the part of the Government of the Province of Saskatchewan, of rights guaranteed [them] by the Dominion in respect of certain religious and educational privileges."[137] The delegation based its claim on clause 10 of John Lowe's July 23, 1873, letter to the Mennonite delegates, which read:

> The fullest privilege of exercising their religious principles is by law afforded to the Mennonites, without any kind of molestation or restriction whatever, and the same privilege extends to the education of their children in schools.

Interior Minister Arthur Meighen, responding to the Hague delegation on behalf of the federal government, upheld the view of Premier Martin "that the exercise of the privilege guaranteed your community in clause 10,... is not inconsistent with the fullest provision ... of the essential elements of education for all children in your community."[138]

The first plank of the Saskatchewan Liberal Party platform adopted at its convention in Moose Jaw in March 1917 dealt with education, and was concerned especially that every child obtain a thorough knowledge of the English language.[139] As a result, Dr. Harold W. Foght, a specialist in rural school practice with the U.S. Bureau of Education, was employed to make a survey of education in Saskatchewan. In spite of his strong commitment to an assimilationist policy, Foght interpreted with some sensitivity the basis of Reinländer Mennonite opposition to public schools. This may account for the moderation and care with which the Department of Education initially proceeded in enforcing its school laws.[140] But it did not lessen the government's determination to enforce its laws.

Other groups joined the Liberal Party in calling on the government not to relax its efforts to bring English schools to all parts of the province. The Saskatchewan Rural Municipalities Association in March 1918 deplored the fact that large tracts of land were not assessed for school purposes and almost unanimously passed a resolution urging "the government to bring these lands into school districts and to enforce the teaching of English in all schools."[141] A mass meeting at Swift Current resolved that "the children of these people must be educated up to our standards of British and Canadian citizenship, so that they may, in the future, voluntarily relinquish their claims to an unjust exemption."[142]

Under this kind of pressure, the government decided at first "to pursue a policy in the Mennonite settlements of building public schools wherever there is reason to believe that the Mennonites, or some of them, will send their children to such institutions when built."[143] By spring it had practically decided to erect four public schools in the Swift Current area and from one to three in the Hague district. In the latter area, Lily School District had to be placed under an official trustee, A. J. Sparley.[144] To prepare the Mennonite leadership for these proposed new developments, Education Minister Martin wrote all Mennonite clergy to inform them of the administration of the School Attendance Act.

Leaders of the Mennonite community of the Swift Current district objected to the government's plan to establish public school districts in their area, but to no avail.[145] During the summer of 1918 the Department of Education took steps to create five new public school districts in the Mennonite area, two in the communities around Hague and three in the Swift Current district (see table 9). The official trustees J. J. Friesen, A. H. Klassen, and B. Klassen were Mennonites or of Mennonite background. But as in Manitoba, the names assigned to the new districts ignored the local communities. Some of them, in fact, appeared to be clearly inspired by persons or places made famous by the Great War.

The press reported favourably on this decisive action by the government.[146] The Reinländer at Hague appealed once more to Ottawa "to restore our ancient rights."[147] But the Saskatchewan government had made up its mind and proceeded with its policy of implementing a national school system. Three additional public school districts were created in the Hague area in December 1918 and the remaining unorganized territories in both the Swift Current and Hague Reserves were divided into public school districts in March 1919. Table 9 summarizes these actions and maps 9 and 10 locate the new districts.

Meanwhile, the government had further modified its education legislation in such a way as to make English the sole language of instruction in all schools.[148] The government rationalized this move by pointing out that in the last year of the old law, which permitted the teaching of a language other than English for one hour a day, only 118 of the 4,157 public schools in the province took advantage of this provision.[149] The elimination of the use of languages other than English obviously did not make it easier for the resisting Mennonite communities to adopt public schools.

There were other problems in making the newly created school districts operative. One of the Mennonite official trustees, J. J. Friesen, ran into difficulties over the high cost of buildings and equipment.[150] The idea of appointing two small commissions to act as official trustees in the Hague and Swift Current areas was explored.[151] The suggestion was well received and a committee consisting of Municipal Councillor John Bell, Inspector W. S. Cram, and Major Roy Graham, President of the Great War Veterans in Swift Current, was almost appointed to serve as joint official trustees for the nine Mennonite school districts in the area.[152] In the end the idea was dropped because the government did not have the power to

## Table 9
## Saskatchewan Mennonite School Districts Created by the Department of Education, 1918–1919

| District | District No. | Date Erected | Official Trustee or Board | Appointed/ Elected |
|---|---|---|---|---|
| Hague Area | | | | |
| Scarpe | 4076 | July 2, 1918 | C. Holz Board | July 2, 1918 Jan. 22, 1923 |
| Passchendaele | 4084 | Aug. 5, 1918 | B. Klassen C. Holz Board | Aug. 5, 1918 Sep. 25, 1919 Oct. 16, 1922 |
| Venice | 4117 | Dec. 9, 1918 | J. J. Friesen C. Holz | Mar. 7, 1919 July 1, 1919 |
| Pembroke | 4115 | Dec. 9, 1918 | J. J. Friesen A. H. Klassen | Mar. 7, 1919 Aug. 15, 1922 |
| Renfrew | 4116 | Dec. 9, 1918 | J. J. Friesen A. H. Klassen | Mar. 7, 1919 Aug. 15, 1922 |
| La Bassee | 4156 | Mar. 27, 1919 | | |
| Embury | 4157 | Mar. 27, 1919 | | |
| Steele | 4158 | Mar. 27, 1919 | | |
| Swift Current Area | | | | |
| Flora | 4087 | Aug. 12, 1918 | W. S. Cram | Aug. 12, 1918 |
| Amphion | 4088 | Aug. 12, 1918 | W. S. Cram Board | Aug. 12, 1918 Feb. 4, 1922 |
| Clemenceau | 4089 | Aug. 12, 1918 | W. S. Cram | Aug. 12, 1918 |
| Flowerville | 4150 | Mar. 27, 1919 | W. S. Cram | Mar. 19, 1919 |
| Balfour | 4151 | Mar. 27, 1919 | | |
| Maharg | 4152 | Mar. 27, 1919 | | |
| Falkland | 4153 | Mar. 27, 1919 | No official trustee Board | Aug. 17, 1923 |
| Iris | 4154 | Mar. 27, 1919 | W. S. Cram | May 19, 1920 |
| Versailles | 4155 | Mar. 27, 1919 | W. S. Cram | May 17, 1920 |

Source: Report dated September 7, 1923, SAB, M 5, 6.

appoint such a committee.[153] That left Inspector Cram as the sole official trustee of the Mennonite districts in the Swift Current area. Education Minister Martin wondered whether that was appropriate.

> Of course there is the question of whether an inspector should be an official trustee or not. Generally speaking I think that he should not be but the Mennonite problem is one so different from other problems

## Map 9
## Hague Reserve Showing Reinländer School Districts

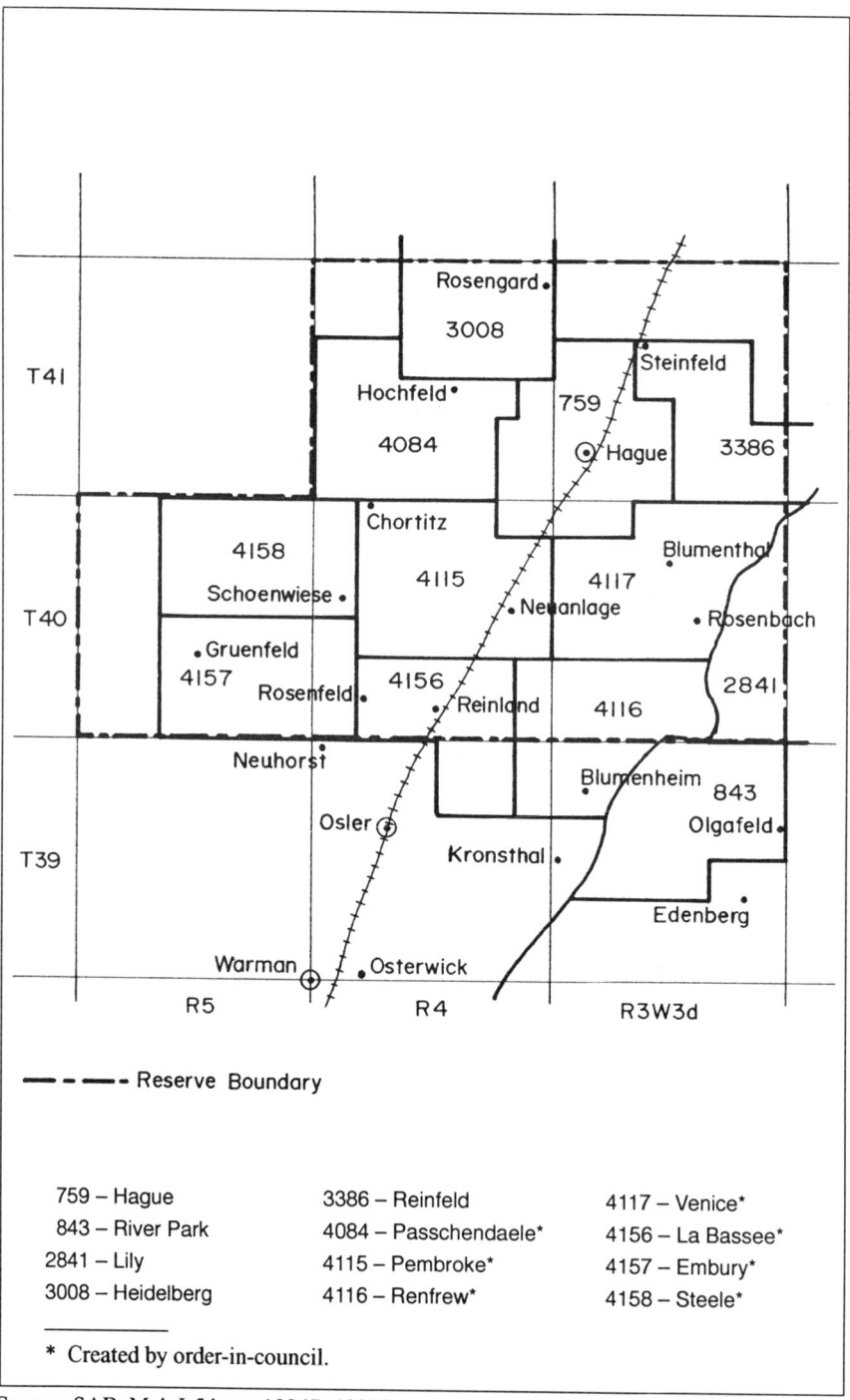

– – – Reserve Boundary

759 – Hague
843 – River Park
2841 – Lily
3008 – Heidelberg
3386 – Reinfeld
4084 – Passchendaele*
4115 – Pembroke*
4116 – Renfrew*
4117 – Venice*
4156 – La Bassee*
4157 – Embury*
4158 – Steele*

\* Created by order-in-council.

Source: SAB, M 4, I-54, pp. 18847, 18998.

# Map 10
## Swift Current Reserve Showing Reinländer School Districts

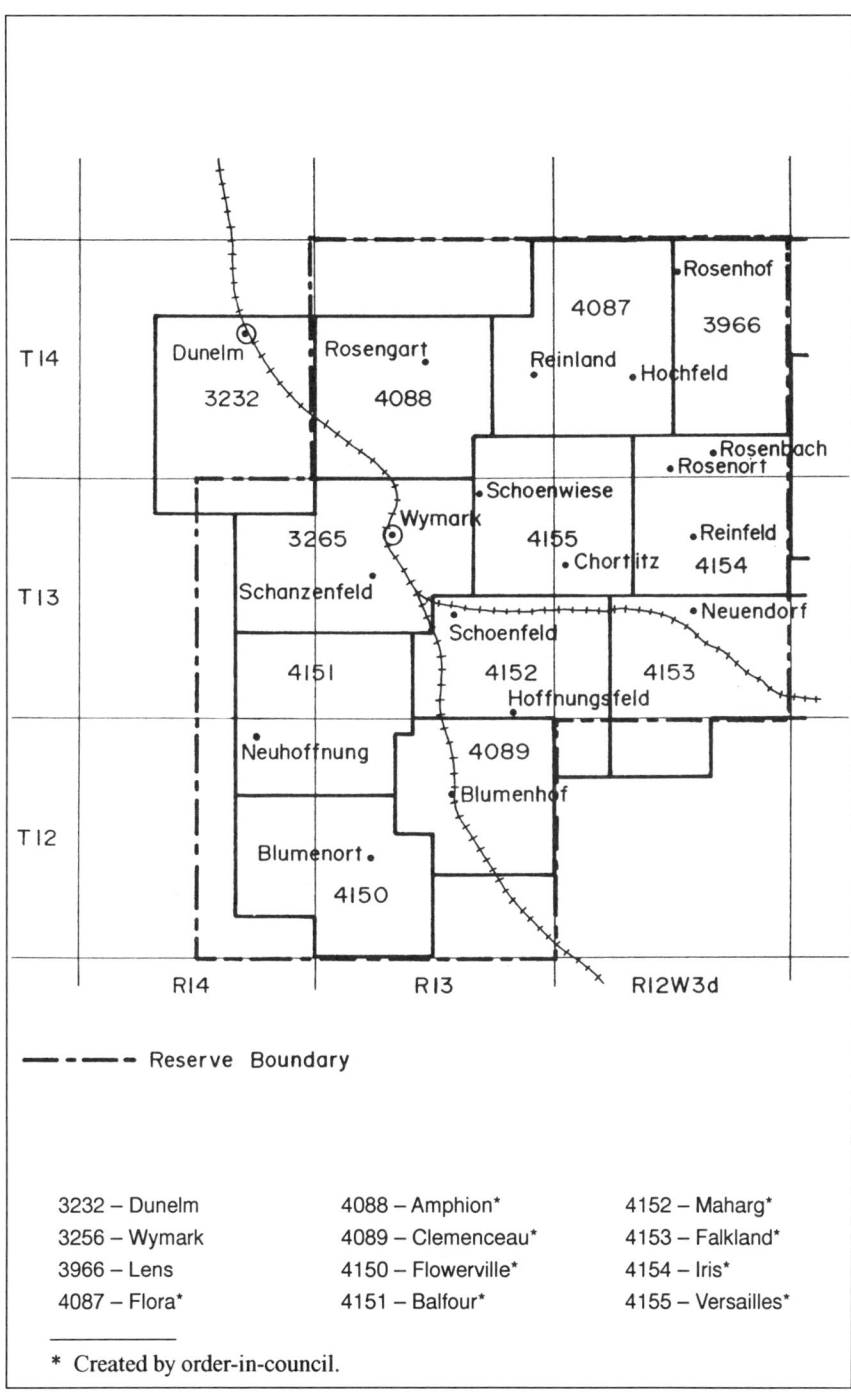

— - — - Reserve Boundary

3232 – Dunelm
3256 – Wymark
3966 – Lens
4087 – Flora*

4088 – Amphion*
4089 – Clemenceau*
4150 – Flowerville*
4151 – Balfour*

4152 – Maharg*
4153 – Falkland*
4154 – Iris*
4155 – Versailles*

\* Created by order-in-council.

Source: SAB, M 4, I-54, p. 18999.

that we have had to face that in this case we might very well depart from precedent.[154]

Cram responded quite sensitively to the Mennonite communities as official trustee, thereby raising new questions for the Department. As in Manitoba, some of the districts created in August 1918 included more than one village. This made it difficult to decide where to place the school buildings. He therefore suggested declaring each village a school district. "Schools should be placed where the children are," he argued.[155] As part of their passive resistance to the public schools, Mennonites in the new districts refused to sell land for the erection of school buildings. The official trustee then resorted to expropriation of school sites.[156] This naturally raised costs and Cram was anxious not to add unduly to the tax burden.[157]

Cram was able to open three new public schools in the Swift Current area during the summer and fall of 1919. In Amphion the school opened on July 14 with six children attending even though the teacher, Miss Moon, spoke only English. The returned serviceman who was appointed teacher in Flora had no pupils, although he spoke German as well as English.[158] Clemenceau school at Blumenhof opened on October 14 but also had no pupils.[159] Cram's choice of two young women and a returned soldier as the first three teachers to impose on the Reinländer community reflects a lack of sensitivity or of sensibleness. That a recent veteran would hardly be acceptable to a pacifist community was obvious. But Cram must also have known that teachers in Reinländer communities were not "slips of girls, but men of character and mature judgement."[160] The six children attending at Amphion were all from the Bergthal group; Reinländer resistance remained firm.[161]

Premier Martin visited Bishop Abram Wiebe of the Reinländer congregation at Swift Current during the summer of 1919 in an effort to enlist his co-operation.[162] When the Reinländer steadfastly refused even to give the names of their children, the government turned to police action and the use of the courts to enforce its laws.[163] By then it was also aware of the existence of a Reinländer delegation from Swift Current, Hague, and Manitoba appointed "to discover, if advisable, ways and means towards a new home elsewhere."[164]

## Compulsory Attendance: Boycott and Court Enforcement

Now that both Manitoba and Saskatchewan possessed compulsory attendance legislation, it was only a matter of time before this would be applied against Mennonite offenders. Sommerfelder parents in both provinces lived in some communities together with Mennonites who had accepted the public schools. Their children, who were attending private schools, could now be held to be in violation of the law if those private schools did not meet the government's standards.

In April 1918 prosecutions under the Act began in Saskatchewan, with fourteen Mennonites charged at Aberdeen, just outside of the Hague Reserve. By mid-May some fifty prosecutions had been registered in Saskatchewan.[165] In July several (probably Reinländer) families, who were part of the non-Mennonite school district of Dunelm on the edge of the Swift Current Reserve, were fined for sending their children to their own private school instead of the public school.[166] Before appearing in court they sent a delegation to Regina asking for a postponement in the enforcing of the Act at least until the next spring. In September 1918 eleven Mennonite families in the formerly non-Mennonite school district of Wakeham, Manitoba, were fined for not sending their children to the public school maintained in operation by the government's official trustee.[167]

In November the Reinländer congregation in Saskatchewan forbade its members to pay fines. Eleven men of the Swift Current area, convicted under the Act on November 30 and fined one dollar and costs in each case, refused to pay and were sent to Regina to serve ten days in jail. The press interpreted this as a defiance of the government.[168] The *Swift Current Sun* called for more severe legislation, including a provision by which the prosecution could "put the church heads in the coop as well as the other fellows."[169] The government, however, moved in the other direction and decided in early 1919 that no more jail sentences would be imposed on those who incurred penalties under the School Attendance Act. Instead of being allowed to "pose as martyrs for their religion," Mennonite offenders would have their goods and chattels seized to pay the fine. The *Sun* now considered this a wise move on the part of the government.[170]

All Mennonite groups resisting government schools based their action on clause 10 of the 1873 agreement with Ottawa. The Reverend J. P. Wall of Hague took this position before a justice of the peace in the spring of 1918.[171] A petition to Ottawa from the Mennonites around Swift Current in May of the same year also quoted this clause.[172] In the Wakeham case referred to earlier, magistrates Noble of Winnipeg and Milne of Morden had ruled that plea irrelevant since the provinces enjoyed full control of education by the provisions of the British North America Act.[173] Justice of the Peace J. E. Hemenway, in a trial at Swift Current in November 1918, "pointed out that he had nothing to do with the Treaty of 1873 as he was dealing with the Saskatchewan School Attendance Act alone." But he advised the Mennonites that they had the right of appeal from his decision.[174] By May 1919 it was reported that the Swift Current Mennonites were planning to carry such an appeal to the Supreme Court of Canada.[175]

It was the Sommerfelder of Manitoba, however, who launched an appeal.[176] In July 1919 the Manitoba Department of Education laid nine charges against Mennonite parents of the Houston School District for violations of the School Attendance Act.[177] Since this was to be made into a test case, the government was represented by H. J. Symington and Archie Campbell, with the defence being conducted by A. E. Hoskin and J. T. Haig. Magistrate C. C. Milne of Morden presided at the law courts in Winnipeg.[178] The defence argued that

> by the Immigration Act of 1869, by the Act establishing the Department of Agriculture in 1868, and by the Act of British North America, immigration was placed under the control of the Federal Department of Agriculture. It was the duty of the Minister of Agriculture, in the Dominion Government, to carry out the order-in-council in respect to the Mennonites.[179]

The prosecution objected to the order-in-council on the grounds that there was no statutory power for the federal government to agree to its terms. In any case, the rights conferred on the Mennonites by the order-in-council were not in any way infringed on by the School Attendance Act, since the matter of language was not mentioned at all and since the Attendance Act did not interfere in any way with the teaching of religion.

The cases of two of the nine defendants, immigrant John Hildebrand and Manitoba-born Dietrich Doerksen, were chosen for appeal by the Mennonites.[180] Their case was argued before the Manitoba Court of Appeals on August 5, and dismissed by a unanimous decision of the four Justices hearing the evidence.[181] In its decision the Court addressed three key questions: (a) Did the government of Manitoba have the power to pass its School Attendance Act of 1916? (b) If so, was this Act binding upon the accused, John Hildebrand, a Mennonite who had come to this country from Russia about 1874? (c) Did the Manitoba government have the power to legislate as to schools, school attendance, or education insofar as the Mennonites coming from Russia were concerned? The answer to all three questions was affirmative.[182]

The Mennonites had in their possession only the July 26, 1873, letter from John Lowe, and always quoted it as their *Privilegium*. Clause 10 read:

> The fullest privilege of exercising their religious principles is by law afforded to the Mennonites, without any kind of molestation or restriction whatever; and the same privilege extends to the education of their children in schools.

Counsel for the province in turn quoted from the corresponding order-in-council of August 13, 1873, in which clause 10 read:

> that the Mennonites will have the fullest privilege of exercising their religious principles, and educating their children in schools, as provided by law, without any kind of molestation or restriction whatever.

Justice Cameron in his written judgment drew attention to the difference between these two readings, particularly to the phrase "as provided by law," not found in Lowe's letter. He then interpreted the clause as follows:

> What it means is that the Mennonites are to have the unhampered and unrestricted privilege of educating their children in the schools provided by the laws of the country in which they proposed to settle. In my judgement this undertaking is in no wise interfered with by the compulsory provisions of the Act in question, and we are left to conjecture what the real motive may be that underlies the opposition to that beneficial legislation.

The court held that "Mr. Lowe's letter must be taken as merged" in the August 13 order-in-council. The difference in wording between the two was, in fact, irrelevant, because section 22 of the Manitoba Act provided that "in and for the province the said legislature may exclusively make laws in relation to education."[183]

> Nothing can be plainer. The Dominion Parliament itself could and can pass no legislation affecting education in this province save in the circumstances indicated in sub-sections 2 and 3 of Section 22, which have absolutely no application here; and if that cannot be done by a Statute of Canada, how is it possible that it could be accomplished by an order of the Governor-General-in-Council, or by the letter of an official of the department of the Dominion Government?

Both versions of clause 10 were, according to this ruling, worthless "scraps of paper." Arguments about differences in wording between them or about their relative legality are thus irrelevant. Nevertheless, the discovery that there were two versions of the *Privilegium*, which in the key tenth clause contained significantly different wording, has led to a kind of "conspiracy theory" among later interpreters.

Hildebrand sees the government's action of 1873 as substituting the August 13 order-in-council for a document of the same status, which it had given the Mennonite delegates on July 26, and then keeping the Mennonites unaware of the official one until the court process of August 1919.[184] Francis considers clause 10 of Lowe's letter "a definite misrepresentation" in that the Department of Agriculture "deliberately or unconsciously failed to mention the fact that under the provisions of the British North America Act jurisdiction over schools was reserved to the individual provinces." The "legal inaccuracies" of Lowe's letter, Francis continues, had been "quickly discovered" and altered in the Minister's July 28 submission to the Privy Council. The August 13 order-in-council was marked "secret" and

> thus remained unknown to the public for forty-five years, so that the Mennonites were made to believe that Lowe's wording was the official

one. This devious procedure was the direct cause of the serious conflicts which later on arose with the Manitoba school question.[185]

Bergen also considers the differences in the phrasing of clause 10 between the Lowe letter and the order-in-council significant, and goes to some length to ascertain that the Mennonites had indeed not been informed of the change.[186] Friesen holds that the latter part of the tenth clause of Lowe's letter was invalid to begin with, and contends that the addition of the four words "as provided by law" voided the whole article of its previous meaning. He also stresses the fact that the order-in-council was kept secret and that the Mennonites had no knowledge of the difference between it and the letter handed to them by Lowe.[187]

Gerbrandt implies that only the wording of privilege no. 10 was kept secret from the Mennonites. He then makes matters worse by assuming that Lowe had at hand the official wording of the later order-in-council when he wrote his letter on July 26, and that he was therefore aware of the phrase "as provided by law" in the order-in-council. He adds:

> Apparently Lowe purposely slipped over this important point and the Mennonites did not know until many years later that they only received the privilege of educating their children in schools, as provided by law.... The "privileges," in fact, gave the Mennonites no special protection. All other immigrants also had the right to have their children educated in schools as provided by law, the law of the province in which they would be residing.[188]

Epp notes that it was outside of federal jurisdiction to give the Mennonites the right to educate their own children. The inclusion of this clause

> in the federal offer led to very serious misunderstanding in years to come. Three days after the Privilegium had been handed over, John Pope, Minister of Agriculture, eliminated the education provision from the official document, having recognized its legal discrepancies. The document was placed before the cabinet for approval without advising the Mennonites of the change.[189]

There is very little foundation for this "conspiracy theory." The reasons for marking the August 13 order-in-council "secret" had nothing whatever to do with the change in the wording of clause 10. As has been shown in chapter 1 under "Negotiating a *Privilegium*," it was done in direct response to British diplomatic fear about the consequences of premature Canadian governmental negotiation with the Russian Mennonites. Once the 1873 order-in-council had been brought back into circulation by the Deputy Minister of Agriculture on March 3, 1916, the government certainly made no effort to keep it from the Mennonites.[190] Before the end of the month, John P. Wall, chief government contact person of the Saskatchewan Reinländer, was provided with the full text of clause 10 of the order-in-council, and his attention was drawn to the words "as provided by law" and to their possible significance.[191]

When the Military Service Act of 1917 was before Parliament, the 1873 order-in-council became the basis of Mennonite exemption and was accordingly tabled in the House of Commons by Arthur Meighen.[192] This made it so much of a public document that by 1918 individual Mennonites in Nebraska and Kansas, as well as at least four branches of the Mennonite church in Saskatchewan, were aware of it or even had possession of copies of it.[193] There was thus no conspiracy to keep the order-in-council secret from the Mennonites.

It is equally unlikely that Lowe, or the Department of Agriculture, was deliberately trying to deceive the Mennonites on the point of educational freedom. It is much more likely that both were trying to offer to the Mennonites "an authoritative interpretation of the existing laws of the Dominion."[194] In 1873 in Manitoba the law provided for confessional schools to operate "without any kind of molestation or restriction whatever." Indeed, the debates in Parliament and the arguments in the courts from 1890 to 1896 revealed that many, especially among the Ottawa Conservatives, who had drafted the Manitoba Act in 1870 and had negotiated with the Mennonites three years later, were convinced that such educational freedom was incorporated into the very constitution of Manitoba.

Lowe and the federal government thus acted in good faith when they offered Mennonites assurance of the right to denominational schools. Cameron and the Canadian court system, however, were no longer free to make such a legal interpretation in 1919. Although that understanding had been unanimously endorsed by Canada's Supreme Court on October 28, 1891 in the Catholic challenge of the Manitoba School Act of 1890, it was overturned by the Judicial Committee of the Privy Council in London, England, in 1892.[195] Cameron's verdict in 1919 was thus virtually a foregone conclusion.

The Manitoba Mennonites nevertheless decided to pursue their case through the entire legal route. The August 1919 decision of the Manitoba Court of Appeal was accordingly taken to the Judicial Committee of the Privy Council. Almost a year later, in July 1920, that body announced its decision.[196] By refusing to grant leave to appeal against the judgment of the Manitoba Court, it gave full legal sanction to the Manitoba legislation of 1916. It also confirmed that Mennonites were subject to the School Attendance Act in spite of clause 10 of their *Privilegium*.

Although the Manitoba Department of Education was now legally armed to force Mennonite acceptance of its schools, it apparently acted with restraint. Dawson refers to "an epidemic of fining" in Manitoba during

1920 and 1921, and mentions that a half dozen Mennonite preachers were jailed for a time at Winnipeg.[197] Former inspectors Ewert and Willows also speak of fines and imprisonment being imposed, but not in a wholesale way.[198] There are scattered reports of prosecutions in the press, but they do not suggest "an unbending policy of coercion."[199]

Even without extensive court enforcement, the Department was making some progress toward its goal. Near the end of 1919 Greenway was able to resign as official trustee from three school districts in the Bergthal–Sommerfeld area of the West Reserve, to be replaced by local trustees.[200] In other districts tension continued, with both public school and private school teachers attempting to occupy the same building or with two schools dividing community loyalties.[201] They also divided the income of parents, who now paid taxes for the district school, levies for the private school, and fines for non-attendance at the former.

In the Reinländer communities on the West Reserve the boycott of the new public school districts was maintained with tenacity. As in the Swift Current communities, Mennonites refused to sell land or building materials to Greenway, forcing the Department to expropriate school building sites and to bring in building supplies from Winnipeg.[202] In view of this opposition and of the announced emigration plans of the Reinländer Mennonites, which would probably result in the break-up of the existing villages if carried out, the Department decided in 1920 to defer the location of school sites in these new districts.[203] Two years later Inspector Finn was able to report six of these new districts in operation, although two of them had zero enrolment.[204] In the spring of 1922 the Reinländer emigration to Mexico began, making it possible for many of their members to maintain the boycott of the public schools to the end of their stay in Canada. Prosecutions under the Attendance Act seem to have been suspended in 1924 in view of the emigration in progress.[205]

The Chortitzer congregation on the East Reserve also resisted the *Zwangsschulen*. In the summer of 1919, after public school districts had been created in its communities by order-in-council, a delegation visited the Minister of Education to explain their situation and to ask to be able to retain their own schools.[206] Since Dr. Thornton gave them no satisfactory reply, they made arrangements for another audience with the government at which Agriculture Minister Winkler, who spoke German, would also be present. This second delegation, which also included representatives from the *Kleine Gemeinde*, met with Premier Norris and five of his ministers, including Winkler and Education Minister Thornton, in October.[207] In response to their request to retain their own schools, Thornton assured them that the 1916 school legislation applied to all Manitoba residents. It was indeed possible to continue private schools, but only if the children attending them were educated in English up to the Department's standard. Since, in his judgment, the Mennonites in Hanover had not met these conditions, the School Attendance Act had to be applied by the government.[208]

In a further petition in early 1920 the Chortitzer announced that they were now prepared to accept the Department's standards and to introduce instruction in English in their schools. They were anxious, however, to make this transition with their own teachers and hence asked the co-operation of the Department during the interval when some of these teachers would not yet fully meet government qualifications.[209] Thornton had by now had a measure of success in his own program of converting the area into functioning public school districts, and was unwilling to wait for the upgrading of the Chortitzer private schools.[210] E. K. Francis correctly perceived that

> it was no more a question of educational standards which prompted the authorities to destroy [the parochial schools] once and for all, and to replace them with English public schools. It was part of a consistent national policy aimed at the assimilation of ethnics to safeguard national unity and cultural uniformity.[211]

With this seeming impasse in their attempts to work out an acceptable form of co-operation with the Department of Education, the Chortitzer and Sommerfelder began to give serious consideration to the possibility of emigrating. A large joint meeting in September 1920 decided to make one more approach to the government. A brief, signed by the bishops and ministers of both churches, was presented to the Norris government in October. After reiterating the earlier pleas to be allowed their own schools, the statement announced that emigration was the only alternative.[212] Thus, for the Chortitzer also, continuing boycott of the public schools was strengthened by the hope of leaving. But since their emigration was delayed until 1926, the resistance of many was worn down before the actual move could take place.

The Saskatchewan government acted much more decisively. When Reinländer Mennonites of the Swift Current Reserve boycotted the newly opened public schools in their communities in the summer of 1919, Premier Martin instructed the provincial police to issue a summons against every family in the districts involved.[213] Within a month seventeen offending parents had been fined, eight in Flora School District and nine in Amphion.[214] The eight Flora ratepayers sentenced refused to pay the fine, so distress warrants were issued to cover the amount of the fine and costs. Three horses, a hog, and five cured hams were seized by the police and sold at a public auction in Wymark on November 6. The total proceeds of $129.50 were not enough to pay the assessed costs.[215] A second auction at Swift Current brought better prices for the five cows, two heifers, and two horses seized by the police.[216]

At least twenty-eight more men were fined in three separate court actions during the balance of 1919. Some paid their fines, while others refused to do so. Most of them refused to promise to send their children to the public school.[217] The idea of appealing any of these court sentences by Saskatchewan Mennonites was dropped when the Manitoba Court of Appeals handed down its ruling in August 1919. Inspector Cram drove the point home to the Swift Current area Mennonite parents in January 1920:

> There is no doubt that if the School Attendance Act of the Province of Manitoba is binding on the Mennonites of that province, the School Attendance Act of the Province of Saskatchewan is binding on the Mennonites in this province.[218]

The Reinländer Mennonites of the Swift Current area were so incensed at the government over its handling of the education matter, that they refused to accept any seed grain or other relief from municipal officials.[219] Inspector Cram, on the other hand, felt that the problem had been handled well by the police. "The first steps represent the problem in its most awkward stages," he remarked philosophically.[220] Others were not as detached. W. W. Cooper of Swift Current warned Premier Martin that "there are a number of the families being reduced to destitution through the fines being imposed upon them."[221]

Cooper proposed, on behalf of a Mennonite delegation from the Swift Current community, that the School Attendance Act not be enforced for two years to give families intending to emigrate an opportunity to get away. The Mennonite land-seeking delegation was on its way home from Brazil.[222] Premier Martin, however, had determined on a firm course of action and would not agree to exempting the Mennonites from the school law "because it would have a most detrimental effect on certain other people that we have in the province."[223] The government was backed in this tough position by groups such as the Great War Veterans' Association, whose Swift Current branch on October 8 passed a resolution supporting compulsory attendance enforcement because "we are convinced that the only method by which these groups and sects can be Canadianized is by inculcation in the schools through the English language the elementary principles of freedom and democracy we enjoy."[224] Martin also had support for this course of action from his Department's Director of Education among New Canadians, J. T. M. Anderson, M.A., LL.B., D. Paed. After a very satisfactory meeting with twenty-three Mennonites in River Park School he condescendingly reported: "I cannot but feel that these Mennonites are after all human like ourselves and will respond to firm but just and fair treatment." He then went on to recommend keeping up the enforcement of the School Attendance Act.[225]

Another approach toward alleviating the Mennonite problem was suggested by Inspector Cram. It consisted of either some form of licence system for private institutions or some clauses in the School Act itself having reference to private institutions and the directors of such institutions.[226] That option had already been considered and rejected by Premier Martin. He questioned very much "whether any law with respect to private schools would simplify our difficulties among the Old Colony people."[227]

The government therefore decided to continue its policy of relentless prosecution of offenders against the School Attendance Act. A summary of the action for 1920 and 1921 is given in table 10. It includes the much publicized case at Hague in March 1921 where sixty Mennonites were assessed fines amounting to one thousand dollars and one was sentenced to thirty days in Prince Albert jail.[228] If court costs are added to the fines, the total paid in 1920–1921 came to about $26,000. This amount may be compared with the $65,000 Greenway raised 1919–1921 for the erection of school and teacherage buildings for twelve new districts in Manitoba (see table 7). That meant that the Saskatchewan public school resisters paid in fines over two years approximately forty percent of what the Manitoba resistors would repay in loans over the next twenty years. For the Reinländer Mennonites, who as a congregation and on principle opposed the public schools, this continuous prosecution presented a dilemma.

> If we send our children to public schools, we violate God's commands in not holding to that which we promised our God and Saviour at holy baptism. If we do not send them, we offend against your laws. Does Mr. Martin want us to transgress against God's commands in order to keep his? ... Oh how difficult it is to be a true Mennonite! ... And we came here precisely because of the freedom which the government promised us in full.[229]

The letter went on to quote Romans 13:1 and added: "We want to be subject to the authorities. But you must also allow us our rights ['das Unsere lassen']. If you force us to violate our teaching, who will then bear the punishment?"

The heart of the dilemma was focussed more sharply by barrister H. Vogt, who had already earlier interceded for the Swift Current Reinländer. For them, Vogt wrote, "the school is the church" and "if the school is changed the church is changed." Their objection was not to the English language but to the system the government was attempting to force on them, whose objective they perceived as seeking "to change the church principles even so far as the military question is concerned."[230] Vogt then proposed that the government give the Reinländer Mennonites their own school system provided they would undertake to give the children a knowledge of the English language up to the required standard.

Premier Martin felt that a reasonable agreement could be made "with the people themselves" but did not think that the leaders would allow it.

## Table 10
### School Attendance Prosecutions in Mennonite Districts, Saskatchewan, 1920 and 1921

|  | 1920 | 1921 |
|---|---|---|
| Number of schools | 25 | 20 |
| Number of cases | 1,131 | 1,804[a] |
| Number fined | 874 | 1,472[a] |
| Amount of fines | $7,834 | $13,150 |
| Number dismissed | 76 | 133 |
| Number pending | 43 | 70 |
| Number sent to jail | 6 | 6 |
| Number cancelled | 5 | — |

a. Latta to R. S. Thornton, Minister of Education, Manitoba, March 6, 1922, indicates 2,018 cases referred to the police in 1921 and adds $4,823.80 in court costs to the amount collected in fines.

Source: A. H. Ball to S. J. Latta, Minister of Education, December 6, 1921. SAB, M 5, 6(2).

Vogt, who had a branch office in Wymark, pursued his idea with the church leaders and found that they were prepared to teach English as long as they could train their own teachers, run their own system (the government system being too militaristic and "not good enough to raise Christians"), and keep up their own language. He recommended that the government pursue this idea and bring in H. H. Ewert from Manitoba to help implement the new arrangement. The Premier, however, was convinced that the Mennonites would not agree to use the authorized textbooks and so the idea died.[231]

Some Mennonites who had accepted the public school system continued to have their problems with it. The required physical exercises seemed quite militaristic and some parents wanted their children exempted from them.[232] In spite of some good reasons for granting this request, Premier Martin dismissed it with the argument:

> Physical drill is surely a good thing for children. It has nothing whatever to do with military training and it appears to me to be impossible to change the course of work in our schools in every case where some individual happens to object to it. If we were to pursue this policy the Province over, it would be very difficult to have any systematic course of instruction at all.[233]

Since government policy had obviously become quite inflexible, the Reinländer Mennonites pursued their plans to emigrate. By March 1920 they were negotiating the sale of their lands with a Saskatoon firm, which in turn put pressure on the government to suspend enforcement of the School Attendance Act for at least sixty days to allow the Mennonites to leave the country. Throughout the spring of 1920 the government stood firm in its refusal "to suspend the operation of an Act of the Legislature in this way."[234]

In May the Reinländer Mennonites of the Hague area agreed to give exclusive authority to J. P. Murphy and his Saskatoon company to sell their lands, comprising about 80,000 acres, on the condition that the provincial government would discontinue prosecutions under the School Attendance Act for the balance of 1920.[235]

About the same time the Swift Current Reinländer signed an agreement with barrister A. McWilliams of Swift Current to sell their land, comprising 106,000 acres. McWilliams now joined Murphy in seeking to persuade Premier Martin to suspend enforcement of the Attendance Act.[236] But it was not until January 1921 that the government showed any willingness to reconsider its position on this point.[237] In September, the Premier finally agreed that, in view of the Mennonites' agreement to sell and the purchasers' request to have them operate the farms in 1922, it would be "in the best interests of the Province" to enact a special measure exempting the townships in question from the operation of the School Attendance Act.[238]

When the Hague Reinländer sold their land to the Union Liberty Company of Winnipeg on October 10, Education Minister Latta instructed his staff to draft "an Act to exempt the Old Colony Mennonites from the School Attendance Act."[239] In fact, Deputy Minister Ball had already early in October advised the inspector of the Hague area to suspend any further investigations or prosecutions against Mennonites in his inspectorate.[240]

The threatened emigration of large numbers of Mennonites brought a warning to the government from a Saskatoon businessman. A. J. E. Sumner felt that the country, and particularly the West, could not afford the loss of many of "the best farmers Canada possesses." He asked the government to have patience—"twenty-five years in the history of a nation are nothing"—and urged an "earnest impartial non-political concentration of purpose" to solve the impasse.[241] Not satisfied with the Premier's curt response that no reasonable compromise was possible, Sumner pressed his point:

> I believe the reason the negotiations have failed is primarily due to lack of sympathy and failure to appreciate the deadly earnestness of these people by your colleagues and officials. There has been no change of attitude upon the part of the Mennonites, they are still endeavouring to carry out the tenets of their faith and creed, in identically the same way as when they were invited to the Dominion and which privilege they were told they could always enjoy.[242]

Martin remained unmoved by this plea, and since pressure on the government to resume prosecutions under the Attendance Act mounted, its truce with the Hague Mennonites proved to be a short one.[243]

Prosecutions in the Swift Current area continued uninterrupted. As table 11 shows, in 1922 this resulted in an average of slightly over four convictions per pupil enrolled. The pressure of that kind of prosecution through the courts moved the leaders of the Swift Current Reinländer to request once more that enforcement of the Attendance Act be suspended until they could leave the country.[244] But it did not happen. The decrease in prosecutions for 1923 indicated in table 11 resulted rather from the fact that the first groups of Reinländer left the Swift Current area for Mexico in March 1922. An estimated 1,200, well over one-third of the Reinländer group of the Swift Current Reserve, left the country over the next several years.[245] The rest eventually accepted the public schools.[246]

In the Hague area the resumption of law enforcement in 1922 showed that the Reinländer resistance to public schools there had not decreased. Table 12 compares the number of cases investigated or prosecuted during October 1921, when enforcement of the Attendance Act had been temporarily suspended, with the corresponding month in 1922.

The Hague group was not yet ready to emigrate in 1922. As a result, prosecutions there continued quite intensely for several years more. Table 13, which summarizes prosecutions for 1923 to 1925, shows that resistance was especially strong in the four school districts arbitrarily created by the Department.

Table 11
**School Attendance Prosecutions in Five Mennonite Districts, Swift Current Area, Saskatchewan, 1922 and 1923**

| | | 1922 | | | 1923 | | |
|---|---|---|---|---|---|---|---|
| District | District No. | Enrolment | Prosecutions | Convictions | Enrolment | Prosecutions | Convictions |
| Flora | 4087 | 26 | 87 | 75 | 12–18 | 22 | 22 |
| Amphion | 4088 | 26 | 45 | 16 | 22–24 | 6 | 4 |
| Clemenceau | 4089 | 17 | 197 | 167 | 21 | 122 | 117 |
| Versailles | 4155 | 20 | 59 | 51 | 29–33 | 12 | 6 |
| Iris | 4154 | 38 | 257 | 219 | 31 | 40 | 35 |
| Totals | | 127 | 645 | 528 | | 202 | 184 |

Source: Compiled for Education Minister S. J. Latta, SAB, M 5, 6(3).

Table 12
**Mennonite School Attendance Cases Sent to Provincial Police, Hague Area, Saskatchewan, October 1921 and 1922**

| District | District No. | Number of Cases October 1921 | October 1922 |
|---|---|---|---|
| Hague | 759 | – | 3 |
| River Park | 843 | 2 | 2 |
| Lily | 2841 | – | 4 |
| Heidelberg | 3008 | 1 | 4 |
| Reinfeld | 3386 | – | 6 |
| Passchendaele | 4084 | 10 | 59 |
| Pembroke | 4115 | – | 46 |
| Renfrew | 4116 | 1 | 21 |
| Venice | 4117 | 6 | 47 |
| Totals | | 20 | 192 |

Source: "Mennonite cases sent to Provincial Police for investigation and prosecution if necessary during the month of October 1921 and 1922," SAB, M 5, 6.

Table 13
**School Attendance Prosecutions in Six Mennonite Districts, Hague Area, 1923–1925**

| District | District No. | Number of Convictions |
|---|---|---|
| Hague | 759 | 38 |
| Reinfeld | 3386 | 34 |
| Passchendaele | 4084 | 278 |
| Pembroke | 4115 | 618 |
| Renfrew | 4116 | 165 |
| Venice | 4117 | 269 |
| Total | | 1,402 |

Source: A. H. Ball, Deputy Minister, to S. J. Latta, Minister of Education, SAB, M 5, 6(4).

In early 1923 the Reinländer of the Hague area appealed once more for a suspension of the Attendance Act, at least for a few years during which they could settle their affairs and emigrate. "Would you not be inclined to show your sympathy as well as the Russian government did, who granted [our forefathers] sufficient time in which they were free to carry out their move?" asked J. P. Wall.[247] Education Minister Latta was moved to sympathy for them, but was "powerless to do anything outside of that which the law says."[248]

## Table 14
### Summary of School Attendance Prosecutions of Saskatchewan Mennonites, 1918–1925

| Year | No. of Prosecutions | Source |
|---|---|---|
| 1918 | 61 | Press reports (incomplete) |
| 1919 | 56 | Press reports (incomplete) |
| 1920 | 1,131 | Table 10 |
| 1921 | 1,804 | Table 10 |
| 1922 | 645 | Table 11 (Swift Current only) |
| 1922 | 192 | Table 12 (Hague, October only) |
| 1923 | 202 | Table 11 (Swift Current only) |
| 1923–1925 | 1,402 | Table 13 (Hague only) |
| Total | 5,493 | |

Note: These figures are incomplete for the years 1918 and 1919, where the press search did not attempt to be exhaustive and where only those prosecutions, in which the actual number of defendants was reported, were tabulated. The 1922 figure for Hague covers only one month, and there are no figures for Swift Current for 1924–1925.

Deputy Minister Ball was also moved. In the summer of 1923 he observed that it was now six years since the School Attendance Act had come into force "and there has been no appreciable headway in the direction of getting into our schools the children of the Old Colony Mennonites." In his opinion the government "would be amply justified in attempting a compromise with the Mennonite leaders." He therefore suggested that the government allow traditional Mennonite instruction to take place in the afternoons with English school in the mornings, on the understanding that their teachers would gradually be upgraded in their qualifications. "Considerations of humanity almost compel an attempt at compromise."[249] But there was no compromise. Like their members in the Swift Current region, the Hague Reinländer solved the school problem partly by emigrating to Mexico,[250] partly by giving in to the government system. Some of those who remained continued to pay school fines regularly into the 1930s.[251]

Table 14 summarizes prosecutions of Saskatchewan Mennonites under the Attendance Act to 1925. In view of this record in Saskatchewan it is difficult to accept Dawson's claim that there

> the conflict was not so severe, since the Saskatchewan Old Colonists were not so completely sectarian in outlook as their Manitoba brethren. The Saskatchewan government, realizing the nature of the group with which it had to deal and the probable results of drastic action, was inclined to avoid a direct clash.[252]

Even less accurate is Weir's evaluation of the actions of the man who served as Premier from 1916 to 1922 and Minister of Education from 1916 to 1921:

> Hon. W. M. Martin ... refused to resort to strongarm methods of coercion, but with commendable foresight and almost inexhaustible patience adopted a policy of tolerance and enlightened firmness which finally won over all but the hopelessly obdurate old-colony reactionaries.[253]

The above evidence instead supports the conclusion, tentatively stated by Ewert in 1920 and by Friesen in 1934, that the clash in Saskatchewan was much more severe than it was in Manitoba.[254]

The reasons for this difference are not clear. On the one hand, Saskatchewan's "Mennonite problem" was much smaller than Manitoba's. In the fall of 1918 there were approximately thirty private and sixty public schools in the Mennonite areas in Saskatchewan compared to some eighty private and thirty public schools among the Mennonites in Manitoba.[255] On the other hand, the Manitoba Mennonites provided a more complete spectrum in their attitude to the public schools. The Reinländer and Chortitzer, with a combined membership of just under 3,000, maintained private schools exclusively. The Sommerfelder and *Kleine Gemeinde* groups, with a combined membership of just over 3,000, opposed public schools in principle but a good number of their communities accepted them in practice. The remaining four groups, with a total membership of slightly over 1,200, offered little or no resistance to the public schools. In Saskatchewan this latter group had almost 2,500 members and was even more favourably inclined to the public schools than its Manitoba counterpart. The Sommerfelder group, numbering fewer than 1,000 members, was scattered and so offered even less resistance to the public schools than the Manitoba Sommerfelder did. That left only the two Reinländer groups, with a combined membership of slightly over 2,000, who adamantly resisted the public schools in Saskatchewan.[256] Table 15 gives a summary of the various Mennonite groups in Manitoba and Saskatchewan together with membership statistics for 1917.

## The Petitions: Articulating the Issues

During the decade of the school struggle from 1916 to 1926, interaction with the two provincial governments was almost continuous and took a variety of forms. The Mennonite position in these encounters was articulated most clearly in the several briefs or petitions that were formally addressed either to the government or to the legislature. Although all of these have been referred to previously, they are listed in chronological order in table 16.

## Table 15
## Mennonite Groups in Manitoba and Saskatchewan, 1917

| Congregation | Area | Origin | Date | Population | Members |
|---|---|---|---|---|---|
| Reinländer | W. Reserve, MB | Russia | 1875 | 4,496 | 1,893 |
| | Hague, SK | Manitoba | 1895 | 3,068 | 1,135 |
| | Swift Current, SK | Manitoba | 1905 | 2,344 | 880 |
| Chortitzer | E. Reserve, MB | Russia | 1874 | 2,320 | 955 |
| Sommerfelder | W. Reserve, MB | Bergthaler split | 1890 | 6,452 | 2,692 |
| Bergthaler[a] | Herbert, SK | Manitoba | 1900 | 1,353[b] | 483[b] |
| | Rosthern, SK | Manitoba | 1902 | 1,332[b] | 475[b] |
| Kleine Gemeinde | E. Reserve, MB | Russia | 1874 | 837 | 307 |
| | Morris, MB | Russia | 1874 | 342 | 141 |
| Holdemann | E. Reserve, MB | Kleine Gemeinde | 1881 | 491 | 182 |
| | Morris, MB | split | | 87 | 44 |
| Bruderthaler | E. Reserve, MB | Kleine Gemeinde split | 1897 | 199 | 87 |
| | Rosthern, SK | U.S.A. | 1912 | | |
| Mennonite Brethren | W. Reserve and Winnipeg, MB | Manitoba revivals | 1893 | | 274 |
| | Rosthern, SK | U.S.A. | 1901 | | 774 |
| | Herbert, SK | Russia; U.S.A. | 1905 | | 505 |
| Krimmer M.B. | Rosthern, SK | U.S.A. | 1899 | | |
| M.B. in Christ | Alsack, SK | Alberta | 1910 | | |
| (Old) Mennonite | Guernsey, SK | Ontario; U.S.A. | 1905 | | |
| Canadian Conference (total members = 2,002) | | | | | |
| - Bergthaler | W. Reserve, MB | Russia | 1874 | 1,311 | 660 |
| - Rosenorter | Rosthern, SK | Russia; MB; Prussia; U.S.A. | 1891 | 1,510[b] | 668 |
| - Nordstern | Drake, SK | U.S.A. | 1906 | 286 | 155 |
| - Other | Rosthern, SK Lost River, SK | | | 961 | 519 |

a. Saskatchewan Bergthaler were similar to Manitoba Sommerfelder.
b. Extrapolated from data available for 1914–1916, 1918.

Source: Statistics compiled by B. Ewert, *Mitarbeiter*, February 1918, p. 8, and similar annual reports. Epp, *Mennonites in Canada*, pp. 317, 323.

Table 16
**Mennonite School Petitions to the Governments of Manitoba and Saskatchewan, 1916–1922**

| Group | Date | Presented to |
|---|---|---|
| MB Bergthaler–Sommerfelder | Jan. 7, 1916 | Hon. V. Winkler |
| All MB groups except Reinländer | Feb. 15, 1916 | MB government |
| MB Reinländer | Feb. 1919 | MB legislature |
| Chortitzer–*Kleine Gemeinde* | Oct. 21, 1919 | MB government |
| Chortitzer | Jan. 13, 1920 | MB government |
| Chortitzer–Sommerfelder | Oct. 14, 1921 | MB government |
| Swift Current Reinländer | Jan. 7, 1922 | SK government |

An analysis of the content of these official church statements shows that they have a number of points in common while they differ significantly on others. Since all of the Manitoba Mennonite groups are represented in these briefs, a brief summary of these points will help to see the spectrum of their positions in relation to the government on the issue of education.

First, all base their claim to educational "rights" on the *Privilegium*, the 1873 agreement between the Mennonite delegates and the Dominion government. All groups expect the government to keep its promise and honour its side of the agreement. The decision of the courts, that the provincial Departments of Education were not bound by clause 10 of the 1873 order-in-council, did not alter this basic position of the Mennonites.

Second, the briefs all agree that "as a matter of conscience [the Mennonites] cannot delegate to others the all important responsibility of educating their children."[257] The educational legislation of the provinces on the other hand, assumed, as a *Free Press* editorial put it: "The children are the children of the state of which they are destined to be citizens; and it is the duty of the state to see that they are properly educated." By that was meant "seeing that children are suitably educated to discharge the duties of citizenship."[258] In the context of World War I, this so clearly meant military participation that it was relatively easy for the Mennonites to reject this claim of the state.[259]

Third, all groups insisted that the right to teach religion in their schools was essential. Indeed, one of the reasons that the state was incapable of providing the child with a rounded education was the fact that it could not teach religion since it had none itself.[260] One brief emphasized the need to teach "both religious and secular truth as a part of one whole,"[261] while another stated that without religious instruction in the schools the Mennonite church could not survive.[262]

Instruction in the German mother tongue was considered essential only in the two briefs presented in 1916. Naturally, all Mennonite groups at this time were opposed to the elimination of German from the curriculum, since it was almost without exception still the sole language of the church. But the assertion that the Reinländer placed greater emphasis on the importance of German than the others is not substantiated in the briefs.[263] Only the brief of February 1916, which did not represent the Reinländer Mennonites, indicated that Mennonites would rather emigrate than lose the right of instruction in the mother language in their schools.[264] The Manitoba Reinländer brief of 1919 does not mention language at all, while the 1922 Swift Current petition explicitly says that the group was preparing to emigrate "not for the sake of language but for the sake of our religious grounds."[265] The Manitoba Reinländer bishop, Johann Friesen, made the same point: "The issue for us is not language; rather, we could impossibly allow our children to be shaped into proper citizens of this world under the flag and under a militarist ideology."[266]

While all the briefs emphasized the central role of the church and parents in the education of their children, only the Chortitzer, with mixed support from the Sommerfelder, and the Reinländer stressed that this meant retaining full control over their own schools.[267] The Bergthaler leadership took formal action in 1919 not to participate in a representation to the government planned by the Sommerfelder–Chortitzer at that time.[268] They, along with the Mennonite Brethren and *Kleine Gemeinde*, had already basically accepted the government-controlled public schools.[269]

In the nature of their appeal there is a significant difference among the briefs. The Manitoba Reinländer statement follows a clear theology of the state.

> We immigrated to this country wholly on account of having received the privileges given us by the government. And believing then as we do now that the word of the government is inviolate because the government is ordained of God, we started our own schools right from the beginning.[270]

In contrast to this Biblical basis for placing faith in the promises of government, the Bergthaler brief of January 1916 begins with a clearly political appeal.

> The majority of the Mennonites have so far put their confidence in the Liberal Party and have uninterruptedly sent a Liberal representative to the legislature. They would not like to be betrayed by the Liberal Party. If they were betrayed, they would feel so offended that they would cease to support the Liberal government.[271]

The non-voting Reinländer, of course, could not make such a threat. In keeping with their understanding of Romans 13, they clearly subjected themselves to the government "ordained of God," but for them that did not carry the implications of full citizenship.

## Notes

1. Lowe to David Klassen et al., 26 July 1873, NA, RG 15, vol. 1507, pp. 167–169.

2. Manitoba, *Statutes*, 1890, 53 Vic., chap. 38, sec. 8, 108(3).

3. Quoted in Lovell Clark, ed., *The Manitoba School Question: Majority Rule or Minority Rights?* (Toronto: Copp Clark, 1968), p. 102.

4. Morton, p. 187.

5. Ibid.

6. Hildebrand, p. 254, claims that their eight-point reform plan did not succeed at the time because of the government's preoccupation with abolishing the Legislative Council.

7. Gerald Friesen, *The Canadian Prairies. A History* (Toronto: University of Toronto Press, 1984), pp. 216–217.

8. Morton, pp. 241–250.

9. Dr. George Bryce offered his services to the government to help the Society find a new principal in Kansas. Hon. Joseph Martin to Premier Thomas Greenway, 17 August 1890, PAM, MG 13, E 1, p. 3204. Bryce had apparently been contacted for this purpose by Julius Siemens of Gretna who knew Ewert and was also acquainted with Bryce. Paul J. Schaefer, *Heinrich H. Ewert. Lehrer, Erzieher, und Prediger der Mennoniten. Züge aus seinem Leben und Wirken* (Gretna, Man.: Jugendorganisation der Mennoniten=Konferenz von Canada, 1945), pp. 46–47 (24–26). (Numbers in parentheses refer to the English translation by Ida Toews, *Heinrich H. Ewert. Teacher, Educator and Minister of the Mennonites* [Winnipeg: CMBC Publications, 1990]).

10. A. A. Taché, "Are the Public Schools of Manitoba the Continuation of the Protestant Schools of the Same Province?", pamphlet, 20 April 1893, quoted in Clark, p. 71. Since two Mennonites had served previously as inspectors of Mennonite schools, Ewert's position was not a completely new creation, even though his immediate predecessor, W. Thiem-White, had been a non-Mennonite.

11. John Schultz, Lieutenant Governor of Manitoba, to Prime Minister John Thompson, 28 December 1893, quoted in Margaret Scott MacGregor, *Some Letters from Archbishop Tache on the Manitoba School Question* (Toronto: by the author, 1967), p. 47.

12. Canada, Parliament, *Sessional Papers*, 1895, no. 20; quoted in Clark, p. 148.

13. *Manitoba Statutes*, 60 Vict., chap. 26.

14. Oscar Douglas Skelton, *Life and Letters of Sir Wilfrid Laurier*, ed., with an introduction by David M. L. Farr, Carleton Library no. 22, 2 vols. (Toronto: McClelland and Stewart, 1965), 2:8.

15. Schaefer, *Ewert*, p. 56 (31–32); Gerbrandt, p. 90.

16. The summary of events above is based largely on Gerbrandt, pp. 254–257, and Schaefer, *Ewert*, pp. 45–49 (23–27).

17. See, for example, *Mitarbeiter*, January 1907, pp. 28–29, for a list of thirty-four schools in Manitoba and four in Saskatchewan served by graduates of the Gretna school.

18. Schaefer, *Ewert*, p. 59 (34); Gerbrandt, p. 259; *MFP*, 6 February 1913, p. 3; Gerhard J. Ens, *"Die Schule muss sein." A History of the Mennonite Collegiate Institute* (Gretna: Mennonite Collegiate Institute, 1990), pp. 27–29.

19. Gerbrandt, pp. 259–274, gives a comprehensive summary of this unfortunate division.

20. *MFP*, 8 February 1913, p. 3; Gerbrandt, p. 268.

21. Manitoba, Legislative Assembly, *Sessional Papers*, 1892, no. 24, "Report of the Department of Education, Manitoba, for the Year Ending December 31, 1891," p. 143.

22. *MFP*, 6 February 1913, p. 3.

23. Manitoba, Legislative Assembly, *Sessional Papers*, 1903, no. 2, "Report of the Department of Education for the Year Ending December 31, 1902," p. 598.

24. Bergthaler Church, Ministerial, *Minutes*, 1893–1926, pp. 61, 76; 4 August 1902, 10 September 1904; MHCA, vol. 716. Bergthaler Church, Brotherhood, *Minutes*, 1901–1934, 4 December 1902, MHCA, vol. 715.

25. Schaefer, *Ewert*, p. 65 (40). The Bergthaler congregation leaders decided to make a joint representation with Mennonite Brethren representatives to the provincial government about Ewert's firing. Bergthaler Church, Ministerial, *Minutes*, p. 69, 14 September 1903, MHCA, vol. 716.

26. See their annual reports in "Report of the Department of Education" for 1904–1909. A typographical error on Friesen's first report, Manitoba, Legislative Assembly, *Sessional Papers*, 1907, no. 6, p. 390, identifies him as A. M. Friesen. The list of inspectors of Mennonite schools in *Gedenkfeier*, p. 85, perpetuates the error. Friesen obtained his teaching certificate at the Gretna school in 1900 and Graff in 1901. Mennonite Educational Institute, *Erster Katalog*, 1900.

27. For a brief biographical sketch, see Gerbrandt, pp. 155–156, and Gerhard I. Peters, *Remember Our Leaders. Conference of Mennonites in Canada 1902–1977* (Clearbrook, B.C.: Mennonite Historical Society of British Columbia, 1982), p. 2.

28. *Canadian Annual Review*, 1906, p. 448.

29. Ibid., p. 449.

30. *Mitarbeiter*, November 1906, pp. 12–13. Inspector J. M. Friesen expressed almost the same concerns in his 1907 report. Manitoba, Legislative Assembly, *Sessional Papers*, 1908, no. 8, pp. 498–499.

31. Ältester Peter Toews, Kleefeld, *Mitarbeiter*, December 1906, pp. 17–18.

32. Ältester Peter R. Dueck, Steinbach, *Mitarbeiter*, December 1906, p. 18.

33. Johann Gerbrandt, Nordstern Congregation, Humboldt, Saskatchewan, *Mitarbeiter*, February 1907, pp. 36–37.

34. Ibid., p. 36.

35. Jacob Hoeppner, *Mitarbeiter*, January 1907, pp. 29–30. The letter to Premier Roblin was dated 22 December 1906.

36. Johann M. Friesen, secretary, Bergthaler *Predigerkonferenz*, *Mitarbeiter*, March 1907, p. 47. Friesen was also inspector of schools.

37. Bergthaler Church, Brotherhood, *Minutes*, 11–13 November 1907, MHCA, vol. 715. *Mitarbeiter*, November 1907, pp. 9–10; December 1907, pp. 20, 23.

38. *Mitarbeiter*, January 1908, pp. 25–27.

39. *Mitarbeiter*, February 1908, pp. 36–37.

40. I. I. Friesen, pp. 107–108; *Gedenkfeier*, p. 89; *MFP*, 26 November 1910, p. 44. They included Rosenort no. 60, Rosenhof no. 61 (RM of Morris); Blumenort no. 62, Grünfeld no. 63, Blumenhof no. 64, Steinbach no. 65, Hochstadt no. 66, Greenland no. 893, Neuanlage (RM of Hanover); and Houston no. 214, Neu Kronsthal no. 1137 (RM of Rhineland).

41. The British, he wrote, did not view their flag in the way portrayed in patriotic German songs like *"Ich bin ein Preuße, kennt ihr meine Farben?"* or *"Die Wacht am Rhein."* *Mitarbeiter*, February 1908, p. 37.

42. Willows, p. 95. I. I. Friesen, p. 107, uses almost the same words, but adds that the Mennonites who thought this way "misunderstood the purpose of this Act."

43. *MFP*, 26 November 1910, p. 44.

44. *Morden Chronicle*, 16 January 1908, p. 4; 23 January 1908, p. 8.

45. Manitoba, Legislative Assembly, *Sessional Papers*, 1914, no. 2, "Report of the Department of Education for the Year Ending June 30, 1913," p. 176.

46. *MFP*, 21 January 1916, p. 1; Willows, p. 96. Bergen, "A Historical Study of Education," p. 97, lists the twenty-eight district schools in Rhineland Municipality, 1884–1926, giving the founding date of each.

47. Schaefer, *Ewert*, p. 80 (54).

48. Ibid., p. 82 (57). In later years reports of its annual meetings were carried in the *Mitarbeiter*.

49. Constitution of "The German-English Teachers' Association of Southern Manitoba," Object, 2, d., MHCA, vol. 544, no. 47.

50. *Mitarbeiter*, April 1913, p. 49; Schaefer, *Ewert*, p. 85 (60). *Mennonite Encyclopedia*, s.v. "Manitoba School Commission," by Cornelius Krahn, erroneously credits Ewert for the initiative in organizing the commission. A nine-point list of duties of the Commission is found in MHCA, vol. 544, no. 47. Ens, *Die Schule*, p. 100, sees the organizing of the Commission as a response to the *Free Press* campaign against bilingual schools.

51. *Mitarbeiter*, March 1914, pp. 43–45, reports on the delegation of 18 February and publishes the brief in German translation.

52. Ibid., May 1914, pp. 62–63.

53. Weidenhammer to Valentine Winkler, MLA, 17 May 1915, PAM, MG 14, B 45, box 2: Should the new Minister of Education "deem it advisable to enact a Compulsory Education law, my support is his through thick and thin."

54. Epp, *Mennonites in Canada*, p. 350.

55. Ibid., p. 351; Frank H. Epp, *Education with a Plus. The Story of Rosthern Junior College* (Waterloo: Conrad Press, 1975), pp. 13–14.

56. David Toews, "Einiges über die Ansiedlung bei Rosthern," *Mitarbeiter*, August 1907, p. 86.

57. T. W. Scott to W. F. A. Turgeon, 20 August 1908, SAB, M 1, IV-18d, p. 34536.

58. Scott to Education Minister J. A. Calder, 2 September 1908, SAB, M 1, IV-18d, p. 34537.

59. The one hundred pages of evidence of the Ford-McColl Commission of Inquiry are in SAB, RC M 28 and also in M 5, 6(1); copy in MHCA, vol. 2623. The Reinländer deputation that met with the Commission on 4 January 1909 consisted of John P. Wall, Hague, Rev. John Wall, Hague, and Mr. Overseer Klassen.

60. I. P. Friesen to Hon. Walter Scott, 20 January 1909, SAB, M 1, IV-18d, p. 34543; Friesen to J. A. Calder, Minister of Education, 20 January 1909, M 2, 18, p. 2892.

61. J. A.Calder to Mr. Barrett, 3 October 1910, M 2, 17, p. 2801.

62. H. V. Meyer, "Report re Organization Work in Mennonite Districts, in German Parochial Schools and in Hungarian and Roumanian Settlements," 1915, SAB, M 12, II-77, pp. 11444–50; also in M 4, I-50, pp. 17329–35.

63. SAB, M 12, II-77, p. 11445. See map 10.

64. W. B. Bashford, MLA, Rosthern, to W. Scott, Premier and Minister of Education, 13 September 1915, SAB, M 1, IV-18d, pp. 34645–46. Ratepayers of Hochfeld were sending their children to the private school instead of to the Heidelberg public school to which they belonged.

65. Scott to J. W. Brady, 8 September 1915, SAB, M 1, IV-18d, p. 34643.

66. David Toews, report in *Mitarbeiter*, February 1914, pp. 36–37.

67. H. V. Meyer, "Report," SAB, M 12, II-77, p. 11445.

68. Gerald Friesen, *The Canadian Prairies*, p. 241.

69. Quoted in Clark, p. 148.

70. J. T. M. Anderson, *The Education of the New Canadian. A Treatise on Canada's Greatest Educational Problem* (London and Toronto: J. M. Dent, 1918), p. 8.

71. "How Shall the Foreigners Govern Us?" *The Christian Guardian*, 23 February 1910, p. 8.

72. Ralph Connor, *The Foreigner. A Tale of Saskatchewan* (Toronto: The Westminster Company, 1909).

73. Harold W. Foght, *A Survey of Education in the Province of Saskatchewan, Canada. A Report to the Government of the Province of Saskatchewan* (Regina: King's printer, 1918), p. 147.

74. Ibid., pp. 15, 18.

75. Anderson, p. 9.

76. Ramsay Cook, *Canada and the French-Canadian Question*, quoted in Clark, p. 226.

77. Morton, *Manitoba*, p. 351.

78. *Morden Empire*, 26 January 1899, p. 4.

79. Dawson, pp. 103–104. C. B. Sissons, "The Mennonites of Western Canada," *The New Outlook*, 7 March 1928, made a similar observation: "When the war spirit got hold of the West, and to poor equipment were added the dual sins of pacifism and German speech, the patience of public and officials could no longer stand the strain. Recourse was had to compulsion." Quoted in Francis, *In Search of Utopia*, p. 180, n. 19.

80. Willows, pp. 96–97. V. Winkler to John D. Klassen, Secretary, Mennonite School Commission, Rosenfeld, 30 December 1915, PAM, MG 14, B 45, box 3.

81. MHCA, vol. 544, no. 47.

82. Ibid. The report of this meeting in the *Mitarbeiter*, January 1916, pp. 2–4, gives the eleven-point petition in German translation.

83. Benjamin Ewert to Hon. V. Winkler, 10 January 1916, PAM, MG 14, B 45, box 3.

84. Winkler to John D. Klassen, Secretary, Mennonite School Commission, 7 February 1916, PAM, MG 14, B 45, box 4.

85. *Mitarbeiter*, March 1916, pp. 1–4; Epp, *Mennonites in Canada*, p. 356.

86. The text of Ewert's brief is given in German in *Mitarbeiter*, March 1916, pp. 4–6; April 1916, pp. 1–2.

87. B. Ewert's brief in English and German is found in MHCA, vol. 544, no. 47. See also *Mitarbeiter*, April 1916, pp. 2–3.

88. *Mitarbeiter*, March 1916, p. 3.

89. *MFP*, 22 January 1916, p. 15.

90. *MFP*, 24 January, p. 7.

91. *MFP*, 26 January, p. 9.

92. H. H. Ewert, editorial, *Mitarbeiter*, February 1916, pp. 4–5: "*den engsten, beschränktesten Nativismus.*"

93. *Canadian Annual Review*, 1916, pp. 673–674, 676. Manitoba, Legislative Assembly, *Statutes*, 1916, 6 Geo. V, chap. 88, assented to 10 March 1916. A revised school attendance act, chap. 97, received assent on the same date.

94. *Mitarbeiter*, May 1916, p. 1.

95. Willows, pp. 96–97.

96. The meeting was called at the initiative of Sommerfelder bishop Abraham Doerksen. Bergthaler Church, Ministerial, *Minutes*, p. 147, 25 April 1916, MHCA, vol. 176. For reports on the proceedings of the 11 May 1916 meeting in Bergfeld, see *Mitarbeiter*, May 1916, pp. 1–3.

97. *Mitarbeiter*, June 1916, p. 3.

98. Bergthaler Church, Brotherhood, *Minutes*, 5 June 1916, MHCA, vol. 715.

99. Ibid., 26 June 1916. *Mitarbeiter*, July 1916, p. 3. MLA Valentine Winkler had already been informed of this move on 6 June 1916 by the Mennonite Brethren representative, P. H. Neufeld. PAM, MG 14, B 45, box 4.

100. Ewert, *Mitarbeiter*, July 1916, pp. 4–5.

101. Manitoba, Legislative Assembly, *Sessional Papers*, 1917, no. 2, "Report of the Department of Education for the Year Ending June 30, 1916," p. 369. In his M.A. thesis, p. 90, written eight years later, Willows is much less critical.

102. *Mitarbeiter*, August 1916, pp. 6–7. They were Edenthal, Halbstadt, Blumenthal, Reichenbach, Rosenheim, Kronsweide, Grünfarm, Edward, Rosefarm, and Steinreich.

103. Ibid., October 1916, p. 6.

104. Ibid., September 1916, p. 4.

105. Edmund H. Oliver, *The Country School in Non-English Speaking Communities in Saskatchewan* (Regina: Saskatchewan Public Education League, 1915), pp. 3, 9.

106. Deputy Minister of Education, to A. P. McNab, Minister of Public Works, 29 March 1916, SAB, M 12, II-36, p. 5375.

107. Ibid., p. 5376.

108. W. Scott, Minister of Education, to H. B. Wiebe, Herbert, 18 February 1916, SAB, M 1, IV-18, p. 34676.

109. Reinfeld S.D. passed a resolution to convert its school to private status, but the government did not agree. *Mitarbeiter*, October 1916, p. 6.

110. W. S. Cram, Inspector of Schools, to Deputy Minister of Education, 15 December 1916, SAB, M 4, I-54, p. 18835.

111. Francis, *In Search of Utopia*, p. 183; *MFP*, 11 May 1920, p. 15.

112. Editorial, *Mitarbeiter*, January 1918, p. 4.

113. J. D. Dyck and J. Giesbrecht, Councillors, and J. A. Klassen, Reeve, R.M. of Rhineland; Peter Bückert, Mayor, Town of Winkler; John Schwartz and J. E. Schwartz, Altona; petition to Hon. Valentine Winkler, 24 February 1918. The municipality solved that problem by appointing its reeve as School Attendance Officer. Winkler to R. S. Thornton, 1918, 13 March 1918. PAM, MG 14, B 45, box 5.

114. Order-in-Council no. 29601, 4 June 1918, PAM, MG 14, B 45, box 5. The districts were Glencross no. 71 and Wakeham no. 773, both originally English districts that had since been taken over by Mennonites, and Heabert no. 1282, north of the Mennonite reserve.

115. *MFP*, 25 September 1918, p. 11.

116. Greenway was appointed Supervisor of School Attendance for the province by Order-in-Council no. 25779, 17 March 1916, and served as Assistant Deputy Minister of Education since 1 September 1917. Order-in-Council no. 28546, 30 October 1917, PAM, RG 2, A 1. The wording of Order-in-Council no. 29748, 5 July 1918, is as follows:

> The Honourable the Minister of Education submits to Council a report setting forth
>
> WHEREAS the trustees of the S.D. of Edenburg Number 330, have notified the Department of Education that the ratepayers of the said District at a special meeting held on the 15th day of June, A.D. 1918, decided by a unanimous vote to have their school henceforth operated as a private school,
>
> AND WHEREAS the trustees of the said district have intimated to the Department that they have resigned as trustees,
>
> AND WHEREAS it is desirable that the public school in the said district be continued in operation under the provisions of the Public Schools Act,
>
> On the Recommendation of the Hon. the Minister, Committee advise
>
> THAT John Franklin Greenway be appointed Official Trustee of the said S.D. of Edenburg no. 330, as provided in section 269 of the Public Schools Act, this appointment to date from the date passing of the Order-in-Council.

The other orders-in-council listed in table 4 have similar wording.

117. Dr. R. S. Thornton, *Address to the Legislature of Manitoba, January 30th, 1920* (Winnipeg: Legislation Assembly of Manitoba, n.d.), p. 12, PAM, MG 14, B 36, no. 45.

118. Bergthaler Church, Ministerial, *Minutes*, 5 August 1918, 2:171, MHCA, vol. 716.

119. *MFP*, 25 September 1918, p. 11.

120. Ibid., 28 September 1918, p. 2.

121. Ibid., 12 February 1919, p. 13.

122. PAM, MG 14, B 45, box 6. The document is dated February 1919. It is reproduced in German in Walter Schmiedehaus, *Die Altkolonier-Mennoniten in Mexiko* (Winnipeg: CMBC Publications, 1982), pp. 9–15, and in English translation in Redekop, pp. 245–250.

123. *MFP*, 18 May 1920, p. 15. An unidentified insider reported the incident to the Reinländer leader, Johann P. Wall, Hague, Saskatchewan, 12 March 1919, MHCA, microfilm no. 66. Arrangements had been made with V. Winkler "that we should be advised when the Bill ... went before the Law Amendments Committee." But Winkler spent a day at the Brandon fair and "they had put the thing through when he was away... I do not know what my Liberal friends are coming to when they play this kind of game."

124. Order-in-Council no. 31208, 8 April 1919, PAM, RG 2, A 1.

125. C. G. Unruh, "The history of Goodwill S.D. #1967," p. 18, PAM, MG 9, D 41. The Grunthal private school continued to function until the spring of 1921. In January of that year a public school opened under the name of "Goodwill."

126. "Profile: James Gordon Fletcher," *University of Manitoba Financial Planner* (Spring 1993): 1, 4.

127. Erdman Nikkel et al. to J. F. Greenway, 1 April 1919, PAM, MG 14, B 45, box 6.

128. Greenway to Johann D. Klassen, 21 June 1919, PAM, MG 14, B 45, box 6.

129. Klassen to Winkler, 18 and 23 June 1919, PAM, MG 14, B 45, box 6.

130. J. A. Braun et al. to Hon. R. S. Thornton, Minister of Education, 2 May 1919, PAM, MG 14, B 45, box 6.

131. Ibid.

132. The "Memorandum of Agreement," 13 November 1919, between S.D. of Randolph no. 1964, and the Department of Education, signed by Greenway and Thornton, provided for a loan of $3,000 repayable in twenty annual instalments at six percent interest and was confirmed by Order-in-Council no. 32565 on 14 November 1919, PAM, RG 2, A 1, box 83. An identical agreement was made with the school district of Arran no. 1960.

133. The Saskatchewan School Trustees' Association on 2 March 1916 passed a resolution that regretted the large number of private schools in the province, "devised with the intent to defraud the child of a Canadian education," and urged the application of compulsory education or compulsory inspection by the Department of Education. Opposition leader W. B. Willoughby on 8 November 1916 urged that English should be "the sole language of instruction in schools." *Canadian Annual Review*, 1916, p. 727.

134. H. V. Meyer, Supervisor of School Districts among Germans, Hungarians and Roumanians, to R. F. Blacklock, Acting Deputy Minister of Education, 17 March 1917, SAB, M 4, I-50, p. 17324. Meyer passed on a suggestion from Neville barrister Henry Vogt that a committee of "higher" Mennonites be used by the Department to bring the new School Act into effect in the Reinländer areas.

135. Edwin S. Bartel, principal, Osler S.D. no. 1238 on 15 June 1917 reported to the Department of Education that the Reinländer Mennonites in the village of Neuhorst refused co-operation on the basis of their 1873 agreement with Ottawa. SAB, M 4, I-54, p. 18849.

136. W. M. Martin to Rev. Jacob Wiens, Hague, 23 April 1918, NA, MG 26, H 1(c), vol. 214, p. 121123.

137. Arthur Meighen, Minister of the Interior, Ottawa, to Rev. J. P. Wall, Hague, 14 May 1918, NA, MG 26, H 1(c), vol. 214, p. 121124.

138. Ibid., p. 121125.

139. Editorial, *Regina Morning Leader* (hereafter *RML*), 2 September 1918, p. 4.

140. The Foght report is found in SAB, M 4, I-62. The Reinländer Mennonites feared that the introduction of English would bring with it *Hochmut* (pride) and the gradual disintegration of the community spirit.

141. *RML*, 8 March 1918, p. 2. Some delegates cautioned the meeting not to ask the government to abrogate any treaty under which Mennonites had entered Canada. National obligations "must be held sacred and not treated as a scrap of paper."

142. *Canadian Annual Review*, 1918, p. 427.

143. Memo, [Premier Martin], to Mr. Blacklock, 21 March 1918, SAB M 4, I-54, p. 18851.

144. *RML*, 15 May 1918, p. 14.

145. *Swift Current Sun* (hereafter *SCSun*), 17 September 1918, p. 5.

146. The *RML*, 31 August 1918, p. 17, ran its headline "Department of Education deals drastically with the Mennonites" across the entire front page of its second news section. The *SCSun*, 16 August 1918, p. 1, was more subdued but gave the event front-page coverage.

147. Rev. J. P. Wall, to Hon. Arthur Meighen, 7 September 1918, NA, MG 26 H, 1(c), vol. 214, p. 121126. Wall wrote on behalf of the Reinländer groups of both the Hague and Swift Current areas.

148. C. B. Sissons, *Church and State in Canadian Education: An Historical Study* (Toronto: Ryerson, 1959), p. 293. Saskatchewan, *Statutes*, 1918–1919, chap. 48, sec. 14. French could be used in Grade 1 as the language of instruction where necessary. Agriculture Minister W. R. Motherwell so absolutely disapproved of this legislation that he resigned from the cabinet before it was passed. Motherwell to Sir Wilfrid Laurier, 13 December 1918, SAB, M 12, II-36, p. 5382.

149. W. M. Martin to Mrs. G. H. Smith, Education Secretary, I.O.D.E., 28 April 1919, SAB, M 4, I-62.

150. Deputy Minister of Education to Premier Martin, 20 March 1919, SAB, M 4, I-54, p. 18867.

151. Martin to D. J. Sykes, MLA for Swift Current, 22 April 1919, SAB, M 4, I-54, p. 18875.

152. Sykes to Martin, 3 May 1919, SAB, M 4, I-54, p. 18876; W. S. Cram, Inspector of Schools, to Martin, 9 May 1919, p. 18878. Sykes suggested that the GWV president might not be acceptable to the pacifist Mennonite communities.

153. Martin to Cram, 16 May 1919, SAB, M 4, I-54, p. 18881.

154. Martin to Cram, 18 August 1919, SAB, M 4, I-54, p. 18892.

155. Cram to Martin, 27 March 1919, SAB, M 4, I-54, p. 18869.

156. Report of W. S. Cram, Inspector and Official Trustee, 14 August 1919, SAB, M 4, I-54, p. 18889. Expropriation procedures were required in both Amphion S.D. no. 4088 and Clemenceau S.D. no. 4089.

157. Cram to Premier Martin, 10 February 1920, SAB, M 4, I-54, p. 18924.

158. Cram, Report, 14 August 1919, SAB, M 4, I-54, p. 18889. *RML*, 9 September 1919, p. 8; 25 September 1919, p. 9.

159. Lou Emmons, teacher, to Deputy Minister of Education, 4 November 1919, SAB, M 4, I-54, p. 18900.

160. C. B. Sissons, *Bilingual Schools in Canada* (London: J. M. Dent and Sons, 1917), p. 132.

161. Cram to Martin, 24 November 1919, SAB, M 4, I-54, p. 18908.

162. *RML*, 13 June 1919, p. 16.

163. Martin to Deputy Minister of Education Ball, 8 September 1919, SAB, M 4, I-54, p. 18898; Martin to Attorney General W. F. A. Turgeon, 9 September 1919, p. 18899.

164. Cram to Martin, 14 July 1919, SAB, M 4, I-54, p. 18909.

165. *RML*, 15 May 1918, p. 14. Reference has already been made to a few series of fines in the Hague area in the fall of 1915. Abraham Friesen, "Emigration in Mennonite History with Special Reference to the Conservative Mennonite Emigration from Canada to Mexico and South America after World War I" (M.A. thesis, University of Manitoba, 1960),

p. 58, errs in claiming that the first court action against Mennonites in regard to compulsory school attendance was in September 1918.

166. *SCSun*, 30 July 1918, p. 1.

167. *MFP*, 28 September 1918, p. 2.

168. *RML*, 2 December 1918, p. 9; *SCSun*, 3 December 1918, 13 December 1918, p. 1. Guenther, p. 14, mentions that his father was one of those jailed.

169. Editorial, 6 December 1918, p. 4.

170. Editorial, 4 February 1919, p. 2.

171. *RML*, 15 May 1918, p. 14.

172. Petition, Rev. Abram J. Peters et al., Dunelm, Saskatchewan, enclosed in W. D. Scott, Superintendent of Immigration, to W. W. Cory, Deputy Minister of the Interior, 4 May 1918, NA, RG 76, vol. 173, no. 58764-2. The Manitoba Chortitzer also appealed to this clause. William Jennings O'Neill to Hon. R. S. Thornton, 14 July 1919; quoted in J. H. Doerksen, p. 91.

173. *MFP*, 28 September 1918, p. 2.

174. *SCSun*, 3 December 1918.

175. Ibid., 2 May 1919, p. 1; *RML*, 3 May 1919, p. 39.

176. A. Friesen, p. 59, mistakenly claims that the appeal was made by the Old Colony, or Reinländer group, probably because he thought Houston S.D. was located near Morden, rather than its actual location in township 1-1E in the Sommerfeld-Bergthal area. I. I. Friesen, p. 125, is also under the impression that it was the Old Colony Mennonites who launched this appeal. Their conviction against initiating litigation, or even of defending themselves through the judicial process, would hardly have permitted such action.

177. *MFP*, 11 July 1919, p. 4.

178. Ibid., 17 July 1919, p. 1. Charges were read to the accused before magistrate Milne in Altona on 16 July and trial proceeded with at Winnipeg when the accused pleaded not guilty.

179. Ibid., 18 July 1919, p. 1.

180. Ibid., 29 July 1919, p. 5.

181. Ibid., 6 August 1919, p. 7. In fact, the court made its decision without even hearing counsel for the Province.

182. The entire text of the court's decision is found in *The Manitoba Reports* (Calgary: Law Society of Manitoba, 1921), 30: 149–154; also in Manitoba, Legislative Assembly, *Sessional Papers*, "Report of the Department of Education for the Year Ending June 30, 1919," pp. 149–154. *MFP*, 24 September 1919, p. 9; *SCSun*, 5 December 1919, p. 2; and I. I. Friesen, pp. 122–125, quote extensive portions. A. Friesen, pp. 59–62, has a lengthy summary.

183. 33 Victoria, chap. 3, confirmed by the Imperial Act, 34 and 35 Victoria, chap. 28.

184. Hildebrand, pp. 242–243, 338.

185. Francis, *In Search of Utopia*, pp. 47–49.

186. Bergen, "The Manitoba Mennonites," pp. 75, 135–136.

187. A. Friesen, pp. 27, 59.

188. Gerbrandt, pp. 59, 83.

189. Epp, *Mennonites in Canada*, pp. 192–193.

190. A notation on the original Privy Council minute, P.C. no. 957, 13 August 1873, indicates the date on which the first copy was made after it had been withdrawn from circulation on 22 August 1873; NA, RG 2, 1, vol. 283.

191. G. E. McCraney, House of Commons, to J. P. Wall, 29 March 1916, MHCA, microfilm no. 66. See also Arthur Meighen to Wall, 7 November 1916, NA, MG 26 H, 1(c), vol. 214, p. 121065.

192. Canada, Parliament, House of Commons, *Debates*, 1917, 4:3368–69.

193. W. D. Scott, Superintendent of Immigration, 24 October 1917, sent a copy to J. C. Koehn, Canadian Government Agent, Omaha, Nebraska. Koehn was wooing U.S. Mennonites to migrate to Canada. G. W. Giesbrecht, Montezuma, Kansas, 11 March 1918, requested a copy of the order-in-council from R. B. Bennett, Director General of National Service. NA, RG 76, vol. 173, no. 58764-1. The General Conference, Mennonite Brethren, Krimmer Mennonite Brethren, and Defenceless Mennonites attached a printed copy of the order-in-council to their 4 November 1918 petition to the Governor-General-in-Council. RG 2, 3, vol. 199, P.C. no. 2897/1918.

194. Francis, *In Search of Utopia*, p. 48.

195. Clarke, pp. 104–106.

196. *Winnipeg Evening Tribune*, 30 July 1920, p. 1. *MFP*, 3 August 1920, p. 11; *Canadian Annual Review*, 1920, p. 740. George W. Weir, *The Separate School Question in Canada* (Toronto: Ryerson, 1934), p. 107; *Gedenkfeier*, p. 89; and E. K. Francis, "The Mennonite School Problem in Manitoba, 1874-1919," *MQR* 27 (July 1953): 232; *In Search of Utopia*, p. 185, n. 30, gives the date as 30 July 1930. *Canadian Annual Review*, 1919, p. 548, and Abraham Friesen, p. 61, mention that the case was taken to the Canadian Supreme Court before it went to the Privy Council, but do not report its verdict.

197. Dawson, p. 105. A. Friesen, p. 90, talks of "wholesale prosecutions" against Mennonites in the Rhineland district. Isaak M. Dyck, *Auswanderung der Reinländer Mennoniten Gemeinde von Canada nach Mexico* (Cuauhtemoc, Mexico: Imprenta Colonial, 1970), p. 46, and David Harder, *Schule und Gemeinschaft. Erinnerungen des Dorfschullehrers* (Gretna, Man.: mimeographed by Jacob Rempel, 1969), p. 6, seem to know of only Rev. Peter Friesen, Schanzenfeld, among the Reinländer ministers to have been jailed. Henry J. Gerbrandt, *En Route. Memoirs. Hinjawäajis* (Winnipeg: CMBC Publications, 1994), p. 39, writing from a Sommerfelder perspective, also mentions imprisonments.

198. H. H. Ewert, *Mitarbeiter*, April 1920, pp. 26–27, 29–30: Willows, p. 97.

199. The expression is attributed to Official Trustee J. F. Greenway by the *Christian Science Monitor*, 12 October 1920, in connection with its report of five Mennonites being fined $20 and costs each under the Manitoba School Attendance Act. Fines imposed on Mennonite offenders are also reported for the Hamburg district, *MFP*, 25 March 1920, p. 1, and the Spencer and Goodwill districts, *MFP*, 22 June 1925, p. 5.

200. Amsterdam, Edenburg, and Kleinstadt. See tables 4 and 20.

201. *Mitarbeiter*, April 1920, p. 29, reports such difficulties in the West Reserve communities of Gnadenfeld, Silberfeld, and Grünthal.

202. *MFP*, 3 February 1920, p. 11; Dawson, p. 105.

203. Manitoba, Legislative Assembly, *Sessional Papers*, Department of Education, "Report for 1919–1920," p. 69.

204. Ibid., 1921–1922, p. 71. The districts in operation, with enrolment figures added, were Grimsby (28), Calder (15), Birkenhead (13), Exeter (4), Snowdon (0), Mersey (0). Actually, Snowdon, which was open for seventeen days in December 1921, had one

pupil. In the spring of 1922 it was open seventy-eight days with nine pupils (including two non-Mennonites) producing a total of sixty-six and one half pupil days. Zacharias, p. 259.

205. The *Morden Times*, 27 February 1924, p. 6, reports summons to one hundred and sixty Mennonites compared to some sixty the year before. Court to hear these cases was supposed to sit in Chortitz on 28 February but was postponed, apparently indefinitely. 3 March 1924, p. 6.

206. J. H. Doerksen, pp. 91–95, reproduces in German translation the letter of William Jennings O'Neill presented to Education Minister Thornton on 14 July 1919 in the presence of Bishop J. K. Dueck, Johann Braun, and H. Doerksen.

207. The petition in English of Johann K. Dueck, Jacob R. Dueck, Heinrich Doerksen, and H. R. Reimer, Niverville, to the Honourable Ministers of the Provincial Government, 21 October 1919, is found in Doerksen, pp. 95–96.

208. Doerksen, pp. 98–99.

209. This six-point petition of 13 January 1920 is reproduced in German without date or signatures, Doerksen, pp. 102–104. Quiring, *Russlanddeutsche suchen eine Heimat*, p. 34, claims that this statement was made by Rev. H. Derksen, Schöntal, in the name of the Chortitzer congregation but without its authorization. He also dates the first delegation 14 June and the second 8 October 1919 (p. 31). I. I. Friesen, appendix 17, reproduces a longer version of the petition in English, signed by Johann K. Driver [Dueck?] and nine others, including Heinrich Doerksen and probably five other ministers.

210. R. S. Thornton, Minister of Education, to T. J. Murray, 17 February 1920, reproduced in German by J. H. Doerksen, pp. 104–106.

211. Francis, "The Mennonite School Problem," p. 233.

212. J. H. Doerksen, pp. 107–109, reproduces in German this "Petition to the Provincial Government of Manitoba, submitted by the Sommerfelder Church, Altona district, and the Chortitzer Church, Niverville District," dated 14 October 1921, with twenty-one signatories. His chronology of closely related events, pp. 110–111, suggests that the date should be 1920. But I. I. Friesen, who has the petition in English with twenty signatories, appendix 18, also gives the date as 1921. So does Sawatzky, p. 26, n. 83.

213. *RML*, 25 September 1919, p. 9.

214. *SCSun*, 3 and 24 October 1919, p. 1; *RML*, 4 October 1919, p. 20. W. S. Cram, Inspector, to Premier Martin, 24 November 1919, SAB, M 4, I-54, p. 18908.

215. *SCSun*, 7 November 1919, p. 1.

216. Ibid., 21 November 1919, p. 1.

217. Ibid., 21 November 1919, p. 1 (eleven more fined); 19 December, p. 1 (eleven fined in Blumenhof); 30 December (six more fined).

218. W. S. Cram to Mennonite parents, 9 January 1920, quoted in I. I. Friesen, p. 136.

219. *SCSun*, 11 November 1919, 1.

220. Cram to Premier Martin, 18 November 1919, SAB, M 4, I-54, p. 18904.

221. Cooper to Martin, 22 November 1919, SAB, M 4, I-54, p. 18941.

222. This request had already been expressed to Inspector Cram in July, shortly after the delegation to South America left. Cram to Minister of Education, 14 August 1919, SAB, M 4, I-54, p. 18890.

223. Martin to Cooper, 24 November 1919, SAB, M 4, I-54, p. 18913.

224. *RML*, 15 October 1919, p. 16.

225. Anderson to W. M. Martin, 14 June 1919, SAB, M 4, I-56, p. 19115.

226. Cram to W. M. Martin, 18 November 1919, SAB, M 4, I-56, p. 18904.

227. Martin to Cram, 21 November 1919, SAB, M 4, I-56, p. 18906.

228. Dawson, p. 106; *Steinbach Post*, 31 March 1921; I. I. Friesen, p. 138.

229. Johann F. Peters, Neuanlage, to Premier Martin, 13 April 1920, SAB, M 4, I-54, p. 18941; translation mine; an "official" translation by N. Goldsmith is found p. 18943. Guenther, p. 14, describes the dilemma in very similar terms.

230. H. Vogt, Neville, to Premier Martin, 29 May 1920, SAB, M 4, I-54, p. 18955. For a brief biography of Vogt, see Harold J. Dyck, *Lawyers of Mennonite Background in Western Canada Before the Second World War* (Winnipeg: Legal Research Institute of the University of Manitoba, 1993), pp. 117–127.

231. Martin to Vogt, 7 June 1920, SAB, M 4, I-54, p. 18956; Vogt to Martin, 30 June 1920, p. 18957; Martin to Vogt, 3 July 1920, p. 18959.

232. Lt.-Col. J. McAughey, O.B.E., of Locke and McAughey, Barristers, Saskatoon, to Martin, 21 August 1920, on behalf of P. M. Friesen, SAB, M 4, I-54, p. 18964.

233. Martin to McAughey, 16 September 1920, SAB, M 4, I-54, p. 18970.

234. Premier W. M. Martin to J. P. Murphy, Saskatoon, 17 May 1920, SAB, M 4, I-54, p. 18950. Pressure had been put on the government in a steady stream of correspondence by Murphy and his partner, C. H. Johnson, since mid-March.

235. Jacob Wiens and eight others, Hague, to J. P. Murphy and W. J. Jauhlfs, Saskatoon, 8 May 1920, SAB, M 4, I-54, p. 18949.

236. W. S. Cram to Martin, 10 May 1921, SAB, M 4, I-54, p. 18987.

237. Martin to Murphy, 4 January 1921, SAB, M 4, I-54, p. 18918. He quickly pointed out however, "that we can give no assurance that the School Attendance Act will not be enforced." Martin to Murphy, 7 January 1921, p. 18922.

238. Memo, Premier Martin to S. J. Latta, Minister of Education, 23 September 1921, SAB, M 5, 6(2). "In the best interests of the Province" presumably meant to prevent the lands "from being overrun with noxious weeds," as Martin had written to Murphy on January 4.

239. Memo, Latta to Mr. Shannon, 21 October 1921, SAB, M 5, 6(2). A copy of the draft, dated 25 October 1921, is found with the memo.

240. S. H. Braund, Chief Attendance Officer, to Inspector E. L. J. Sparkman, 4 October 1921, SAB, M 5, 6(2).

241. A. J. E. Sumner of R. M. Buchanan Co. Ltd., Saskatoon, to Premier Martin, 29 November 1921, SAB, M 4, I-54, p. 18991.

242. Sumner to Martin, 9 December 1921, SAB, M 4, I-54, p. 18994.

243. A. H. Ball, Deputy Minister, to S. J. Latta, 6 December 1921, SAB, M 5, 6(2). Latta on 6 March 1922 assured R. S. Thornton that the Act was again being strictly enforced.

244. Bishop Abraham Wiebe and six ministers to Hon. Members of the Legislative Assembly of the Province of Saskatchewan, 7 January 1922, SAB, M 5, 6.

245. I. I. Friesen, p. 140, estimates 1,500, but see table 19.

246. Inspector Cram reported 24 September 1926 to Latta that attendance in Versailles and Clemenceau districts was still poor, approx. 38% and 28% respectively. SAB, M 5, 6(4).

247. Johann P. Wall, Hague, to Minister of Education, 12 February 1923, SAB, M 5, 6. His remark refers to the ten years during which the Russian government allowed Mennonites to emigrate when military exemption and control of their schools were cancelled in 1870.

248. Latta to Wall, 19 February 1923, SAB, M 5, 6.

249. A. H. Ball to Latta, 21 August 1923, SAB, M 5, 6(2).

250. The Durango settlement was founded by Hague Reinländer in 1924 and numbered 946 by 1925. See table 19.

251. Dawson, p. 166, reports this in the chapter on "Canadian Mennonite Communities Today."

252. Dawson, p. 106.

253. Weir, p. 108. Martin's view of tolerance is reflected in a speech he gave at Swift Current, 3 October 1919: "It is folly to talk of having [the Mennonites] deported in large bodies. They have been here a long time and while they are deluded in thinking that they have special privileges in Saskatchewan over other citizens, at the same time we have to use reasonable toleration in our treatment of them. Quoted in *Canadian Annual Review*, 1919, p. 552.

254. *Mitarbeiter*, March 1920, p. 27; I. I. Friesen, p. 140. However, even from a perspective of a fifty-year time lapse, *"Strafgelder and Gefängnis"* (fines and prison) were severe enough in Manitoba to remind the Reinländer leaders of the people in Israel in the iron furnace of Egypt, 1 Kings 8:51. Isaak M. Dyck, p. 70.

255. H. H. Ewert to S. F. Coffman, Vineland, 12 November 1918, MHCA, vol. 554. Ewert was as familiar with the Manitoba scene as anyone, and his figures for Saskatchewan are confirmed by the Minister of Education, W. M. Martin to Mrs. G. H. Smith, 28 April 1919, SAB, M 4, I-62, p. 21691.

256. This analysis follows in part that given by Ewert to Coffman, 12 November 1918, MHCA, vol. 554; Francis, *In Search of Utopia*, p. 176; David Toews at the Ford-McColl Commission hearings, 1908; Epp, *Education with a Plus*, p. 37.

257. Chortitzer church to Government of Manitoba, 13 January 1920, in I. I. Friesen, app. 17. See also H. H. Ewert brief of 15 February 1916, referred to earlier.

258. *MFP*, 18 May 1920, p. 15.

259. H. H. Ewert, *"Gehört das Kind dem Staate?"* (Does the child belong to the state?) *Mitarbeiter*, November 1920, pp. 81–82. Harder, p. 3, wrote: "In the government schools the children are taught that it is their proper duty to defend their country with the natural sword in time of war."

260. Ewert, *"Gehört das Kind dem Staate?"*

261. Manitoba Reinländer, February 1919, *MFP*, 18 May 1920, p. 15.

262. Chortitzer–Sommerfelder, 14 October 1921, in J. H. Doerksen, p. 108.

263. Dawson, p. 104, is correct in his observation that "the more liberal groups, which had come to use English increasingly, could conceive of a separation between the German language and the Mennonite religion," but not in his implication that the more "conservative" saw the two as inseparable. Thielman, p. 310, is similarly correct in pointing out that the Reinländer were most consistent in their "rejection of the English language in their private schools," but not, as he claims, because "they saw in English the biggest threat to their cultural integrity." Quiring, *Rußlanddeutsche suchen eine Heimat*, pp. 32, 39, and even Ewert, *Mitarbeiter*, October 1921, p. 80, place considerably more emphasis on the German language as the basis of Chortitzer–Sommerfelder opposition to the Manitoba schools than these groups themselves did.

264. Johann D. Klassen, report in *Mitarbeiter*, March 1916, p. 3.

265. Abraham Wiebe et al. to Saskatchewan MLAs, 7 January 1922, SAB, M 5, 6. Reinländer leaders realized that "language and religion are so interwoven" that it is difficult

to separate them (J. P. Wall, Hague, to Hon. Arthur Meighen, 7 September 1918, NA, MG 26, H, 1(c), vol. 214), just as Ewert did (*Mitarbeiter*, March 1916, p. 6).

266. My translation. The original reads: "Es handelt sich bei uns nicht um die Sprache, sondern wir könnten es unmöglich zugeben, unsere Kinder unter der Flagge, und unter der Ausübung des Militärismus zu rechte Bürger dieser Welt ausüben oder bilden zu lassen." I. M. Dyck, p. 45.

267. Gerhard Wiebe, p. 76 (English, p. 63), lamented the fact that only the bishops of these three groups (Stoesz, Doerksen, and Johann Wiebe) opposed the Gretna teacher training institute and the district schools for which it was preparing teachers. "These schools and their founders do not stem from Bethlehem, where the kings knelt at the manger to worship the child Jesus; rather they stem from Babylon, that is, they produce confusion." He was particularly upset that their school at Gretna was endorsed by the government (p. 82).

268. Bergthaler Church, Ministerial, *Minutes*, 2:179, 26 May 1919, MHCA, vol. 716. The leadership also decided a year later not to become involved with plans to emigrate. 30 December 1920, p. 195.

269. When the government reopened discontinued Mennonite district schools in 1918–1919, only three *Kleine Gemeinde* ones (Blumenort, Blumenhof, Grünfeld — see table 5) were still operating as private schools. *Gedenkfeier*, p. 89. During 1921–1922 all three returned to local board control (table 20); i.e., the communities voluntarily conducted public schools.

270. *MFP*, 18 May 1920, p. 15. Romans 13:1.

271. MHCA, vol. 544, file no. 47. This brief, as can be seen from the several preliminary drafts, was clearly the work of Benjamin Ewert.

CHAPTER V

# THE WAR ISSUES

Prime Minister Robert Borden had the difficult task of leading Canada through Britain's first major war since Confederation. In the 1911 election his Conservatives defeated the Laurier government, whose aggressive immigration policies had radically altered the demographic character of western Canada. A Maritimer with a strong concern for the British connection, he alienated French Canadians early in his first term by introducing legislation that would provide $35 million for three dreadnoughts to sail as part of the British navy. Relations between the two official language groups in Canada were further strained by the restrictions that Ontario placed on the use of instruction in French in its primary schools in 1913, and by the abolition of the bilingual provision of the Manitoba School Act in 1916. When the war dragged on longer than first expected and casualties mounted, voluntary enlistments seemed inadequate to sustain the level of Canadian involvement that the government deemed necessary.

In 1917, with Russia out of the war and American involvement just beginning, Borden moved to introduce conscription. In preparation for the wartime election of 1917, Borden sought to ensure victory for his government on the conscription issue by forming a coalition with Liberals, mostly Anglophones from western Canada, led by Clifford Sifton. In the somewhat tense atmosphere after the election anyone withholding full support from the war effort was increasingly suspect. This applied in a special way to German-speaking, pacifist Mennonites. They were not used to having their church meetings monitored by the police and their church periodicals censored.

While there was a considerable range of response among the various Mennonite groups to the provincial governments with respect to public school education and the introduction of municipal government, their response to the issues arising as a result of World War I was much more united. Their strong commitment to pacifism made all of them resist active participation in the war effort. However, in their approach to specific issues such as the national registrations, or contributing to the Red Cross or Victory Bond drives, differences between the groups again emerged.

## Military Exemption Provisions

The first clause of the 1873 *Privilegium* assured the immigrants "that an entire exemption from military service, as is provided by law and order-in-council, will be granted to the denomination of Christians called Mennonites." The law referred to was the Militia Act of 1868, which provided that

> any person bearing a certificate from the Society of Quakers, Mennonists or Tunkers ... who, from the doctrines of his religion, is averse to bearing arms and refuses personal service shall be exempt from such service when balloted in time of peace, or war, upon such conditions and under such regulations, as the Governor-in-Council may from time to time prescribe.[1]

The order-in-council referred to was that of September 25, 1872, passed in order to assure the Mennonites intending to emigrate from Russia

> that the Governor General in Council cannot prescribe any conditions or regulations under which, under any circumstances, the persons referred to in the above quoted section can be compelled to render any military service.[2]

Those Mennonites who in the 1870s had gone from Russia to the United States instead of to Canada had been unable to obtain similar assurances of military exemption from the American government. As a result, the Spanish-American War (1898) created anxiety among some U.S. Mennonites and led them to explore emigration to Canada.[3] This provided an occasion to clarify once more the status of Canadian Mennonites with respect to military exemption.[4]

At approximately the same time, Doukhobors from Russia and Hutterites from the United States were also negotiating entry into Canada as pacifist immigrants. Both groups were assured that they would "be exempted, unconditionally, from service in the militia, upon production in each case of a certificate of membership from the proper authorities of their community."[5] These events helped to assure the Canadian Mennonites that Ottawa was still aware of and was reaffirming their own exemption.

The issue of Mennonite participation with the voluntary Canadian forces in the Boer War (1899–1902) does not seem to have arisen. Nor is there any evidence that Mennonites in western Canada took any action at the time of the 1911 naval debate, although some of the Swiss Mennonites from Ontario did.[6]

## The Early Years of the War

News of the outbreak of war in Europe evoked an immediate editorial response from the *Mitarbeiter*, deploring the fact that civilized nations would resort to bloodshed.[7] Before the end of the year the Bergthaler Church in Manitoba, probably at the initiative of Swiss Mennonites from America, began voluntarily to raise funds for the war victims in Europe and Asia.[8] By 1915 some of the private schools of the *Kleine Gemeinde* were contributing to the Red Cross.[9]

At its meeting in the summer of 1916, the Conference of Mennonites of Central Canada passed a resolution thanking the Dominion government for the considerate treatment they had received with respect to military service. The promise given at the time of the immigration from Russia had been scrupulously kept, not only in the government's not conscripting Mennonites, but also in its not trying to persuade them to volunteer.[10] Perhaps they spoke too soon, for the first signs of problems were beginning to appear. That same summer the Bergthaler congregation in Manitoba served notice that any of its members who volunteered for active service in the military thereby automatically excommunicated themselves.[11] And in the fall of that year, some anxiety was caused by the much publicized refusal of entry into Canada of Bishop E. L. Frey of Ohio and his party of ten people. Entry was refused under the War Measures Act because Frey admitted that he did not encourage military recruiting but rather discouraged it.[12]

For the federal government also questions were raised about its "willingness to exempt from service on religious grounds the Mennonites, Doukhobors, and Quakers, while refusing to recognize the French Canadian sentiment against military service except in the defence of Canada."[13]

## The National Service Registration, 1917

In December 1916 the government announced that under the authority of the War Measures Act 1914, the first week of the New Year was to be observed as "national service week" for the taking of an inventory of the manpower of Canada. Cards were provided for this purpose through the

Post Office authorities, to be completed by all males between the ages of sixteen and sixty-five (see appendix 5). Although only one of the twenty-four questions on the cards referred to the war, its inclusion, and the fact that the inventory was done under the authority of the War Measures Act, led to immediate and deep apprehensions among the Mennonites.[14] Was this going to be the beginning of conscription? Fearing this to be the case, many Mennonites decided initially not to fill in the cards.

Outright disobedience, however, was not a natural Mennonite reaction to a national law. Meetings were consequently held in the various areas to elect delegates to go to Ottawa to investigate the matter. The delegation of Klaas Peters for the Herbert area of Saskatchewan, David Toews for the Rosthern area, Heinrich Doerksen for the Manitoba East Reserve, Abraham Doerksen for the West Reserve Sommerfelder, and Benjamin Ewert for the Bergthaler, represented all Mennonite groups except the Reinländer and showed the largest measure of Mennonite solidarity since their coming to Canada.[15]

This five-man delegation met with R. B. Bennett, Director General, National Service, and other government representatives on January 8, 1917, and presented its petition. The delegates were assured that agriculture was a national service essential to the military, and that their status was being fully respected by the government. Canada would not regard the *Privilegium* as "a scrap of paper" as Germany had done with its neutrality pact with Belgium. Bennett emphasized, however, that the cards must be completed, and suggested that the word "Mennonite" be written across the face of each card by members of that denomination. The delegation was also assured that it was possible for Mennonites who had enlisted "under misapprehension or otherwise" to be released if they applied for a discharge to their battalion commander.[16] With these assurances from the government, the Mennonite groups represented in the delegation were relieved and cooperated with the national registration.[17]

The Reinländer Mennonites had not participated in this delegation. Instead, at a brotherhood meeting attended by some 450 of its members, the church decided against filling in the national service cards.[18] Bishop Johann Friesen of the Manitoba Reinländer communicated this decision to Prime Minister Borden early in the New Year, reminding him of their *Privilegium* and of the assurance which the government had given the three Reinländer bishops on this point in November of 1916. Against that background, wrote Friesen, "we are therefore confident that you ... will justify our sending these cards back by return mail."[19] The solution was not quite that simple, however, for the Reinländer leaders were promptly summoned to Winnipeg by the Manitoba District Director of National Service. Here they were urged to provide the government with a list of all males from sixteen to sixty-five years of age in their church, since they resisted filling out the cards. When the leaders felt unable to comply with even this request, that was accepted by the government representative.[20] The Manitoba Director of National Service continued as late as March to attempt to get Reinländer to co-operate "in order to make the inventory of manpower complete" but was not successful.[21]

When Manitoba Sommerfelder discovered that their Reinländer co-religionists had not filled in the cards, some of them complained that their leaders had not obtained exemption from the government for them also. This led Bishop Abraham Doerksen to urge a joint Sommerfelder–Bergthaler delegation to go to Winnipeg to attempt to "discover whether our high government has a different law for the Old Colony church than it does for our churches."[22]

In Saskatchewan there was general co-operation although some young men apparently decided to spend the winter months in California lest the January registration have more serious implications.[23]

The delegates who had gone to Ottawa in January now suggested to their constituency that a special collection be held in all of their churches for those who had been widowed, orphaned, or crippled as a result of the war. This money was to be sent to the government as an expression of thanks for its considerate treatment of the Mennonites in regard to military exemption.[24] The organizers of this fund drive made it clear that their purpose was not to support the war but rather to provide some relief for war victims. It was also observed that such an action might help to obtain the goodwill of their Canadian neighbours, who would be less likely to press for Mennonite enlistment if they saw evidence of voluntary sacrifices.[25] While the hoped-for $25,000 was not raised, an initial contribution of $5,777.17 was forwarded to R. B. Bennett, Director General of National Service, in April.[26] The Canadian government, after consultation with Mennonite leaders, turned the contribution over to the Canadian Patriotic Fund for disbursement in keeping with the donors' request.[27] The Reinländer congregations of Manitoba and Saskatchewan, which had not participated in the delegation to Ottawa, sent in their contributions separately.[28] These groups also participated in local relief efforts during the war.[29]

## Implementing Mennonite Exemption: Military Service Act, 1917

By April 1917 voluntary enlistments in the Canadian forces no longer matched casualties at the front. Prime Minister Borden returned from the latest Imperial War Conference convinced that Canada must introduce conscription. The Military Service Act, passed on August 29, 1917, provided enabling legislation for this step.

The Act provided seven categories of persons who were excepted from its provisions. Included in the seventh exception were "those persons exempted from military service by the order-in-council of 13th August 1873 and the order-in-council of 6th December 1898."[30] In the opinion of Solicitor General Arthur Meighen, all the descendants of those originally exempted, who had remained part of their community, were excepted from the Military Service Act.[31]

The government was therefore clear that conscription would not apply to western Canadian Mennonites who had come from Russia nor to their descendants.[32] Accordingly, when the first recruits were called up under the new conscription law, the Military Service Branch Registrars in both Manitoba and Saskatchewan were clear in their instructions that Mennonites were excepted from the terms of the law.[33] They therefore did not need to "fill in and sign the Reports for Service or Claims for Exemption." The much smaller Mennonite community in Alberta received the impression from the papers and from official announcements that they were required to register under the Military Service Act. The absence of regular official communication among the leaders in the three provinces prevented the Alberta Mennonites from discovering that their brethren in Manitoba and Saskatchewan were not registering. Accordingly, they arranged a day when all their young men were registered. Now some of them were being called before the military tribunal and were having difficulty obtaining exemption.[34]

In Manitoba and Saskatchewan difficulties in the administration of the Act also soon appeared. In part this was caused by a misleading announcement in the *Mitarbeiter* of October 1917.[35] It advised all single males from twenty to thirty-four years of age, explicitly including Mennonites, to apply for exemption either by completing a "Claim for Exemption" form available at the Post Office or by appearing personally before a military tribunal. That meant that they were seeking *exemption under* the Military Service Act instead of *exception from* its terms, as the two provincial registrars had advised.

In part the problem lay with some of the local tribunals appointed under the Military Service Act who were not aware that Mennonites were excepted from its provisions.[36] In the large block settlements in Manitoba and in those Saskatchewan communities where the Mennonite leadership became personally acquainted with members of the local tribunal this did not present a problem.[37] But persons living outside of the Mennonite communities in Saskatchewan were frequently inducted.[38]

An underlying cause of these difficulties was the lack of clarity in government circles as to who was a Mennonite. The delegation of January

1917 had raised the question of the status of unbaptized Mennonite youth at the ministerial level and had been assured that children of Mennonite parents were considered Mennonite by the government. A year later the public press reported that the government was intending to restrict military exemption among Mennonites to baptized members only.[39] That was indeed the interpretation now held in the upper echelons of the civil service in Ottawa. The Deputy Minister of the Interior, for example, wrote:

> I would say that any young man of military age who has not yet joined the church should not be exempt. To my mind the whole thing hinges on whether the man is a member of the church or not.[40]

With the legal induction age at eighteen, and many Mennonite young men not baptized until twenty or twenty-one, this presented a serious problem for the Mennonite church.

When the Saskatchewan military district office decided to appoint a special police commissioner to organize the entire province and round up all draft-aged males who could not show exemption, the Saskatchewan Mennonite ministers unanimously agreed that another delegation should be sent to Ottawa as soon as possible.[41] Their invitation to Manitoba Mennonites to add representatives to the delegation was discussed by twenty-eight ministers on April 3. Since the problem in Manitoba was not a serious one at this point, they did not see sufficient reason to join the delegation.[42]

The three-man Saskatchewan delegation met in Ottawa on April 12, 1918, with Colonel H. A. C. Machin, Director of the Military Service Branch, and Judge Duff, the top official dealing with exemptions. Their brief suggested that every Mennonite of military age be required to have a certificate signed by an ordained minister stating that he is a Mennonite and exempt from all military service. This certificate was to be countersigned by a Mennonite person recognized by the government, one such person to be designated for each of the main Mennonite areas. The military registrars would be provided with the names of these designated persons so that they could instruct their entire staff to recognize the certificates.[43] The delegation received verbal assurance that the 1873 order-in-council applied also to unbaptized Mennonite youth, but the official written response reported that the whole question of Mennonite exemption had been assigned for study to a special commissioner.[44]

The suggestion that every draft-aged Mennonite carry a military exemption certificate was implemented, however.[45] David Toews did not accept Registrar Haining's suggestion that he be the official person to countersign all Saskatchewan certificates, but he was elected by a large meeting of representatives at Waldheim to do so for the Rosthern and

Drake areas.[46] He immediately ordered five thousand certificates to be printed. The hoped-for uniformity of Mennonite identification was not achieved through these certificates, however. The government published its own form near the end of June 1918 (see appendix 6).

In Alberta the results of the Saskatchewan delegation to Ottawa were positive. When Registrar Carson in Calgary was informed he cancelled all orders to Mennonites to report.[47] In Saskatchewan the problems persisted. By mid-May there still was no written decision from Ottawa regarding the exemption of unbaptized Mennonite youth. In the absence of a clear directive from the government, it was suggested that the matter be tested in the courts.[48] This Bishop Toews wanted to avoid if at all possible. Could a judge decide this dangerous, precedent-setting case neutrally in these turbulent times, he wondered?[49] The presence in Saskatchewan of some Swiss Mennonites, who did not come under the terms of the 1873 order-in-council, complicated matters and made it difficult to deal with lower level officials. Obtaining the release of one inducted Mennonite youth created such tensions in the community that he was advised to go to Manitoba for the duration of the war.[50]

In Manitoba, where things had been relatively quiet, the Military Board in Winnipeg decided in June 1918 to have the matter of unbaptized Mennonite youth clarified. Abraham Dyck from Lowe Farm was inducted and taken to the barracks as a test case. Leaders of the Manitoba Mennonite churches were then called to Winnipeg to testify before the Board about the church status of unbaptized Mennonite children. Five ministers, including the Sommerfelder and Bergthaler bishops, presented a fifteen-point brief to the Board on June 10.[51] The brief explained that on birth a Mennonite child is not only registered with the state but also entered into the church register and belongs to the *Gemeinschaft* from that day on. On reaching sufficient maturity, usually at age twenty-one, the child is baptized and received into full membership. Those not requesting baptism nevertheless attend worship, support the church, and have their marriage, place of abode, and death recorded in the church register. The difference between these and the baptized members is that the latter are admitted to communion and have a vote in church decisions. "In summary," the brief concluded, "our *Gemeinschaft* considers its children and young people its own as much as the baptized members."

A few days later there was a broad sigh of relief when word came from Winnipeg that the explanation given was acceptable and would serve as basis for future action by the military boards. The inducted Abraham Dyck was forthwith released.[52]

In Saskatchewan, however, the situation remained intolerable. Registrar Haining had admitted to Bishop Toews in mid-May that his earlier advice that Mennonites register and claim exemption had been wrong. In the future, if a conscript could be shown by an ordained minister to be a member of a Mennonite church, he would be considered as "outside the Act." If he could not be shown to be a member of a Mennonite church, he would have to "obey the order to report for duty when it is sent, or apply to the courts for a decision as to his status."[53] After thorough consideration the Mennonite leaders decided not to follow that course because they did not want to arouse undesirable publicity or embarrass the authorities, but mostly because

> our faith rested and continues to rest in the successors in office of those with whom our fathers entered into a solemn contract. It is unthinkable to us that they should violate this contract and we are quite sure that it only requires a thorough presentation of our case to cause them to so act that we may again have that peace for which we long so much.[54]

The result of this decision was an endless series of conferences with the military authorities in Regina, accusations of fraud in connection with the issuing of certificates of church membership, and demands for all kinds of documentary proof regarding the ordination of ministers, bishops, and presiding elders, church and conference records, and confessions of faith.[55] To meet these demands, Bishop Toews prepared an affidavit listing fifty-eight "properly qualified and duly ordained ministers of the denomination of Christians called Mennonites" in fourteen districts of Saskatchewan.[56] At a conference in the Military District No. 12 office in Regina between Commanding Officer Lieutenant Colonel Cross, Registrar Haining, and a Mennonite delegation on June 28, the military authorities agreed that they would not attempt "to distinguish between Mennonites born and brought up as such, and unbaptized on the one hand and baptized on the other hand."[57] A further delegation to Regina on July 11 "brought along numerous voluminous church records from various sections of the province, declarations from bishops showing induction of ministers, minutes of meetings of congregations and several translations of articles of faith and other material."[58] In view of the conclusions reached at that conference the delegation thought that its troubles were now over and that all the Mennonite youths who had already reported for duty would be discharged and the order to report to the others cancelled.[59]

It did not happen. The military police at Regina less than a month before the armistice still had not received a clear ruling whether, in the case of Mennonites, "bona fide membership" meant only "baptized communicant members," or whether the broader Mennonite interpretation held.[60] So the difficulties in Saskatchewan persisted.

Finally, four branches of the church in Saskatchewan, whose membership included approximately two-thirds of the Mennonite population of that province, compiled a twenty-seven-page brief with fourteen exhibits documenting the sequence of events outlined above. It was addressed to the Governor General of Canada in Council and dated one week before the armistice. By the time it was received in Ottawa conscription had ceased and the document ended up among the Privy Council "dormants."[61]

It must be admitted that the government was under considerable criticism for its policy of allowing Mennonite exemption. The Great War Veterans' Association, the Loyal Orange Lodge, and the Sons of England criticized the undue power conferred upon the Mennonite clergy by the government. In giving them authority to determine who was entitled to military exemption under "the Mennonite Treaty of 1873," the government was "constituting a Mennonite priest a one man tribunal."[62] Methodist ministers also "played a leading part in alerting the Saskatchewan government to the 'Mennonite menace' and suggested that the policy of exempting Mennonites be reviewed."[63] But Ottawa had determined that "the rights granted to the Mennonites under the orders-in-council must be respected, for we could not afford to convert what was really a treaty into a 'scrap of paper.'"[64] The federal government therefore stood firm on western Canadian Mennonite exemption from military service even though it was apparently unable to prevent its Saskatchewan officials from making that exemption very difficult to obtain in practice.

The trial and conviction of ex-Mennonite Klaas Peters—who was now a Swedenborgian minister—for illegally issuing military exemption certificates might well have damaged the Mennonite cause in Saskatchewan further had the court proceedings occurred any earlier. Peters had left the Bergthaler congregation in Manitoba in 1897 and was ordained a minister of the Church of the New Jerusalem (Swedenborgian) in 1902.[65] In spite of this, he represented the Herbert area Mennonites in both of the wartime delegations to Ottawa. Bishop Toews and the Rosthern area congregations were uneasy about this and warned the Mennonites in southern Saskatchewan to sever their connections with him.[66] They chose H. M. Klassen from Herbert to countersign identification cards for their area.[67] When some difficulty arose in regard to Klassen's countersigning Peters' certificates, the latter went to Ottawa to arrange with the Deputy Minister of Justice that a certain certificate bearing only the signature of an ordained minister be acceptable.[68] Peters then began issuing Mennonite identity cards on his own.[69] The police soon laid charges and he was brought to trial three days after the armistice, found guilty, and fined $200 plus costs.[70]

## U.S. Mennonite Immigrants and the Military Service Act

When the United States entered the war in 1917 it soon became obvious that Mennonites there had considerably more difficulty in obtaining exemption from military service than their Canadian brothers did. In February 1918 there were a hundred and thirty Mennonite conscientious objectors in Camp Funston, Kansas.[71] Both Mennonites and Hutterites were beginning to emigrate to Canada to escape induction, and it was expected that this would become a large movement if they would be assured of exemption from military service there.[72]

When the Canadian government's agent in Omaha, Nebraska, inquired about the status of U.S. Mennonite immigrants under the Military Service Act in September 1917, he was assured on the advice of the Minister of the Interior "that the provisions of the Military Service Act do not apply to these people,—that they are exempt."[73] In the late months of 1917 the Canadian government still considered Mennonites "a desirable class of agriculturalists" and encouraged its U.S. agents to facilitate their immigration into Canada.[74] This attitude also applied to Hutterites and continued well into 1918.[75] When in August 1918 a Member of Parliament from British Columbia suggested to immigration officials that local feeling was beginning to turn against the influx of Mennonites from America,[76] Ottawa's official position began to be less enthusiastic.

> My own opinion is that we ought to handle the movement with considerable care. I doubt if we should offer any great encouragement, but, at the same time, if these people are interested in Western Canada ... we should not put any special hindrance in their way.[77]

Throughout this time U.S. Mennonites were assured that anyone who could produce a certificate from a recognized bishop of the church showing that he was a bona fide member would be regarded as exempt from the provisions of the Military Service Act.[78] By September, Immigration Minister Calder maintained that Mennonite immigrants from the U.S. were American citizens subject to the U.S. draft even in Canada.[79] A few days later Registrar Haining announced that U.S. immigrant Mennonites were not excepted from the Military Service Act, but, like Ontario Mennonites, could seek exemption from combatant service only.[80] This interpretation was confirmed in October by an order-in-council passed at the recommendation of the Minister of Justice, which provided that only those Mennonites who had come directly to Canada under the provisions of the *Privilegium*, and their descendants, who had continued without interruption to be members of the denomination and had resided permanently in Canada, were exempted from military service within the seventh exception to the Military Service Act of 1917.[81]

## The 1918 National Registration

While the Mennonites were still struggling to clarify their status under the Military Service Act of 1917, a new threat appeared in the form of "The

Canada Registration Board" created by order-in-council in February 1918.[82] The Bergthaler congregation promptly instructed Benjamin Ewert, its member on the 1917 Ottawa delegation, to attempt to discover whether Mennonites had to participate in the proposed new registration.[83] Ewert turned to Bishop Toews in Saskatchewan for information and counsel, and the two of them became the focal points of further consultation among the Mennonites.[84]

In response to early inquiries Mennonites were assured that the registration had "no military significance whatever."[85] The chairman of the Registration Board, Senator Robertson, in his official communication to the provincial premiers stated:

> We expect it will prove a valuable aid to the military and naval authorities in securing men for Canada's first line of defense, which for the present is overseas.[86]

Mennonite leaders were aware of this military significance of the registration despite reassurances to the contrary.

The national registration of all persons age sixteen to sixty-five was to take place on June 22. The Bruderthaler of the Manitoba East Reserve were apparently the first Mennonite group to agree to register.[87] In early June a number of bishops and ministers met with Senator Robertson in Winnipeg to discuss the implications for Mennonites if they participated in the registration. Senator Robertson assured them that the government intended to honour fully its promise regarding Mennonite exemption from military service, but at the same time emphatically warned that everyone without exception had to register.[88] As protection against military recruiters Robertson suggested that question 4 for females and question 9 for males (see appendix 7) be answered with "exempted as Mennonite."[89] Instructions prepared for the registration by the Reinländer *Obervorsteher* in Manitoba suggest in addition that males answer with "Mennonite" questions 3 ("Speak English (E) or French (F)?") and 4 ("British subject? By birth? By naturalization?").[90]

Three days after the Winnipeg meeting with Senator Robertson, leaders of the Bergthaler congregation met in Altona to discuss their response. Although some brethren had serious misgivings regarding the registration, suggesting that this might be the beginning of the fulfilment of Revelation 13, the meeting decided not to hinder anyone who wanted to register and agreed to have persons available at every place of registration to help their members complete the forms.[91] In Saskatchewan also "the mark of the beast" (Revelation 13:16–17) was being widely applied to the registration. Nevertheless, at a meeting at Hepburn on June 20 delegates reluctantly decided to endorse participation in it.[92]

Manitoba Reinländer leaders had already gone to Winnipeg in May to meet with the chief registrar for Manitoba, Philip Locke. The latter's decision to have Mennonites handle the registration themselves under his direction was welcomed for its accommodating spirit.[93] But it was not an easy matter for Mennonites to accept appointment as deputy registrar when they were not yet convinced that their people should even register.[94]

The Manitoba Reinländer had a brotherhood meeting to decide this issue on June 13 with representatives of the two Saskatchewan Reinländer groups also present.[95] Registrar Locke was invited to attend the meeting but when he arrived at the announced time it was already over. Together with Morden attorney Alex McLeod, who frequently served the Reinländer Mennonites, and W. J. Rowe, Registrar for the electoral division of Lisgar, Locke visited the Mennonite leaders who were still assembled in Reinland. Since the brotherhood meeting had decided not to register, Locke was faced with a dilemma. Threats of imprisonment and fines did not accomplish anything. In the end his appeal to the example of the willingness of Joseph and Mary to participate in the Roman registration as recorded in the Gospel of Luke, chapter 2, persuaded the Mennonite leaders to reconsider.[96] A second brotherhood meeting on the following Sunday then decided unanimously to participate in the registration.[97] Thus, in the end, all Mennonite groups in western Canada co-operated in the 1918 registration.

## Financial Involvement: Red Cross and Victory Loans

Reference has already been made to Mennonite contributions as early as 1915 to the Red Cross, and to the special collection for the Patriotic Fund in early 1917. These organizations continued to receive financial support throughout the war years from all Mennonite groups. The Bergthaler congregation of Manitoba made this into a carefully planned annual affair, urging its members to contribute sacrificially, and even developing an informal property tax for this purpose by 1918.[98] In the Reinländer Church such contributions caused some uneasiness in spite of official assurances that the funds were entirely used for the relief of war victims. As far as the more sensitive consciences were concerned, all these contributions helped to strengthen the total war effort.[99] It is estimated that overall Mennonite contributions to these relief organizations amounted to about $50,000 by the end of 1917, with close to $100,000 more contributed during 1918.[100]

The Victory loan question was much more vexatious. To help pay for the enormous cost of the war, the Borden government in February 1917 introduced measures for a five-hundred-million-dollar National War Loan. Funds for this loan were to be raised through the periodic issue of government bonds called Victory bonds. While the purchase of such bonds represented a loan rather than a gift, the proceeds were to be used for war purposes only. An initial $150,000,000 bond issue was announced in March.[101] Saskatchewan Mennonite leaders, meeting to discuss this issue as the second Victory loan was issued in November 1917, had little difficulty in agreeing that their congregations could not participate.[102] To Manitoba Bergthaler leaders the issue was not that clear. They considered it their duty to support the government financially when such support was requested. But in keeping with their pacifist stance they would ask the government not to use their funds for military purposes but only for the purchase of foodstuffs.[103] Accordingly, they recommended to their brotherhood meeting that participation in the Victory loan be a matter of individual decision.[104]

Most of the Mennonite churches apparently followed the lead of the Saskatchewan Mennonites rather than the Bergthaler congregation. In lieu of participation in the Victory bond drive they held special collections for the Red Cross and in one case offered the government a five-year interest-free loan for relief purposes.[105]

Refusal to participate in the Victory bond drive was not a popular move in wartime Canada. When Jacob Friesen, editor and publisher of the *Steinbach Post*, refused to accept a paid advertisement for the Victory loan, a chain reaction of responses was triggered. The President of the Canadian Press Association complained to Lieutenant-Colonel E. J. Chambers, the Chief Press Censor in Ottawa,

> that a newspaper published by a man with a name like that and devoted to the purposes specified, ["a German-Mennonite family paper devoted to the interests of the German speaking public of this country"] and which will not accept, even at proper rates, advertising for a Canadian war loan, should not be permitted to publish in this country.[106]

Although the Censor had "never had any complaints made against this publication since the commencement of the war," he nevertheless requested that Friesen explain "at length" just why he had taken this action.[107]

Friesen apologized for his inability to co-operate in this respect and then explained that "the one and only reason why we did not publish said advertisement is because our faith forbids us to partake of anything which aids to harm or kill any human being whatever, direct or indirect."[108] Not satisfied with this explanation, Chambers submitted the matter to the Deputy Minister of Justice.[109] At the same time, he advised the Deputy Postmaster General,

> that as this paper, published ... "in the interest of the German-speaking public of this country", shows itself absolutely indifferent to the public

interests, that the Post Office Department as a public service may not feel itself under any obligation to assist the publishers in the circulation of their publication.[110]

The Post Office Department made it clear that since the *Post* "complied with all the conditions necessary" for the granting of statutory postal privileges, only the Secretary of State could take any action against it.[111] The Deputy Minister of Justice had meanwhile forwarded the matter to the Finance Department, which found Friesen's explanation reasonable and advised against the government's taking any action as long as objection to publishing the Victory loan advertisement was not widespread.[112]

The Censor still felt that Friesen's refusal to run the advertisement was "certainly an unfriendly attitude to assume by one who enjoys special privileges from the government."[113] But when the next issue of the *Post* included a front page editorial explaining the loan and advising its readers "that the possession of one or more of the Victory bonds might rightly be considered as a test of true patriotism," Chambers was somewhat mollified.[114] The President of the Canadian Press Association, who had initiated the investigation, found Friesen's excuse "probably just a plain, ordinary falsehood induced by fear," and was sceptical of the "religious principles to which he seems suddenly so attached." While he appreciated the government's motives for tolerance, he objected to the "unnecessary leniency toward alien enemies in our midst" and thought that "an example should be made of some of these people."[115] The government, however, wanted as little of the mailed-fist approach in censorship as possible.[116]

A year later the government took strong initiative in attempting to resolve Mennonite objection to the Victory bonds. Finance Minister White met with church leaders in Winnipeg and Regina to announce an unusual concession. In order to meet their conscientious objections to participation in the Victory bond drive, the government promised to devote "an amount equivalent to the total subscriptions of your people to the loan, for relief purposes, namely convalescent homes and hospitals."[117] This arrangement apparently was quite acceptable to most of the Mennonite groups.[118] Within a year Manitoba Mennonites had purchased an estimated $600,000 to $700,000 worth of Victory bonds.[119]

## Press Censorship

Early in 1917 the government strengthened and consolidated its censorship powers, which had been in existence since the beginning of the war.[120] The first Mennonite publication to feel the effect of these new powers was *Der Christliche Bundesbote*, official organ of the General Conference Mennonite Church of North America, published in Berne, Indiana. A recommendation that distribution in Canada of the *Bundesbote* be prohibited was quickly implemented by the Secretary of State.[121] For Canadian members of the General Conference, possession of their official church paper now became an offence punishable by a fine up to a $5,000 and/or imprisonment.[122] When Canadian Mennonite leaders inquired how they might advise their editor to make the *Bundesbote* acceptable for distribution in Canada, the irony of the Censor's response must have struck them:

> It is contrary to the principles of British freedom and liberty and British respect for international obligations, to endeavour to dictate a policy to publications which are printed in countries which are not under the jurisdiction of the British flag.[123]

In spite of a staff censor's report that the contents of the *Bundesbote* were "quite inoffensive," its publishers were unable to have Canadian postal privileges restored through U.S. diplomatic intervention.[124] Since at least part of the offensiveness of the *Bundesbote* was the fact that it was printed in German, its publishers solved the problem by sending Canadian subscribers the denomination's English-language paper, *The Mennonite*. This successfully passed the criteria of the Censor despite the presence of an article regarding the Mennonite position on bearing arms.[125]

The other German-language periodical published in the U.S.A. with a wide readership in western Canada was *Die Mennonitische Rundschau*. In August 1918 it was still surviving the periodic scrutiny of the Canadian Press Censor.[126]

Of the two German-language papers published by Mennonites in western Canada, the *Steinbach Post* had already come to the attention of the Chief Press Censor by its refusal to publish Victory loan advertising. In the summer of 1918 its publishers were again severely criticized by Lieutenant-Colonel Chambers for printing, in pamphlet form, resolutions passed by the Holdemann Conference (Church of God in Christ Mennonite) held at Lonetree, Kansas.

> I have secured through the United States authorities copies of this pamphlet, and regret to find that it contains a great deal of most objectionable matter, matter which is in distinct contravention of the Canadian censorship orders-in-council inasmuch as it encourages opposition to practically all the war measures of the government.[127]

Jacob Friesen, publisher of the *Post*, apologized for having accepted this printing job and assured Chambers that the pamphlet was not intended "to do any harm to our beloved government or country; it was simply meant to serve as a memorandum" for members of the pacifist denomination involved and was not intended to be in the possession of any person not belonging to that denomination.[128] In response to Chambers' request,

Friesen identified Reverend Jacob T. Wiebe as the person who had placed the printing order. Wiebe also now received a stiff warning not to repeat this offence or anything like it. The Censor added

> that while the laws of this country concede certain well defined rights to those who conscientiously object to military service, they provide clear and distinct punishment for those who would appeal to those who are not conscientious objectors to become so at this particular crisis of the country's affairs.[129]

In September 1918 the government introduced new measures to control literature in enemy alien languages.[130] *Der Mitarbeiter*, official organ of the Conference of Mennonites in Central Canada, was forced to suspend publication,[131] even though the staff censor described it as "a paper devoted to religious and missionary subjects ... perfectly harmless."[132] The *Steinbach Post*, however, still circulated its October 2 and 9 issues in German even though the new law had taken effect October 1. It was promptly reported to the Chief Press Censor by the Royal Northwest Mounted Police, to whose attention it had been drawn by one of the force's special operatives.[133] The latter found it offensive because "the whole edition does not contain even one reference to the War, neither editorially nor in its news which in itself is proof of its pro-Germanism."[134]

The *Post* was then forced to publish in English even though it was "one of the least objectionable enemy language publications circulated in Canada."[135] Friesen offered his readers no public explanation for the abrupt change in language. But since two-thirds of its readers did not understand English adequately, he applied for permission to use German again as soon as the war was over.[136] In recommending against granting permission, the Chief Press Censor referred back to the Victory loan advertisement and the Holdemann pamphlet incident, while making no mention of the harmless nature of the paper itself. He would consider it a gain for the country if the *Post* should cease publication entirely.[137]

Both popular feeling against and government restriction of periodicals in "enemy alien language" continued to increase after the conclusion of the war. A new cabinet order in April 1919, however, seemed to offer new hope.[138] Both the *Steinbach Post* and the *Mitarbeiter* attempted, unsuccessfully once more, to be reinstated under this order. Editor Friesen of the former offered to "arrange our little paper to be literary, scientific and religious only,"[139] but found out that it could not even legally print auction sale handbills in German.[140]

The editor of the *Mitarbeiter* felt that his paper was "purely a religious paper" that never dealt with "economic or political matters" and would therefore qualify for permission to publish again in German.[141] However, when he found out that the government's understanding of a purely religious publication meant that "all features of a newspaper must be eliminated, such as trade advertising and news of all kinds, even news of church meetings or denominational meetings," he reluctantly concluded "to desist from publication of this paper until the conditions in the country will warrant you to remove this restriction."[142]

The entry of German-language materials from abroad was also severely curtailed by the new measures. The *Mennonitische Rundschau*, which earlier had passed censorship standards, was now excluded.[143] Non-periodic literature, both books and pamphlets, began to be affected. Rudolf Wolkan's scholarly historical work, *Die Hutterer: österreichische Wiedertäufer und Kommunisten in Amerika*, was admitted, but not before the Chief Censor had checked with the Superintendent of Immigration his "idea that the Hutterites are subject to some outlawry."[144] The Mennonite Publishing Company of Elkhart, Indiana, received a licence to fill Canadian orders for its *Gesangbuch* (hymnal)[145] but not for a booklet entitled "Christianity and War: A Sermon Setting Forth the Sufferings of Christians," written by a minister of the Old Mennonite Church and first published in 1863.[146] A circular letter and order form for Bibles, hymn-books, catechism, and other similar literature, was seized by the Postal Censorship Office and retained on instruction from the Chief Press Censor, who felt that such action "will indicate to foreign language publishers in the U.S. that we are doing something in the way of enforcing the new Order-in-Council."[147] The Mennonite Brethren Publishing House in Hillsboro, Kansas, apparently was only marginally affected by the censorship laws.[148]

By early 1920 matters were getting back to normal and Mennonite publications in German cautiously began to make their reappearance. The *Mitarbeiter* resumed publication in January 1920 and editorially noted its enforced vacation. The *Steinbach Post* switched back to German in its January 7 issue and finally explained to its readers why English had been used during the past year.[149] The school struggle in Saskatchewan and Manitoba, described in the previous chapter, took place against this background of anti-German feeling and governmental action.

# Notes

1. 31 Vic., chap. 40, sec. 17.
2. P.C. no. 1043D, 25 September 1872, NA, RG 2, 1.
3. Hugo Carotens, Winnipeg, to Clifford Sifton, Minister of the Interior, 6 June 1898, NA, RG 15, vol. 571, no. 179925(2).
4. J. A. Smart, Deputy Minister of the Interior, to Hon. David Mills, Minister of Justice, 15 June 1898, NA, RG 15, vol. 571, no. 179925(2).
5. P.C. no. 2747, 6 December 1898; P.C. no. 1676, 12 August 1899; NA, RG 2, 1. Copies of both orders are found in RG 76, vol. 173, no. 58764(1). The statute that provided

the basis of exemption was now found in the Militia Act, *Revised Statutes of Canada*, chap. 41, sec. 21, sub-sec. 3. For a fuller discussion of the WWI experiences of these two groups, see Janzen, chap. 8.

6. L. J. Burkholder to Sir Wilfrid Laurier, 20 February 1911, NA, MG 26 G, vol. 667, p. 181870, microfilm no. C-900.

7. H. H. Ewert, editorial, *Mitarbeiter*, August 1914, p. 84.

8. Bergthaler Church, Ministerial, *Minutes*, 30 December 1914, MHCA, vol. 716.

9. Valentine Winkler, Minister of Agriculture and Immigration, to D. D. Driedger, Blumenhof private school, 16 November 1915, PAM, MG 14, B 45, box 3. Driedger to Winkler, 1 December 1916, sent a further contribution (box 5).

10. *Mitarbeiter*, October 1916, pp. 4–5, reproduces the 15 July 1916 letter of thanks, together with Prime Minister Borden's response.

11. Bergthaler Church, Brotherhood, *Minutes*, 5 June 1916, MHCA, vol. 715.

12. G. Adams, Windsor Immigration Inspector, to W. D. Scott, Superintendent of Immigration, Ottawa, 14 November 1916, NA, RG 76, vol. 173, no. 58764-1. The *Toronto Daily Star*, 25 November 1916; the *Globe*, 17 November; the *London Advertiser*, 16 November; and the *Windsor Recorder*, 16 November, also reported the incident. See Epp, *Mennonites in Canada*, pp. 368–369, for a longer account of this incident.

13. Mason Wade, *The French Canadians, 1760–1967*, rev. ed., 2 vols. (Toronto: Macmillan, 1968), 2:738, referring to Henri Bourassa's position in the 1916 conscription debate.

14. B. Ewert in *Mitarbeiter*, January 1917, p. 1; P. M. Friesen, Rush Lake, Saskatchewan, to R. L. Borden, 22 December 1916, NA, MG 26 H, 1(c), vol. 214, pp. 121076–77. J. C. Koehn, Mountain Lake, Minnesota, to W. J. White, 2 January 1917, RG 76, vol. 173, no. 58764-1. Question 23 of the inventory card reads: "Would you be willing to change your present work for other necessary work at the same pay during the war?" A copy of the registration card is given in appendix 5. A complete packet of the material sent by R. B. Bennett, Director General, National Service, to members of the provincial legislatures is found in PAM, MG 14, B 45, box 5, dated 9 December 1916.

15. *Mitarbeiter*, January 1917, p. 2.

16. B. Ewert's official report of the delegation's negotiations, a German translation of the petition and of R. B. Bennett's written summary of 8 January 1917 to Abraham Doerksen et al., are reproduced in *Mitarbeiter*, January 1917, pp. 1–4, 4–6, and 6–7; in B. Ewert, comp., *Wichtige Dokumente betreffs der Wehrfreiheit der Mennoniten in Canada* (Gretna, Man.: by the author, 1917), and in J. H. Doerksen, pp. 76–88. See MHCA, vol. 544, no. 46, and I. I. Friesen, appendixes 20 and 21 for these documents in English. For a later recollection of this event by a Reinländer leader see I. M. Dyck, pp. 33–34.

17. E. R. Chapman, Director of National Service, M. D. no. 10, Winnipeg, to Valentine Winkler, 7 March 1917, PAM, MG 14, B 45, box 5.

18. Report by Cpl. C. T. Hildyard, Rosthern Detachment of the R.N.W.M.P., 5 April 1917, NA, MG 26 H, 1(c), vol. 214, p. 121098. The meeting was held in Reinland, Manitoba.

19. Johann J. S. Friesen, Neuenburg, to Sir Robert Borden and Hon. Arthur Meighen, 4 January 1917, NA, MG 26 H, 1(c), vol. 214, p. 121078.

20. Ältester Abraham Doerksen, Sommerfeld, to Benjamin Ewert, Gretna, 7 April 1917, MHCA, vol. 542, no. 3. The R.N.W.M.P. report had indicated their willingness to furnish a list of male members.

21. E. R. Chapman to V. Winkler, 7 March 1917; Winkler to J. W. Rempel, Gretna, 8 March 1917, PAM, MG 14, B 45, box 5.

22. Doerksen to Ewert, 7 April 1917; Ewert to Doerksen, 18 April, agreed with the suggestion, but apparently nothing came of it. MHCA, vol. 542, no. 3. This sequence of events seems more likely than that suggested by Epp, *Mennonites in Canada*, pp. 369–370.

23. Doell, *The Bergthaler Mennonite Church*, pp. 19–21; *Mitarbeiter*, January 1917, p. 7.

24. B. Ewert, "*Aufforderung zum Dankopfer*," *Mitarbeiter*, February 1917, p. 2. At least one Reinländer community had already begun contributions ($341.50 and $31.00) to the Patriotic Fund in 1916. MHCA, Gnadenthal Papers, vol. 2198, no. 6.

25. *Mitarbeiter*, March 1917, pp. 7–8.

26. Abraham Doerksen, Heinrich Doerksen, David Toews, Klaas Peters, and Benjamin Ewert, to R. B. Bennett, 17 April 1917, MHCA, vol. 542, no. 3. A German translation is found in MHCA, vol. 542, no. 7, and is reproduced in *Mitarbeiter*, May 1917, pp. 7–8. A detailed breakdown of the sources of most of these contributions is given in *Beilage* to the *Mitarbeiter* of May 1917.

27. R. B. Bennett to Abraham Doerksen, 28 May, 11 June and 23 June 1917, MHCA, vol. 542, no. 3. *Mitarbeiter*, June 1917, pp. 2–3.

28. Benjamin Ewert to Klaas Peters, Waldeck, 23 April 1917, MHCA, vol. 542, reports a contribution of $2,044.75 from Manitoba and $1,383 from Hague. The latter amount, however, had already been sent by Bishop Jacob Wiens on 17 January to Hon. Arthur Meighen. It was sent as an expression of thanks for Meighen's sympathetic response to a November 1916 delegation of the three Reinländer bishops who had petitioned the federal government to provide their church with some protection against lawsuits by excommunicated members. Arthur Meighen to R. L. Borden, 29 January 1917; Meighen to Jacob Wiens, 29 January, NA, MG 26 H, 1(c), vol. 214, pp. 129091–95. *Morden Times*, 6 November 1916, p. 1. Jacob Heinrichs, Laird, had sued the Hague Reinländer congregation for business losses resulting from his excommunication. The Church decided at the last moment not to contest the suit, as a matter of principle, and was assessed $1,000 and costs amounting to $3,212. A special collection was held in order to raise this amount, and it is likely that the $1,383 forwarded to Ottawa in January was the surplus of this collection after fine and costs had been paid. *Mitarbeiter*, October 1916, p. 5; November 1916, p. 3; April 1917, p. 8.

Epp, *Mennonites in Canada*, p. 370, gives a quite misleading interpretation of Bishop Wiens' letter and contribution, although it is true that Meighen turned the contribution over to the Patriotic Fund, just as Bennett did with contributions from the other Mennonite groups at this time.

29. I. M. Dyck, p. 45.

30. The orders-in-council referred to are the Mennonite *Privilegium* and the order providing for military exemption for Doukhobors.

31. Meighen to E. B. Robertson, Assistant Superintendent of Immigration, 8 August 1917; W. W. Cory, Deputy Minister of the Interior, to W. D. Scott, Superintendent of Immigration, 20 October 1917; NA, RG 76, vol. 173, no. 58764-1. See also Canada, Parliament, House of Commons, *Debates*, 1917, 4:3368–69.

32. Janzen, pp. 184–197, and Epp, *Mennonites in Canada*, pp. 372–386, indicate that the status of Swiss Mennonites in Ontario was much less clear, even though they had been in Canada much longer.

33. E. R. Chapman, Registrar, Military Service Branch, Winnipeg, to D. W. Friesen, Postmaster, Altona, 18 October 1917; A. Haining, Registrar, Saskatchewan, to Rev. P. J.

Epp, Neville, (October 1917), quoted in John Vogt, Neville, to Benjamin Ewert, 2 November 1917, MHCA, vol. 542, no. 3. To an inquiry from Langham, Haining replied that he was not too clear about the status of Mennonites under the Act and so advised them to register and file for exemption. Quoted in the Genral Conference, Mennonite Brethren, Crimean Mennonite Brethren, and Defenceless Mennonite petition to the Governor General of Canada in Council, 4 November 1918, p. 12. P.C. no. 2897/1918, NA, RG 2, 3, vol. 199.

    34. Abram W. Klassen, Swalwell, Alberta, to Benjamin Ewert, 25 October 1917, MHCA, vol. 542, no. 3; Rev. Peter Berg, Swalwell, *Mitarbeiter*, February 1918, p. 4.

    35. "*Was haben Glieder wehrloser Gemeinschaften zu tun, um sich bei der bevorstehenden Aushebung Befreiung vom Militärdienst zu sichern?*" p. 1.

    36. Unsigned letter to Prime Minister R. L. Borden, 17 November 1917, MHCA, vol. 542, no. 3.

    37. Benjamin Ewert, Gretna, to David Toews, Rosthern, 25 March 1918; Klaas Peters, Waldeck, to B. Ewert, 23 January 1918, MHCA, vol. 542, no. 4.

    38. David Toews to B. Ewert, 21 March 1918, MHCA, vol. 542, no. 4. Ben P. Jantz, Drake, *Mitarbeiter*, February 1918, p. 4; March 1918, p. 7. The Herbert and Drake communities, and some areas north of Saskatoon were having considerable difficulties.

    39. B. Ewert to Klaas Peters, 28 January 1918, MHCA, vol. 542, no. 4, referring to a report in the *Winnipeg Tribune* of 26 January 1918. *Mitarbeiter*, editorial, February 1918, pp. 4–5.

    40. W. W. Cory to W. D. Scott, Superintendent of Immigration, 11 March 1918; Scott to Rev. Thomas A. Simpson, Waldeck, 18 June 1918; NA, RG 76, vol. 173, no. 58764-1.

    41. David Toews to B. Ewert, 21 and 26 March 1918, reports on the 25 March meeting. Toews to Ewert, 29 March, expresses regret that the Herbert committee again chose the Swedenborgian, Klaas Peters, as its representative. MHCA, vol. 542, no. 4.

    42. Ewert to Rev. Heinrich Doerksen, Niverville, 10 April 1918; Ewert to David Toews, Rosthern, 30 March 1918; MHCA, vol. 542, no. 4. The twenty-eight ministers represented the Sommerfelder (14), Bergthaler (9), Mennonite Brethren (1), *Kleine Gemeinde* (2), and Holdemann (2) churches.

    43. David Toews, Rosthern, Klaas Peters, Waldeck, and H. M. Klassen, Herbert, to Col. Machin, Ottawa, 12 April 1918, MHCA, vol. 542, no. 4. *Mitarbeiter*, April 1918, pp. 5–6, "*Unsere ungetauften Jünglinge und der Militärdienst*" has a report on the Ottawa meeting, a German translation of the brief, and a sample form of the proposed certificate.

    44. David Toews to B. Ewert, 1 May 1918, reporting content of his letter from Col. Machin; MHCA, vol. 542, no. 4.

    45. Machin to the Provost Marshal for Canada, 1 July 1918, asks him to instruct police to honour these certificates. NA, RG 24, vol. 115, HQ 7168-1.

    46. Toews to B. Ewert, 22 and 25 April 1918, MHCA, vol. 542, no. 4.

    47. J. M. Carson, Registrar, Province of Alberta, Calgary, to David Toews, 3 May 1918, Exhibit "J," P.C. no. 2897/1918; Toews to B. Ewert, 1 and 14 May 1918, MHCA, vol. 542, no. 4.

    48. Toews to B. Ewert, 14 May 1918, MHCA, vol. 542, no. 4. "*Advocatenfutter!*" (lawyer feed) ejaculated Toews in exasperation.

    49. Toews to B. Ewert, 19 May 1918, MHCA, vol. 542, no. 4.

    50. Toews to B. Ewert, 11 June 1918, MHCA, vol. 542, no. 4.

    51. Undated brief signed by Abraham Doerksen, Bishop of Sommerfeld Mennonite Church, Jacob Hoeppner, Bishop of Bergthal Congregation, and Johann Warkentin,

Leading Minister of Mennonite Brethren Church; NA, RG 24, vol. 115, HQ 7168-1. *Mitarbeiter*, June 1918, pp. 3–5, "*Bemühungen zur Sicherung der Wehrfreiheit für unsere ungetauften Jünglinge*," includes a German translation of the fifteen-point brief. A copy of the document is found in MHCA, vol. 542, no. 4. The delegation consisted of Doerksen, Hoeppner, and Warkentin, who signed the brief, and W. J. Bestvater and H. H. Ewert. An eleven-point statement, "Unbaptized Members of the Church," submitted by four Saskatchewan Mennonite groups to the authorities in their province repeats points 5–11 and 13–15 of the Manitoba brief. See Exhibit "B" of P.C. no. 2897/1918.

52. B. Ewert to D. Toews, 14 June 1918, MHCA, vol. 542. *Mitarbeiter*, June 1918, pp. 5–6, "*Die Frage wegen der Wehrfreiheit der ungetauften Jünglinge entschieden*."

53. A. L. Haining to David Toews, 16 May 1918, quoted in P.C. no. 2897/1918, p. 17.

54. Ibid., p. 19.

55. When the Chief Inspector of the Military Police requested a Mennonite *Calendar* for 1918, the government bureaucracy finally caught up with itself, since both the *Bundesbote* and *Familienkalendar* had already been banned by the Chief Press Censor. D. Toews to B. Ewert, 8 October 1918; Ewert to Toews, 12 October 1918; MHCA, vol. 542, no. 4.

56. David Toews, Regina, 4 June 1918; a copy is attached as Exhibit "E" to P.C. no. 2897/1918.

57. J. E. Doerr of Doerr and Guggisberg, Solicitors, to David Toews, 28 June 1918; Exhibit "H" of P.C. no. 2897/1918.

58. Ibid., p. 16.

59. J. E. Doerr to Lieut. McKenzie, Headquarters Staff, Regina, 11 July 1918, Exhibit "I," of P.C. no. 2897/1918.

60. J. H. Reid, Chief Inspector, Civil Section, Canadian Military Police Corps, Regina, to Provost Marshall, Ottawa, 15 October 1918, NA, RG 24, vol. 115, HQ 7168-1.

61. Western Canadian branch of the General Conference of Mennonites of North America, Mennonite Brethren, Crimean Mennonite Brethren, and Defenceless Mennonites, to the Governor General of Canada in Council, 4 November 1918, received in Ottawa 19 November 1918, P.C. no. 2897/1918, NA, RG 2, 3, vol. 199.

62. R. M. Stewart, Acting Secretary-Treasurer, Great War Veterans' Association of Canada, Ottawa, to Prime Minster R. L. Borden, 21 October 1918, NA, MG 26 H, 1(c), vol. 214, p. 121177; G.W.V.A., Loyal Orange Lodge, and Sons of England, Regina, to J. A. Calder, Minister of Colonization and Immigration, 15 October 1918, SAB, M 12, II-77, p. 11436; Great War Next of Kin Association, Lethbridge, to P. M. Robert Borden, 22 September 1918, NA, RG 24, vol. 115, HQ 7168-1. See also reports in *RML* on meetings of the G.W.V.A. (24 September 1918, p. 9) and Orange Lodge (7 October 1918, p. 9).

63. J. M. Bliss, "The Methodist Church and World War I," *Canadian Historical Review* 49 (September 1968): 222. See also "The Church, the War and Patriotism," report prepared by the Army and Navy Board of the Methodist Church and adopted by the General Conference at Hamilton in 1918; copy in PAM, MG 14, B 45, box 6. It contains nine recommendations dealing specifically with the Mennonite situation in the prairie provinces.

64. R. B. Bennett to R. L. Borden, 22 January 1917, NA, MG 26 H, 1(c), vol. 214.

65. Doell, "Klaas Peters," p. 72.

66. D. Toews to B. Ewert, 29 March, 18 April 1918, MHCA, vol. 542, no. 4.

67. B. Ewert to P. H. Neufeld, Vanderhoof, B.C., 4 June 1918, MHCA, vol. 542, no. 4; "Synopsis of Evidence to be Expected of H. M. Klassen" at the trial of Klaas Peters, NA, RG 24, vol. 115, HQ 7168.

68. J. H. Reid, Chief Inspector, Civil Section, Canadian Military Police Corps, Regina, to the Provost Marshall, Ottawa, 15 October 1918, NA, RG 24, vol. 115, HQ 7168.

69. That some of these cards were issued to young men of the New Church is probably the reason for Klassen refusing to countersign them. The non-pacifist Church of the New Jerusalem now sought to distance itself from Peters. F. E. Waelchli, Rosthern, "The New Jerusalem Community of the Mennonites," *New Church Life*, October 1918, pp. 645–647.

70. *RML*, 9 November 1918, p. 17; 15 November, p. 15; 29 November, p. 11; *SCSun*, 15 and 29 November 1918; Doell, "Klaas Peters," pp. 79–80. For extensive documentation of this court case see NA, RG 24, vol. 115, HQ 7168-1.

71. *Mitarbeiter*, February 1918, p. 7; see also April 1917, p. 3; October 1917, p. 6; November 1917, p. 2.

72. Ibid., editorial, April 1918, p. 4. Hutterite purchase of a 122,000-acre ranch in Alberta was reported. For an extensive account of this movement from the perspective of the American emigrants, see Allan Teichroew, "World War I and the Mennonite Migration to Canada to Avoid the Draft," *MQR* 45 (July 1971): 219–249.

73. J. C. Koehn, Canadian Government Agent, Omaha, to W. J. White, Inspector of U.S. Agencies, 28 September 1917; W. W. Cory, Deputy Minister of the Interior, to W. D. Scott, Superintendent of Immigration, 20 October 1917; NA, RG 76, vol. 173, no. 58764-1; cf. Adjutant-General, Canadian Militia, to John P. Thiessen, Jansen, Nebraska, 2 October 1917, RG 24, vol. 115, HQ 7168-1.

74. M. J. Johnstone, Canadian Government Agent, Watertown, S.D., to W. J. White, 23 October 1917; White to Johnstone, 6 November 1917, NA, RG 76, vol. 173, no. 58764-1.

75. J. B. W., Commissioner of Immigration, Winnipeg, to W. D. Scott, 30 January 1918, regarding Hutterites: "these people are very desirable." NA, RG 76, vol. 173, no. 58764-1. Cf. Valentine Winkler, Manitoba Minister of Agriculture and Immigration, to Arthur Meighen, Minister of the Interior, 31 January 1918. In April Inspector White was still encouraging Agent Koehn in Mountain Lake, Minn., to try to "get as many of the [Mennonites] to move to Canada as possible."

76. F. J. Fulton, M.P., Kamloops, to W. D. Scott, 20 August 1918, NA, RG 76, vol. 173, no. 58764-2.

77. Scott to W. W. Cory, 27 August 1918. Writing to Canadian government agent J. C. Koehn in Omaha on 31 August 1918, Scott indicated the reasons "for deciding on a somewhat neutral policy with regard to strongly encouraging a heavy movement of Mennonites to Canada at this time." NA, RG 76, vol. 173, no. 58764-2.

78. W. D. Scott to Mennonite Emigration Committee in Kansas, 13 June 1918, quoted in *Canadian Annual Review*, 1918, p. 427.

79. *RML*, 20 September 1918, p. 9; 24 September, p. 9.

80. Ibid., 25 September 1918, p. 9; 26 September, p. 1.

81. P.C. no. 2622, 25 October 1918, NA, RG 2, 1, vol. 1518. Epp's claim, *Mennonites in Canada*, p. 382, that after June 1918 "all Mennonites in Western Canada were *excepted from* the Act upon simple proof of identity" is thus not supported by the facts. Mennonites from the U.S.A. clearly did not come into this category, and even those in Saskatchewan, who had come to Canada directly under the 1873 agreement, had difficulty in practice gaining exception right to the end of the war.

82. P.C. no. 404, 23 February 1918, NA, RG 2, 1, vol. 1485.

83. Bergthaler Church, Ministerial, *Minutes*, 2:165, 7 March 1918, MHCA, vol. 716.

84. B. Ewert, Gretna, to D. Toews, Rosthern, 15 May 1918; H. M. Klassen, Herbert, Saskatchewan, to B. Ewert, 5 June 1918; P. H. Neufeld, Vanderhoof, B.C., to B. Ewert, 29 May 1918, MHCA, vol. 542, no. 4.

85. V. Winkler, Minister of Agriculture, Winnipeg, to Rev. Peter Goertz, Inman, Kansas, 13 May 1918, PAM, MG 14, B 45, box 5. Peter B. Schmidt, Steinbach, to B. Ewert, 29 May 1918, reports an almost identical response from Registrar Philip Locke, Winnipeg, MHCA, vol. 542, no. 4.

86. G. D. Robertson, Chairman, Canada Registration Board, Ottawa, to Premier W. M. Martin, Regina, 18 May 1918, SAB, M 4, I-101, p. 30088.

87. Peter B. Schmidt, Steinbach, to B. Ewert, 29 May 1918, MHCA, vol. 542, no. 4.

88. *Mitarbeiter*, June 1918, pp. 6–7. Present at the June 8 meeting were bishops Jacob Hoeppner and Peter Schmidt, and ministers H. Doerksen, H. H. Ewert, Johann Warkentin, and Heinrich Reimer.

89. Question 9 of the "Card for Males" reads: "If registered under Military Service Act, what is your serial number?" Question 4 of the "Card for Females" asks for the person's nationality. Copies of the cards are given in appendix 7.

90. JWR[empel], *"Fragen für die Registrierung am 22sten Juni 1918, für Männliche Personen,"* MHCA, vol. 1099.

91. *Mitarbeiter*, June 1918, p. 7; B. Ewert to D. Toews, 14 June 1918, MHCA, vol. 542, no. 4.

92. Toews to B. Ewert, 11 June 1918, MHCA, vol. 542, no. 4.

93. *Mitarbeiter*, May 1918, pp. 6–7.

94. Peter S. Buhr, Haskett, to B. Ewert, 30 May 1918, MHCA, vol. 542, no. 4.

95. B. Ewert to D. Toews, 14 June 1918, MHCA, vol. 542, no. 4. See also p. 4 of account of P. C. Locke, submitted by Judge J. E. Adamson and attached to memo of L. E. Westman to A. MacNamarra, 27 March 1944, NA, RG 27, 601.3-6, vol. 4.

96. Adamson to MacNamarra, 27 March 1944, p. 8, NA, RG 27, 601.3-6, vol. 4. Ewert to D. Toews, 15 June 1918, MHCA, vol. 542, no. 4.

97. I. M. Dyck, pp. 30–32. Some details of Dyck's version of this highly interesting incident are clearly wrong, understandably so since he wrote some fifty years after the event, largely from memory. But his claim that a second brotherhood meeting was called to reverse the decision of June 13 is much more plausible than Locke's more dramatic version in which the leaders made the decision on the spot.

Gerhard Rempel, *"Erinnerungen,"* undated MS, Blumenort, Chihuahua, Mexico, copy in MHCA, vol. 1028, pp. 1–3, includes another variation of this incident, according to which the Swift Current *Obervorsteher* Rempel tried to persuade the *Bruderschaft* with Luke 2 even before Locke used it with the leaders. See also Epp, *Mennonites in Canada*, pp. 383–384.

98. Bergthaler Church, Brotherhood, *Minutes*, 15 November 1917, 9 October 1918, MHCA, vol. 715; idem, Ministerial, *Minutes*, 2:163, 172, 174; 6 November 1917, 5 August and 13 September 1918, MHCA, vol. 716. *Mitarbeiter*, November 1917, p. 6.

99. I. M. Dyck, pp. 29–30; cf. pp. 45, 55. Redekop, pp. 13–14, erroneously claims that the Old Colony Mennonites did not support the Red Cross at all. The *Mitarbeiter*, November 1917, p. 6, for example, reported Reinländer contributions of $2,044.75 for the Patriotic Fund in March and $2,335.50 more recently for the Red Cross.

100. *Mitarbeiter*, January 1918, p. 4. The editor compared the $50,000 Mennonite total with the reported $53,000 contribution of Manitoba Jews to the Patriotic Fund and

wondered whether Mennonites had done enough. William J. O'Neill to R. S. Thornton, Manitoba Minister of Education, 14 July 1919, quoted in J. H. Doerksen, pp. 91–95.

101. *Canadian Annual Review,* 1917, pp. 291, 293, 300.

102. P. J. Friesen, secretary, report on 1 November 1917 meeting at Waldheim of Mennonite ministers, MHCA, vol. 542, no. 3. D. Toews, Rosthern to B. Ewert, 17 November 1917, reported that the Drake community had agreed with the Waldheim decision. See also *Mitarbeiter,* November 1917, p. 6.

103. Bergthaler Church, Ministerial, *Minutes,* 2:163, no. 4.A, 6 November 1917, MHCA, vol. 716.

104. Bergthaler Church, Brotherhood, *Minutes,* 15 November 1917, MHCA, vol. 715; *Mitarbeiter,* November 1917, p. 6.

105. *Mitarbeiter,* January 1918, p. 5. The northern Saskatchewan churches raised $16,000 for the Red Cross; the Manitoba Sommerfelder contributed over $4,000, the Reinländer over $3,000, and the Manitoba East Reserve churches offered a $12,800 interest-free loan in addition to their gift.

106. J. H. Woods, Chairman, Victory War Loan Press Publicity Committee, to Chambers, Chief Press Censor for Canada, 1 November 1917, NA, RG 6, E-1, vol. 21, no. 119-S-2.

107. Chambers to Woods, 2 November 1917; Chambers to Jacob S. Friesen, Steinbach, 2 November 1917, NA, RG 6, E-1, vol. 21, no. 119-S-2.

108. Friesen to Chambers, 7 November 1917, NA, RG 6, E-1, vol. 21, no. 119-S-2.

109. Chambers to E. L. Newcombe, 12 November 1917, NA, RG 6, E-1, vol. 21, no. 119-S-2.

110. Chambers to R. M. Coulter, 12 November 1917, NA, RG 6, E-1, vol. 21, no. 119-S-2.

111. Coulter to Chambers, 14 November 1917, NA, RG 6, E-1, vol. 21, no. 119-S-2.

112. Newcombe to Chambers, 14 November 1917; T. C. Boville, Deputy Minister of Finance, to Chambers, 15 November 1917, NA, RG 6, E-1, vol. 21, no. 119-S-2.

113. Chambers to Coulter, 15 November 1917, NA, RG 6, E-1, vol. 21, no. 119-S-2.

114. Chambers to Woods, 15 November 1917. To the Deputy Minister of Finance the Censor admitted: "I am unable to say whether the publication of this editorial was the result of our correspondence or was prompted by some spontaneous impulse which it is impossible for the ordinary mortal to fathom." Chambers to Boville, 16 November 1917, NA, RG 6, E-1, vol. 21, no. 119-S-2.

115. Woods to Chambers, 15 November 1917, NA, RG 6, E-1, vol. 21, no. 119-S-2.

116. Chambers to Woods, 16 November 1917, NA, RG 6, E-1, vol. 21, no. 119-S-2.

117. Manitoba Mennonites Rev. H. Doerksen, Chortitzer Church, and Rev. H. J. Friesen, Sommerfelder Church, met with the Minister in Winnipeg on 8 October 1918. Bishop J. Wiens and Rev. J. P. Wall, Hague Reinländer Church, Bishop David Toews and Rev. J. Gerbrandt, Rosenorter Church, and J. H. Friesen, Mennonite Brethren Church, met with the Minister in Saskatchewan a week later. The letter (T. White, Finance Minister, to the Bishops of the Mennonite Church, 8 October 1918) is found in German translation in J. H. Doerksen, p. 90; in English (W. T. White, Minister of Finance, to the Bishops in the Mennonite churches in Saskatchewan) it is found in *RML,* 16 October 1918, p. 2.

118. The Manitoba Bergthaler approved participation in the bond drive at their brotherhood meeting on 9 October 1918. MHCA, vol. 715. The *Mitarbeiter,* May 1918, pp. 5–6, had already prepared the way for this decision by reporting a similar arrangement

made by the Mennonite Church in the U.S.A. H. H. Ewert to S. F. Coffman, Vineland, Ontario, 21 October 1918, reported that western Canadian Mennonites generally had accepted White's proposal. MHCA, vol. 554. The *RML*, 16 October 1918, p. 2, reported that White's letter was "perfectly satisfactory to the representatives of the Mennonites."

119. William J. O'Neill to R. S. Thornton, 14 July 1919, reproduced in J. H. Doerksen, p. 91.

120. P.C. no. 146, 17 January 1917, "Consolidated Orders Respecting Censorship," NA, RG 2, 1, vol. 1430. Four orders-in-council of 1914 and four of 1915 were replaced by the new one.

121. Col. E. J. Chambers, Chief Press Censor, to Secretary of State, 1 February 1917; Acting Under-Secretary of State to Chambers, 22 February 1917, NA, RG 6, E-1, vol. 13, 116-C-5.

122. Chambers to B. C. Johnson, Arizona, 23 February 1917, NA, RG 6, E-1, vol. 13, 116-C-5.

123. Chambers to Rev. Peter Goertz, Carnduff, Saskatchewan, 16 March 1917, replying to Goertz's inquiry of 12 March 1917; cf. Chambers to Bishop David Toews, Rosthern, 3 August 1917, NA, RG 6, E-1, vol. 13, 116-C-5.

124. Censor "EB" examined the 12 and 17 April 1917 issues of the *Christlicher Bundesbote*. The request to restore postal privileges was made through J. F. Foster, U.S. Consul General, to Thomas Mulvey, Under-Secretary of State, 22 July 1917. The Chief Press Censor replied to Foster, 24 July 1917, that "under no consideration whatever" would he think of advising that the ban be lifted. NA, RG 6, E-1, vol. 13, 116-C-5.

125. R. M. Coulter, Deputy Postmaster General, to Chambers, 19 March 1917; Chambers to Herbert Vanderhoof, Chicago, 20 March 1917, NA, RG 6, E-1, vol. 13, 116-C-5.

126. J. P. D. van Veen on 16 August 1918 reported to the Censor Bureau that the *Rundschau* was devoted exclusively to religious subjects. It was published weekly by Mennonite Publishing House, Scottdale, Pa. NA, RG 6, E-1, vol. 15, no. 116-M-6.

127. Chambers to The Publishers, "Steinbach Post," 7 June 1918, NA, RG 6, E-1, vol. 21, no. 119-S-2.

128. Jacob S. Friesen to Chambers, 12 June 1918, NA, RG 6, E-1, vol. 21, no. 119-S-2.

129. Chambers to Jacob T. Wiebe, Greenland, Manitoba, 17 June 1918, NA, RG 6, E-1, vol. 21, no. 119-S-2.

130. P.C. no. 2381, 25 September 1918, NA, RG 2, 1, vol. 1515.

131. B. Ewert, Gretna, to David Toews, Rosthern, 12 October 1918, MHCA, vol. 542, no. 4. H. H. Ewert, editor, to Secretary of State, 30 June 1919, NA, RG 6, E-1, vol. 138, no. 370-G-A-25. B. Ewert could not resist pointing out the irony of this form of suppression: "*Es wird auch in unserm schönen Canada immer dunkler. Wir kämpfen ja auch für Freiheit und gegen Unterdrückung.*" (Even in our beautiful Canada it is getting darker and darker. But then, we are fighting for freedom and against oppression.)

132. J. P. D. van Veen to J. Leslie, Press Censor of Canada, 10 October 1918, NA, RG 6, E-1, vol. 21, no. 119-S-2.

133. J. A. McGibbon, Asst. Commissioner, Royal North-West Mounted Police, Regina, to Chief Press Censor, Ottawa, 9 October 1919, NA, RG 6, E-1, vol. 21, no. 119-S-2.

134. "No. 50," Regina, report to [RNWMP], 6 October 1918, NA, RG 6, E-1, vol. 21, no. 119-S-2.

135. Chambers to RNWMP, Regina, 12 October 1918, NA, RG 6, E-1, vol. 21, no. 119-S-2; cf. J. P. D. van Veen to Leslie, 10 October 1918, describing the *Post* as "a Mennonite family paper for young and old ... perfectly harmless."

136. Jacob S. Friesen to Department of the Secretary of State, 18 November 1918, NA, RG 6, E-1, vol. 21, no. 119-S-2.

137. Chambers to Secretary of State, 22 November 1918, NA, RG 6, E-1, vol. 21, no. 119-S-2.

138. P.C. no. 703, 2 April 1919, NA, RG 2, 1, vol. 1538.

139. Friesen to Department of Secretary of State, 2 May 1919, NA, RG 6, E-1, vol. 138, no. 370-G-A-14.

140. Chambers to Friesen, 20 May 1919, NA, RG 6, E-1, vol. 138, no. 370-G-A-14.

141. H. H. Ewert to Secretary of State, 30 June 1919, NA, RG 6, E-1, vol. 138, #370-G-A-25.

142. Chambers to Ewert, 10 July 1919; Ewert to Chambers, 17 July 1919, NA, RG 6, E-1, vol. 138, #370-G-A-25.

143. "Censorship Notice," *Canada Gazette*, 26 June 1919, p. 30; quoted in Epp, *Mennonites in Canada*, p. 393. The Amish *Herold der Wahrheit*, ed. S. D. Guengerich, Wellman, Ohio, unsuccessfully attempted to regain permission to circulate among its 270 Canadian (Ontario) subscribers. Guengerich to Chambers, 7 and 13 May 1919; Chambers to Guengerich, 13 and 19 May 1919, NA, RG 6, E-1, vol. 138, no. 370-G-A-17.

144. Chambers to W. D. Scott, 7 October 1919; Scott pointed out to Chambers, 16 October 1919, that a recent order-in-council prohibited Hutterite immigration, but did not relate in any way to literature. NA, RG 6, E-1, vol. 146, no. 371-H-2.

145. John F. Funk, President, Mennonite Publishing Company, Elkhart, Indiana, to Chambers, 10 and 15 May 1919; Chambers to Funk, 17 May 1919, NA, RG 6, E-1, vol. 146, no. 371-M-1.

146. Chambers to Funk, 4 June 1919, NA, RG 6, E-1, vol. 146, no. 371-M-1.

147. Chambers to R. M. Coulter, Deputy Postmaster General, 5 May 1919, NA, RG 6, E-1, vol. 146, no. 371-M-1.

148. Chambers to M. B. Publishing House, 8 May 1919, NA, RG 6, E-1, vol. 146, no. 371-M-3.

149. Dennis Stoesz, "Jacob S. Friesen and the *Steinbach Post*," *Mennonite Historian*, March 1985, p. 2.

CHAPTER VI

# EMIGRATION AND ACCOMMODATION

The four years of war changed many aspects of Canadian life. The initial boost to the economy, which was sparked by a rapid increase in value of grain and flour exports, was offset by serious inflation in the latter years of the war. Accelerated mechanization of farming and growth of industry encouraged a population shift to urban areas. The end of wartime manufacture and the demobilization of troops brought a new competitiveness to the labour market, stimulating the growth of industrial unions. The formation of the One Big Union and the Winnipeg general strike of 1919, in the context of much socialist rhetoric, alarmed the government. As a result it tended to overreact to perceived threats to national security or unity. Mennonites were only one group to become the target of such overreaction.

At the same time, Canada's new recognition in international circles as a result of its contribution to the war effort stimulated the nationalist mood, especially in English Canada. Immigration regulations temporarily reflected a nativist bias and some extreme nationalists even talked of deporting undesirable "aliens" such as Mennonites.[1] This led to enormous pressures on minority groups to conform. Some Mennonites chose to emigrate rather than compromise. Others, especially those who had accepted public schools before the war, decided to stay, confident that matters would quickly return to normal. Far from emigrating, they expended considerable energy and resources in the next decade to help about twenty thousand of their co-religionists immigrate to Canada from the newly founded U.S.S.R.

Still others wanted to emigrate but either lacked the financial resources to do so or were kept back by family ties.

## The Postwar Situation

The series of crises experienced by the Mennonite communities in Manitoba and Saskatchewan since the beginning of the war has been described in the preceding chapters. In Manitoba this began with the loss of German language rights in the public schools with the abolition of the bilingual provisions in 1916. This was intensified when the option of maintaining their own private schools was removed in 1918 and compulsory attendance legislation was increasingly used to force all Mennonite children to attend government-controlled public schools. By 1920, education under the flag was the only legal option open to them.

The direct effects of the war were less threatening. The extent and the manner of financial participation raised some delicate questions of conscience. Contributing to the relief of war sufferers through the Red Cross seemed generally acceptable while subscription to the Victory loans was for the most part rejected. In neither case was there direct governmental pressure to participate. On the other hand, Ottawa's insistence that Mennonites take part in the national registrations of 1917 and 1918 created considerable consternation. Neither registration, as it turned out, led to any significant increase in Mennonite enlistment. But they were reminders that the exemption promised the Mennonites in their *Privilegium* was exemption from direct military service only.

The exclusion of Mennonites from participating in federal elections by the Dominion Elections Act 1916, and the War-Time Elections Act 1917, does not seem to have aroused any apprehension or resentment among them.[2] Several Mennonite groups refused in principle to participate in any elections. Several of the others had already decided during the summer of 1917 against voting in the conscription plebiscite proposed by Sir Wilfrid Laurier, or in a federal election in which conscription would be an issue.[3] While Mennonites were not immediately affected by the voting legislation, they keenly felt the effects of the official press censor. By the end of 1919, all of their official church periodicals had suspended publication, and difficulties were encountered in the free circulation of liturgical and church educational material.

Public agitation against German-speaking peoples and pacifists led to one further disturbing development. By late summer of 1918 local opposition was beginning to develop toward Mennonite immigrants from the U.S.A.[4] This intensified during the last few months of the war and led to official protests to the Borden government about its immigration policy. Leading these protests was the Great War Veterans' Association, who considered it "a gross breach of faith to returned men" for the government to sell land to Mennonites when it was needed for returning soldiers.[5] Joining this protest were politicians[6] and church groups.[7] Under that kind of pressure Immigration Minister J. A. Calder was publicly saying by mid-October that "a law should be enacted to the effect that no man should be allowed to come to this country unless he is prepared to carry his full share of the military burden."[8] Even before Ottawa took any official action, Premier Oliver of British Columbia implemented a policy of "no crown lands for pacifists" in his province.[9]

The federal government waited until the following spring before it acted, and then it did so not by new legislation but by order-in-council. Using the authority of section 38 of the Immigration Act, it decided that

> whereas the Minister of Immigration and Colonization reports that, owing to conditions prevailing as the result of the War, a widespread feeling exists throughout the Dominion, and more particularly in Western Canada, that steps should be taken to prevent the entry to Canada of all persons who may be regarded as undesirables because, owing to their peculiar customs, habits, modes of living and methods of holding property, they are not likely to become readily assimilated or to assume the duties and responsibilities of Canadian citizenship within a reasonable time;
>
> and whereas the Minister further reports that numerous representations have been received by the Department of Immigration and Colonization indicating that persons commonly known as Doukhobors, Hutterites and Mennonites are of the class and character described and consequently that it is desirable to prohibit the entry to Canada of such;
>
> therefore ... on and after the second day of May, 1919, and until further ordered, the entry to Canada of immigrants of the Doukhobor, Hutterite and Mennonite class shall be and the same is hereby prohibited.[10]

While this action did not affect Mennonites already in Canada, it added to their growing sense of uneasiness about their future status in the country. For those already inclined toward emigration, this provided reinforcement. For those who had decided to stay, it meant political lobbying to get the order-in-council repealed.

## The Emigration Option

The possibility of being forced to participate in military service was a strong factor in the decision to emigrate from Prussia to Russia in the late eighteenth century and from Russia to Canada in the nineteenth. It is thus not surprising that for a significant portion of the Canadian Mennonite community this option would again be taken in the political climate after 1918.[11]

The first warning that Mennonites might well choose to leave the country on the issue of control of their own schools was sounded by the *Free Press* in 1910. Reviewing the compulsory flag-flying issue of 1907, it wrote:

> the conservative people who constitute the large majority of the people are to this day so tenacious of their principals [sic] that if any attempt should be made on the part of the government to force public schools upon them ... they would leave the country in spite of the large material interests which they have here.[12]

That warning was reiterated in the presentation of H. H. Ewert to the Premier of Manitoba and three cabinet ministers made on behalf of the large Mennonite delegation in February 1916: "If Mennonites are deprived of something they deem necessary for the preservation of their faith, they would always be prepared to leave their homes and seek another country with a greater measure of freedom."[13]

In Saskatchewan, P. M. Friesen of Rush Lake warned Prime Minister Borden in December 1916 that the announced 1917 national registration had caused some leading Mennonites to suggest emigration.[14] Klaas Peters feared that the federal pre-election legislation of 1917 might lead to a termination of the *Privilegium*. Should Mennonites choose to emigrate, he already had a location in mind. "With the government of the Argentines we have a good agreement in reserve, and the opportunity of establishing a colony there," he wrote to one of his friends in the Swift Current area.[15] When funds were raised in several Saskatchewan communities in 1918 to send a delegation to South America to pursue this possibility, an investigation by the military police kept the government informed.[16] Nevertheless, a semi-official three-man delegation led by Klaas Peters of Wymark left in early 1919 and negotiated with the governments of Brazil, Uruguay, and Argentina, but without success.[17]

Two groups seriously pursued the emigration option. The three Reinländer congregations in the Manitoba West Reserve and in the Hague and Swift Current reserves in Saskatchewan were strongly committed. In most of their explorations and negotiations they acted as one body. Several congregations of Bergthal descent also promoted emigration. Led by the Chortitzer of the Manitoba East Reserve, a loose coalition was formed with the Sommerfelder in the West Reserve and their related groups in Saskatchewan. This group had informal ties with the Reinländer and generally followed that group's leads.

## Reinländer

A conference of Reinländer Mennonites at Hague announced in the fall of 1918 that if the School Attendance Act were enforced in their schools they would arrange immediate migration to the Argentine.[18] By the following summer the decision to emigrate had been made by all three Reinländer groups, and a joint delegation of six men was sent to South America to look for suitable land and to negotiate a *Privilegium*.[19] The delegates, listed in table 17, returned from their long trip in November without any success. As the earlier group led by Klaas Peters had found, neither Argentina nor Brazil was prepared to offer suitable concessions.[20]

Equally discouraging was the delegation's report from Ottawa, where they had stopped on their way to South America to attempt once more to have the federal government guarantee their school privileges. Ottawa, of course, could not do this for constitutional reasons. But the Reinländer leadership, at least in retrospect, blamed the war for having ruined everything.[21]

With South America apparently closed, the Reinländer now explored possibilities in the southern states of the U.S.A. Land offers were received from Mississippi, Alabama, and Louisiana. Negotiations were undertaken with officials of the state of Mississippi, to which a Reinländer delegation was sent in January 1920. The delegates, listed in table 17, presented a six-point petition to the governor asking for exemption from military service, the right to affirm instead of taking an oath, religious freedom, complete responsibility for and control of their schools (including the right to use German), freedom to administer their *Waisenamt*, and control over the disposition of all colony lands by their Society.[22]

Table 17
**Reinländer Land-Seeking Delegations, 1919–1921**

| Date | Destination | Groups Represented | Members[a] |
|---|---|---|---|
| Aug. 4 to Nov. 24, 1919 | Argentina Brazil | Hague | Rev. Johann Wall Rev. Johann P. Wall |
| | | Manitoba | Klaas Heide Cornelius Rempel |
| | | Swift Current | Rev. Julius Wiebe David Rempel |
| Jan. 15 to 29, 1920 | Mississippi | Hague | Jacob E. Friesen |
| | | Manitoba | Franz F. Froese Peter P. Harms |
| | | Swift Current | Rev. Julius Wiebe Bishop Abraham Wiebe |

## Table 17
## Reinländer Land-Seeking Delegations, 1919–1921 *(Continued)*

| | | | |
|---|---|---|---|
| April 12 to 29, 1920 | Mississippi | Hague | Rev. Johann P. Wall |
| | | | Benjamin Goertzen |
| | | | Rev. Franz Peters |
| | | Manitoba | Bishop Johann Friesen |
| | | | Cornelius Rempel |
| | | | Johann W. Rempel |
| May 14 to 25, 1920 | Mississippi | | |
| Aug. 19, 1920 | Quebec | Manitoba | Bishop Johann Friesen |
| | | Swift Current | Bishop Abraham Wiebe |
| | | | Jacob Friesen |
| | | | David Rempel |
| Sept. 8 to Oct. 9, 1920 | Mexico | Hague | Rev. Johann P. Wall |
| | | | Benjamin Goertzen |
| | | | ? Klassen |
| Oct. 9 to Dec. 1920 | Paraguay | Hague | Abram Klassen |
| | | | Jacob Friesen |
| | | | Franz Dyck |
| | | | ? Wiens |
| Nov. 11 to end Dec. 1920 | Mexico | Hague | |
| | | Swift Current | |
| Jan. 24 to Mar. 12, 1921 | Mexico | Hague | Rev. Johann Loeppky |
| | | | Benjamin Goertzen |
| | | Manitoba | Rev. Julius Loewen |
| | | | Klaas Heide |
| | | | Cornelius Rempel |
| | | Swift Current | David Rempel |
| April 5 to May 9, 1921 | Mexico | Hague | Rev. Johann P. Wall |
| | | Manitoba | Klaas Heide |
| | | Swift Current | |
| July 1921 | Mexico | Manitoba | Abram Giesbrecht |
| | | | ? Peters |
| | | | ? Baumann |
| | | | ? Klassen |
| | | Swift Current | Rev. Julius Wiebe |
| | | | David Rempel |
| Aug. 12 to Sept. 10, 1921 | Mexico | Manitoba | |
| | | Swift Current | |

a. In a number of cases the lists given are incomplete.

Source: Compiled from I. M. Dyck, pp. 53, 75; Harder, pp. 3–6; Quiring, *Rußlanddeutsche suchen eine Heimat,* pp. 37–38, 54; Sawatzky, pp. 31, 43; Gerhard Rempel, p. 6; Schmiedehaus, pp. 18–21; Johan M. Loeppky, *Ein Reisebericht von Kanada nach Mexiko im Jahre 1921* (n.p., n.d.); *MFP,* May 8, 1920, p. 11; August 20 and 21, 1920; *Mennonite Encyclopedia,* s.v. "Old Colony Mennonites," by Cornelius Krahn.

A week after their return, Governor Russell confirmed in writing what he had told the delegation. State laws would guarantee the Mennonites "the fullest privilege of exercising their religious principles without any molestation or restriction, and the same privilege [would] be extended to the education of their children in their own schools of their own language."[23] He also assured them of the privilege of giving the oath by affirmation instead of swearing and the liberty to administer their own benevolent society according to their system.

On the basis of this encouraging offer, a second delegation left for Mississippi in April 1920. In addition to exploring concrete settlement possibilities, it also called on U.S. Attorney General A. Mitchell Palmer to discuss exemption from military service. Palmer could only point to existing legislation, which provided that proven conscientious objectors "shall be exempted from military service in a combatant capacity."[24] While this was considerably less than the Mennonites were currently enjoying in Canada, it was sufficient for the Reinländer church to decide formally on May 4 to emigrate to Mississippi.[25]

A third delegation in May 1920 negotiated the purchase of 125,000 acres of land. On their return the *Bruderschaft* decided on June 1 to ratify the deal and instructed each prospective purchaser to provide a two-dollar-per-acre down payment.[26] A fourth delegation authorized to close the deal was mysteriously refused entry into the U.S.A. The Reinländer leadership accepted this as a sign from God that kept them from moving into an unhappy situation, and turned their attention elsewhere.[27]

Governor Russell of Mississippi was not prepared to give up the project that readily, however, and asked the Immigration Department in Washington to investigate fully why U.S. authorities at Winnipeg had stopped the movement of Mennonites to Mississippi.[28] The Commissioner-General of Immigration in Washington responded that "this Bureau has no advice that immigration authorities at Winnipeg have stopped movement of Mennonites to Mississippi, or any other state."[29] In response to a more general subsequent inquiry from Neche, North Dakota, as to why the Mennonites from Manitoba and Saskatchewan had not been allowed into the country, Washington replied: "As to the numbers in the particular class of people to whom you refer, the Bureau knows of no particular reason why they should not be allowed to enter."[30] The proposed migration to Mississippi therefore appears to have been halted, not by policy decision, but by the arbitrary action of the Immigration official who turned back the land-buying delegation.

It is clear, however, that the U.S. authorities were not prepared to arrange in advance for a group immigration.

> Whether they will or will not be admitted is a question which, under the immigration law, can not be determined in advance of their physical

application at one of our ports. When they do so apply, their cases will be given careful consideration in the light of all the circumstances which may be known as to them at that time.[31]

But neither were they closed to the immigration of Mennonites. H. M. Kratz, a Mennonite attorney from Philadelphia, inquiring on behalf of the General Conference Mennonite Church's Executive Committee, received this rather self-evident response: "So far as the Bureau is aware, there is no particular reason why Mennonites should not be admitted if they satisfactorily meet the requirements of the immigration law."[32] A decision of sorts was reached when, in response to pressure from Senators from the Southern states and a specific case submitted by Inspector Carr of Winnipeg, the Secretary of the Department of Labor ruled that "Mennonites as such are not inadmissible."[33]

The correspondence generated by this emigration attempt also sheds some interesting light on Canadian official attitudes to the Mennonites.

It appears from the information which the Bureau has on file concerning the Mennonites, as a class, that they are "persona non grata" in Canada. This by reason of their peculiarities, religiously, politically and otherwise.[34]

Strong objections have been made to the attitude of this sect by provincial and municipal authorities in Canada by reason of the fact that they absolutely refuse to comply with civil laws with reference to sending their children to school or to meeting the requirements of the vital statistics with reference to births or deaths.... During the War these people were the most radical of conscientious objectors.... The writer in conversation with civil officers has been told repeatedly that the continued presence in Canada of this sect was detrimental to the interests of the country and that every pressure would be brought to bear to influence them to leave Canada.[35]

As late as the summer of 1921, the Commissioner-General of the U.S. Bureau of Immigration indicated that he was aware that Canada was "exerting more or less pressure with the view to effecting their [the Mennonites'] departure."[36] The Bureau was faced at the same time with strong protest from within the U.S.A. against admitting Mennonite immigrants. Much of this came from the American Legion, but other groups were also represented.[37] That the Bureau did not seek a ban on Mennonite immigrants was due to the fact that these were being vigorously sought as settlers by various agencies in Alabama, Colorado, South Carolina, Arkansas, Florida, and Georgia.[38] Settlement possibilities in Florida were seriously explored and promoted by Klaas Peters as late as the spring of 1921.[39]

When the attempts to emigrate to South America and to the Southern states both failed, the Reinländer Mennonites explored alternatives within

Canada and even considered North Africa and Australia.[40] Their final attempt to gain educational freedom in Manitoba by settling in some more remote part of the province, possibly in "the Hudson Bay district," need not be taken too seriously.[41] More serious were explorations undertaken in the Abitibi region and with the Government of Quebec. On August 19, 1920, a seven-man delegation (see table 17) representing the Reinländer Mennonites of Manitoba and Swift Current met with Premier L. A. Taschereau, Colonization Minister J. E. Perreault, and J. N. Miller, Secretary of the Catholic Committee of the Council of Public Instruction, to state their case.[42] The five points of their requested *Privilegium* were as follows:

> 1. To grant and assure (or have ratified by the Dominion Government) an entire exemption from any military forces as defenceless Christians called Mennonites;
>
> 2. The privilege of affirming with the simple "Yes" or "No" instead of making oath in or out of courts;
>
> 3. The fullest privilege of exercising our religious principles and rules of our church without any kind of molestation or restriction whatever;
>
> 4. The privilege of our own private school buildings and maintaining them at our own expense, and to educate our children in the same, according to our creed in our customary German language without any restrictions;
>
> 5. To administer and invest the estates and inherited property of our people, especially that of widows and orphans, in our own trust system, called the "*Waisenamt*," according to our own rules and religion without any restrictions.[43]

It will be noted that the main points in this list of requests are identical to those in the 1873 *Privilegium*. The education clause is made more specific and includes explicit mention of the German language, just as it did in the Mississippi petition. The clause on the *Waisenamt* did not appear in the 1873 *Privilegium* but was included in the Mississippi petition.

The Mennonites were now aware that there was a division of powers between the federal and provincial governments. Accordingly, the two bishops left the next day for Ottawa to gain reassurance on the question of military exemption and to obtain federal government approval of the proposed move to Quebec. The five lay delegates meanwhile left for the Abitibi district to explore settlement possibilities.

The initial response of the Quebec press to the proposed Mennonite migration was quite favourable. *Le Matin* considered the Mennonite requests "not incompatible with the normal administration of the law," while *La Patrie* found "nothing in their demands which conflicts with our laws."[44] The Reinländer were encouraged and sent several subsequent delegations to Quebec. But in the end, the migration did not materialize, partly because the land was unsuitable for agriculture, partly because the requested governmental guarantees were not forthcoming.[45]

While the Manitoba and Swift Current Reinländer were exploring possibilities in Quebec, the Hague group dispatched a delegation to Mexico. This country was first drawn to their attention by the Mexican Consul in Buenos Aires whom Johann P. Wall met quite incidentally while the first Reinländer delegation was waiting on the pier to return to Canada.[46] A second delegation was sent to Paraguay to follow up the slim hope brought back by the group that explored Argentina and Brazil.[47] When the first group returned with a positive report, the Manitoba and Swift Current groups abandoned the Quebec negotiations and agreed on November 1, 1920, to pursue investigations in Mexico with the Hague group.[48] Because the Manitoba delegates did not get their passports in time, the second Mexico delegation represented only the Hague and Swift Current groups of Saskatchewan. While the second Reinländer delegation was in Mexico from November 11 to the end of December 1920, delegates A. A. Friesen and C. H. Warkentin from the Mennonites in the U.S.S.R. were also exploring settlement possibilities there.[49]

The return of the Saskatchewan delegates with an encouraging report in December 1920 led to the sending of a third delegation, this time representing all three Reinländer groups. The delegates met with President Alvaro Obregon and Agriculture Minister A. I. Villareal to negotiate their terms of entry. Eight days later, on February 25, 1921, their desired *Privilegium* was signed by the President. Its five points follow the outline of the Reinländer petition submitted to the governments of Mississippi and Quebec.[50]

With the necessary governmental guarantees in hand, the Reinländer leaders now proceeded to locate suitable land for a settlement. The Manitoba and Swift Current groups in September 1921 purchased adjacent tracts of 155,000 and 74,125 acres respectively, in the state of Chihuahua.[51] The departure of so many farmers from a relatively small area severely depressed the price of land and goods.[52] The first chartered trainload of Mennonites from Manitoba left Plum Coulee on March 1, 1922; the first departure from Swift Current came about a week later.[53] Between 1922 and 1925 some 3,200 Reinländer from Manitoba and about 1,200 from the Swift Current area emigrated to the Chihuahua settlement. The Hague group purchased approximately 35,000 acres of land in the state of Durango, where they founded a settlement in 1924 with about 950 immigrants coming during the first two years.[54]

Both of the Saskatchewan groups experienced some final irritation from the federal and provincial governments in the disposal of their lands prior to emigration. The Swift Current group sold 107,000 acres to a syndicate of Florida capitalists for almost five million dollars in June 1921. When the deal ultimately fell through, they forfeited 10,200 acres to their agent as commission in lieu of a judgment of $221,000 and court costs.[55] The long, drawn-out court proceedings (through the Judicial Court of Saskatchewan, the Saskatchewan Court of Appeal, and the Supreme Court of Canada, all of which gave judgment to the Mennonites) were distasteful to the Reinländer leaders, who in principle preferred not to settle disputes in worldly courts. Even more upsetting was the final ruling by the Privy Council in London, reversing the Canadian courts' decision, which appeared to them unjust.[56] Some saw this misfortune as part of a government design to get them to leave Canada.[57]

The sale of 80,000 acres by the Hague group in 1920 also fell through, delaying the immigration. By 1923, when the Swift Current and Manitoba migration was well under way, the Hague group had difficulty in selling its lands. Poor crops the last few years may have been part of the reason, but the church leadership was convinced that its prospects were seriously undermined by an inspection and valuation of their holdings, ordered, as they understood it, by the Dominion government. The report of this inspection turned out to be quite negative, and they felt that it was now "being used to keep prospective purchasers from buying [their] lands."[58] This is one of the reasons why emigration from the Hague Reinländer colony was so small.

## Bergthal Groups

The final petition of the Sommerfelder and Chortitzer congregations to the Manitoba government in October 1920 had stated explicitly that "if the limitations and the pressure to which Mennonites are currently subjected will continue, then we will be forced to look for a new homeland in which we and our children can live according to our faith."[59] When this petition remained unanswered, a decision to emigrate was made on December 1.[60]

The *Bruderschaft* had apparently already decided in September to send a delegation to Paraguay.[61] But this was now delayed until the Hague Reinländer delegation would return.[62] Representatives were then selected by the East Reserve Chortitzer, the West Reserve Sommerfelder, and the Saskatchewan Bergthaler. By the time this group of six people, listed in table 18, was ready to leave, the second Reinländer delegation had returned from Mexico with increasingly favourable reports. Accordingly, the delegates left in February 1921 with instructions to visit Mexico also on their return trip from Paraguay.[63]

## Table 18
## Sommerfelder–Chortitzer–Bergthaler Land-Seeking Delegations

| Date | Destination | Groups Represented | Members |
|---|---|---|---|
| February 1919 | Argentina<br>Brazil<br>Uruguay | Local groups | Klaas Peters, Wymark<br>Johann Hamm, Rosthern<br>Johann Heinrichs, Rosthern |
| Feb. 11 to Sept. 2, 1921 | Paraguay<br>Mexico | Bergthaler,<br>Saskatchewan<br><br>Chortitzer<br>Sommerfelder | Johann Priess (Adviser)<br>Rev. Jacob W. Neufeld<br>Rev. Johann J. Friesen<br>Jacob Doerksen<br>Bernhard Toews<br>Isaak Funk |
| February 1921 | Mexico | Bergthaler,<br>Saskatchewan | Rev. Heinrich A. Neufeld<br>Johann C. Schellenberg<br>Peter Epp<br>Peter H. Goertzen<br>Cornelius F. Andres<br>Heinrich H. Reimer<br>Benjamin E. Redekopp |
| Oct. to Nov. 1921 | Mexico | Chortitzer<br>Sommerfelder | A. Doerksen<br>Dietrich Doerksen<br>Abram Hiebert |
| Early summer 1922 | Mexico | Chortitzer<br>Sommerfelder | D. Doerksen<br>Julius Harder<br>Franz Voth |

Source: Compiled from Quiring, *Rußlanddeutsche suchen eine Heimat*, pp. 39, 41; M. W. Friesen, *Kanadische Mennoniten*, pp. 16–17; *Neue Heimat*, pp. 69–70; J. H. Doerksen, p. 120; Sawatzky, p. 51; *RML*, February 18, 1919, p. 20; *Mitarbeiter*, February 1921, p. 12; Doell, *Bergthaler Mennonite Church of Saskatchewan*, p. 27; Fred Kaita, ed. *Niverville: A History, 1878–1986* (Niverville, Man.: Niverville District Historical Society, 1986), pp. 81–82.

Following the lead of the Hague delegation to Paraguay, this second group contacted General Samuel McRoberts, a New York financeer who had connections with large landowners and high government officials in Paraguay.[64] In Buenos Aires they were met by Fred Engen, a Norwegian pacifist and Chaco expert employed by McRoberts. Engen introduced the delegates to the Argentinean Casado brothers, who owned about five million hectares of land in the Chaco, and then accompanied them to Asunción. Here he introduced them to Senator Eusebio Ayala who arranged an audience with President Manuel Gondra for them. They submitted their petition for a *Privilegium* to him on April 4, 1921, and in a fifty-minute interview were able to reach agreement on all points.[65] Before the end of July the Paraguayan Senate and Congress had passed the necessary legislation to guarantee these privileges.[66] This did not take place without some heated debates among both legislators and general public, especially over the granting of military exemption.[67]

At the end of April, when weather and scenery in the Chaco are at their best, Engen took the delegation on a four-week tour of the prospective settlement area in the Casado holdings. The delegates were sufficiently impressed to recommend the land as "well adapted for agriculture, stock raising, fruit growing and the raising of vegetables. We believe that grain such as wheat, etc., can be grown at certain times of the year."[68]

When the delegation arrived back in New York on July 24, the two Saskatchewan delegates returned home while the Manitoba representatives continued on to Mexico. An unidentified man from Chicago had meanwhile appeared in Manitoba and attempted to persuade Bishop Abraham Doerksen to call off the Mexican part of the delegates' trip.[69] After looking at various lands there for about a month under the guidance of realtor Johann Wiebe of Herbert, Saskatchewan, the delegation finally left for home near the end of August, having been on the road almost seven months.[70] Its report on Mexico was very discouraging. In fact, the delegation seems to have decided against Mexico even before it left Paraguay. On June 3 Priess cabled from Asunción that "Mexico and other places become very unattractive in comparison with the advantages here."[71]

An important reason for recommending against settling in Mexico was the fact that the Reinländer *Privilegium* was only signed by the President and the Minister of Agriculture, and not ratified by Congress and Senate like the one given by Paraguay.[72] However, the enthusiasm of the Reinländer groups for Mexico, supported by reports of individual Sommerfelder who had investigated Mexico on their own and had actually purchased land there,[73] created a division among potential emigrants among Manitoba Sommerfelder, with some deciding for Paraguay and others wanting to pursue the Mexico option.[74]

A new delegation of three persons, listed in table 18, was elected to return to Mexico in the fall of 1921. They took with them a ten-point request for privileges, dated at Sommerfeld, October 5, 1921, and signed by Bishop Abraham Doerksen and fourteen ministers, addressed to the government, the congress, and the President of Mexico.[75] The petition naturally requested exemption from military service and the swearing of oaths, the right to complete control of their own church and school, including the use of German in them, and the right to administer their own inheritance laws and fire insurance. In addition to these basic privileges, it asked for the following: (6) permission to bring into the country all members of their community, including the sick and crippled; (7) protection of property and life; (8) a ten-year period of duty-free entry of agricultural implements and seeds; (9) freedom to leave the country; and (10) incorporation of all the above requests into the constitution of the country.

President Obregon on October 30, 1921, responded positively to all requests except the sixth and eighth ones.[76] In their meeting with the President on November 4, he assured them that all of their requests were met except the eighth one, on which the government was prepared to grant a two-year duty-free period. The delegates asked specifically whether the *Privilegium* would have the full force of law without having been passed on by congress and whether all of the state governments would recognize it. They were emphatically reassured by Obregon on both points.[77]

With the necessary *Privilegium* in hand, a number of Manitoba West Reserve Sommerfelder were now prepared to join the Reinländer groups in their migration to Mexico. A third delegation went to Mexico in the summer of 1922 and purchased 12,000 acres of land at Santa Clara, Chihuahua, just north of the Manitoba and Swift Current Reinländer lands.[78] The actual migration did not begin until October and involved a total of about six hundred Mennonites during the next few years, mostly West Reserve Sommerfelder.[79]

The leaders of the movement to Paraguay meanwhile attempted to bridge geographical barriers and create one congregation out of the intending emigrants from the East Reserve Chortitzer, the West Reserve Sommerfelder, and the Saskatchewan Bergthaler congregations.[80] While this proved unsuccessful for the moment, even though all three groups originated from the same Bergthal congregation in Russia less than fifty years before, it was possible for them in late 1922 to strike a common *Fürsorgekomitee* to organize and lead the emigration.[81]

On the Manitoba East Reserve negotiations had been taking place with McRoberts of New York since the fall of 1921 and an agreement regarding the sale of Manitoba lands and the purchase of a block of the Paraguayan Chaco had been negotiated.[82] But the economic recession, which depressed Canadian land prices in the early 1920s, caused McRoberts to withdraw his offer for the time being, thus delaying the emigration. By the time he reopened contact with the Mennonites in late 1924, Chortitzer resistance to the School Attendance Act had largely been broken and the enthusiasm for emigration had strongly diminished.[83] The matter was further complicated by Bolivia's announcement in 1923 of its claim to that part of the Chaco granted by the Paraguayan government for Mennonite colonies.[84]

When the economic situation improved in 1925, McRoberts organized the Intercontinental Company in Winnipeg to buy and resell the land of the immigrants, and the Corporación Paraguaya in Asunción to buy land from Casado and sell it to immigrants. Finally, in June 1926 the *Fürsorgekomitee* was able to complete the transaction by which the Mennonites sold 44,000 acres of Canadian lands for $903,000 ($20.52 per acre) and in return bought 138,000 acres of Paraguayan Chaco for $690,000 ($5 per acre).[85] The actual emigration began in late November and involved fewer than 2,000 persons in all, the majority of them Chortitzer from the Manitoba East Reserve.[86] A more detailed breakdown of their origin is given in table 19.

Just before their departure, the emigrants addressed a letter to the Minister of Agriculture in Ottawa expressing their thanks to the governments of Canada and Britain for the half century of peace and goodwill that they had experienced as the first Mennonite settlers on the Prairies. They expressed a special appreciation for the free homestead they had received on their arrival and for the large loan in the early pioneer years. The letter indicated clearly that they were leaving because of their conviction that no Christian church could survive without having the word of God taught in its schools. They hoped that their leaving would stimulate both government and society to a greater vigilance in the face of encroaching atheism and a greater tolerance toward Christian schools. In looking back to Canada with warm love they promised to continue to pray for the government, "including those who, in the matter of the school question, have not hesitated to attack and to violate the promise of 1873" which they considered sacred.[87]

The lack of official concern of the Canadian government for the Mennonite emigrants is in sharp contrast to this attitude. In response to the British Colonial Secretary's request for information regarding Canadian Mennonite plans to settle in Paraguay, the Governor-General pointed out that the vast majority of Mennonites were content in Canada and that the few who had left or were thinking of seeking other homes had publicly stated "that they are not leaving Canada through any lack of appreciation of the farming opportunities in this country."[88] In response to a similar request for information about the settlement plans of Mennonites in Mexico, Lord Byng admitted that "the Canadian government has no definite information as to the settlement of these people in the Republic of Mexico."[89]

Ottawa reflected similar indifference or ignorance in regard to their status. When the British Vice-consul in Chihuahua inquired about the national status of Canadian Mennonites on arrival in Mexico, the government speculated that most of them would probably "possess Russian or German nationality or American citizenship, very few being British

## Table 19
## Manitoba and Saskatchewan Mennonite Emigrants to Latin America, 1922–1930

| Group | Origin | Years | Approx. No. | % | Destination |
|---|---|---|---|---|---|
| Reinländer[a] | Swift Current, SK | 1922–1926 | 1,200 | 37 | Chihuahua, Mexico |
| Reinländer[b] | West Reserve, MB | 1922–1926 | 3,200 | 64 | Chihuahua, Mexico |
| Reinländer[c] | Hague, SK | 1924–1925 | 950 | 24 | Durango, Mexico |
| Sommerfelder[d] | West Reserve, MB; Herbert, SK | 1922–1925 | 600 | 8 | Chihuahua, Mexico |
| Chortitzer[e] | East Reserve, MB | 1925–1930 | 1,201 | 41 | Chaco, Paraguay |
| Sommerfelder[f] | West Reserve, MB | 1926–1930 | 357 | 5 | Chaco, Paraguay |
| Bergthaler[g] | Rosthern, SK | 1926–1927 | 227 | 18 | Chaco, Paraguay |
| Total to Latin America | | | 7,735 | | |
| Total Reinländer (groups 1–3) | | | 5,350 | | |
| Total Bergthal (groups 4–7) | | | 2,385 | | |
| Total to Mexico | | | 5,950 | | |
| Total to Paraguay | | | 1,785 | | |

a. Sawatzky, p. 64, gives the actual population of the Swift Current colony in Mexico as 1,258 in 1926. Allowing for an excess of births over deaths of 58 during the immigration period, this leaves approximately 1,200 immigrants, or 37% of the 1923 population of 3,250.
b. Johann P. Wall, statistical compilation in MHCA microfilm no. 66, gives the 1926 population total for the Manitoba colony in Mexico as 3,340. I. M. Dyck, pp. 180–181, shows a growth rate (excess of births over deaths) in 1922 of 23 in a population of 1,798. At that rate of growth the actual number of immigrants in Wall's 3,340 total would have been about 3,200, which represents 64% of the approximately 5,000 total population in 1923.
c. Johann P. Wall, statistical compilation, gives the population of Hague colony in Mexico as 946 in 1925. This means that only about 24% of the total population of 3,932 emigrated.
d. The 600 total given by John H. Warkentin, "The Mennonite Settlements," p. 228, is used rather than the 1,000 estimated by I. I. Friesen, p. 141. That represents 8.4% of the 1925 year end total of 7,124 Sommerfelder reported in *Der Mitarbeiter*, February 1926, p. 5.
e. Quiring, *Rußlanddeutsche*, p. 72, and *Deutsche erschließen den Chaco*, p. 11, uses the figure 1,181, likely as a result of the error in his tabulating of the October 16, 1927, group as 337 instead of 357 ("The Canadian Mennonite Immigration into the Paraguayan Chaco," p. 37). M. W. Friesen, *Kanadische Mennoniten*, pp. 17–18, gives the 1,201 which Quiring's data would also produce. This represents 41% of the 1926 total of 2,930 Chortitzer reported in *Mitarbeiter*, February 1927, p. 9. M. W. Friesen, *Neue Heimat*, pp. 69, 129–130, uses a slightly lower total.

Table 19
Manitoba and Saskatchewan Mennonite Emigrants to
Latin America, 1922–1930 *(Continued)*

f. Quiring, *Rußlanddeutsche*, p. 72; M. W. Friesen, *Kanadische Mennoniten*, pp. 17–18. The 357 represent only 5% of the 7,124 Sommerfelder total at year end of 1925.
g. Quiring, *Rußlanddeutsche*, p. 72; M. W. Friesen, *Kanadische Mennoniten*, pp. 17–18. Doell, pp. 30–31, 35, 119, reports a slightly smaller total. The 227 represent about 18% of the 1925 total of 1,254 reported by Doell, p. 114. The *Mitarbeiter*, February 1927, p. 8. reported that 75% of the Rosthern Bergthaler church had accompanied Bishop Aron Zacharias to Paraguay.

Source: The summaries given by I. I. Friesen, pp. 141–142; John H. Warkentin, "The Mennonite Settlements," p. 228; Francis, *In Search of Utopia*, p. 192; and by other scattered sources are not in agreement with each other. The figures above represent a new calculation based on what appear to be the most reliable sources for each group.

subjects, so that the question of the loss of their right to British protection is one which in the majority of cases would not arise."[90] The government based this guess on the assumption "that Mennonites do not as a rule take steps to become naturalized." According to the Secretary of the Department of Immigration and Colonization, Mennonite

> peculiarities are of such a nature as to bring them into conflict with some of the obligations usually understood to be inseparable from citizenship. I do not suppose that any Mennonite ever acquires citizenship otherwise than by birth. I have never heard of any of our Western Mennonites becoming naturalized."[91]

As was pointed out in chapter 1, the majority of the immigrants of the 1870s were naturalized.

The British chargé d'affaires in Mexico City at the time of the Mennonite migration to Mexico was informed that "the Canadian government felt no regret at their departure" and that "protection should be afforded them only in extreme circumstances with the object of saving life if threatened."[92] It is true that on request the Canadian government used British diplomatic connections in Argentina and Paraguay to ascertain that there was a clear title to the Casado lands being purchased by the Mennonites in the Chaco.[93] But neither the accuracy of its information about the Mennonite immigrants, nor its attitude toward them, had improved in the intervening years. As late as 1927, the External Affairs Department still held that the emigrants to Paraguay would

> probably be American, Russian or German citizens. Any born in Canada who have not subsequently renounced British nationality, would be regarded by our law as entitled to the full rights of British subjects. In the protection of those born in British territory outside Canada, or

naturalized in the Dominion, who have abandoned or lost their Canadian domicile under the provisions of the Immigration Act, the Canadian government has no interest, though applications from such persons to return to the Dominion to assume residence would be received and considered.[94]

## The Accommodation Option

The emigration of almost eight thousand Mennonites to Latin America during the 1920s left Canada with two major groups from the 1870s immigration from Russia. The largest group consisted of those denominations that had fairly readily accepted the public schools and had at no point seriously considered leaving the country. The other group consisted of those portions of the Reinländer, Sommerfelder, and Chortitzer who had been unable or unwilling to join the emigration. To these must be added a substantial number of colonies of communal Hutterites who had come to Canada from the U.S.A. during 1917–1918, having immigrated to America from Russia during the 1870s. Coming to join them as refugees from the communist regime in the Union of Soviet Socialist Republics during the 1920s were approximately twenty thousand additional Mennonites.[95] The latter had experienced fifty years of fairly rapid accommodation in Russia after 1870. Hence, their coming added new dimensions to the relationship of Canadian Mennonites to their governments.

The Reinländer, Sommerfelder, and Chortitzer who remained in Manitoba and Saskatchewan were generally left without leaders and only gradually re-established a sense of corporate identity. All three Reinländer bishops and almost all ministers emigrated to Mexico without installing any successors to serve their non-emigrating members. Johann Friesen of the Manitoba Reinländer made it clear that only those emigrating to Mexico would be considered members of the church. As a result the approximately thirty-six percent who remained in Canada were in limbo or joined other Mennonite congregations until their own was reorganized as the Old Colony Mennonite Church under Jacob F. Froese (1885–1968) in 1936. Froese was ordained as the new bishop by an Old Colony bishop from Saskatchewan.[96]

Bishop Jacob Wiens of the Hague Reinländer emigrated to Mexico in 1925 but continued to serve both Hague and Durango until 1929. By then he considered those remaining in Canada (about seventy-six percent of the total) as not taking the matter of emigration seriously enough and refused to serve them further. In fact, a good number of them were so poor that they were unable to clear up their debts as they were supposed to, and could not afford to emigrate. Reverend Johann Loeppky, a member of the

1921 delegation to Mexico who had not joined the emigration, was then ordained as the new bishop by the Bergthaler bishop Cornelius Hamm.[97] Bishop Abraham Wiebe of the Swift Current Reinländer, together with two other "outstanding church leaders," had moved to Mexico by early 1925. In the next year the rest of the ministers apparently also emigrated, leaving the sixty-three percent of the congregation, which remained in Canada largely leaderless.[98]

In the Sommerfelder and Chortitzer groups the departure of key leaders was less disruptive of community and church life. Chortitzer bishop Johann K. Dueck died in 1923. His successor, Martin C. Friesen, led some forty-one percent of the group to Paraguay in 1927. Since only two active ministers planned to remain in Canada, the congregation elected three more in December 1926 to give leadership to the group remaining in Canada.[99] Sommerfelder bishop Abraham Doerksen of the Manitoba West Reserve preached his last Canadian sermon in Altona on December 3, 1923, and then left for Mexico with a small portion of his congregation. H. J. Friesen had been ordained as new bishop in October 1922 so that the disruption for the large remaining body was minimal.[100] Saskatchewan Bergthaler bishop Aron Zacharias left for Paraguay with part of his congregation in 1926. The majority who remained in Canada were served by Bishop David Doerksen of their co-religionists in southern Saskatchewan until a new bishop of their own, Cornelius Hamm, was ordained in 1928.[101]

The emigration to Latin America broke any organized resistance to the public schools. The editor of the *Mitarbeiter* reflected the position of most of those remaining in Canada when he wrote that the issues of private or district schools, of German or English as the medium of instruction, and of teacher qualifications were no longer debatable. The government had decided.[102] One might deplore the resulting separation of church and school and hope for a reversal, but in practice the basic fact of governmental control had been accepted.[103] Consequently, church leaders now operated with an effort at political realism within this new situation.

Already in late 1922 the non-emigrating leaders of the Chortitzer and Sommerfelder churches invited representatives of the *Kleine Gemeinde*, Holdemann, Bergthaler, and Mennonite Brethren groups to a strategy session. A committee representing these six groups was created to negotiate once more with the Manitoba government.[104] The committee decided to negotiate on three basic points. First, it would seek permission to teach German in the schools in accordance with clause 10 of the *Privilegium*, at the same time promising the government that Mennonite children would master the English language as thoroughly as children in the province generally did. Second, it agreed to support other efforts in the province to reduce the length of the school year. Third, it would urgently request the government to return the administration of public schools in Mennonite districts into the hands of local school boards.[105] It should be noted that only the first of these points represents a request for a special privilege and does so on the basis of a promise to co-operate with the system. The second makes common cause with other groups in the province, and the third asks for its schools to be made fully a part of the public system.

In planning its next strategy, the committee decided to look for maximum support from influential persons in conducting its lobby. Feelers extended to leading business and financial people in Winnipeg as well as to many lawyers and doctors were so encouraging that the committee sought the formal support of the Chamber of Commerce.[106] A delegation from the committee met with Premier Bracken in March 1923 but received no hope for German instruction and only the promise of a limited, experimental return of Mennonite schools to local administration. As table 20 shows, the *Kleine Gemeinde* districts and most of the Bergthaler ones had already regained local control prior to 1923, but progress in the Sommerfelder, Reinländer, and Chortitzer areas was as slow as the government had promised. In the spring of 1930, as seen in table 21, a dozen Mennonite schools were still under official trustee administration. The committee was disappointed both in its results and in the failure of any support from "influential persons" to materialize.[107]

Table 20
**Return to Local Control of Manitoba Mennonite District Schools**

| District | District No. | Greenway as Official Trustee | | Resignation Order-in-Council No. |
| --- | --- | --- | --- | --- |
| | | Appointed | Resigned | |
| Amsterdam | 885 | Aug. 6, 1918 | Nov. 25, 1919 | 32666 |
| Edenburg | 330 | July 5, 1918 | Dec. 29, 1919 | 32945 |
| Kleinstadt | 781 | July 19, 1918 | Dec. 30, 1919 | 32966 |
| Reichenbach | 1198 | Jan. 28, 1919 | June 14, 1921 | 36827 |
| Glencross | 71 | July 23, 1918 | Oct. 20, 1921 | 37722 |
| Blumenort | 62 | Jan. 17, 1919 | Dec. 16, 1921 | 38145 |
| Blumenhof | 64 | Jan. 17, 1919 | Jan. 23, 1922 | 39556[a] |
| Rosefarm | 1577 | Oct. 18, 1918 | Mar. 17, 1922 | 38538 |
| Grossweide | 786 | Oct. 4, 1918 | April 18, 1922 | 38649 |
| Neu Kronsthal | 1137 | Jan. 28, 1919 | May 10, 1922 | 39556[a] |
| Silberfeld | 1590 | Mar. 25, 1919 | May 31, 1922 | 38827 |

## Table 20
## Return to Local Control of Manitoba Mennonite District Schools *(Continued)*

| | | | | |
|---|---|---|---|---|
| Gruenfeld | 63 | Jan. 17, 1919 | Oct. 12, 1922 | 39330 |
| Edenthal | 756 | Aug. 23, 1918 | Nov. 17, 1922 | 39556[a] |
| Neu Hoffnung | 1310 | July 5, 1918 | June 18, 1923 | 40465 |
| Grimsby | 1993 | Feb. 21, 1920 | June 18, 1923 | 40465 |
| Halbstadt | 886 | Jan. 28, 1919 | June 18, 1923 | 40465 |
| Neu Bergthal | 1594 | Oct. 4, 1918 | Nov. 13, 1923 | 41155 |
| Houston | 214 | Jan. 28, 1919 | Jan. 4, 1924 | 41365 |
| Clyde | 1990 | Feb. 21, 1920 | Mar. 1, 1924 | 41584 |
| Weidenfeld | 988 | Jan. 28, 1919 | Mar. 1, 1924 | 41584 |
| Bothwell | 1961 | April 8, 1919 | Mar. 1, 1924 | 41584 |
| Hoffnungsort | 821 | May 19, 1920 | May 12, 1924 | 41849 |
| Sommerfeld | 2058 | Feb. 11, 1921 | Sept. 30, 1924 | 42416 |
| Gnadenfeld | 1593 | Mar. 25, 1919 | Nov. 28, 1924 | 42611 |
| Alt Bergthal | 1296 | Oct. 4, 1918 | Dec. 10, 1924 | 42644 |
| Steinreich | 820 | Aug. 6, 1918 | Dec. 12, 1924 | 42658 |
| Steinreich | 820 | Aug. 6, 1918 | Jan. 31, 1925 | 42831 |
| Kronsweide | 1030 | Oct. 18, 1918 | Feb. 28, 1925 | 42958 |
| Steinfeld | 1128 | July 30, 1918 | Mar. 14, 1925 | 43013 |
| Rudnerweide | 1752 | Mar. 25, 1919 | April 22, 1925 | 43146 |
| Eigenhoff | 1591 | Aug. 20, 1918 | Dec. 22, 1925 | 44085 |
| Moray | 1963 | April 8, 1919 | Apr. 15, 1926 | 44505 |
| Wakeham | 773 | July 16, 1918 | April 21, 1926 | 44544 |
| Thames | 1991 | Feb. 21, 1920 | June 17, 1926 | 44835 |
| Meath | 1992 | Feb. 21, 1920 | June 17, 1926 | 45159 |
| Calder[b] | 2075 | Feb. 21, 1920 | Oct. 23, 1926 | 45353 |
| Carmichael | 1959 | April 8, 1919 | Nov. 30, 1926 | 45499 |
| Exeter | 1994 | Feb. 21, 1920 | Feb. 11, 1927 | 152-27 |
| Greenland | 893 | July 3, 1926 | Sept. 24, 1927 | 1141-27 |
| Wells | 1998 | Feb. 21, 1920 | Dec. 31, 1927 | 1501-27 |
| Kronsgart | 2151 | Sept. 15, 1926 | Feb. 14, 1928 | 156-28 |
| Birkenhead | 1996 | Feb. 21, 1920 | May 11, 1929 | 606-29 |
| Schanzenfeld | 420 | Jan. 28, 1919 | May 11, 1929 | 607-29 |
| Mersey | 1997 | Feb. 21, 1920 | May 30, 1929 | 739-29 |

a. Date of order-in-council was December 5, 1922.
b. Calder was created out of Meath on July 26 and August 16, 1921.
Source: Compiled from PAM, RG 19, B 1, box 5.

Table 21
**Manitoba Mennonite Schools Under Official Trustee Administration as of May 6, 1930**

| District | District No. | Official Trustee Appointed |
| --- | --- | --- |
| Arran | 1960 | April 8, 1919 |
| Barkfield | 1951 | March 5, 1918 |
| Ekfrid[a] | 2061 | May 6, 1921 |
| Goodwill (Aldershot) | 1967 | April 8, 1919 |
| Gruenthal | 1592 | March 25, 1919 |
| Heabert | 1282 | |
| Mitchell | 1965 | April 8, 1919 |
| Newfield (Neufeld) | 1580 | June 14, 1928 |
| Randolph | 1964 | April 8, 1919 |
| Rosengard | 2168 | Sept. 15, 1927 |
| Shakespeare | 2069 | May 31, 1926 |
| Spencer | 1969 | April 8, 1919 |

a. Ekfrid became a Hutterite *Bruderhof* when the Reinländer Mennonites moved to Mexico.
Source: Order-in-Council no. 582-30, May 6, 1930, PAM, RG 19, B 1, box 5. The order appointed Albert Tomlinson as official trustee, replacing the recently deceased J. F. Greenway.

Following their rebuff by the new government, the non-emigrating groups looked for ways of teaching religion and German in the context of the new public school system. In doing so, they were quite aware that this was their alternative to emigrating.[108] Where a Mennonite local school board was in charge it was frequently possible to teach these subjects during the half hour immediately preceding the official school day and in the half hour immediately after its official closure. Other communities conducted a Saturday school for this purpose.[109] In both cases, the district school building and the Mennonite district school teacher were normally used for this purpose.

To make the public school system reasonably acceptable to the Mennonites, it was necessary to have local control of the school and to have a supply of well-trained Mennonite teachers. The joint school committee appointed in 1922 continued to work at obtaining local control. In 1926, when many of the public school resisters had left for Latin America and been replaced by new immigrants from Russia, the committee applied to the provincial government for permission for these new Mennonite immigrants to vote and hold office in local school boards.[110]

For a continuing supply of its own well-trained teachers the congregations depended very heavily on the three Mennonite teacher training institutions in Altona, Gretna, and Rosthern. It is not accidental that two of the leading men of the non-emigrating Mennonites, H. H. Ewert and David Toews, were also principals of two of these teacher training institutes.[111] It was to teachers prepared in these schools that the congregations looked for instruction in religion and German in their public schools and for help in maintaining Mennonite distinctives.[112] The vital role of these schools in the survival of the Mennonite church in the new circumstances may be seen in the fact that the Sommerfelder, who had parted company with the Bergthaler in 1890 as an expression of their rejection of higher education, now became very strong supporters of the Mennonite Educational Institute of Altona.[113] In spite of the tremendous help that teachers from these schools gave to Mennonite society, church leaders still noted with regret that the local teachers' conventions had accommodated themselves to the new circumstances by becoming totally English.[114]

Some of the non-emigrating groups were quite concerned to maintain a relative geographic isolation in Canada. In both of the major Mennonite communities in Manitoba there was concern about the possibility of non-Mennonite settlers moving in when the Reinländer and Chortitzer attempted to sell their lands *en bloc*.[115] They were relieved when efforts to sell these lands to incoming Mennonites from the U.S.S.R. proved successful, thereby maintaining the virtually closed settlements on the former East and West Reserves.

The Sommerfelder church of Manitoba made one more concerted effort to relocate its entire community of some eight thousand people to a new block settlement in northern Alberta. For this purpose they petitioned the Minister of Agriculture in 1927 to grant them a reserve of some ten to twenty townships of land in the vicinity of Fort Vermillion together with the right to operate parochial or separate schools.[116] This attempt, as well as a similar one by the Reinländer Mennonites, was unsuccessful because Ottawa had abandoned the practice of granting reserves to facilitate the block settlement of particular groups.[117]

On the issue of exemption from military service, H. H. Ewert raised the question of Mennonite responsibility to their country now that the war was over.[118] Reflecting on the fact that the Canadian government had no provisions for non-combatant service nor a system of sending conscientious objectors to farm work, he wondered whether the Mennonites should create a standing organization to make contact with the government regarding possible service of non-resisters during a war.

The Conference of Mennonites in Central Canada formed a committee to contact other Mennonite groups to discuss together with them the question of whether to offer the government some kind of alternative service during wartime. Responses from the Church of God in Christ Mennonite, the Mennonite Brethren, and the Old Mennonites (Swiss) were mildly favourable, but the matter does not seem to have gone beyond the discussion stage.[119] In the Manitoba Bergthaler Church the matter was raised in a meeting of the ministers as well as in the larger brotherhood meeting, but apparently without reaching any conclusion.[120]

The political realism with which some of the Mennonite groups now approached the school and alternative service issue grew out of a few decades of increasing political awareness and involvement. At the first annual sessions of the Conference of Mennonites in Central Canada in 1903, Bergthaler bishop Jacob Hoeppner presented a paper on the question of whether it was contrary to Scripture and conscience for Mennonites to hold public office or vote.[121] While Hoeppner was unable to find much Scriptural evidence against this, he nevertheless thought it best for Mennonites to abstain from public participation, except at the municipal level. Discussion from the floor revealed a considerable range of opinion.

The firing of H. H. Ewert from his school inspectorate as a result of political manoeuvring in the Manitoba provincial election that same year gave a new dimension to Mennonite political awareness.[122] In the 1904 federal election several prominent Mennonites of the Altona area were actively campaigning for the Conservative party.[123] Reference has already been made to the election of Cornelius Hiebert (Conservative) to the Alberta legislature and ex-Mennonite Gerhard Ens (Liberal) to the Saskatchewan legislature in the 1905 elections. Ewert's reappointment as inspector in May 1908, and his dismissal "for purely political purposes" three months later, alienated many Mennonite supporters of the Conservative party.[124] When the Roblin Conservatives were finally swept out of power in Manitoba by the Norris Liberals in the 1915 election, Valentine Winkler carried every poll except Altona in the largely Mennonite riding of Rhineland.[125] Several prominent Mennonites applauded this result, some of them even expressing pride in the part played by their people in the "cleanup of the province."[126]

As a result of this gradually increasing political involvement, a Mennonite delegation in 1916 could say to its representative in the provincial legislature in Manitoba: "The majority of the Mennonites have so far put their confidence in the Liberal party and have uninterruptedly sent a Liberal representative to the legislature."[127] Their keen sense of disappointment at the action of the Norris government on the school issue, together with the larger events of World War I, brought this rapid accommodation on the political front to a temporary halt.[128]

The coming of twenty thousand new Mennonites from Russia and two decades of relative world peace provided the environment for the tempo of accommodation to pick up again in the 1920s. And the fact that it was the federal Liberal government of William Lyon McKenzie King that repealed the offending order-in-council barring Mennonite immigration, when the previous Conservative government had refused to do so, ensured that western Mennonites would again be Liberal for at least another generation.[129]

# Notes

1. The Rev. (Captain) Wellington Bridgman, *Breaking Prairie Sod. The Story of a Preacher in the Eighties with a Discussion of the Burning Question of Today, "Shall the Alien Go?"* (Toronto: Musson Book Company, 1920).

2. Francis, *In Search of Utopia*, pp. 189–190; Epp, *Mennonites in Canada*, p. 388.

3. Bergthaler Church, Ministerial, *Minutes*, 2:159–160; no. 8, 11 June 1917; no. 4, 27 August 1917, MHCA, vol. 716. The Manitoba Bergthaler ministers were apparently unaware of Mennonite disfranchisement under the War-Time Elections Act, since they decided on 6 November 1917 that their members should not vote in the coming federal election. *Minutes*, 2:163, no. 5. Saskatchewan Bergthaler reached a similar decision. Doell, *Bergthaler Mennonite Church*, p. 22. *Mitarbeiter*, July 1917, p. 4, reports that Sommerfelder and *Kleine Gemeinde* ministers of Manitoba and Saskatchewan, meeting in Chortitz near the end of June, agreed to advise their members not to vote in the proposed plebiscite, since that might jeopardize their exemption from military service.

4. Reference to this development has already been made in chap. 5.

5. F. W. Law, Secretary-Treasurer, The Great War Veterans' Association, Winnipeg, to Prime Minister Robert L. Borden, 18 September 1918, NA, MG 26 H, (1c), vol. 214, p. 121122. Similar protests to the Prime Minister came from the Dominion headquarters of the G.W.V.A. in Ottawa, Acting Secretary-Treasurer R. M. Stewart, 18 September 1918, p. 121131, and Mrs. Elizabeth Longworth, President, Great War Next-of-Kin Association, Lethbridge, 22 September 1918, p. 121140.

6. Alberta MLA W. A. Rae on 7 October 1918 wrote Prime Minister Borden to protest Mennonite immigrants coming into the Grande Prairie area. For returning soldiers to "find they have in many cases only Mennonites for neighbours is so base a treachery to Canadians that very undesirable results are inevitable." NA, MG 26 H, (1c), vol. 214, p. 121165.

7. The Executive of the Board of Home Missions and Social Service of the Presbyterian Church in Canada on 18 September 1918 took action to oppose block settlement in Canada of foreigners, school instruction in German, and the admission of pacifists as immigrants. NA, MG 26 H, (1c), vol. 214, p. 121162. Reference to similar action by the Methodist Church has already been made in chap. 5.

8. *Canadian Annual Review*, 1918, p. 428, reporting on Calder's remarks in Regina on 15 October 1918.

9. *Vancouver Daily Province*, 7 November 1918; press clipping in NA, RG 76, vol. 173, no. 58764-2.

10. P.C. no. 923, 1 May 1919, NA, RG 2, 1, vol. 1541. An almost identical order-in-council, P.C. no. 1204, was passed on 9 June 1919, vol. 1546. Before taking this action the Canadian government checked, via the British Ambassador in Washington, whether the U.S.A. would object if it would "for the time being debar entry into Canada" of Mennonites

and Hutterites. Reading to Hon. William Phillips, Department of State, 16 April 1919, NARS, RG 85, 54623/130. The American Secretary of State was provided with a copy of P.C. no. 923 by the U.S. Consul in Ottawa on 7 May 1919.

11. For an extended discussion of the emigration to Latin America in the 1920s, see Frank H. Epp, *Mennonites in Canada 1920–1940. A People's Struggle for Survival* (Toronto: Macmillan, 1982), chap. 3.

12. *MFP*, 26 November 1910, p. 44.

13. *Mitarbeiter*, March 1916, p. 6.

14. Friesen to Borden, 22 December 1916, NA, MG 26 H, (1c), vol. 214.

15. Klaas Peters to Abram Reimer, Wymark, 16 October 1918, NA, RG 24, HQ7168-1, vol. 115.

16. *RML*, 18 November 1918, p. 11.

17. Quiring, *Russlanddeutsche suchen eine Heimat*, p. 39; *RML*, 18 February 1919, p. 20; Martin W. Friesen, *Neue Heimat in der Chacowildnis* (Altona and Asunción: D. W. Friesen and Chortitzer Komitee, 1987), pp. 52–53. It is not clear how officially this delegation represented the Saskatchewan Bergthaler.

18. *RML*, 1 October 1981, p. 9; *MFP*, 3 October 1918, p. 9.

19. Harder, p. 3; I. M. Dyck, pp. 53–66; Schmiedehaus, p. 19; Harry Leonard Sawatzky, *They Sought a Country. Mennonite Colonization in Mexico* (Berkeley: University of California Press, 1971), pp. 31–32; *RML*, 29 August 1919, p. 2.

20. A diary of the trip kept by Johann P. Wall, 4 August to 24 November 1919, is found in MHCA, microfilm no. 66. Harder, p. 4, indicates that Paraguay had offered a glimmer of hope.

21. I. M. Dyck, p. 56.

22. Representatives of the Reinland Mennonite Church (Old Church) near Reinland, Manitoba, and Hague and Wymark, Saskatchewan, to the Governor and the U.S. Attorney of the State of Mississippi, U.S.A., or to whom it may concern, 12 April 1920; MHCA, microfilm no. 66. For extensive discussion of this emigration attempt, see Abraham Friesen, esp. pp. 74–75, 82–86, 102–103. Shorter summaries are found in Sawatzky, pp. 33–34, Schmiedehaus, pp. 17–18, and Harder pp. 4–5.

23. Governor Lee M. Russell, Jackson, Miss., to Julius Wiebe et al., 6 February 1920, NARS, RG 85, 54623/130; MHCA, microfilm no. 64.

24. Portions of Palmer's letter of 26 April 1920 to Bishop Johann Friesen et al. are quoted in *MFP*, 8 May 1920, p. 11.

25. Harder, p. 5; *MFP*, 6 May 1920, p. 1.

26. Harder, p. 5.

27. Ibid.; I. M. Dyck, p. 68, quoted Scripture: "This also comes from the Lord of Hosts; he is wonderful in counsel, and excellent in wisdom." Isaiah 28:29. Sawatzky, p. 34, indicates that the land purchase negotiations had proceeded to the point where litigation was narrowly avoided when the deal fell through.

28. Russell to Chief of Immigration Department, Washington, telegram, 1 July 1920, NARS, RG 85, 54623/130.

29. Commissioner-General to Russell, telegram, 3 July 1920, NARS, RG 85, 54623/130.

30. Assistant Commissioner-General of Immigration to N. L. DeMars, Farmers State Bank, Neche, N.D., 27 August 1920, responding to DeMars' 17 August inquiry. NARS, RG 85, 54623/130.

31. Assistant Commissioner-General to Rock Island Railway, 26 July 1920, NARS, RG 85, 54623/130.

32. W. J. Peters, Special Immigrant Inspector, to Kratz, 9 December 1920, NARS, RG 85, 54623/130.

33. Asst. Comm.-Gen., telegram, 3 January 1921, NARS, RG 85, 54623/130. The U.S. Bureau of Immigration apparently considered Doukhobors to be a branch of the Mennonites. The former were held to be extremely fanatical and were classified as "philosophical anarchists." Idem, to T. W. Conway, 15 August 1921. When a Winnipeg official of the Bureau used this expression of Manitoba Mennonites, the Editor of the *Mitarbeiter* could not suppress his astonishment. January 1921, p. 4.

34. Commissioner-General, Bureau of Immigration, to W. E. Price, General Immigration Agent, Southern Railway Development Service, Washington, D.C., 12 April 1920, NARS, RG 85, 54623/130; MHCA, microfilm no. 64.

35. Inspector J. Zubrick, Vancouver, to Commissioner of Immigration, Seattle, Washington, 10 May 1920, NARS, RG 85, 54623/130; MHCA, microfilm no. 64.

36. Letter to T. W. Conway, Chicago, 15 August 1921, NARS, RG 85, 54623/130; MHCA, microfilm no. 64.

37. NARS, RG 85, 54623/130, has on file protests against Mennonite "undesirables" from the American Legion, Mississippi Division, to U.S. Secretary of State, 23 December 1920; National Legion Committee to Secretary of State, 29 December 1920; Tennessee Division to Senator J. K. Shields and others, 30 December 1920; resolutions from Legion Conventions held 17 August 1920, 11 June 1921, 3 October 1921. Protests also came from such diverse groups as the Prentiss Club, Natchez, Miss., to Commissioner-General, U.S. Immigration, 29 June 1920; and the Punxsutawney, Pa., Lodge no. 669, International Association of Machinists, (AF of L), 28 March 1921. MHCA, microfilm no. 64.

38. At the invitation of W. L. Henderson, Industrial and Immigration Agent, Southern Railway System, Mobile, Ala., Governor Thomas E. Kilby of Alabama on 17 February 1920 assured Mennonites of the privilege of making an affirmation instead of taking the oath, of operating their own benevolent societies, and of using any language desired in their private schools. Charles Hootman, Sedalia, Mo., 13 July 1920, assured the U.S. Immigration Bureau that he had the full co-operation of Governor Shoup of Colorado to settle 4,000 Mennonites on 200,000 acres of land in the southern part of that state. Hagwood Realty Co., New Bern, N.C., 21 July 1920, informed the Department of Labor in Washington that it wanted some of the 10,000 Mennonite immigrants for the cotton and tobacco belt in the northeastern parts of the state. T. W. Conway, Chicago, 2 August 1921, wanted assurance from the Commissioner-General of Immigration that Mennonite immigrants would be admitted to the country, so that he could settle them on a large tract of land in Florida. Rev. F. G. Hartman, Washington, Ga., 20 September 1923, wrote the Secretary, Department of Labor, that he would like some Mennonites as settlers for the "boll weevil sections" of Georgia. NARS, RG 85, 54623/130, MHCA, microfilm no. 64. R. D. McMullen, Ola National Farm Loan Association, Ola, Ark., 17 May 1920, wrote to the Mayor of Regina, Sask., for addresses of Mennonite leaders to persuade them to settle in Arkansas. SAB, M 4, I-54, p. 18952.

39. *Mennonitische Rundschau*, 30 March, 4 and 25 May, 1, 8 and 15 June 1921.

40. C. J. Dyck, "Die Mennonitenkolonien in Südamerika," in Hans Jürgen-Goertz, ed., *Die Mennoniten* (Stuttgart: Evangelisches Verlagshaus, 1971), p. 206.

41. *MFP,* 13 May 1920, p. 2; *Canadian Annual Review,* 1920, p. 249.

42. *MFP,* 20 August 1920, p. 1. For a brief summary of the Quebec story see I. M. Dyck, p. 67; Abraham Friesen, pp. 87–88; Harder, p. 5; Schmiedehaus, p. 18.

43. Bishop Johann Friesen et al., Reinländer Mennonite Church, to Government of Quebec, 13 August 1920, quoted in *MFP,* 21 August 1920, p. 2.

44. Quoted in *MFP,* 21 August 1920, p. 2.

45. Harder, p. 5; I. M. Dyck, p. 67. Dyck's reference is probably to Ottawa rather than to Quebec City. *Mitarbeiter,* July 1920, p. 52, and February 1921, p. 14, reported favourably on school freedoms in Quebec.

46. Fretz, *Mennonite Colonization in Mexico,* p. 10; Cornelius Krahn, "Johann P. Wall, 1875–1961," *Mennonite Life* 16 (October 1961): 186; G. Rempel, pp. 6–7. This distinction is also claimed for John F. D. Wiebe, a Krimmer Mennonite Brethren who owned a real estate business in Herbert, Saskatchewan, by Sawatzky, p. 36; and for D. Salas Lopez by I. M. Dyck, p. 73.

47. Quiring, *Russlanddeutsche suchen eine Heimat,* pp. 37–38; Walter Quiring, "The Canadian Mennonite Immigration into the Paraguayan Chaco, 1926–1927," *MQR* 8 (January 1934): 33–34; J. Winfield Fretz, *Pilgrims in Paraguay. The Story of Mennonite Colonization in South America* (Scottdale: Herald Press, 1953), pp. 12–13; H. Hack, *Die Kolonisation der Mennoniten im Paraguayischen Chaco* (Amsterdam: Königliches Tropeninstitut, n.d.), pp. 45–46.

48. The Mexico explorations are described by Harder, pp. 6–10; I. M. Dyck, pp. 72–87; Sawatzky, pp. 36–40; and Schmiedehaus, pp. 20–26. The latter includes portions of the diary kept by delegate David Rempel.

49. *Mitarbeiter,* December 1920, p. 93; Harder, p. 6.

50. The *Privilegium* of 25 February is reproduced in German by Schmiedehaus, pp. 25–26; in English by Redekop, p. 251, Sawatzky, pp. 39–40, and the *MFP,* 17 September 1921, p. 4. The latter omits the crucial fourth point. It also reproduces the 8 July 1921 reply of Vincente Guerrero of the government of the State of Durango to the Mennonite petition of 30 June 1921.

51. Schmiedehaus, pp. 27–28.

52. Peter Elias, *Memoirs,* 4: 23, MHCA, vol. 3523, no. 4, notes land prices dropping from about $100 per acre when emigration talk first began in 1920, to as low as $16 per acre in 1922. *Mitarbeiter,* June 1922, p. 43, reports emigrants selling possessions at half price.

53. *MFP,* 7 March 1922, p. 3; 9 March, p.6; 13 March, pp. 5, 8. Schmiedehaus, p. 29.

54. *Mennonite Encyclopedia,* s.v. "Durango Mennonite Settlement," by Cornelius Krahn. A clash between delegates Klaas Heide of Manitoba and Johann P. Wall of Hague resulted in the two groups purchasing land tracts five hundred miles apart. Guenther, p. 15; Sawatzky, p. 43.

55. *Canadian Annual Review,* 1921, pp. 797–798; *MFP,* 5 October 1921, p. 4; 6 October, p. 4; 7 October, p. 9; 10 October, p. 4; Sawatzky, pp. 41–42. The complicated legal proceedings of this case have not yet been adequately reconstructed.

56. Sawatzky, p. 42, n. 32, suggests that "the fact that British financial interests were involved makes the Privy Council's reversal of the Canadian Supreme Court's ruling appear all the more as a 'managed' miscarriage of justice."

57. Ibid., p. 42, n. 34.

58. Johann P. Wall, Hague, to Minister of Education, Regina, 12 February 1923, SAB, M 5, 6.

59. J. H. Doerksen, p. 108, Petition of 14 October 1920, clause 2. Doerksen gives the date as 1921.

60. Ibid., p. 110.

61. Martin W. Friesen, comp. and ed., *Kanadische Mennoniten bezwingen eine Wildnis. 50 Jahre Kolonie Menno, Chaco, Paraguay, 1927–1977* (Loma Plata, Paraguay: Verwaltung der Kolonie Menno, 1977), p. 16. Idem, *Neue Heimat*, pp. 46–47.

62. J. H. Doerksen, p. 110. This delegation had left for Paraguay on 9 October and returned just before Christmas 1920.

63. Ibid., p. 111; Friesen, *Kanadische Mennoniten*, p. 16. One of the reasons for the delay was the fact that one of the Manitoba delegates, Bernhard Toews of Weidenfeld, had neglected to take out Canadian citizenship papers, and hence took a longer time to obtain a passport. Quiring, *Rußlanddeutsche suchen eine Heimat*, p. 41.

64. The following summary is based on Fretz, *Pilgrims in Paraguay*; Walter Quiring, *Deutsche erschließen den Chaco* (Karlsruhe: Heinrich Schneider, 1936) and *Rußlanddeutsche suchen eine Heimat*; and Friesen, *Neue Heimat*, pp. 53-66, 73-110.

65. Quiring, *Rußlanddeutsche*, p. 42; Friesen, *Neue Heimat*, pp. 82–83.

66. See appendix 8. An English version of this *Privilegium* of 26 July 1921 is found in Fretz, *Pilgrims in Paraguay*, pp. 229–231; German ones are found in J. H. Doerksen, pp. 111–114, and Quiring, *Rußlanddeutsche*, pp. 51–52; and Friesen, *Neue Heimat*, pp. 125–126.

67. F. W. Paris, British Chargé d'Affaires, Asunción, to Secretary of State for Foreign Affairs, London, 28 July 1921; included in Winston S. Churchill, Secretary of State for the Colonies, to Governor General of Canada, 15 September, 1921, NA, RG 7, G 21, vol. 653, no. 37523. See also Friesen, *Kanadische Mennoniten*, pp. 98–100. Fretz, *Pilgrims in Paraguay*, p. 15, advances some reasons why the generous terms of the *Privilegium* were not opposed by the Catholic Church.

68. From the written report of the delegates to the churches in Canada, quoted in Quiring, "The Canadian Mennonite immigration," p. 35.

69. J. H. Doerksen, p. 120. Other anonymous parties used a forged telegram and unsigned letters to warn against settling in Paraguay because of its political instability. Quiring, *Rußlanddeutsche*, p. 57.

70. Ibid., pp. 54–55.

71. Ibid., pp. 49–50; cf. J. H. Doerksen, p. 115.

72. Quiring, *Rußlanddeutsche*, p. 57.

73. Ibid., pp. 54–55; J. H. Doerksen, p. 120; Sawatzky, p. 52.

74. J. H. Doerksen, p. 115. Friesen, *Neue Heimat*, p. 129, reports the Sommerfelder vote split evenly with 123 choosing Paraguay and 125 Mexico. Chortitzer clearly preferred Paraguay (227–3), as did the small Bergthaler groups at Rosthern (40–0) and Herbert (8–0) in Saskatchewan.

75. J. H. Doerksen, pp. 121–125. The delegation's letter of introduction, signed by Bishop A. Doerksen, was dated 10 October 1921.

76. This *Privilegium*, translated from J. H. Doerksen, pp. 125–126, is included as appendix 9.

77. According to the report of Johann F. Wiebe, in J. H. Doerksen, pp. 126–129. The delegates' persistence on the point of legality of the *Privilegium* may have been inspired in part by a *MFP* report of 17 September 1921, p. 4, which published the Reinländer *Privi-*

*legium* and pointed out various points at which the Mexican constitution appeared to be "in direct contradiction to the promises made by President Obregon."

78. Sawatzky, pp. 51, 71.

79. Sawatzky, p. 58; John H. Warkentin, "The Mennonite Settlements," p. 228.

80. Quiring, *Rußlanddeutsche*, p. 61. Friesen, *Neue Heimat*, pp. 137, 141 ff., discusses this at greater length.

81. Quiring, *Rußlanddeutsche*, p. 62. The committee consisted of Martin C. Friesen and Abram A. Braun of the Chortitzer; Heinrich Unruh and Abram J. Friesen for the Sommerfelder; and Peter Peters and Peter J. Dyck of the Saskatchewan Bergthaler.

82. Ibid., p. 58. A German translation of the form of the sale-purchase agreement is given by J. H. Doerksen, pp. 115–120.

83. Quiring's estimates, *Rußlanddeutsche*, pp. 58–59, that in 1920 about ninety-five percent of all the Mennonite farmers favoured the emigration compared to a mere twenty-five percent by 1925, are exaggerated whether he is referring only to Chortitzer as the context suggests, or to all Manitoba and Saskatchewan Mennonites. The Chortitzer correspondent to the *Mitarbeiter* reported March 1926, p. 10, that half of his church, some two hundred families, expected to emigrate. By November, p. 5, his estimate was down to one hundred and sixty families.

84. E E and M P of Bolivia, Legación de Bolivia, Washington, D.C., to the Governor of Canada, 26 May 1923, NA, RG 7, G 21, vol. 653, no. 37523. Quiring, *Rußlanddeutsche*, p. 59, reports a letter of 9 June 1924 from the Bolivian ambassador directly to the East Reserve Mennonites.

85. Ibid., p. 63; Friesen, *Neue Heimat*, chap. 6.

86. Friesen, *Kanadische Mennoniten*, pp. 17–18.

87. The letter is given in German in Quiring, *Rußlanddeutsche*, pp. 65–66.

88. Lord Byng of Vimy, Ottawa, to Winston S. Churchill, Secretary of State for Colonies, 5 January 1922, NA, RG 7, G 21, vol. 653, no. 37523.

89. Byng to Churchill, 11 January 1922, NA, RG 7, G 21, vol. 653, no. 37523.

90. Byng to Churchill, 22 February 1922, NA, RG 7, G 21, vol. 653, no. 37523.

91. F. C. Blair, Ottawa, to J. H. Clark, U.S. Commissioner of Immigration, Montreal, 14 May 1920, NARS, RG 85, 54623/130; MHCA, microfilm no. 64.

92. H. A. C. Cummin, Asunción, to Sir Malcolm Robertson, Buenos Aires, 14 April 1926, NA, RG 7, G 21, vol. 653, no. 37523.

93. Lord Byng to H. B. M. Chargé d'Affaires, Buenos Aires, telegram, 14 April 1926, NA, RG 7, G 21, vol. 653, no. 37523.

94. Assistant Under-Secretary of State for External Affairs to Governor General's Secretary, 29 April 1927. The Deputy Governor General on 29 April 1927 sent that information unchanged to V. A. L. Mallet, H. M. Chargé d'Affaires in Buenos Aires. NA, RG 7, G 21, vol. 653, no. 37523.

95. For an account of their coming see Frank H. Epp, *Mennonite Exodus. The Rescue and Resettlement of the Russian Mennonites since the Communist Revolution* (Altona, Man.: Canadian Mennonite Relief and Immigration Council, 1962), and John B. Toews, *Lost Fatherland, The Story of the Mennonite Emigration from Soviet Russia, 1921–1927* (Scottdale: Herald Press, 1967).

96. I. M. Dyck, p. 85; Gerbrandt, p. 76; *ME*, s.v. "Froese, Jacob J." by Jacob Peters (5:314).

97. Guenther, p. 16.

98. W. S. Cram to A. H. Ball, Deputy Minister of Education, 13 January 1925, SAB, M 5, 6(3); J. E. Friesen to S. J. Latta, 1 June 1926, ibid., 6(4).

99. Quiring, *Rußlanddeutsche*, p. 61; *Mitarbeiter*, November 1926, p. 5; February 1927, p. 8.

100. Quiring, *Rußlanddeutsche*, p. 56; *Mitarbeiter*, December 1922, p. 92; Abraham Doerksen papers, MHCA, vol. 2230, no. 2, indicate that Friesen was elected 6 October and ordained 15 October.

101. Doell, *The Berthaler Mennonite Church*, p. 35.

102. *Mitarbeiter*, December 1922, p. 92.

103. Ibid., April 1926, p. 7; October 1926, pp. 1–2.

104. Ibid., December 1922, p. 92. The committee appointed by the 9 November meeting in Altona consisted of Johann Rempel—Chortitzer; Wilhelm Berg, Johann D. Klassen and Abram Sawatzky—Sommerfelder; Johann D. Goossen and H. H. Ewert—Bergthaler; H. R. Reimer and Johann K. Friesen—*Kleine Gemeinde*; Johann P. Toews—Holdemann; P. G. Neufeld—Mennonite Brethren.

105. Ibid., pp. 92–93; decisions of the committee at its 27 November meeting in Winnipeg.

106. Ibid., February 1923, pp. 11–12.

107. Ibid., April 1923, p. 28.

108. Ibid., July 1923, pp. 52–53.

109. Ibid., January 1926, p. 4; March 1926, pp. 9–10.

110. Ibid., March 1926, p. 3.

111. Ewert served the Mennonite Collegiate Institute, Gretna, Manitoba, as principal until his death in 1934; Toews was principal of Rosthern German-English Academy until 1917 and then served for many years as chairman of its board. Both were immigrants from the U.S.A.

112. *Mitarbeiter*, October 1925, pp. 75–76; November 1925, p. 81; August 1921, p. 65.

113. The *Mitarbeiter*, October 1925, p. 80, announced that the Sommerfelder had actually taken over the school. Gerbrandt's reconstruction of MEI events of 1925–1926 on the basis of its minutes does not clearly corroborate the reported Sommerfelder takeover, but it is unable to explain why all board members by the summer of 1926 were from the Sommerfelder church. Gerbrandt, *Adventure in Faith*, p. 270.

114. *Mitarbeiter*, November 1925, p. 87.

115. A. P. Elias, Winkler, quoted in F. C. Blair, Secretary, Department of Immigration and Colonization, to J. M. Roberts, Secretary, Department of the Interior, 8 November 1923, NA, RG 15, vol. 571, no. 179925. Elias wanted the government to allow only Mennonites to buy lands on the "reserve." In the former East Reserve, there was considerable consternation in 1925 when an Italian Countess Garibaldi was negotiating to purchase the entire block being sold by McRoberts for the Mennonites leaving for Paraguay. Quiring, *Rußlanddeutsche*, p. 60; *Mitarbeiter*, March 1926, p. 10.

116. Sommerfelder Gemeinde per H. J. Friesen, Bishop, and Johann D. Klassen, Secretary, to W. R. Motherwell, Minister of Agriculture, 28 January 1927; Klassen to Motherwell, 9 April 1927; H. J. Friesen et al. to Motherwell, 2 June 1927; Klassen to Motherwell, 16 August 1927, NA, RG 15, vol. 233, no. 3129(5).

117. Department of the Interior, to P. M. Friesen, Enderby, B.C., 15 March 1928, NA, RG 15, vol. 233, no. 3129(5). Friesen had applied for a reserve for Reinländer Mennonites in the Peace River district.

118. *Mitarbeiter*, April 1920, p. 31, *"Welche Aufgaben haben wir jetzt nach dem Kriege unserm Lande gegenüber?"*

119. Ibid., October 1920, pp. 78–80.

120. Bergthaler Church, Ministerial, *Minutes*, 2:204, no. 9, 21 June 1921; MHCA, vol. 716; Brotherhood, *Minutes*, no. 9, 22 June 1921, MHCA, vol. 715.

121. Conference of Mennonites in Central Canada, *Minutes*, 1903–1913, 21 July 1903, MHCA, vol. 525.

122. *MFP*, 26 November 1910, p. 44; 6 February 1913, p. 3.

123. Gerbrandt, *Adventure in Faith*, p. 315, lists Klaas Peters, Peter Friesen, F. F. Siemens, and John M. Wall among them. Peters had already become a Swedenborgian minister in 1902, and so should not properly be considered a Mennonite even though he continued to regard himself as one. *Germania*, a fiercely partisan Conservative German weekly, reported on Mennonite involvement in the election campaign in its issues of 20 October 1904, p. 5; 27 October, pp. 1, 5, 7, 8; and 3 November, p. 1.

124. *MFP*, 7 and 8 February 1913, p. 3.

125. V. Winkler to H. H. Hamm, 11 August 1915, PAM, MG 14, B 45, box 2.

126. H. H. Hamm, Secretary-Treasurer, R.M. of Rhineland, to V. Winkler, 7 August 1915; H. H. Ewert, MCI, Gretna, to Winkler, 17 May 1915. Even the former Conservative campaigner, F. F. Siemens, 13 May 1915, expressed his satisfaction to V. Winkler at the "downfall of the Roblin-Rogers & Co. organization." Winkler expressed some surprise at Siemens' feelings, but assured him in good Methodist manner that it was "never too late for a sinner to return." PAM, MG 14, B 45, box 2. It should also be noted that in the 1909 Alberta elections, Cornelius Hiebert left the Conservatives and ran as Independent, only to be badly defeated in the Didsbury riding by ex-Mennonite J. E. Stauffer, running as Liberal. *Canadian Parliamentary Guide*, 1912, p. 534.

127. Mennonite School Commission brief to Hon. Valentine Winkler, 7 January 1916, MHCA, vol. 544, no. 47.

128. Gerbrandt, p. 317. But not for long. By 1931 the Bergthaler Ministerial gave almost unanimous support to one of its members (Dr. C. W. Wiebe) in his proposal to run for the Liberals in the provincial election. *Minutes*, 3:74, no. 6, 6 February 1931, MHCA, vol. 716.

129. *Mitarbeiter*, October 1921, p. 80; March 1922, p. 20; June 1922, p. 44. P.C. no. 1204, the order barring Mennonite immigrants, was rescinded by P.C. no. 1181, 2 June 1922, NA, RG 2, 1, vol. 1676. A recommendation by the Minister of Immigration and Colonization to have this done on 26 May 1922 was not acted on by cabinet. P.C. no. 1130/22, RG 2, 3, vol. 210. The War-Time Elections Act, 1917, which had disenfranchised Mennonites, was repealed in 1920. Canada, *Statutes*, chap. 46, schedule 3.

# CONCLUSION

About one-third of the Mennonites in Russia emigrated to North America during the 1870s. For the most part they were the ones who found unacceptable the threatened loss of "separate" status (full control of their schools and total exemption from military service) in Russia. The two-thirds that remained accepted the compromise of teaching Russian in their schools and performing alternative service to military duty.

About one-third of the immigrants from Russia came to Canada. For the most part they distinguished themselves from their co-religionists who settled in the United States by the importance they attached to a *Privilegium*, which would once more define for them a separate status in their new home. This twofold selection process meant that the three groups that came to Canada initially held very similar positions on the question of the relationship of a believers' church to the state. The delegates of Bergthal and the *Kleine Gemeinde* were thus able jointly to negotiate terms of entry into Canada. The Fürstenland–Chortitza group, which did not send delegates to North America, also found these terms acceptable.

The understanding that they brought with them from Russia of separation from the state involved formal recognition of their group as a separate community within Canadian society. The *Privilegium* that they negotiated with the federal government indicated that this included at least full freedom of religion, total exemption from military service and the swearing of oaths, and the right to their own schools. Implied in the granting of reserves for the creation of closed communities, but not explicitly stated, was the right to local self-government. Given these conditions, they were quite prepared to become obedient subjects of the realm.

All three Russian Mennonite immigrant groups that came to Canada thus recognized that negotiations with the national government in Ottawa were necessary and unavoidable. It was fully acceptable not only to negotiate a *Privilegium*, i.e., to define their separate status, but also to continue the ongoing administrative relations necessary to have that separate status recognized in practice by local officials. The federal government in Ottawa, more naturally than the provincial governments, was seen as the authority ordained of God (Romans 13) to which Christians are to submit. Throughout the fifty-year span covered by the present study, Mennonite relations with the government in Ottawa were characterized by mutual respect, trust, and cordiality. At no point did there appear a hesitation on the part of the churches to send a delegation to Ottawa to meet with the Prime Minister or other cabinet officials when some issue seemed impossible to resolve by mail.

Significant differences emerged among the three initial Mennonite groups in the way they sought to resolve difficulties relating to the introduction of municipal government and public schools. The former was not explicitly mentioned at all in the *Privilegium* and the latter ambiguously defined. In both cases Mennonites had to deal with provincial governments rather than with Ottawa. In both cases the initiative came from the governments rather than from the Mennonite churches. And in both cases the issue was not one of defining their separate status, but rather one of developing an ongoing relationship that implied increasing involvement with each other.

Since the province of Manitoba was still in its infancy when the Mennonites first arrived, self-government on their reserves was initially totally independent of the provincial government. Administratively it was not difficult to adapt their system of a *Gebietsamt* with *Oberschulze* and village *Schulzen* to the new municipal system with its council, reeve, and councillors. On the Manitoba East Reserve this happened, in fact, with an apparently smooth transition. The minority *Kleine Gemeinde*, which did not participate in local government at all, was indifferent as to whether the majority Bergthal group handled local administrative matters as *Chortitzer Gebietsamt* or as Hanover Municipal Council, and so offered no resistance to the change. The majority Bergthal group was divided between East and West Reserves and suffered from a church leadership crisis just as the new municipal government was introduced. It, too, offered no significant practical resistance, and no resistance in principle.

The West Reserve Reinländer, however, saw this as much more than a changing of titles. Since they lived in closed communities by choice, local government was necessarily in the hands of their own members. These could not be allowed to hold offices that functioned under an outside authority without threatening their concept of church. A municipal council received its authority from an act of the provincial government, not from the church or the consent of the villagers. In addition, the municipal system could function with, indeed was designed for, a landholding system without villages and the communal commitments involved in the village form of life. The municipality thus meant not merely a new form of local government; it could spell the end of the old way of life. The Reinländer threat of emigration did not become reality in the early 1880s because the government allowed the old *Gebietsamt* and all of its local village commitments to function alongside the new municipal councils. These parallel systems of administration continued in operation into the 1920s, when the emigration took place over other issues.

The local government issue thus revealed a difference in principle between the Reinländer and the other Mennonite groups by 1885. The former refused to be "unequally yoked" with state authorities in the ordering of their own communities. While remaining obedient subjects, even to the municipal regulations, they refused (like the *Kleine Gemeinde*) to exercise citizenship rights by electing the municipal councils or serving on them.

The Mennonites discovered only gradually that their *Privilegium* had not unambiguously defined their separate status in the area of education. Until 1890 Manitoba's publicly supported schools functioned with such a large measure of autonomy that the *Kleine Gemeinde* and its splinter groups (Holdemann and Bruderthaler) had no objection in principle to accepting such support. Even after the denominational public schools were abolished in 1890 the school Act seemed generous enough for these groups and the West Reserve Mennonite Brethren and Bergthaler to move increasingly toward incorporation into the public school system. Having basically accepted the idea of working together with the government in the area of education, these groups took a pragmatic approach and were ready on any specific issue to withdraw from the system. The compulsory flag-flying law and the abolition of the bilingual clause in Manitoba were such issues, causing the withdrawal of a number of schools from public support.

The Reinländer and Chortitzer viewed the matter of schools from a different perspective. In their reading of the *Privilegium* they had been given the right to their own schools without any interference from the government whatsoever. They accepted the fact that this also meant taking full responsibility for the cost of such schools. To them this was important because education was clearly the responsibility of the church and the parents. It was far too important to be given to the state. Until about 1916 this position was acceptable to the governments of Saskatchewan and Manitoba, and these two groups maintained their own private schools alongside the public school system that functioned all around them and even in some of their immediate communities. When the right to autonomous administration of their own private schools was denied them, they refused to yield.

The Bergthaler and their allies, who had taken a pragmatic position, also did not like the changes in the school system that were introduced during the First World War. But in their pragmatism they used the accepted means of the Canadian democratic process, the ballot box and the political lobby, to attempt to change the school system in such a way as to make it tolerable for them. They acted like enfranchised citizens. The Reinländer and Chortitzer, in their opposition in principle to state-controlled education for their children and their rejection of a "political" approach, were left with only three options. First, they appealed to Ottawa to have their *Privilegium* upheld. When that was unsuccessful, they deliberately chose faithfulness to their religious conviction over obedience to the provincial law. When even that drastic language did not persuade the provincial governments to modify their positions, both Reinländer and Chortitzer resorted to a repetition of the cycle with another emigration.

The public school issue thus confirmed the division among the Mennonites that the local government issue had first suggested. However, in this case the Chortitzer group shared the convictions of the Reinländer and sided with them in maintaining a separatist position. The *Kleine Gemeinde*, reluctant to participate in municipal government, had been the first to accept public schools and continued to do so.

On a third issue, exemption from military service, the *Privilegium* had clearly defined Mennonite status and the federal government faithfully kept its promise. It was therefore only indirectly a contributing factor to the decision of some groups to emigrate. The two issues that created the most tension between Ottawa and the Mennonites during the war (i.e., obtaining exception from the Military Service Act of 1917 and coping with press censorship) affected the emigrating Reinländer and Chortitzer least. This is in sharp contrast with the situation of the Russian Mennonites in the United States, where "the abrasive encounter of Mennonite nonresistance with American nationalism" not only produced a significant emigration already during the war years, but also strongly influenced the process of Mennonite accommodation to the dominant society.[1]

Since the groups emigrating from Canada in the 1920s took care to negotiate a new *Privilegium* with the national governments of the countries to which they planned to move, it is clear that their faith in government as ordained of God had basically not been shaken by their experiences with Canada and Russia. Another aspect of their theology was helpful to them in maintaining this faith. They were convinced that the true church had always been persecuted in this world, but that a faithful God would never fail to provide a new place of refuge in which the church could once more live out its faith for a while.

The governments of Canada and the two provinces most directly involved with the Mennonites responded in quite diverse ways. Ottawa had the advantage over the other two in that it was an active partner in the initial negotiations that produced the *Privilegium*. This advantage was enhanced by the fact that it had control over crown lands in Manitoba and the Northwest Territories (and later in Alberta and Saskatchewan) and thus became both the donor of the land for Mennonite settlements and the primary outside influence in the early shaping of their communities. In advancing the loan during the financial crisis of the 1870s, in extending the life of the reserves long beyond their initially intended duration, and in supporting an active recruitment program to gain new Mennonite immigrants, the federal government laid the basis for a very positive relationship. This, and its determination to honour its commitment in the matter of exemption from military service, helped that relationship to survive the inevitable tensions between a nation at war and its pacifist communities.

The provinces lacked these initial advantages. In fact, in Saskatchewan and Alberta Mennonite settlement preceded the achievement of provincial status. In the matter of extending provincially regulated local self-government to these communities, the Manitoba government moved with patience and flexibility. It did not insist on eliminating the old *Gebietsamt* system when it introduced municipal councils, but allowed the two to function side by side. By doing so, it avoided what could well have been a confrontation leading to the emigration of a sizable portion of the Mennonite community.

In the matter of education, both provinces initially showed the same kind of flexibility. Church-controlled and -funded private schools were allowed at first to function alongside government-supported and -regulated public schools. But the twin pressures of an intense Protestantism and a narrow nationalism that Canada experienced from 1890 to 1920 found less resistance in Winnipeg and Regina than they did in Ottawa. The first manifested itself as anti-Catholicism, but in school matters showed as little tolerance for the non-Protestant Mennonite system as it did for the non-Protestant Catholic one. The second argued in effect "that unless English was made the sole language of all schools in the West, a Canadian 'nation' could never emerge from the polyglot western population,"[2] and opposed German Mennonite schools with the same intensity as it did French Catholic or Ukrainian Orthodox ones.

When the patriotic fervour of the First World War intensified these pressures, the governments of Manitoba and Saskatchewan capitulated.

The inflexible methods used in both cases to impose "national schools" on the Mennonite communities produced the kind of confrontation that confirmed the worst fears of the public school resisters. Manitoba had already seen in the reaction to its 1906 flag legislation how deep Mennonite objection to imposed nationalism was. But that lesson did not prevent the government in 1919 from taking every measure necessary to bring the entire Mennonite population under the jurisdiction of the School Attendance Act. Its construction of one-room school buildings to serve the combined population of three Mennonite villages (where a minimum of three classrooms was required) in school districts created by order-in-council and operated single-handedly by an official appointed by the Department of Education can hardly be given a charitable interpretation.

In Saskatchewan the government had been well informed of Mennonite convictions in the area of education by the reports of several special studies, beginning with a commission of inquiry in 1908. But the insights of those studies were not applied in its postwar school policy. The resulting clash with a sizable portion of the Mennonite community was much more severe than previous studies have shown. The emigration to Mexico and Paraguay, together with the new immigration from the U.S.S.R. in the 1920s, so altered the nature of the western Canadian Mennonite community that the specific issues of the 1918–1921 clash in Manitoba and Saskatchewan were never resolved in a definitive way. Both the group that remained in Canada and the group that arrived were for the most part quite open to incorporation as full Canadian citizens.

## Notes

1. Juhnke, p. 153.

2. Ramsay Cook, *Canada and the French Canadian Question* (Toronto: Macmillan, 1966), quoted in Clark, p. 226.

# APPENDIX 1

# Order-in-Council of April 26, 1872

P.C. #827B. Certified copy of a Report of the Committee of the Privy Council, approved by His Excellency the Governor General on the 26th April, 1872.

The Committee of Council have had under consideration a Despatch No. 51 of the 7th of March, 1872 from the Right Honourable the Secretary of State for the Colonies transmitting Copy of a Letter from the Foreign Office with a Despatch from Her Majesty's Consul at Berdiansk enclosing Letters from German Menonites established in Russia enquiring whether if they emigrate to Canada they would be allowed certain privileges there as to exemption from Military Service.

This Despatch having been referred to the Hon. the Minister of Militia and Defence, that Officer reports that the body of Religionists known as Menonites, is by Statute put on the same footing as Quakers and he calls attention to the 17th Section of the "Act respecting the Militia and Defence of the Dominion of Canada" by which it is enacted that "any person bearing a Certificate from the Society of Menonists shall be exempt from Military Service when balloted in time of peace or war, upon such conditions and such regulations as the Governor-in-Council may, from time to time prescribe."

The said Despatch and enclosures having been also referred to the Hon. the Minister of Agriculture for report with respect to the other matters therein alluded to the Minister recommends that the applicants be informed that a free grant of 160 acres of best land in the possession of the Dominion in the Province of Manitoba, or in other parts of the North West Territory during the years 1872 and 1873 will be made to any person among them, or to as many persons as may apply over the age of 21 years, upon the condition of settlement, and further that, in the other Provinces of the Dominion either free grants of land may be obtained or purchases made on easy terms and at merely nominal prices. The settlers may obtain contiguous lots of land, so as to enable them to form their own communities.

That as related to their enquiry touching a possible application for aid he respectfully recommends that they be informed, it is not the policy of the Dominion Government to grant aid to any settlers in Canada.

That as relates to the information with which they ask to be furnished he recommends that a supply of the several publications of the Provinces and of the Department of Agriculture, containing information for intending Emigrants, be sent to them – and further that in view of the proposed large movement of population, that they should be invited to send to Canada one or two persons from among themselves in whose statements they would have confidence, in order to see the Country in general and the localities in particular, in which they could obtain lands for settlement, and the terms on which they could obtain them, the Department of Agriculture paying the expenses of such persons while engaged on such Mission.

The Committee submit the above reports and the recommendations they contain for Your Excellency's approval and recommend that a Copy of this Minute be transmitted by Your Excellency to the Earl of Kimberley.

Clerk of the Privy Council.

---

Source: NA, RG 2, 1, vol. 108.

# APPENDIX 2
# Order-in-Council of September 25, 1872

P.C. #1043D. Certified Copy of a Report of a Committee of the Honourable the Privy Council, approved by His Excellency the Governor General in Council on the 25th September, 1872.

The Committee of Council have had under consideration a despatch from the Right Hon. the Secretary of State for the Colonies, dated August 23rd ultimo, covering a letter from Mr. Zahrabs, Her Majesty's Consul at Berdiansk, dated July 26th last, and a letter from Mr. Cornelius Janzen, of Berdiansk, dated June last, addressed to Your Excellency.

The Hon. the Minister of Agriculture, to whom the above despatch and enclosures were referred, reports that it is expedient to give the German Mennonites in Russia the fullest assurances of absolute immunity from military service if they settle in Canada.

That a sub-section, of section 17, of the Act 31 Victoria, chapter 40, is as follows:

"Any person bearing a certificate from the Society of Quakers, Menonists or Tunkers, or any inhabitant of Canada, of any religious denomination, otherwise subject to military duty, but who, from the doctrines of his religion, is averse to bearing arms and refuses personal military service shall be exempt from such service when balloted in time of peace or war, upon such conditions and under such regulations as the Governor in Council may, from time to time, prescribe."

That under this section all the persons above mentioned, and the Mennonites are expressly included, are absolutely free and exempted by the law of Canada, from military duty or service, either in time of peace or war.

That the Governor General in Council cannot prescribe any condition or regulations under which, under any circumstances, the persons referred to in the above quoted section can be compelled to render any military service.

That the intention of the Act in conferring upon the Governor General in Council the power of making conditions and regulations was to enable the Government to provide, if necessary, for the registration of the exempted persons in such manner as to prevent persons belonging to any other denominations than those specified in the section of the Act above quoted from avoiding military duty under false pretences.

That the Constitution does not confer upon the Governor General in Council any power to over-ride or set aside, under any circumstances, the plain meaning of statute law and he recommends that this explanation be conveyed to the Mennonists in Russia.

The Committee concur in the foregoing report, and advise that a copy of this Minute be transmitted by Your Excellency to the Earl of Kimberley.

(Signed) John J. McGee, Clerk, Privy Council.

---

Source: NA, RG 2, 1.

# APPENDIX 3

# Capital Brought into Canada by Russian Mennonite Immigrants, 1874–1880

| Year | No. of Immigrants | Capital Brought in According to | |
|---|---|---|---|
| | | P. Wismer | Immigration Dept. |
| 1874 | 1,533 | $143,000 | $200,000[a] |
| 1875 | 3,261 | 242,000 | 324,000[b] |
| 1876 | 1,352 | 119,000 | 170,000[c] |
| 1877 | 184 | 19,000 | 25,600[d] |
| 1878 | 324 | – | 79,500[e] |
| 1879 | 208 | 60,000 | – |
| 1880 | 69 | 7,000 | – |
| Totals | 6,931 | 590,000 | 866,100[f] |

a. Canada, Parliament, *Sessional Papers*, 1875, vol. 8, no. 40, "Annual Report of the Department of Agriculture," appendix 5, p. 31.
b. Ibid., 1876, vol. 9, no. 8, appendix 1, p. 7; appendix 21, p. 86.
c. Ibid., 1877, vol. 10, no. 8, p. xvi; appendix 28, p. 89.
d. Ibid., 1878, vol. 11, no. 9, appendix 43, p. 166; 40,000 rubles calculated at the 1876 exchange rate.
e. Ibid., 1879, vol. 12, p. xxiv; appendix 40, p. 163; 124,000 rubles calculated at the 1876 exchange rate.
f. Since the Immigration Department did not report any figures for 1879 and 1880, the amounts given by Wismer for these years have been included in the total.

Source: The Wismer amounts are calculated from more detailed data given by Frank H. Epp, *Mennonites in Canada, 1786–1920* (Toronto: Macmillan, 1974), p. 201.

## APPENDIX 4

## Sample Homestead Entry Receipt

Source: NA, RG 15, vol. 233, no. 3129(3).

APPENDIX 5

## National Service Registration Card, 1917 (Front)

THIS CARD MUST BE FILLED IN AND PROMPTLY RETURNED BY ALL MALES BETWEEN THE AGES OF 16 AND 65 INCLUSIVE.

### NATIONAL SERVICE.
CANADA.

1. What is your full name?..................................................... 2. How old are you?..................years.
3. Where do you live? Province..................................
4. Name of city, town, village or Post Office }
   Street.................................................... Number..................
5. In what country were you born? }
6. In what country was your father born? }
7. In what country was your mother born? }
8. Were you born a British subject?..................
9. If not, are you naturalized?..................
10. How much time have you lost in last 12 months from sickness? }
11. Have you full use of your arms?..................
12. Of your legs?.................. 13. Of your sight?..................
14. Of your hearing?..................
15. Which are you—married, single or a widower? }
16. How many persons besides yourself do you support? }
17. What are you working at for a living?..................
18. Whom do you work for?..................
19. Have you a trade or profession?.................. 20. If so, what?..................
21. Are you working now?.................. 22. If not, why?..................
23. Would you be willing to change your present work for other necessary work at the same pay during the war?..................
24. Are you willing, if your railway fare is paid, to leave where you now live, and go to some other place in Canada to do such work?..................

INSTRUCTIONS FOR FILLING IN THIS CARD ARE ON THE OTHER SIDE. IT ASKS 24 QUESTIONS. COUNT YOUR ANSWERS.

Source: MHCA, XX-1, vol. 542, no. 9.

APPENDIX 5

# National Service Registration Card, 1917 (Back)

## INSTRUCTIONS FOR FILLING IN CARD.

1. This card is to be filled in by all males between the ages of 16 and 65 inclusive.

2. Write plainly.

3. Answer correctly every question. Each is important.

4. This card must be filled in and mailed to the Director General ot National Service, Ottawa, in accompanying official envelope, within 10 days of its receipt by you. No postage is required.

5. If you lose your card or envelope any Postmaster will supply another on request.

6. DO NOT FOLD THIS CARD.

Source: MHCA, XX-1, vol. 542, no. 9.

APPENDIX 6

# Mennonite Identification Certificate, World War I

## MILITARY SERVICE ACT, 1917

To Whom It May Concern:

I .................................................. of .................................................. in the Province of .................................................., being a duly ordained and authorized minister of the denomination of Christians called Mennonites, do hereby certify that .................................................. of .................................................. in the Province of .................................................., who is of the age of ........ years, is a Mennonite and a member of the denomination of Christians aforesaid and that he is a descendant of one of those Mennonites who came to Canada from Russia subsequent to the order of the Governor-General in Council of 13th August, 1873, pursuant to the arrangement thereby sanctioned.

.................................................. Ordained Minister

Dated at .................................................., in the Province aforesaid, this ........ day of .................., 1918.

.................................................. 
Signature of Bearer

Police will be instructed to recognize certificates duly executed in above form as PRIMA FACIE, entitling the bearer named therein to immunity.

(Sgd) E. L. NEWCOMBE,
Deputy Minister of Justice.

Ottawa, 28 June, '18.

Source: MHCA, XX-1, vol. 542, no. 4.

APPENDIX 7

# Canada Registration Board Cards, 1918 (Card for Females)

CANADA REGISTRATION BOARD

## CARD FOR FEMALES

| DATE OF REGISTRATION | | | | SERIES NUMBER |
|---|---|---|---|---|
| MONTH | DAY | YEAR 1918 | | |

TO BE FILLED IN BY DEPUTY REGISTRAR

1. Name in full (surname last)? ........................ 2. Age? ......

3. Address (permanent)? ........ NUMBER ........ STREET ........ RURAL DELIVERY OR POST OFFICE ........ CITY, TOWN, ETC. ........ PROVINCE

4. Nationality? ........ can you speak English? ........ French? ........

5. British subject? ........ by birth? ........ naturalization? ........ marriage? ........

6. Are you single? ........ married? ........ widow? ........ divorced? ........

7. How many children or wards under 16? ........ Will these children be recorded by another registrant? ........

8. Do your health and home ties permit you, if required, to give full-time paid work? ........
(Registrants answering "NO" here, need not answer any of the following questions; if answering "YES" or, if in doubt, should fill up rest of card. All must sign affirmation.)

9. Do your circumstances permit you to live away from home? ........

10. What is your present main occupation? ........
    (a) If in business as employer, state number of employees.
    (b) If an employee, state name, business and address of employer.
    (c) If full-time voluntary worker, state name of Society served.

11. State particulars of each, if you have
    (a) Trade or profession?
    (b) Degree, diploma or certificate?
    (c) Special training?

12. State length of experience, if any In:-

| | Years |
|---|---|
| (a) General farming ... | |
| (b) Truck farming ... | |
| (c) Fruit farming ... | |
| (d) Poultry farming ... | |
| (e) Dairy farming ... | |

13. Can you
    (a) Drive a tractor? ...
    (b) Drive a motor car? ...
    (c) Drive a horse? ...
    (d) Harness a horse? ...
    (e) Do plain cooking? ...

14. Indicate here any qualification or practical experience which you possess, not already recorded.

15. Considering your health, training and experience, and the national needs, in what capacity do you think you could serve best?

16. Do your circumstances permit you to give regular full-time service without remuneration?

I affirm that I have verified the above answers and that they are true.

........................ Signature of Registrant.

Source: W. M. Martin Papers, SAB, M 4, I-101, p. 30094.

# APPENDIX 7

## Canada Registration Board Cards, 1918 (Card for Males)

DATE OF REGISTRATION | CANADA REGISTRATION BOARD | SERIES NUMBER

MONTH | DAY | 1918 YEAR

CARD FOR MALES

TO BE FILLED IN BY DEPUTY REGISTRAR

1. Name in full (surname last)?

Address (permanent)?
STREET AND NUMBER | RURAL DELIVERY OR POST OFFICE | TOWN OR CITY | PROVINCE

2. Age?     Date of birth?     Country of birth?     3. Race?     Speak English (E) or French (F)?

4. British subject?     By birth?     By Naturalization?     5. If not a British subject, to what country do you owe allegiance?
   If naturalized, Which year?     What place?

6. Single (S), Married (M), Widower (W), or divorced (D)?     7. How many children under 16 years?

8. Physical disabilities, if any?     9. If registered under Military Service Act, what is your serial number?

10. (a) Present occupation (if any)?
    (b) What is your regular occupation?     Length of experience in (a) (b) (c)
    (c) What other work can you do well?

11. If an employee, state employer's name:
    Address:     Nature of business:

12. Do your circumstances permit you to serve in the present national crisis, by changing your present occupation to some other for which you are qualified, if the conditions offered be satisfactory?     (a) Where you can return home daily?     (b) Away from home?

13. (a) Were you brought up on a farm?     Until what age?     (b) Have you worked on farm?     How long?
    (c) Are you retired farmer?     (d) Can you handle horses?     Drive tractors?     Use farm machinery?
    (e) Are you willing to do farm work?     Where?     During what periods?

I affirm that I have verified the above answers and that they are true.

...................................................... Signature of Registrant.

Source: W. M. Martin Papers, SAB, M 4, I-101, p. 30092.

# APPENDIX 8

# Excerpts of the Paraguayan Mennonite Privilegium

Translation of Law granting to the Mennonites exemption from compulsory military service.

Art. 1. The members of the community named Mennonite that arrive in the country as components of a colonization enterprise, and their descendants, shall enjoy the following rights and privileges:-

1) To practice their religion and their cult with entire freedom, without restriction, and consequently to make affirmations before justice by simple Yes or No instead of taking the oath, and be exempt from compulsory military service in time of peace and in time of war in combatant or non-combatant forces;

2) Found, administer and maintain schools and educational establishments, and teach and learn their religion and their language, which is the German, without any restriction.

3) Administer residuary property and effects and especially the property and effects belonging to widows and orphans, by means of the special system of trust-guardianship known as "*Waisenamt*", and in accordance with the peculiar rules of the community, without any restriction;

4) Administer the mutual fire insurance that is established in the colonies.

Art. 2. The sale of alcoholic and intoxicating beverages is prohibited within the limits of a zone that extends for five kilometres from the properties belonging to the mennonite [*sic*] colonies unless the competent authorities of those colonies request from the Government, and the Government grants the admission of such sale.

. . . . . . . . . . . . . . . . . . . . . . . . . .

Art. 4. No immigration Law, or other, existing or that may be promulgated, can prevent the entry into the country of mennonite immigrants for reasons of age, mental or physical disability.

Art. 5. The franchise referred to in paragraph 3) of Article 1 should be understood as not affecting the rights of persons capable of managing their own property and effects. Dealing with incapables, the Judges, once they have proved the fact of their belonging to the mennonite communities, shall designate as executors or curators the respective trust institutions. Such executorship, or curatorship, shall be governed by the rules of those trust institutions.

. . . . . . . . . . . . . . . . . . . . . . . .

Art. 7. The privileges and franchises accorded by this Law shall be extended to individuals of the same mennonite community that may reach the country separately, provided that, through the competent authorities of the community, they prove that they are mennonites and form part of the colonization undertaking referred to in Article 6.

Art. 8. Let it be communicated to the Executive.

>Asunción, July 22nd, 1921.
>(Sd.) Felix Paiva
>(Sd.) Enrique Bordenave, President of Senate. President of Chief of Deputies.

>Asunción, July 26, 1921.
>To be held as Law, complied with, published, and given to the Official Registry.
>(SD.) GONDRA; José P. Guggiari; Ramón Lara Castro; Eligio Ayala; Rogelio Ibarra; A. Chirife.

---

Source: F. W. Paris, British Chargé d'Affaires, Asunción, despatch no. 16 to Secretary of State for Foreign Affairs, July 28, 1921; included in Winston S. Churchill, Secretary of State for the Colonies, despatch no. 501 to Governor General of Canada, September 15, 1921, NA, RG 7, G 21, vol. 653, no. 37523.

## APPENDIX 9

# Sommerfelder Mexican Privilegium

To Bishop Abraham Doerksen
Representative of the Sommerfelder Mennonite Church of Canada

In reply to your submission of the 5th of this month, in which you express your wish to settle in our country as agriculturalists, I have the honour to answer as follows the questions contained in the above mentioned submission:

In no case will you be obliged to render military service.

In no case will you be obliged to render an oath.

You have the most far-reaching right to exercise your religious principles and the prescriptions of your church without any molestation or restriction.

You are fully authorized to found your own schools with your own teachers, and to teach and practise your religion in the German language without being hindered in any way by the government.

In regard to the administration of your estates and the founding of a Mennonite mutual fire insurance, our laws are so liberal that you can regulate your estates in the way and manner you consider right. This government will raise no objection if the members of your sect introduce among themselves economic regulations which they voluntarily adopt.

You will receive the protection of the law at all times for your property and life wherever such protection is necessary.

You have full freedom to emigrate from this republic whenever you deem it right to do so.

It is the emphatic wish of this government to support the settlement of order-loving, moral and industrious elements, which includes the Mennonites, and it will be pleased if you will find the foregoing answers satisfactory, since the privileges mentioned are guaranteed by our laws, and you as well as your descendants shall positively and forever enjoy them.

Sufragio Efectivo No Reelección

Mexico, October 30, 1921

The Constitutional President of the
United States of Mexico
(sgd) A. Obregon

Minister of Agriculture and Economic Affairs
(sgd) A.J. Villarreal

---

Source: J. H. Doerksen, *Geschichte und Wichtige Dokumente der Mennoniten von Russland, Canada, Paraguay und Mexico* (n.p., 1923), pp. 125–126. My translation.

# BIBLIOGRAPHY

## Books

ANDERSON, J. T. M. *The Education of the New Canadian. A Treatise on Canada's Greatest Educational Problem.* London and Toronto: J. M. Dent, 1918.

BENDER, HAROLD S., and SMITH, C. HENRY, eds. *The Mennonite Encyclopedia. A Comprehensive Reference Work on the Anabaptist-Mennonite Movement,* 4 vols. Scottdale: Mennonite Publishing House, 1955–1959.

BERG, BALDWIN, comp. *Our 1–6 Heritage. A History of the School Districts of Deer Creek—Lindal—Elk Creek—Diamond.* Morden, Man.: One–Six History Book Committee, 1976.

BLANKE, FRITZ. *Brothers in Christ. The History of the Oldest Anabaptist Congregation in Zollikon, Near Zurich, Switzerland,* trans. Joseph Nordenhaug. Scottdale: Herald Press, 1961.

BRIDGMAN, THE REV. (CAPTAIN) WELLINGTON. *Breaking Prairie Sod. The Story of a Preacher in the Eighties with a Discussion of the Burning Question of Today, "Shall the Alien Go?"* Toronto: Musson Book Company, 1920.

CLARK, LOVELL, ed. *The Manitoba School Question: Majority Rule or Minority Rights?* Toronto: Copp Clark, 1968.

DAWSON, C. A. *Group Settlement: Ethnic Communities in Western Canada,* vol. 7, W. A. Mackintosh and W. L. G. Jörg, eds., Canadian Frontiers of Settlement. Toronto: Macmillan, 1936.

DOELL, LEONARD. *The Bergthaler Mennonite Church of Saskatchewan, 1892–1925.* Winnipeg: CMBC Publications, 1987.

DOERKSEN, J. H. *Geschichte und Wichtige Dokumente der Mennoniten von Russland, Canada, Paraguay und Mexico.* N.p., 1923.

DYCK, CORNELIUS J. *An Introduction to Mennonite History,* 2nd ed., Scottdale, Pa.: Herald Press, 1981.

DYCK, CORNELIUS J., and MARTIN, DENNIS D., eds. *The Mennonite Encyclopedia.* Vol. 5. Scottdale: Herald Press, 1990.

DYCK, HAROLD J. *Lawyers of Mennonite Background in Western Canada Before the Second World War.* Winnipeg: Legal Research Institute of the University of Manitoba, 1993.

DYCK, ISAAK M. *Auswanderung der Reinländer Mennoniten Gemeinde von Canada nach Mexico.* Cuauhtemoc, Mexico: Imprenta Colonial, 1970.

DYCK, JOHN. *Oberschulze Jakob Peters 1813–1884. Manitoba Pioneer Leader.* Steinbach, Man.: Hanover Steinbach Historical Society, 1990.

DYCK, JOHN, ed. *Working Papers of the East Reserve Village Histories, 1874–1910.* Steinbach: Hanover Steinbach Historical Society, 1990.

DYCK, JOHN, ed. *Bergthal Gemeinde Buch.* Steinbach: Hanover Steinbach Historical Society, 1993.

ENNS, F. G. *Gretna: Window on the Northwest.* Gretna, Man.: Village of Gretna History Committee, 1987.

ENS, GERHARD JOHN. *Volost and Municipality: The Rural Municipality of Rhineland, 1884–1984.* Altona: Rural Municipality of Rhineland, 1984.

ENS, GERHARD J. *"Die Schule muss sein." A History of the Mennonite Collegiate Institute.* Gretna: Mennonite Collegiate Institute, 1990.

EPP, D. H. *Die Chortitzer Mennoniten. Versuch einer Darstellung des Entwickelungsganges derselben.* Odessa: A. Schultz, 1889.

EPP, FRANK H. *Mennonite Exodus. The Rescue and Resettlement of the Russian Mennonites since the Communist Revolution.* Altona, Man.: Canadian Mennonite Relief and Immigration Council, 1962.

EPP, FRANK H. *Mennonites in Canada, 1786–1920. The History of a Separate People.* Toronto: Macmillan, 1974.

EPP, FRANK H. *Education with a Plus. The Story of Rosthern Junior College.* Waterloo: Conrad Press, 1975.

EPP, FRANK H. *Mennonites in Canada 1920–1940. A People's Struggle for Survival.* Toronto: Macmillan, 1982.

EWERT, B., comp. *Wichtige Dokumente betreffs der Wehrfreiheit der Mennoniten in Canada.* Gretna, Man.: by the author, 1917.

FAST, HEINOLD. *Der linke Flügel der Reformation. Glaubenszeugnisse der Täufer, Spiritualisten, Schwärmer, und Antitrinitarier.* Bremen: Scheunemann, 1962.

FOGHT, HAROLD W. *A Survey of Education in the Province of Saskatchewan, Canada. A Report to the Government of the Province of Saskatchewan.* Regina: King's Printer, 1918.

FRANCIS, E. K. *In Search of Utopia. The Mennonites in Manitoba.* Altona, Man.: D. W. Friesen, 1955.

FRETZ, J. WINFIELD. *Pilgrims in Paraguay. The Story of Mennonite Colonization in South America.* Scottdale: Herald Press, 1953.

FRIEDMANN, ROBERT. *The Theology of Anabaptism.* Scottdale: Herald Press, 1973.

FRIESEN, GERALD. *The Canadian Prairies. A History.* Toronto: University of Toronto Press, 1984.

FRIESEN, JOHN, ed. *Mennonites in Russia 1788–1988. Essays in Honour of Gerhard Lohrenz.* Winnipeg: CMBC Publications, 1989.

FRIESEN, MARTIN W., comp. and ed. *Kanadische Mennoniten bezwingen eine Wildnis. 50 Jahre Kolonie Menno, Chaco, Paraguay, 1927–1977.* Loma Plata, Paraguay: *Verwaltung der Kolonie Menno,* 1977.

FRIESEN, MARTIN W. *Neue Heimat in der Chacowildnis.* Altona and Asunción: D. W. Friesen and Chortitzer Komitee, 1987.

J. F. GALBRAITH, *The Mennonites in Manitoba, 1875–1900. A Review of Their Coming, Their Progress, and Their Present Prosperity.* Morden, Man.: Chronicle Press, 1900.

*Gedenkfeier der Mennonitischen Einwanderung in Manitoba, Canada.* Steinbach, Man.: Festkomitee der Mennonitischen Ostreserve, 1949.

GERBRANDT, HENRY J. *Adventure in Faith. The Background in Europe and the Development in Canada of the Bergthaler Mennonite Church of Manitoba.* Altona, Man.: D. W. Friesen, 1970.

GERBRANDT, HENRY J. *En Route. Memoirs. Hinjawäajis.* Winnipeg: CMBC Publications, 1994.

GRANT, GEORGE MONRO, ed. *Picturesque Canada: The Country as It Was and Is,* 2 vols. Toronto: Belden Bros., 1882.

GUENTHER, F. D. *Meine innern und äusseren Erlebnisse in Mexico und Canada.* Inwood, Man.: by the author, 1957.

HACK, H. *Die Kolonisation der Mennoniten im Paraguayischen Chaco.* Amsterdam: Königliches Tropeninstitut, n.d.

HARDER, DAVID. *Schule und Gemeinschaft. Erinnerungen des Dorfschullehrers.* Gretna, Man.: mimeographed by Jacob Rempel, 1969.

HERSHBERGER, GUY F., ed. *The Recovery of the Anabaptist Vision.* Scottdale: Herald Press, 1957.

HIEBERT, CLARENCE. *The Holdemann People. The Church of God in Christ, Mennonite, 1859–1969.* South Pasadena: William Carey Press, 1973.

HILDEBRAND, J. J. *Hildebrand's Zeittafel. Chronologische Zeittafel 1500 Daten historischer Ereignisse und Geschehnisse aus der Zeit der Geschichte der Mennoniten Westeuropas, Russlands und Amerikas.* Winnipeg: By the author, 1945.

HORSCH, JOHN. *Mennonites in Europe,* 2nd rev. ed. Scottdale: Mennonite Publishing House, 1950.

HOSTETLER, JOHN A. *Hutterite Society.* Baltimore: Johns Hopkins, 1974.

JANZEN, WILLIAM. *Limits on Liberty: The Experience of Mennonite, Hutterite, and Doukhobor Communities in Canada.* Toronto: University of Toronto Press, 1990.

JUHNKE, JAMES C. *A People of Two Kingdoms. The Political Acculturation of the Kansas Mennonites.* Newton, Kans.: Faith and Life Press, 1975.

JÜRGEN-GOERTZ, HANS, ed. *Die Mennoniten.* Stuttgart: Evangelisches Verlagshaus, 1971.

KLAASSEN, WALTER. *Anabaptism: Neither Catholic nor Protestant.* Waterloo: Conrad Press, 1973.

KLAASSEN, WALTER. *"The Days of Our Years." A History of the Eigenheim Mennonite Church Community: 1892–1992.* Rosthern, Sask.: Eigenheim Mennonite Church, 1992.

KLIPPENSTEIN, LAWRENCE, and TOEWS, JULIUS B., eds. *Mennonite Memories.* Winnipeg: Centennial Publications, 1977.

LOEPPKY, JOHAN M. *Ein Reisebericht von Kanada nach Mexiko im Jahre 1921.* N.p., n.d.

LOEWEN, ROYDEN. *Blumenort: A Mennonite Community in Transition, 1874–1982.* Steinbach: Blumenort Mennonite Historical Society, 1983.

MACGREGOR, MARGARET SCOTT. *Some Letters from Archbishop Taché on the Manitoba School Question.* Toronto: by the author, 1967.

MORTON, W. L. *Manitoba, A History.* Toronto: University of Toronto Press, 2nd ed., 1967; reprint with additions, 1970.

*Old and New Furrows. The Story of Rosthern.* Rosthern: Rosthern Historical Society, [1977].

OLIVER, EDMUND H. *The Country School in Non-English Speaking Communities in Saskatchewan.* Regina: Saskatchewan Public Education League, 1915.

PENNER, LYDIA. *Hanover: One Hundred Years.* Steinbach: Derksen Printers, 1982.

PETERS, GERHARD I. *Remember Our Leaders. Conference of Mennonites in Canada 1902–1977.* Clearbrook, B.C.: Mennonite Historical Society of British Columbia, 1982.

PETERS, KLAAS. *The Bergthaler Mennonites.* Translated by Margaret Loewen Reimer. Winnipeg: CMBC Publications, 1988.

PETERS, VICTOR. *All Things Common. The Hutterian Way of Life.* Minneapolis: University of Minnesota Press, 1965.

PLETT, DELBERT. *Storm and Triumph. The Kleine Gemeinde (1850–1875).* Steinbach: DFP Publications, 1986.

PLETT, DELBERT, ed. *Profile of the Mennonite Kleine Gemeinde 1874.* Steinbach: DFP Publications, 1987.

QUIRING, WALTER. *Deutsche erschließen den Chaco.* Karlsruhe: Heinrich Schneider, 1936.

QUIRING, WALTER. *Rußlanddeutsche suchen eine Heimat. Die deutsche Einwanderung in den paraguayischen Chaco.* Karlsruhe: Heinrich Schneider, 1938.

REDEKOP, CALVIN WALL. *The Old Colony Mennonites. Dilemmas of Ethnic Minority Life.* Baltimore: Johns Hopkins Press, 1969.

REIMER, P. J. B., ed. *The Sesquicentennial Jubilee: Evangelical Mennonite Conference, 1812–1962.* Steinbach, Man.: Evangelical Mennonite Conference, 1962.

REMPEL, JOHN D. *History of the Hague Mennonite Church, 1900–1975.* Rosthern: Valley Printers, 1975.

REMPEL, JOHN, and HARMS, WILLIAM. *Atlas of Original Mennonite Villages, Homesteaders and Some Burial Plots of the Mennonite West Reserve, Manitoba.* Altona: by the authors, 1990.

SAWATZKY, HARRY LEONARD. *They Sought a Country. Mennonite Colonization in Mexico.* Berkeley: University of California Press, 1971.

SCHAEFER, PAUL J. *Woher? Wohin? Mennoniten!*, vol. 3, *Die Mennoniten in Canada.* Altona, Man.: Mennonite Agricultural Advisory Committee, 1946.

SCHAEFER, PAUL J. *Heinrich H. Ewert. Teacher, Educator and Minister of the Mennonites.* Translated by Ida Toews. Winnipeg: CMBC Publications, 1990.

SCHMIEDEHAUS, WALTER. *Die Altkolonier-Mennoniten in Mexiko.* Winnipeg: CMBC Publications, 1982.

SCHREIBER, WILLIAM I. *The Fate of the Prussian Mennonites.* Göttingen Research Committee, 1955.

SCHROEDER, WILLIAM. *The Bergthal Colony,* rev. ed. Winnipeg: CMBC Publications, 1986.

SHANTZ, J. Y. *Narrative of a Journey to Manitoba, Together with an Abstract of the Dominion Lands Act, and an Extract from the Government Pamphlet on Manitoba.* Ottawa: Department of Agriculture, 1873.

SIMONS, MENNO. *The Complete Writings of Menno Simons, c. 1496–1561,* ed. John Christian Wenger, trans. Leonard Verduin. Scottdale: Herald Press, 1956.

SISSONS, C. B. *Bilingual Schools in Canada.* London: J. M. Dent and Sons, 1917.

SISSONS, C. B. *Church and State in Canadian Education: An Historical Study.* Toronto: Ryerson, 1959.

SKELTON, OSCAR DOUGLAS. *Life and Letters of Sir Wilfrid Laurier.* 2 vols. Toronto: McClelland and Stewart, 1965.

SMITH, C. HENRY. *The Coming of the Russian Mennonites. An Episode in the Settling of the Last Frontier, 1874–1884.* Berne, Ind.: Mennonite Book Concern, 1927.

SMITH, C. HENRY. *Smith's Story of the Mennonites,* 5th ed., rev. and enl. by Cornelius Krahn. Newton, Kans.: Faith and Life Press, 1981.

STEINER, SAMUEL J. *Vicarious Pioneer. The Life of Jacob Y. Shantz.* Winnipeg: Hyperion Press, 1988.

SUDERMANN, LEONHARD. *From Russia to America. In Search of Freedom.* Translated by Elmer F. Suderman. Steinbach, Man: Derksen Printers, 1974.

TOEWS, J. A. *Alternative Service in Canada during World War II.* Winnipeg: Publishing Committee of the Canadian Conference of the M.B. Church, 1959.

TOEWS, JOHN B. *Lost Fatherland, The Story of the Mennonite Emigration from Soviet Russia, 1921–1927.* Scottdale: Herald Press, 1967.

URRY, JAMES. *None But Saints. The Transformation of Mennonite Life in Russia 1789–1889.* Winnipeg: Hyperion Press, 1989.

WADE, MASON. *The French Canadians, 1760–1967,* rev. ed., 2 vols. Toronto: Macmillan, 1968.

WAITE, PETER B. *Canada 1874–1896. Arduous Destiny.* Toronto: McClelland and Stewart, 1971.

WARKENTIN, ABE. *Reflections on Our Heritage. A History of Steinbach and the Rural Municipality of Hanover from 1874.* Steinbach: Derksen Printers, 1971.

WEIR, GEORGE W. *The Separate School Question in Canada.* Toronto: Ryerson, 1934.

WIEBE, GERHARD. *Causes and History of the Emigration of the Mennonites from Russia to America.* Translated by Helen Janzen. Winnipeg: Manitoba Mennonite Historical Society, 1981.

WIEBE, JOHANN. *Die Auswanderung von Russland nach Kanada, 1875.* Cuauhtemoc, Mexico: Campo 6.5 Press, 1972.

WILLIAMS, GEORGE HUNSTON, and MERGAL, ANGEL M., ed. *Spiritual and Anabaptist Writers. Documents Illustrative of the Radical Reformation,* Library of Christian Classics, vol. 25. Philadelphia: Westminster, 1957.

WILLIAMS, GEORGE HUNSTON. *The Radical Reformation.* Philadelphia: Westminster, 1962.

YODER, JOHN H., ed. and trans. *The Legacy of Michael Sattler,* Classics of the Radical Reformation, 1. Scottdale: Herald Press, 1973.

ZACHARIAS, PETER D. *Reinland: An Experience in Community.* Reinland, Man.: Reinland Centennial Committee, 1976.

## Periodical Articles

BAINTON, ROLAND H. "The Left Wing of the Reformation." *Journal of Religion* 21 (April 1941): 124–134.

BENDER, HAROLD S. "Church and State in Mennonite History." *Mennonite Quarterly Review* 13 (April 1939): 83–103.

BLISS, J. M. "The Methodist Church and World War I." *Canadian Historical Review* 49 (September 1968): 213–233.

CORRELL, ERNST. "Mennonite Immigration into Manitoba: Sources and Documents, 1872, 1873." *Mennonite Quarterly Review* 11 (July 1937): 196–227; (October 1937): 267–283.

CORRELL, ERNST. "The Mennonite Loan in the Canadian Parliament." *Mennonite Quarterly Review* 20 (October 1946): 255–275.

CORRELL, ERNST. "Mennonite Immigration into Manitoba: Documents and Sources, 1873–1874." *Mennonite Quarterly Review* 22 (January 1948): 43–57.

CORRELL, ERNST. "Sources on the Mennonite Immigration from Russia in the 1870's." *Mennonite Quarterly Review* 24 (October 1950): 329–352.

DYCK, JOHN. "The Oregon Trail of Manitoba Mennonites." *Mennonite Historian,* September 1988, pp. 1–2; December 1988, pp. 4, 8.

ENS, ADOLF, and DOELL, LEONARD. "Mennonite Swedenborgians." *Journal of Mennonite Studies* 10 (1992): 101–117.

ENS, ADOLF, and PENNER, RITA. "Quebec Passenger Lists of the Russian Mennonite Immigration, 1874–1880," *Mennonite Quarterly Review* 48 (October 1974): 527–531.

ENTZ, WERNER. "William Hespeler, Manitoba's First German Consul," *German–Canadian Yearbook* (1973): 149–152.

EWART, C. "The Municipal History of Manitoba." *University of Toronto Studies: History and Economics* 2 (April 1904): 133–148.

FRANCIS, E. K. "Mennonite Institutions in Early Manitoba: A Study of Their Origins." *Agricultural History* 22 (July 1948): 144–155.

FRANCIS, E. K. "The Mennonite School Problem in Manitoba, 1874-1919." *Mennonite Quarterly Review* 27 (July 1953): 204–237.

HILLERBRAND, HANS. "The Anabaptist View of the State." *Mennonite Quarterly Review* 32 (April 1958): 83–110.

HOFER, J. M., ed. and trans. "The Diary of Paul Tschetter, 1873." *Mennonite Quarterly Review* 5 (July 1931): 198–220.

KRAHN, CORNELIUS. "Johann P. Wall, 1875–1961." *Mennonite Life* 16 (October 1961): 186.

LEIBBRANDT, GEORGE. "The Emigration of the German Mennonites from Russia to the United States and Canada in 1873–1880." *Mennonite Quarterly Review* 7 (January 1933): 5–41.

QUIRING, WALTER. "The Canadian Mennonite Immigration into the Paraguayan Chaco, 1926–1927." *Mennonite Quarterly Review* 8 (January 1934): 32–42.

REMPEL, DAVID G. "The Mennonite Commonwealth in Russia. A sketch of its founding and endurance, 1789–1919." *Mennonite Quarterly Review* 47 (October 1973): 259–308; 48 (January 1974): 5–54.

TEICHROEW, ALLAN. "World War I and the Mennonite Migration to Canada to Avoid the Draft." *Mennonite Quarterly Review* 45 (July 1971): 219–249.

WARKENTIN, JOHN. "Manitoba Settlement Patterns." *Papers of the Historical and Scientific Society of Manitoba*, series 3, no. 16 (1961): 62–77.

## Theses and Dissertations

BERGEN, JOHN JACOB. "A Historical Study of Education in the Municipality of Rhineland." M.Ed. thesis, University of Manitoba, 1959.

DRIEDGER, LEO. "A Sect in Modern Mociety. A Case Study of the Old Colony Mennonites of Saskatchewan." M.A. thesis, University of Chicago, 1955.

FRIESEN, ABRAHAM. "Emigration in Mennonite History with Special Reference to the Conservative Mennonite Emigration from Canada to Mexico and South America after World War I." M.A. thesis, University of Manitoba, 1960.

FRIESEN, I. I. "The Mennonites of Western Canada with Special Reference to Education." M.Ed. thesis, University of Saskatchewan, 1934.

FRIESEN, RICHARD JOHN. "Old Colony Mennonite Settlements in Saskatchewan: A Study in Settlement Change." M.A. thesis, University of Alberta, 1975.

REMPEL, DAVID G. "The Mennonite Colonies in New Russia. A Study of Their Settlement and Economic Development from 1789 to 1914." Ph.D. dissertation, Stanford University, 1933.

STOESZ, DENNIS E. "A History of the Chortitzer Mennonite Church of Manitoba 1874–1914." M.A. thesis, University of Manitoba, 1987.

WARKENTIN, JOHN H. "The Mennonite Settlements of Southern Manitoba." Ph.D. dissertation, University of Toronto, 1962.

WILLOWS, ANDREW. "A History of Mennonites, Particularly in Manitoba." M.A. thesis, University of Manitoba, 1924.

# INDEX

**A**
accommodation, 7, 8
Alberta, 2, 7, 86, 87, 92, 98, 154, 176, 178, 221, 222, 235
aliens, 198
*Ältester*, 5, 98
Altona, 109, 110, 128, 182, 210, 217, 221, 222
Anabaptism, origins of, 1–4
Anabaptist, 6, 61
Anderson, J. T. M., 117, 118, 146
Argentina, 202, 203, 208, 210, 216

**B**
Bennett, R. B., 174, 175
Bergthal colony, 13, 14, 16, 19, 21, 66, 231
　settlers from, 23, 24, 43, 46, 65, 67, 68, 71, 85, 86, 87, 114, 138, 144, 202, 209–213
Bergthal congregation, 20, 23, 26, 27, 38, 39, 40, 45, 63, 64, 75, 98, 108
Bergthaler congregation, Manitoba, 45, 46, 70, 73, 76, 108, 109, 110, 112, 113, 118, 119, 121, 122, 124, 154–156, 173, 174, 175, 178, 180, 182, 183, 184, 217, 218, 221, 222, 233, 234
Bergthaler congregation, Saskatchewan, 209, 210, 212, 215, 217
bilingual schools, 113, 114, 117–123, 126, 200, 233
block settlement, 7, 14, 66, 117, 221
BNA Act, 106

Borden, Prime Minister Robert L., 171, 174, 175, 183, 201, 202
Bowell, Prime Minister Mackenzie, 107
boycott, 115, 138, 144, 145
Bracken, John, 218
Brazil, 146, 202, 203, 208, 210
British Columbia, 12, 181, 201
Bruderthaler congregation, 120, 154, 182, 233
Bryce, George, 108, 109
*Bundesbote*, 185, 186
Bureau of Immigration, 206

**C**
Calder, J. A., 115, 132, 181, 201
Canada Registration Board, 182
Canadian Pacific Railway Company, 32, 33–35, 87, 94, 97
Canadian Patriotic Fund, 175
Catholic, 1, 4, 61, 63, 106, 107, 143, 207, 235
censorship, press, 184, 185–188, 200
Chaco, 210–214, 216
Chihuahua, 208, 212–214
Chortitza colony, 7, 21, 94, 117, 231
　settlers from, 23, 24, 35, 39, 40, 45, 46, 65–67, 68
Chortitzer congregation, 45, 46, 63, 76, 109, 113, 120–122, 126, 127, 144, 145, 153, 154, 155, 156, 202, 209, 210, 212, 213, 214, 216, 217, 218, 221, 233, 234

Church of God in Christ, Mennonite (*see* Holdemann congregation)
citizenship, 5, 38, 39, 46, 77, 96, 98, 112, 117, 123, 132, 155, 156, 157, 181, 201, 213, 216, 233, 234, 236
Commission of Inquiry, 115, 236
Conference of Mennonites of Central Canada, 154, 173
conscientious objectors, 181, 187, 205, 206, 221
conscription, 11, 173, 174, 176, 180, 200
conspiracy theory, 141, 142
Cram, W. S., 134, 135, 136, 138, 146

## D

Didsbury, 86, 98
district schools (*see* public schools)
Doerksen, Abraham, 109, 122, 174, 175, 211, 217
Doerksen, David, 217
Dominion Elections Act (1916) 200
Dominion Lands Act, 12, 13, 17, 31, 35–37, 91, 94, 95
Douglas, Municipality of, 70–71, 73
Doukhobors, 172, 173, 201
Dueck, Johann K., 71, 120, 167, 217
Dufferin, Governor General Lord, 18, 19, 38
Durango, 208, 214, 216

## E

East Reserve, 14, 17, 23–24, 27, 31, 35, 38, 40, 41–44, 46, 63, 67, 68, 70, 76, 85, 109–111, 113, 119, 126, 127, 144, 174, 182, 183, 202, 209, 212, 213, 214
emigration, 5–7, 11, 12, 16, 17, 21, 24, 70, 85, 120, 144, 145, 146, 148, 149, 150, 151, 156, 172, 181, 199, 201–217, 233–236
Ens, Gerhard, 97, 98, 115, 222
Ewert, Benjamin, 119, 120, 154, 174, 182,
Ewert, H. H., 108–114, 119–121, 122, 123, 124, 144, 148, 153, 202, 221, 221, 222

## F

fines, 6, 116, 124, 139, 143, 144, 146–148, 152, 180, 183

flag, 7, 111, 112, 113, 117, 125, 126, 156, 186, 200, 202, 233, 236
Foght, Harold W., 117, 118, 132
French Canadian, 12, 35, 173
Friesen, H. J., 119, 217
Friesen, J. M., 110
Friesen, Jacob, 13, 64, 65, 184, 186, 204
Friesen, Johann, 156, 174, 204, 216
Friesen, Martin C., 217
Froese, Franz, 67, 74, 87, 89, 91, 93, 204
Froese, Jacob F., 216
Funk, Johann, 45, 46, 75, 76, 108
Fürstenland colony, 7, 21, 231
  settlers from, 23, 24, 35, 39, 40, 45, 46, 65–67, 68, 75, 98

## G

*Gebietsamt*, 6, 23, 67, 68, 70, 71, 73, 74, 76, 232, 233, 235
German, 5, 8, 11, 13, 14, 18, 20, 42, 62, 64, 66, 68, 71, 89, 108, 113, 114, 116, 118, 120, 121, 122, 138, 144, 156, 184, 186–188, 200, 203, 207, 211, 213, 216–218, 220, 221, 235
German-English Teachers' Association of Southern Manitoba, 113
German-English Academy, 114
Giesbrecht, Jacob, 70, 73
Graff, Henry, 110
Great War Veterans' Association, 146, 180, 201
Greenway, John F., 124, 125, 126, 127, 129–131, 144, 147, 218, 220
Greenway, Thomas, 106, 107, 117
Gretna, 87, 97, 107, 108, 109, 110, 111, 118, 121, 221

## H

Hague Reserve, 87, 89, 91–92, 94–96, 114, 115, 123, 131, 132, 134, 135, 138, 139, 147, 149–151, 152, 154, 202, 203, 204, 208, 209, 210, 214, 216
hamlet privilege, 35–38, 46, 85, 94, 95
Hamm, Cornelius, 217
Hanover, Municipality of, 44, 45, 68, 127, 128, 145, 232

Hespeler, William, 13, 14, 16, 23, 28, 30, 31, 39, 41, 43, 44, 46, 63, 64, 70
Hoeppner, Jacob, 222
Holdemann congregation, 111, 112, 154, 186, 187, 217, 222, 233
Holdemann, John, 45
homestead grant, 13
homestead right, 31–35, 36, 93–94
Homestead Act, 28, 33, 38
Hutterian Brethren (Hutterites), 1–3, 12, 16, 172, 181, 188, 201, 216

**I**
imprisonment, 183, 186

**J**
jail, 116, 139, 144, 147, 148
Jansen, Cornelius, 12
Judicial Committee of the Privy Council, 143

**K**
Kansas, 21, 86, 97, 98, 107, 108, 109, 112, 114, 143, 181, 186, 188
King, William Lyon McKenzie, 223
*Kleine Gemeinde*, 16, 17, 19–22, 24, 39, 44–46, 63, 64, 65, 67, 68, 75, 87, 110–112, 120, 122, 144, 153–156, 173, 217, 218, 231–234
Klotz, Jacob, 21

**L**
land patents, 38–41
Laurier, Prime Minister Wilfrid, 92, 108, 117, 171, 200
Liberal Party, 119, 132, 156, 222
loan, government, Manitoba Mennonites, 24–27, 39–41, 46, 62, 68, 213, 235 (*see also* Mennonite Aid Committee)
loan, government, Saskatchewan Mennonites, 91–92
local self-government (see *Gebietsamt*; municipal government)
Loeppky, Johann, 204, 216
Lowe, John, 17, 19, 28, 39, 41, 105, 132, 140
Loyal Orange Lodge, 180

**M**
Macdonald, Prime Minister John A., 12, 21, 32, 92
Mackenzie, Prime Minister Alexander, 21, 25
Manitoba Court of Appeals, 140, 146
Manitoba *Free Press*, 70, 112, 118, 120–121, 155, 202
Manitoba School Act, 66, 106, 107, 110, 119, 120, 143, 171
Martin, W. M., 118, 131, 132, 134, 136, 138, 145, 146, 147, 148, 149, 150, 153, 217
McCarthy, D'Alton, 107, 117
McLaren, J. B., 46, 71, 87, 91,
McLeod, Alexander M., 93, 126, 183
Meighen, Arthur, 132, 143, 176
Mennonite Aid Committee (Ontario), 22, 24, 25, 39, 40
Mennonite Brethren congregation, 110, 113, 119, 121, 122, 156, 188, 217, 222, 233
Mennonite Collegiate Institute, 109
Mennonite Educational Institute, 109, 221
Mennonite School Society, 108, 110
"Meno-Canuck" line, 70
Methodist church, 117, 180
Métis, 21, 27, 30, 35, 62
Mexico, 144, 150, 152, 204, 205, 208, 208, 208–211, 211–214, 216, 217, 220, 236
Meyer, H. V., 116
military exemption certificate, 177–178
military service
 exemption from, 4, 5, 11–14, 17, 19, 20, 38, 112, 143, 172, 173, 175, 176, 177, 180–182, 187, 200, 201, 203, 205, 207, 211, 221, 231, 234, 235
 status of unbaptized youths, 177–179
Military Service Act, 143, 175–181, 234
Minnesota, 85
Mississippi, 203, 204, 205, 207, 208
*Mitarbeiter*, 111, 122, 154, 173, 176, 187, 188, 210, 214, 215, 217
*Morden Chronicle*, 112
*Morden Empire*, 118
Mott, Jarvis, 71

Mueller, Isaak, 23, 31, 32, 40, 42, 45, 46, 67, 68, 70, 73, 74
municipal government, 7, 11, 38, 39, 65, 68-74, 75, 76, 122, 134, 146, 172, 206, 222, 232-235
Municipal Act, 67, 68, 71, 73, 74, 75

## N

national registration (1918), 181-184
National Policy, 32, 145
National Service Registration (1917), 173-175, 202
nationalism, 8, 117, 198, 234-236
nativism, 121
naturalization, 38, 39, 96, 182, 215, 216
Nebraska, 86, 97, 143, 181
non-resistance (*see* pacifism)
Norris, T.C., 118-120, 123, 144, 145, 222
North Dakota, 85, 87, 89, 205
Northwest Territories, 2, 26, 44, 86, 87, 94, 96, 235

## O

oath, 4, 5, 17, 38, 39, 71, 203, 205, 207, 211, 231
*Oberschulze (Obervorsteher)*, 6, 36, 67, 98, 182, 232
Obregon, 208, 212
odd-numbered sections, 32-34, 43, 44, 93, 94
official trustee, 124, 125, 127, 128, 130, 131, 134-136, 138, 139, 144, 218, 220
Old Colony, 147, 149, 152, 175, 204, 216
Oliver, Edmund H., 122, 123
Ontario, 2, 12-14, 16, 22, 24, 25, 26, 27, 39, 40, 41, 61, 62, 71, 86, 106, 107, 154, 171, 173, 181, 220
order-in-council
  Manitoba, re Mennonite schools, 124, 125, 128, 130-132, 218, 220, 236
  26 April 1872, 13
  25 September 1872, 13, 38, 172
  13 August 1873, 17-19, 105, 120, 132, 139-144, 155, 176-178, 181, 217
  barring Mennonite immigration, 201, 223
  re government loan, 40
  re press censorship, 188
  re railway lands, 33-34
  re Saskatchewan reserves, 87, 89, 91, 93-97
  re termination of reserves, 42, 43
Oregon, 34, 35, 85, 97

## P

pacifism, 8, 111, 127, 138, 171, 172, 184, 186, 210, 235
Paraguay, 204, 208, 209, 210, 211, 212-217, 236
Patriotic Fund, 175, 183
Peters, Jacob, 14, 16, 23, 45, 46, 67
Peters, Klaas, 87, 97, 174, 180, 202, 203, 206, 210
petition
  against Mennonite reserves, 27, 41
  Mennonite, to government, 43, 71, 74, 92, 95, 112, 119, 139, 145, 153-156, 174, 178, 203, 207, 208, 209, 211, 221
  to create public school, 66
  to erect municipality, 67
Petkau, Gerhard, 86
Presbyterian church, 117, 122
private schools, 105, 111, 113, 114, 116, 120-125, 131, 139, 144, 145, 147, 153, 173, 200, 231, 234, 235
*Privilegium*, 4, 5, 11, 12, 17-20, 22, 31, 35, 41, 46, 61, 98, 112, 115, 116, 172, 174, 181, 200, 202, 203, 207, 208, 211, 212, 231-235
  clause 10 (*see* order-in-council, 13 August 1873)
prosecutions, School Attendance Act, 127, 139, 140, 144, 148-152
Prussia, 2, 4, 6, 7, 16, 35, 62, 86, 109, 154, 201
public schools, 62-66, 73, 75-76, 105-156, 172, 198, 200, 202, 216-218, 220, 221, 232-236
Public Schools Act, 65, 66, 105, 124

## Q

Quakers, 172, 173
Quebec, 21, 22, 45, 61, 118, 204, 207, 208

# R

railway lands, 12, 32, 33, 34, 42, 85, 87, 93, 94
Red Cross, 172, 173, 183, 184, 200
Regier, Peter, 86, 91, 144
Reinländer congregation, 24, 45, 46, 65, 68, 70, 71, 73, 74, 75, 76, 85–87, 91–96, 109, 113–115, 121, 122, 126, 131, 132, 134, 138, 139, 142, 144–157, 174, 175, 182, 183, 202, 203, 205–207, 208, 209, 211, 212, 214, 216–218, 220, 221, 233, 234
religion, 113, 120, 139, 140, 155, 172, 207, 220, 221, 231
Rempel, Wilhelm, 65, 73, 107, 108
reserves, Indian, 41
reserves, Mennonite (see East Reserve; Hague Reserve; Swift Current Reserve; West Reserve)
Rhineland, Municipality of, 65, 70, 71, 73, 74, 75, 131, 222
Roblin, Premier Rodmond, 109–112, 113, 117, 118, 121, 222
Romans 13, 3, 147, 157, 232
Rosthern, 86, 87, 89, 96–98, 114, 115, 116, 154, 174, 177, 180, 210, 214, 215, 221
Royal Northwest Mounted Police, 12, 92, 187
*Rundschau*, 186, 188
Russia, 2, 4, 5, 6, 7, 11–14, 16–18, 20, 21, 23, 24, 28, 35, 37, 45, 62, 66, 67, 71, 75, 86, 97, 98, 109, 140, 154, 172, 173, 176, 201, 202, 212, 216, 220, 222, 231, 234

# S

Saskatchewan Rural Municipalities Association, 132
Schleitheim Confession, 3
school attendance, 113, 114, 120, 124, 131, 134, 139, 140, 143, 145, 146–152, 203, 212
School Act
  Manitoba, 106, 107, 110, 119, 120, 125, 127, 143, 233
  Saskatchewan, 147

School Attendance Act, 113, 114, 120, 124, 131, 134, 139, 140, 143, 144–147, 149, 149–152, 203, 212, 235
  exemption from, 116
School Society, 108, 110
schools, 7, 11, 24, 28, 36, 85, 95, 173, 199, 200, 202, 203, 205, 213, 216–218, 220, 221
*Schulkommission*, 113, 119
*Schulze*, 5, 6, 68, 232
Scott, Walter, 114, 115, 116, 118, 123
Scratching River, 22–24, 45, 63, 110
Shantz, Jacob Y., 14, 16, 22, 25
Sifton, Clifford, 91, 92, 108, 116–118, 171
Sommerfelder congregation, 76, 109, 110, 113, 118, 119, 121, 122, 138, 140, 145, 153–155, 156, 174, 175, 178, 202, 209–211, 212, 214–217, 218, 221
South Dufferin, Municipality of, 41, 71
squatters on Mennonite reserves, 28, 30, 31, 42, 43, 46
Stanley, Municipality of, 131
state
  Anabaptist concept of, 3–4, 233
  Mennonite church relations with, 4–7, 12, 37, 39, 45, 46, 68, 70–74, 75–77, 108–109, 120, 155–157, 178, 231, 234
*Steinbach Post,* 184, 186, 187, 188
Stoesz, David, 38, 45, 46, 75, 109
subjects, 11, 27, 46, 65, 77, 187, 216, 220, 232, 233
Sudermann, Leonhard, 12, 20
Supreme Court, 139, 143, 209
Swedenborgian, 98, 180
Swift Current Reserve, 87, 91, 93–95, 96, 97, 114, 116, 123, 132–134, 134–136, 138, 139, 144–147, 149, 150, 152, 154–156, 202–205, 207–209, 212, 214, 217
*Swift Current Sun,* 139

# T

Taché, Archbishop Alexander, 107
teacher conferences, 113

Thornton, R. S., 120, 124, 125, 127, 144, 145, 148
Toews, David, 112, 114, 116, 174, 177, 178–180, 182, 221
Toews, Peter, 16, 23, 45, 63, 64, 111

## U

U.S.A., 109, 117, 118, 132, 154, 172, 180, 181, 186, 188, 200, 203, 205, 206, 216, 231, 234
U.S.S.R., 199, 208, 216, 221, 236
Union Jack, 110, 113
United States, 2, 12, 16, 17, 19, 20, 21, 22, 23, 31, 45, 85, 87, 96, 97, 98

## V

Victory loan (Victory bonds), 172, 183–185, 186, 187, 200
village(s)
  as local government units, 68, 70, 73–74
  as school districts, 63–66, 110, 131, 138, 144, 234, 236
  landholding system, 76, 85, 92, 233
  settlement pattern, 5–7, 14, 22, 23, 24, 31, 32–38, 39, 42, 45, 46, 87, 94–96, 232
voting, Mennonite attitude to, 68, 70, 73, 74, 119, 157, 178, 200, 220, 222, 233, 234

## W

*Waisenamt,* 24, 68, 122, 203, 207
Wall, Johann P., 139, 142, 151
war, 2, 8, 13, 61, 76, 113, 172–174, 175, 178, 180, 183, 184–188, 199, 200, 201, 203, 206, 221, 222
War Measures Act, 173, 174
War-Time Elections Act (1917), 200, 202
Weidenhammer (*see* Willows)
West Reserve, 23, 26, 27, 31, 32, 33, 35, 36, 39, 40–46, 65, 67, 68, 70, 71, 76, 85, 87, 107–109, 113, 122, 124, 126, 127, 144, 174, 202, 209, 212, 214, 217, 232, 233
Wiebe, Abraham, 204, 217
Wiebe, Gerhard, 16, 20, 21, 23, 26, 45, 46, 63, 64, 75, 76
Wiebe, Heinrich, 14, 16, 19
Wiebe, Johann, 21, 24, 26, 45, 46, 67, 68, 74, 75, 76, 87, 91, 109, 211
Wiens, Jacob, 131, 216
Willows, Andrew A., 112, 113, 122, 144
Winkler, Enoch, 46
Winkler, Valentine, 119, 120, 127, 144, 155, 222
World War I, 116, 118, 124, 134, 155, 177–180, 234, 235

## Z

Zacharias, Aron, 215, 217
Zohrab, James, 12

The paper used in this publication meets the minimum requirements
of American National Standard for Information Sciences –
Permanence of Paper for Printed Library Materials, ANSI Z39.48-1992.

Printed by
Groupe Goulet, Létourneau Imprimeurs Inc.
Sherbrooke — Montreal